Writing Literature Reviews

A Guide for Students of the Social and Behavioral Sciences

Seventh Edition

Jose L. Galvan and Melisa C. Galvan
Maora nuwin

© 2017

All rights reserved. No part of this book may be reprinted or reproduced or utilised in any form or by any electronic, mechanical, or other means, now known or hereafter invented, including photocopying and recording, or in any information storage or retrieval system, without permission in writing from the publishers.

ISBN: 9798392359790 Paperback

Library of Congress Cataloging in Publication Data
Names: Galvan, Jose L., author. | Galvan, Melisa, author.
Title: Writing literature reviews : a guide for students of the social and behavioral sciences / Jose Galvan and Melisa Galvan.
Description: Seventh edition.

Contents

Preface — xv
    Audiences — xvi
    Unique Features — xvi
    New to This Edition — xvii
    Ancillaries — xvii
    Notes to the Instructor — xviii
    Special Acknowledgment — xviii
    Acknowledgments — xix
    Notes — xix

Part I: Managing the Literature Search — 1

1 Writing Reviews of Academic Literature: An Overview — 3

    An Introduction to Reviewing Primary Sources — 3
        Empirical Research Reports 3
        Theoretical Articles 6
        Literature Review Articles 7
        Anecdotal Reports 8
        Reports on Professional Practices and Standards 8
    The Writing Process — 8
        Finding Your 'Writer's Voice': Writing for a Specific Purpose 9
        Writing a Literature Review as a Term Paper for a Class 9
        Writing a Literature Review Chapter for a Thesis or Dissertation 11
        Writing a Literature Review for a Research Article 13
    The Parts of this Text — 13
        Managing the Literature Search—Part I 13
        Analyzing the Relevant Literature—Part II 14
        Writing the First Draft of Your Literature Review—Part III 14
        Editing and Preparing the Final Draft of Your Review—Part IV 15
    Activities for Chapter 1 — 15
    Notes — 16

Contents

2 Learn to Navigate the Electronic Resources in Your University's Library — 18
Step 1: Formalize Your Institutional Affiliation with Your University Library — 18
Step 2: Set Up Your Online Access Credentials and/or Proxy Server — 19
Step 3: Inquire about University Library Research Workshops — 19
Step 4: Select a Search Engine that Best Suits Your Needs — 20
Step 5: Familiarize Yourself with How Online Databases Function — 21
Step 6: Experiment with the "Advanced Search" Feature — 23
Step 7: Identify an Array of Subject Keywords to Locate Your Sources — 24
Step 8: Learn How You Can Access the Articles You Choose — 25
Step 9: Identify Additional Databases that May Be Useful for Your Field of Study — 25
Step 10: Repeat the Search Procedures with Other Databases — 27
Activities for Chapter 2 — 27
Note — 27

3 Selecting a Topic for Your Review — 28
Step 1: Define Your General Topic — 28
Step 2: Familiarize Yourself with the Basic Organization of Your Selected Online Database — 29
Step 3: Begin Your Search with a General Keyword, then Limit the Output — 29
Step 4: Identify Narrower Topic Areas If Your Initial List of Search Results Is Too Long — 31
Step 5: Increase the Size of Your Reference List, If Necessary — 31
Step 6: Consider Searching for Unpublished Studies — 32
Step 7: Start with the Most Current Research, and Work Backward — 33
Step 8: Search for Theoretical Articles on Your Topic — 33
Step 9: Look for Review Articles — 34
Step 10: Identify the Landmark or Classic Studies and Theorists — 35
Step 11: Assemble the Collection of Sources You Plan to Include in Your Review — 37
Step 12: Write the First Draft of Your Topic Statement — 39
Step 13: Redefine Your Topic More Narrowly — 40
Step 14: Ask for Feedback from Your Instructor or Advisor — 41
Activities for Chapter 3 — 41
Notes — 42

4 Organizing Yourself to Begin the Selection of Relevant Titles — 43
Step 1: Scan the Articles to Get an Overview of Each One — 43
Step 2: Based on Your Prereading of the Articles, Group Them by Category — 44

	Step 3: Conduct a More Focused Literature Search if Gaps Appear	46
	Step 4: Organize Yourself before Reading the Articles	47
	Step 5: Create a Spreadsheet or Table to Compile Your Notes	47
	Step 6: Remain Flexible as You Compile Your Notes	49
	Step 7: Take Extra Care When Copying an Author's Exact Words	49
	Activities for Chapter 4	49
	Notes	50

Part II: Analyzing the Relevant Literature 51

5 Conduct a Deep Analysis of the Articles 53

Guideline 1: Look for Explicit Definitions of Key Terms in the Literature 53

Guideline 2: Look for Key Statistics to Use near the Beginning of Your Literature Review 55

Guideline 3: Pay Special Attention to Review Articles on Your Topic 56

Guideline 4: Make Note of Short but Important Quotations that Could Be Used Very Sparingly in Your Review 57

Guideline 5: Look for Methodological Strengths 58

Guideline 6: Look for Methodological Weaknesses 58

Guideline 7: Distinguish between Assertion and Evidence 59

Guideline 8: Identify the Major Trends or Patterns in the Results of Previous Studies 60

Guideline 9: Identify Gaps in the Literature 61

Guideline 10: Identify Relationships among Studies 61

Guideline 11: Note How Closely Each Article Relates to Your Topic 61

Guideline 12: Evaluate Your Reference List for Currency and for Coverage 62

Activities for Chapter 5 63

Notes 63

6 Analyzing Quantitative Research Literature 65

Guideline 1: Note Whether the Research Is Quantitative or Qualitative 65

Guideline 2: Note Whether a Study Is Experimental or Nonexperimental 67

Guideline 3: In an Experiment, Note Whether the Participants Were Assigned at Random to Treatment Conditions 67

Guideline 4: Note Attempts to Examine Cause-and-Effect Issues in Nonexperimental Studies 68

Guideline 5: Consider the Test-Retest Reliability of the Measure 69

Guideline 6: Consider the Internal Consistency Reliability of the Measure 69

Guideline 7: Consider the Validity of the Measure 70

- Guideline 8: Consider Whether a Measure Is Valid For a Particular Research Purpose — 72
- Guideline 9: Note Differences in How a Variable Is Measured Across Studies — 73
- Guideline 10: Note How the Participants Were Sampled — 74
- Guideline 11: Make Notes on the Demographics of the Participants — 74
- Guideline 12: Note How Large a Difference Is—Not Just Whether It Is Statistically Significant — 75
- Guideline 13: Presume That All Quantitative Studies Are Flawed — 76
- Concluding Comment — 76
- Activities for Chapter 6 — 76
- Notes — 77

7 Analyzing Qualitative Research Literature — 79

- Guideline 1: Note Whether the Research Was Conducted By an Individual or By a Research Team — 79
- Guideline 2: When There Is a Research Team, Note Whether Analysis of the Data Was Initially Conducted Independently — 80
- Guideline 3: Note Whether Outside Experts Were Consulted — 80
- Guideline 4: Note Whether the Participants Were Consulted on the Interpretation of the Data — 81
- Guideline 5: Note Whether the Researchers Used a Purposive Sample or a Sample of Convenience — 82
- Guideline 6: Note Whether the Demographics of the Participants Are Described — 83
- Guideline 7: Consider Whether the Method of Qualitative Analysis Is Described in Sufficient Detail — 84
- Guideline 8: Note Whether Quantities Are Provided When Qualitative Researchers Discuss Quantitative Matters — 85
- Concluding Comment — 86
- Activities for Chapter 7 — 86
- Notes — 86

8 Organizing Your Notes by Grouping the Results of Your Analysis — 88

- Guideline 1: Consider Building a Table of Definitions — 88
- Guideline 2: Consider Building a Table of Research Methods — 89
- Guideline 3: Consider Including a Summary of Research Results in the Methods Table — 89
- Guideline 4: When There Is Much Literature on a Topic, Establish Criteria for Determining Which Literature to Summarize in a Table — 91
- Guideline 5: When There Is Much Literature on a Topic, Consider Building Two or More Tables to Summarize It — 92

Guideline 6: Present Tables in a Literature Review Only for Complex Material	92
Guideline 7: Discuss Each Table Included in a Literature Review	92
Guideline 8: Give Each Table a Number and Descriptive Title	93
Guideline 9: Insert *Continued* When Tables Split Across Pages	93
Activities for Chapter 8	93
Notes	94

Part III: Writing the First Draft of Your Literature Review — 95

9 Synthesizing Trends and Patterns: Preparing to Write — 97

Guideline 1: Consider Your Purpose and Voice before Beginning to Write	97
Guideline 2: Consider How to Reassemble Your Notes	98
Guideline 3: Create a Topic Outline That Traces Your Argument	99
Guideline 4: Reorganize Your Notes According to the Path of Your Argument	100
Guideline 5: Within Each Topic Heading, Note Differences among Studies	101
Guideline 6: Within Each Topic Heading, Look for Obvious Gaps or Areas Needing Additional Research	102
Guideline 7: Plan to Briefly Describe Relevant Theories	102
Guideline 8: Plan to Discuss How Individual Studies Relate to and Advance Theory	103
Guideline 9: Plan to Summarize Periodically and Again near the End of the Review	103
Guideline 10: Plan to Present Conclusions and Implications	104
Guideline 11: Plan to Suggest Specific Directions for Future Research near the End of the Review	105
Guideline 12: Flesh out Your Outline with Details from Your Analysis	106
Activities for Chapter 9	107
Notes	108

10 Guidelines for Writing a First Draft — 109

Guideline 1: Begin by Identifying the Broad Problem Area, but Avoid Global Statements	109
Guideline 2: Early in the Review, Indicate Why the Topic Being Reviewed Is Important	110
Guideline 3: Distinguish Between Research Findings and Other Sources of Information	111
Guideline 4: Indicate Why Certain Studies Are Important	112
Guideline 5: If You Are Commenting On the Timeliness of a Topic, Be Specific In Describing the Time Frame	113
Guideline 6: If Citing a Classic or Landmark Study, Identify It as Such	114
Guideline 7: If a Landmark Study Was Replicated, Mention That and Indicate the Results of the Replication	115

Guideline 8: Discuss Other Literature Reviews on Your Topic — 116

Guideline 9: Refer the Reader to Other Reviews on Issues That You Will Not Be Discussing in Detail — 116

Guideline 10: Justify Comments Such As "No Studies Were Found" — 117

Guideline 11: Avoid Long Lists of Nonspecific References — 118

Guideline 12: If the Results of Previous Studies Are Inconsistent or Widely Varying, Cite Them Separately — 119

Guideline 13: Speculate on the Reasons for Inconsistent Findings in Previous Research — 120

Guideline 14: Cite All Relevant References in the Review Section of a Thesis, Dissertation, or Journal Article — 121

Guideline 15: Emphasize the Need for Your Study in the Literature Review Section or Chapter — 121

Activities for Chapter 10 — 122

Notes — 122

11 Guidelines for Developing a Coherent Essay — 124

Guideline 1: If Your Review Is Long, Provide an Overview near the Beginning of the Review — 124

Guideline 2: Near the Beginning of a Review, State Explicitly What Will and Will Not Be Covered — 125

Guideline 3: Specify Your Point of View Early in the Review — 125

Guideline 4: Aim for a Clear and Cohesive Essay and Avoid Annotations — 126

Guideline 5: Use Subheadings, Especially in Long Reviews — 127

Guideline 6: Use Transitions to Help Trace Your Argument — 128

Guideline 7: If Your Topic Spans Two or More Disciplines, Consider Reviewing Studies from Each Discipline Separately — 128

Guideline 8: Write a Conclusion for the End of the Review — 129

Guideline 9: Check the Flow of Your Argument for Coherence — 130

Activities for Chapter 11 — 130

Notes — 131

Part IV: Editing and Preparing the Final Draft of Your Review — 133

12 Guidelines for Editing Your Essay and Incorporating Feedback — 135

Guideline 1: The Reader Is Always Right — 136

Guideline 2: Expect Your Instructor to Comment on the Content — 136

Guideline 3: Concentrate First on Comments about Your Ideas — 136

Guideline 4: Reconcile Contradictory Feedback by Seeking Clarification — 137

Guideline 5: Reconcile Comments about Style with Your Style Manual — 137

Contents

Preface — xv
    Audiences — xvi
    Unique Features — xvi
    New to This Edition — xvii
    Ancillaries — xvii
    Notes to the Instructor — xviii
    Special Acknowledgment — xviii
    Acknowledgments — xix
    Notes — xix

Part I: Managing the Literature Search — 1

1 Writing Reviews of Academic Literature: An Overview — 3
    An Introduction to Reviewing Primary Sources — 3
        Empirical Research Reports 3
        Theoretical Articles 6
        Literature Review Articles 7
        Anecdotal Reports 8
        Reports on Professional Practices and Standards 8
    The Writing Process — 8
        Finding Your 'Writer's Voice': Writing for a Specific Purpose 9
        Writing a Literature Review as a Term Paper for a Class 9
        Writing a Literature Review Chapter for a Thesis or Dissertation 11
        Writing a Literature Review for a Research Article 13
    The Parts of this Text — 13
        Managing the Literature Search—Part I 13
        Analyzing the Relevant Literature—Part II 14
        Writing the First Draft of Your Literature Review—Part III 14
        Editing and Preparing the Final Draft of Your Review—Part IV 15
    Activities for Chapter 1 — 15
    Notes — 16

2 Learn to Navigate the Electronic Resources in Your University's Library — 18
Step 1: Formalize Your Institutional Affiliation with Your University Library — 18
Step 2: Set Up Your Online Access Credentials and/or Proxy Server — 19
Step 3: Inquire about University Library Research Workshops — 19
Step 4: Select a Search Engine that Best Suits Your Needs — 20
Step 5: Familiarize Yourself with How Online Databases Function — 21
Step 6: Experiment with the "Advanced Search" Feature — 23
Step 7: Identify an Array of Subject Keywords to Locate Your Sources — 24
Step 8: Learn How You Can Access the Articles You Choose — 25
Step 9: Identify Additional Databases that May Be Useful for Your Field of Study — 25
Step 10: Repeat the Search Procedures with Other Databases — 27
Activities for Chapter 2 — 27
Note — 27

3 Selecting a Topic for Your Review — 28
Step 1: Define Your General Topic — 28
Step 2: Familiarize Yourself with the Basic Organization of Your Selected Online Database — 29
Step 3: Begin Your Search with a General Keyword, then Limit the Output — 29
Step 4: Identify Narrower Topic Areas If Your Initial List of Search Results Is Too Long — 31
Step 5: Increase the Size of Your Reference List, If Necessary — 31
Step 6: Consider Searching for Unpublished Studies — 32
Step 7: Start with the Most Current Research, and Work Backward — 33
Step 8: Search for Theoretical Articles on Your Topic — 33
Step 9: Look for Review Articles — 34
Step 10: Identify the Landmark or Classic Studies and Theorists — 35
Step 11: Assemble the Collection of Sources You Plan to Include in Your Review — 37
Step 12: Write the First Draft of Your Topic Statement — 39
Step 13: Redefine Your Topic More Narrowly — 40
Step 14: Ask for Feedback from Your Instructor or Advisor — 41
Activities for Chapter 3 — 41
Notes — 42

4 Organizing Yourself to Begin the Selection of Relevant Titles — 43
Step 1: Scan the Articles to Get an Overview of Each One — 43
Step 2: Based on Your Prereading of the Articles, Group Them by Category — 44

	Step 3: Conduct a More Focused Literature Search if Gaps Appear	46
	Step 4: Organize Yourself before Reading the Articles	47
	Step 5: Create a Spreadsheet or Table to Compile Your Notes	47
	Step 6: Remain Flexible as You Compile Your Notes	49
	Step 7: Take Extra Care When Copying an Author's Exact Words	49
	Activities for Chapter 4	49
	Notes	50

Part II: Analyzing the Relevant Literature — 51

5 Conduct a Deep Analysis of the Articles — 53

- Guideline 1: Look for Explicit Definitions of Key Terms in the Literature — 53
- Guideline 2: Look for Key Statistics to Use near the Beginning of Your Literature Review — 55
- Guideline 3: Pay Special Attention to Review Articles on Your Topic — 56
- Guideline 4: Make Note of Short but Important Quotations that Could Be Used Very Sparingly in Your Review — 57
- Guideline 5: Look for Methodological Strengths — 58
- Guideline 6: Look for Methodological Weaknesses — 58
- Guideline 7: Distinguish between Assertion and Evidence — 59
- Guideline 8: Identify the Major Trends or Patterns in the Results of Previous Studies — 60
- Guideline 9: Identify Gaps in the Literature — 61
- Guideline 10: Identify Relationships among Studies — 61
- Guideline 11: Note How Closely Each Article Relates to Your Topic — 61
- Guideline 12: Evaluate Your Reference List for Currency and for Coverage — 62
- Activities for Chapter 5 — 63
- Notes — 63

6 Analyzing Quantitative Research Literature — 65

- Guideline 1: Note Whether the Research Is Quantitative or Qualitative — 65
- Guideline 2: Note Whether a Study Is Experimental or Nonexperimental — 67
- Guideline 3: In an Experiment, Note Whether the Participants Were Assigned at Random to Treatment Conditions — 67
- Guideline 4: Note Attempts to Examine Cause-and-Effect Issues in Nonexperimental Studies — 68
- Guideline 5: Consider the Test-Retest Reliability of the Measure — 69
- Guideline 6: Consider the Internal Consistency Reliability of the Measure — 69
- Guideline 7: Consider the Validity of the Measure — 70

Contents

    Guideline 8: Consider Whether a Measure Is Valid For a Particular Research Purpose   72

    Guideline 9: Note Differences in How a Variable Is Measured Across Studies   73

    Guideline 10: Note How the Participants Were Sampled   74

    Guideline 11: Make Notes on the Demographics of the Participants   74

    Guideline 12: Note How Large a Difference Is—Not Just Whether It Is Statistically Significant   75

    Guideline 13: Presume That All Quantitative Studies Are Flawed   76

    Concluding Comment   76

    Activities for Chapter 6   76

    Notes   77

7 Analyzing Qualitative Research Literature   79

    Guideline 1: Note Whether the Research Was Conducted By an Individual or By a Research Team   79

    Guideline 2: When There Is a Research Team, Note Whether Analysis of the Data Was Initially Conducted Independently   80

    Guideline 3: Note Whether Outside Experts Were Consulted   80

    Guideline 4: Note Whether the Participants Were Consulted on the Interpretation of the Data   81

    Guideline 5: Note Whether the Researchers Used a Purposive Sample or a Sample of Convenience   82

    Guideline 6: Note Whether the Demographics of the Participants Are Described   83

    Guideline 7: Consider Whether the Method of Qualitative Analysis Is Described in Sufficient Detail   84

    Guideline 8: Note Whether Quantities Are Provided When Qualitative Researchers Discuss Quantitative Matters   85

    Concluding Comment   86

    Activities for Chapter 7   86

    Notes   86

8 Organizing Your Notes by Grouping the Results of Your Analysis   88

    Guideline 1: Consider Building a Table of Definitions   88

    Guideline 2: Consider Building a Table of Research Methods   89

    Guideline 3: Consider Including a Summary of Research Results in the Methods Table   89

    Guideline 4: When There Is Much Literature on a Topic, Establish Criteria for Determining Which Literature to Summarize in a Table   91

    Guideline 5: When There Is Much Literature on a Topic, Consider Building Two or More Tables to Summarize It   92

Contents

Preface — xv
    Audiences — xvi
    Unique Features — xvi
    New to This Edition — xvii
    Ancillaries — xvii
    Notes to the Instructor — xviii
    Special Acknowledgment — xviii
    Acknowledgments — xix
    Notes — xix

Part I: Managing the Literature Search — 1

1 Writing Reviews of Academic Literature: An Overview — 3

An Introduction to Reviewing Primary Sources — 3
    Empirical Research Reports 3
    Theoretical Articles 6
    Literature Review Articles 7
    Anecdotal Reports 8
    Reports on Professional Practices and Standards 8

The Writing Process — 8
    Finding Your 'Writer's Voice': Writing for a Specific Purpose 9
    Writing a Literature Review as a Term Paper for a Class 9
    Writing a Literature Review Chapter for a Thesis or Dissertation 11
    Writing a Literature Review for a Research Article 13

The Parts of this Text — 13
    Managing the Literature Search—Part I 13
    Analyzing the Relevant Literature—Part II 14
    Writing the First Draft of Your Literature Review—Part III 14
    Editing and Preparing the Final Draft of Your Review—Part IV 15

Activities for Chapter 1 — 15
Notes — 16

2 Learn to Navigate the Electronic Resources in Your University's Library — 18
- Step 1: Formalize Your Institutional Affiliation with Your University Library — 18
- Step 2: Set Up Your Online Access Credentials and/or Proxy Server — 19
- Step 3: Inquire about University Library Research Workshops — 19
- Step 4: Select a Search Engine that Best Suits Your Needs — 20
- Step 5: Familiarize Yourself with How Online Databases Function — 21
- Step 6: Experiment with the "Advanced Search" Feature — 23
- Step 7: Identify an Array of Subject Keywords to Locate Your Sources — 24
- Step 8: Learn How You Can Access the Articles You Choose — 25
- Step 9: Identify Additional Databases that May Be Useful for Your Field of Study — 25
- Step 10: Repeat the Search Procedures with Other Databases — 27
- Activities for Chapter 2 — 27
- Note — 27

3 Selecting a Topic for Your Review — 28
- Step 1: Define Your General Topic — 28
- Step 2: Familiarize Yourself with the Basic Organization of Your Selected Online Database — 29
- Step 3: Begin Your Search with a General Keyword, then Limit the Output — 29
- Step 4: Identify Narrower Topic Areas If Your Initial List of Search Results Is Too Long — 31
- Step 5: Increase the Size of Your Reference List, If Necessary — 31
- Step 6: Consider Searching for Unpublished Studies — 32
- Step 7: Start with the Most Current Research, and Work Backward — 33
- Step 8: Search for Theoretical Articles on Your Topic — 33
- Step 9: Look for Review Articles — 34
- Step 10: Identify the Landmark or Classic Studies and Theorists — 35
- Step 11: Assemble the Collection of Sources You Plan to Include in Your Review — 37
- Step 12: Write the First Draft of Your Topic Statement — 39
- Step 13: Redefine Your Topic More Narrowly — 40
- Step 14: Ask for Feedback from Your Instructor or Advisor — 41
- Activities for Chapter 3 — 41
- Notes — 42

4 Organizing Yourself to Begin the Selection of Relevant Titles — 43
- Step 1: Scan the Articles to Get an Overview of Each One — 43
- Step 2: Based on Your Prereading of the Articles, Group Them by Category — 44

Step 3: Conduct a More Focused Literature Search if Gaps Appear	46
Step 4: Organize Yourself before Reading the Articles	47
Step 5: Create a Spreadsheet or Table to Compile Your Notes	47
Step 6: Remain Flexible as You Compile Your Notes	49
Step 7: Take Extra Care When Copying an Author's Exact Words	49
Activities for Chapter 4	49
Notes	50

Part II: Analyzing the Relevant Literature — 51

5   Conduct a Deep Analysis of the Articles — 53

Guideline 1: Look for Explicit Definitions of Key Terms in the Literature	53
Guideline 2: Look for Key Statistics to Use near the Beginning of Your Literature Review	55
Guideline 3: Pay Special Attention to Review Articles on Your Topic	56
Guideline 4: Make Note of Short but Important Quotations that Could Be Used Very Sparingly in Your Review	57
Guideline 5: Look for Methodological Strengths	58
Guideline 6: Look for Methodological Weaknesses	58
Guideline 7: Distinguish between Assertion and Evidence	59
Guideline 8: Identify the Major Trends or Patterns in the Results of Previous Studies	60
Guideline 9: Identify Gaps in the Literature	61
Guideline 10: Identify Relationships among Studies	61
Guideline 11: Note How Closely Each Article Relates to Your Topic	61
Guideline 12: Evaluate Your Reference List for Currency and for Coverage	62
Activities for Chapter 5	63
Notes	63

6   Analyzing Quantitative Research Literature — 65

Guideline 1: Note Whether the Research Is Quantitative or Qualitative	65
Guideline 2: Note Whether a Study Is Experimental or Nonexperimental	67
Guideline 3: In an Experiment, Note Whether the Participants Were Assigned at Random to Treatment Conditions	67
Guideline 4: Note Attempts to Examine Cause-and-Effect Issues in Nonexperimental Studies	68
Guideline 5: Consider the Test-Retest Reliability of the Measure	69
Guideline 6: Consider the Internal Consistency Reliability of the Measure	69
Guideline 7: Consider the Validity of the Measure	70

- Guideline 8: Consider Whether a Measure Is Valid For a Particular Research Purpose — 72
- Guideline 9: Note Differences in How a Variable Is Measured Across Studies — 73
- Guideline 10: Note How the Participants Were Sampled — 74
- Guideline 11: Make Notes on the Demographics of the Participants — 74
- Guideline 12: Note How Large a Difference Is—Not Just Whether It Is Statistically Significant — 75
- Guideline 13: Presume That All Quantitative Studies Are Flawed — 76
- Concluding Comment — 76
- Activities for Chapter 6 — 76
- Notes — 77

7 Analyzing Qualitative Research Literature — 79

- Guideline 1: Note Whether the Research Was Conducted By an Individual or By a Research Team — 79
- Guideline 2: When There Is a Research Team, Note Whether Analysis of the Data Was Initially Conducted Independently — 80
- Guideline 3: Note Whether Outside Experts Were Consulted — 80
- Guideline 4: Note Whether the Participants Were Consulted on the Interpretation of the Data — 81
- Guideline 5: Note Whether the Researchers Used a Purposive Sample or a Sample of Convenience — 82
- Guideline 6: Note Whether the Demographics of the Participants Are Described — 83
- Guideline 7: Consider Whether the Method of Qualitative Analysis Is Described in Sufficient Detail — 84
- Guideline 8: Note Whether Quantities Are Provided When Qualitative Researchers Discuss Quantitative Matters — 85
- Concluding Comment — 86
- Activities for Chapter 7 — 86
- Notes — 86

8 Organizing Your Notes by Grouping the Results of Your Analysis — 88

- Guideline 1: Consider Building a Table of Definitions — 88
- Guideline 2: Consider Building a Table of Research Methods — 89
- Guideline 3: Consider Including a Summary of Research Results in the Methods Table — 89
- Guideline 4: When There Is Much Literature on a Topic, Establish Criteria for Determining Which Literature to Summarize in a Table — 91
- Guideline 5: When There Is Much Literature on a Topic, Consider Building Two or More Tables to Summarize It — 92

Guideline 6: Present Tables in a Literature Review Only for Complex Material — 92
Guideline 7: Discuss Each Table Included in a Literature Review — 92
Guideline 8: Give Each Table a Number and Descriptive Title — 93
Guideline 9: Insert *Continued* When Tables Split Across Pages — 93
Activities for Chapter 8 — 93
Notes — 94

Part III: Writing the First Draft of Your Literature Review — 95

9 Synthesizing Trends and Patterns: Preparing to Write — 97
Guideline 1: Consider Your Purpose and Voice before Beginning to Write — 97
Guideline 2: Consider How to Reassemble Your Notes — 98
Guideline 3: Create a Topic Outline That Traces Your Argument — 99
Guideline 4: Reorganize Your Notes According to the Path of Your Argument — 100
Guideline 5: Within Each Topic Heading, Note Differences among Studies — 101
Guideline 6: Within Each Topic Heading, Look for Obvious Gaps or Areas Needing Additional Research — 102
Guideline 7: Plan to Briefly Describe Relevant Theories — 102
Guideline 8: Plan to Discuss How Individual Studies Relate to and Advance Theory — 103
Guideline 9: Plan to Summarize Periodically and Again near the End of the Review — 103
Guideline 10: Plan to Present Conclusions and Implications — 104
Guideline 11: Plan to Suggest Specific Directions for Future Research near the End of the Review — 105
Guideline 12: Flesh out Your Outline with Details from Your Analysis — 106
Activities for Chapter 9 — 107
Notes — 108

10 Guidelines for Writing a First Draft — 109
Guideline 1: Begin by Identifying the Broad Problem Area, but Avoid Global Statements — 109
Guideline 2: Early in the Review, Indicate Why the Topic Being Reviewed Is Important — 110
Guideline 3: Distinguish Between Research Findings and Other Sources of Information — 111
Guideline 4: Indicate Why Certain Studies Are Important — 112
Guideline 5: If You Are Commenting On the Timeliness of a Topic, Be Specific In Describing the Time Frame — 113
Guideline 6: If Citing a Classic or Landmark Study, Identify It as Such — 114
Guideline 7: If a Landmark Study Was Replicated, Mention That and Indicate the Results of the Replication — 115

    Guideline 8: Discuss Other Literature Reviews on Your Topic   116
    Guideline 9: Refer the Reader to Other Reviews on Issues That You Will Not Be Discussing in Detail   116
    Guideline 10: Justify Comments Such As "No Studies Were Found"   117
    Guideline 11: Avoid Long Lists of Nonspecific References   118
    Guideline 12: If the Results of Previous Studies Are Inconsistent or Widely Varying, Cite Them Separately   119
    Guideline 13: Speculate on the Reasons for Inconsistent Findings in Previous Research   120
    Guideline 14: Cite All Relevant References in the Review Section of a Thesis, Dissertation, or Journal Article   121
    Guideline 15: Emphasize the Need for Your Study in the Literature Review Section or Chapter   121
    Activities for Chapter 10   122
    Notes   122

11 Guidelines for Developing a Coherent Essay   124

    Guideline 1: If Your Review Is Long, Provide an Overview near the Beginning of the Review   124
    Guideline 2: Near the Beginning of a Review, State Explicitly What Will and Will Not Be Covered   125
    Guideline 3: Specify Your Point of View Early in the Review   125
    Guideline 4: Aim for a Clear and Cohesive Essay and Avoid Annotations   126
    Guideline 5: Use Subheadings, Especially in Long Reviews   127
    Guideline 6: Use Transitions to Help Trace Your Argument   128
    Guideline 7: If Your Topic Spans Two or More Disciplines, Consider Reviewing Studies from Each Discipline Separately   128
    Guideline 8: Write a Conclusion for the End of the Review   129
    Guideline 9: Check the Flow of Your Argument for Coherence   130
    Activities for Chapter 11   130
    Notes   131

Part IV: Editing and Preparing the Final Draft of Your Review   133

12 Guidelines for Editing Your Essay and Incorporating Feedback   135

    Guideline 1: The Reader Is Always Right   136
    Guideline 2: Expect Your Instructor to Comment on the Content   136
    Guideline 3: Concentrate First on Comments about Your Ideas   136
    Guideline 4: Reconcile Contradictory Feedback by Seeking Clarification   137
    Guideline 5: Reconcile Comments about Style with Your Style Manual   137

Guideline 6: Allow Sufficient Time for the Feedback and Redrafting Process	137
Guideline 7: Compare Your Draft with Your Topic Outline	138
Guideline 8: Check the Structure of Your Review for Parallelism	138
Guideline 9: Avoid Overusing Direct Quotations, Especially Long Ones	138
Guideline 10: Avoid Using Synonyms for Recurring Words	139
Guideline 11: Spell Out All Acronyms When You First Use Them, and Avoid Using Too Many	140
Guideline 12: Avoid the Use of Contractions—They Are Inappropriate In Formal Academic Writing	140
Guideline 13: When Used, Coined Terms Should Be Set Off by Quotations	141
Guideline 14: Avoid Slang Expressions Colloquialisms, and Idioms	141
Guideline 15: Use Latin Abbreviations in Parenthetic Material—Elsewhere, Use English Translations	142
Guideline 16: Check Your Draft for Common Writing Conventions	142
Guideline 17: Write a Concise and Descriptive Title for the Review	143
Guideline 18: Strive for a User-friendly Draft	144
Guideline 19: Make Sure That You Have Enclosed in Quotation Marks and/or Cited All Words and Ideas That Are Not Your Own	146
Guideline 20: Use Great Care to Avoid Plagiarism	148
Guideline 21: Get Help If You Need It	151
Activities for Chapter 12	151
Notes	152

13 Preparing a Reference List — 153

Guideline 1: Consider Using Bibliographic Software to Help Manage the Details of Your References	153
Guideline 2: Place the Reference List at the End of the Review under the Main Heading "References"	154
Guideline 3: A Reference List Should Refer Only to Sources Cited in the Literature Review	154
Guideline 4: List References Alphabetically by Author's Surname	154
Guideline 5: Double-Space All Entries	154
Guideline 6: Use Hanging Indents for the Second and Subsequent Lines of References	154
Guideline 7: Learn How to Create Hanging Indents Using a Word Processing Program	155
Guideline 8: Italicize the Titles of Journals and Their Volume Numbers	155
Guideline 9: Pay Particular Attention to Capitalization	156
Guideline 10: Pay Particular Attention to Punctuation	157
Guideline 11: Do Not Add Extraneous Material Such As Abbreviations for Page Numbers	157

Guideline 12: Journal Articles Accessed Through Online Database Repositories Should Be Cited as if They Were Accessed in Their Print Form 157
Guideline 13: Provide the Date and URL in References for Material Published Online 158
Guideline 14: Format References to Books in Accordance with a Style Manual 159
Guideline 15: If Using Online Bibliographic Tools, Make Sure That Generated Citations Are Listed in Correct Format 159
Guideline 16: Double-Check the Reference List against the Citations in the Body of the Review 160
Concluding Comment 160
Activities for Chapter 13 160
Notes 160

Appendix A Comprehensive Self-editing Checklist for Refining the Final Draft **161**

Appendix B Sample Literature Reviews **167**

Index **283**

Guideline 6: Allow Sufficient Time for the Feedback and Redrafting Process — 137
Guideline 7: Compare Your Draft with Your Topic Outline — 138
Guideline 8: Check the Structure of Your Review for Parallelism — 138
Guideline 9: Avoid Overusing Direct Quotations, Especially Long Ones — 138
Guideline 10: Avoid Using Synonyms for Recurring Words — 139
Guideline 11: Spell Out All Acronyms When You First Use Them, and Avoid Using Too Many — 140
Guideline 12: Avoid the Use of Contractions—They Are Inappropriate In Formal Academic Writing — 140
Guideline 13: When Used, Coined Terms Should Be Set Off by Quotations — 141
Guideline 14: Avoid Slang Expressions Colloquialisms, and Idioms — 141
Guideline 15: Use Latin Abbreviations in Parenthetic Material—Elsewhere, Use English Translations — 142
Guideline 16: Check Your Draft for Common Writing Conventions — 142
Guideline 17: Write a Concise and Descriptive Title for the Review — 143
Guideline 18: Strive for a User-friendly Draft — 144
Guideline 19: Make Sure That You Have Enclosed in Quotation Marks and/or Cited All Words and Ideas That Are Not Your Own — 146
Guideline 20: Use Great Care to Avoid Plagiarism — 148
Guideline 21: Get Help If You Need It — 151
Activities for Chapter 12 — 151
Notes — 152

13 Preparing a Reference List — 153

Guideline 1: Consider Using Bibliographic Software to Help Manage the Details of Your References — 153
Guideline 2: Place the Reference List at the End of the Review under the Main Heading "References" — 154
Guideline 3: A Reference List Should Refer Only to Sources Cited in the Literature Review — 154
Guideline 4: List References Alphabetically by Author's Surname — 154
Guideline 5: Double-Space All Entries — 154
Guideline 6: Use Hanging Indents for the Second and Subsequent Lines of References — 154
Guideline 7: Learn How to Create Hanging Indents Using a Word Processing Program — 155
Guideline 8: Italicize the Titles of Journals and Their Volume Numbers — 155
Guideline 9: Pay Particular Attention to Capitalization — 156
Guideline 10: Pay Particular Attention to Punctuation — 157
Guideline 11: Do Not Add Extraneous Material Such As Abbreviations for Page Numbers — 157

Contents

Guideline 12: Journal Articles Accessed Through Online Database Repositories Should Be Cited as if They Were Accessed in Their Print Form   157

Guideline 13: Provide the Date and URL in References for Material Published Online   158

Guideline 14: Format References to Books in Accordance with a Style Manual   159

Guideline 15: If Using Online Bibliographic Tools, Make Sure That Generated Citations Are Listed in Correct Format   159

Guideline 16: Double-Check the Reference List against the Citations in the Body of the Review   160

Concluding Comment   160

Activities for Chapter 13   160

Notes   160

Appendix A Comprehensive Self-editing Checklist for Refining the Final Draft   161

Appendix B Sample Literature Reviews   167

Index   283

Preface

This book was designed to provide students with practical guidelines for the complex process of writing literature reviews in the social and behavioral sciences.

When *Writing Literature Reviews* was first published in 1999, university libraries had just begun to adopt digital search tools to assist with surveying the available research literature, but at the time most journals were still available only in print form. Today, by contrast, the contemporary university library is almost entirely digital, and this edition of *Writing Literature Reviews* has been recast to reflect this new digital landscape.

The author's daughter, now a university professor herself and a new co-author of *Writing Literature Reviews*, is a product of the modern digital library, and she has lent her expertise with digital databases and her recent experience in completing a doctoral dissertation to reframe the book's content. The result is a thorough rewriting and updating of the book, starting with the steps involved in searching databases, keeping track of citations, organizing the details gleaned from the literature surveyed, and producing a reference list or bibliography, all of which were rewritten to reflect the modern library's digital landscapes.

The seventh edition of *Writing Literature Reviews* maintains its primary focus on reviewing original research published in academic journals and on its relationship to theoretical literature. However, most of the guidelines presented here can also be applied to reviews of other kinds of source materials, and feedback received from readers in other fields suggests that the guidelines presented here can easily be applied across the curriculum. In fact, our book has been adopted for use in a variety of departments representing nearly 100 universities across the U.S., and a Chinese translation[1] was published in 2012 for use in universities in Taiwan and mainland China.

Preface

Audiences

There are three main audiences for *Writing Literature Reviews*.

First, this book was written for students who are asked to write literature reviews as term papers in content-area classes in the social and behavioral sciences. Often, their previous training has not prepared them for the complex task of reviewing existing research reports to produce a cohesive essay with an original point of view. Lower-division college students need guidance in learning to search databases for reports of original research and related theoretical literature, to analyze these particular types of literature, and to synthesize them into cohesive narratives. In high school, they may have relied on secondary sources such as encyclopedias, reports in the mass media, and books that synthesize the work of others. Now, they need to access the original research reports, and they need to learn the conventions for writing academic papers. This book is designed to fill these gaps by giving students detailed, step-by-step guidance on how to conduct a literature search and how to write comprehensive reviews of primary source materials.

Students beginning to work on their theses and dissertations will also benefit from this book if they have not previously received comprehensive instruction on how to prepare critical analyses of published research and the theories on which it is based. Undertaking a thesis or dissertation is stressful. This book serves as a source of calm and logic as students begin to prepare their literature review chapter.

Finally, individuals preparing to write literature reviews for possible publication in journals as well as those who need to include literature reviews in grant proposals will find that this book can serve as a resource in outlining and identifying the key components for such publications.

Unique Features

The following features make *Writing Literature Reviews* unique among textbooks designed to teach analytical writing:

- Its organization follows a systematic, natural progression of steps that writing instructors refer to as the Writing Process.
- Its focus is on writing critical reviews of original research.
- It is fundamentally based in the new digital environment that defines the new twenty-first-century university library.
- The steps and guidelines are organized sequentially and are illustrated with examples from a wide range of academic journals.
- Each chapter is designed to help students develop a set of specific products that will contribute to a competent literature review.

New to This Edition

Readers who are familiar with previous editions of *Writing Literature Reviews* will find a number of new and important additions in this one, including the following:

- This new edition was rewritten and recast to reflect the tools of the modern digital library. When this book was written initially, researchers relied almost exclusively on print materials located in the university library's "stacks." Nowadays, when asked, students look puzzled when we mention the stacks. Their library work in the modern era is done entirely online, either from home or from a computer terminal on campus. This has required us to reframe large sections of *Writing Literature Reviews* to reflect this heavy reliance on digital databases and digital repositories of journal articles.
- This edition has benefited by the addition of a new co-author with specific expertise in today's digital library research tools.
- The book's chapters have been organized into parts aimed at helping students break down the larger holistic *review of literature* exercise into a series of smaller steps. These smaller steps enable students to move easily through the multi-step writing process within the time constraints of a single semester course.
- A new Chapter 2 provides step-by-step guidance for navigating the new digital tools that are now standard components of research libraries.
- A comprehensive reorganization of chapter content throughout the book incorporates feedback from longtime adopters of the book and their students.
- We have added comprehensive discussions of new available digital tools, including bibliographic software and plagiarism detection software.
- New chapter activities were added to reflect the updated content of the reframed chapters.
- Several new model literature reviews complement existing reviews that our longtime adopters have found useful. These can serve as the basis for classroom discussions and as source material for end-of-chapter activities, as needed.

Ancillaries

A password-protected instructor teaching site (www.routledge.com/9780415315746) features resources that have been designed to help instructors plan and teach their courses. These resources include PowerPoint presentations that instructors may use to present the book's key points in a lecture format and notecards with key terms and definitions.

Notes to the Instructor

Many colleges and universities have adopted "writing across the curriculum" programs, in which students are required to write papers in all courses. While the goals of such programs are admirable, many instructors are pressed for time to cover just the traditional content of their courses, leaving them with little time to teach writing. Such instructors will find this book useful because the explicit steps in the writing process are illustrated with examples throughout, making it possible for students to use it largely on their own. In addition, many professors "naturally" write well but have given little thought to—and have no training in—*how to teach writing*. As a supplement, this book solves that dilemma by providing a detailed guide to the writing process.

Much of what most of us know about writing was learned through what Kamhi-Stein (1997) calls the "one-shot writing assignment" (p. 52).[2] This is where the instructor gives an assignment at the beginning of the term, using the prompt, "Write a paper about <*specific topic*>." Conceptually, we tend to view this type of assignment as a single task, even though students may need to go through several discrete and complex steps to complete it. In fact, when one is writing papers that involve library research, the quality of the finished product depends in large measure on the care with which one undertakes each of these steps.

The activities at the end of each chapter guide students through these various steps of the writing process. These activities can be recast as a series of tasks that can easily be incorporated into the syllabus of a survey course in a specific discipline as a multistep writing assignment. Thus, this book has two complementary audiences: (a) instructors who may want to incorporate this multistep writing approach into their course syllabus and (b) students, working independently, who may need help in planning and implementing the various stages involved in completing a major writing assignment, such as the literature review chapter of a thesis or dissertation.

Special Acknowledgment

Both authors are indebted to the founder of Pyrczak Publishing, Dr. Fred Pyrczak, for suggesting the topic for this book. Dr. Pyrczak was a friend and mentor to both co-authors, and we are grateful for his support throughout the earlier versions of the manuscript. Melisa spent her summers as a high school and college student learning the academic publishing trade from Fred, and her academic trajectory has undoubtedly been shaped by his support. From technology assistant, to copy editor, to now professor and co-author, her professional trajectory speaks to the ways in which Fred's support has shaped her career in academia.

Acknowledgments

We would like to thank our partners at Routledge and Pyrczak Publishing for their editorial and conceptual assistance in preparing this new major revision of our book.

In addition, we are indebted to our colleagues on the faculty of California State University, Los Angeles, and California State University, Northridge, especially Dr. Marguerite Ann Snow and Dr. Lia D. Kamhi-Stein, whose work on the multistep writing approach inspired this book's organization. Both of these individuals offered countless helpful suggestions, most of which are now part of the final manuscript.

We would also like to thank the following colleagues from a diverse range of institutions who provided feedback on the sixth edition of *Writing Literature Reviews*: Elizabeth F. Warren, Capella University; Michelle R. Cox, Azusa Pacific University; Nancy H. Barry, Auburn University, and Phyllis Burger, Concordia University St. Paul. The authors would also like to thank Dr. Matthew Giblin of the University of Southern Illinois, Carbondale for his helpful editorial comments.

Errors and omissions, of course, remain our responsibility.

Jose L. Galvan
Professor Emeritus
California State University, Los Angeles

Melisa C. Galvan
Assistant Professor
California State University, Northridge

Notes

1. Galvan, Jose L. (2012). *Writing literature reviews: A guide for students of the social and behavioral sciences*. Complex Chinese Edition. Taipei, Taiwan: Psychological Publishing Co.
2. Kamhi-Stein, L. D. (1997). Redesigning the writing assignment in general education courses. *College ESL, 7,* 49–61.

PART I

Managing the Literature Search

Chapter 1

Writing Reviews of Academic Literature: An Overview

This book is a guide to the specialized requirements of writing a literature review for the social and behavioral sciences. In using this book, you will learn how to write a review of the literature using primary (original) sources of information. Five different types of sources are discussed here. By far, the most common primary sources are (1) reports of empirical research published in academic journals. The first sub-heading in the section that follows refers to this type of source. It is followed by brief descriptions of four other types of material found in journals: (2) theoretical articles, (3) literature review articles, (4) anecdotal reports, and (5) reports on professional practices and standards. The second major section of this chapter consists of an overview of the writing process that you will use as you prepare your review, and it mirrors the organization of the book into its four main parts.

An Introduction to Reviewing Primary Sources

Empirical Research Reports

The focus of this book is on *original* reports of research found in academic journals. We say they are original because they are the first published accounts of particular sets of research findings. As such, they are considered *primary sources* of information, detailing the methodology used in the research and in-depth descriptions and discussions of the findings. In contrast, research summaries reported in textbooks, popular magazines, and newspapers, as well as on television and radio, are usually *secondary sources*, which typically provide only global descriptions of results with few details of the methodology used to obtain them. Furthermore, secondary sources are often incomplete, sometimes inaccurate, and their purpose tends to be more to garner casual readers' interest than to engage scholars' consideration and scrutiny. As scholars, you will want to emphasize primary sources when you review the literature on a particular topic. In fact, your instructor may require you to cite primary sources exclusively in your written reviews of literature.

Journals in the social and behavioral sciences abound with original reports of empirical research. The term *empirical* refers to *observation*, while the term *empirical research* refers to *systematic observation*. Research is systematic when researchers plan whom to observe, what characteristics to observe, how to observe, and so on. While empirical research is the foundation of any science, one could reasonably argue that all empirical research is inherently flawed. Hence, the results obtained through research should be interpreted with caution. For instance, the following is a list of three major issues that arise in almost all empirical studies and the problems they pose for reviewers of research.

- *Issue 1: Sampling.* Most researchers study only a sample of individuals and infer that the results apply to some larger group (often called the *population*). Furthermore, most researchers use samples with some kind of bias that makes them unrepresentative of the population of interest. For instance, suppose a professor conducted research using only students in his or her introductory psychology class, or suppose a researcher mailed a questionnaire and obtained only a 40 percent return from recipients. Clearly, these samples may or may not be representative of the population of interest. In the first instance, the professor may be interested only in describing the behaviors of students in his class; but if his interest is in generalizing to a wider population the limitations of his population need to be noted.

    Problem: A reviewer needs to consider the possibility of errors in sampling when interpreting the results of a study. Deciding how much trust to put in the results of a study based on a flawed sample is a highly subjective judgment.

- *Issue 2: Measurement.* Almost all measures in empirical research should be presumed to be flawed to some extent. For instance, suppose a researcher uses a self-report questionnaire to measure the incidence of marijuana use on a campus. Even if respondents are assured that their responses are confidential and anonymous, some might not want to reveal their illegal behavior. On the other hand, others might be tempted to brag about doing something illegal even if they seldom or never do it. So what are the alternatives? One may conduct personal interviews, but this measurement technique also calls for revelation of an illegal activity. Another alternative is covert observation, but this technique might be unethical. On the other hand, if the observation is not covert, participants might change their behavior because they know they are being observed. As you can see, there is no perfect solution.

    Problem: A reviewer needs to consider the possibility of measurement error. Ask yourself whether the method of measurement seems sound. Did the researcher use more than one method of measurement? If so, do the various methods yield consistent results?

■ *Issue 3: Problem identification.* Researchers usually examine only part of a problem—often just a very small part. Here is an example: Suppose a researcher wants to study the use of rewards in the classroom and their effect on creativity. This sounds manageable as a research problem until one considers that there are many kinds of rewards—many kinds and levels of praise, many types of prized objects that might be given, and so on. Another issue is that there are many different ways in which creativity can be expressed. For instance, creativity is expressed differently in the visual arts, in dance, and in music. Creativity can be expressed in the physical sciences, in oral expression, in written communication, and so on. No researcher has the resources to examine all of these forms. Instead, he or she will probably have to select only one or two types of rewards and only one or two manifestations of creativity and examine them in a limited number of classrooms.

> *Problem*: A reviewer needs to synthesize the various research reports on narrowly defined problems in a given area, looking for consistencies and discrepancies from report to report while keeping in mind that each researcher defined his or her problem in a somewhat different way. Because empirical research provides only approximations and degrees of evidence on research problems that are necessarily limited in scope, creating a synthesis is like trying to put together a jigsaw puzzle for which most of the pieces are missing and with many of its available pieces not fully formed.

Considering the three issues presented, you might be tempted to conclude that reviewing original reports of empirical research is difficult. Undoubtedly, it sometimes is. However, if you pick a topic of interest to you and thoroughly read the research on that topic, you will soon become immersed in a fascinating project. On the vast majority of topics in the social and behavioral sciences, there are at least minor disagreements about the interpretation of the available research data, and often there are major disagreements. Hence, you may soon find yourself acting like a juror, deliberating about which researchers have the most cohesive and logical arguments, which have the strongest evidence, and so on. This can be a difficult, but interesting, activity.

You also might incorrectly conclude that only students who have intensively studied research methods and statistics can make sense of original research reports. While such a background is very helpful, this book was written with the assumption that any intelligent, careful reader can make sense of a body of empirical research if he or she reads extensively on the topic selected for review. Authors of reports of original research do not present statistics in isolation. Instead, they usually provide discussions of previous research on their topic, definitions of basic concepts, descriptions of relevant theories, their reasons for approaching their research in the way they did, and interpretations of the results that are moderated by acknowledgments of the limitations of their methodology. Thus, a skilled author of a report on original empirical research will guide you through the material and make it comprehensible to you even if you do not understand all the jargon and statistics included in the research report.

One final consideration: It is essential that you carefully and thoroughly read all the research articles that you cite in your literature review. Reading only the brief abstracts (summaries) at the beginning of research articles may mislead you because of their lack of detail and, therefore, cause you to mislead the readers of your literature review. Thus, it is your ethical responsibility to read each cited reference in its entirety.

Theoretical Articles

Not every journal article is a report of original research. For instance, some articles are written for the explicit purpose of critiquing an existing theory or to propose a new one. Remember, a *theory* is a general explanation of why variables work together, how they are related to each other, and especially how they influence each other. As a unified set of constructs, a theory helps to explain how seemingly unrelated empirical observations tie together and make sense. Here is a brief example:

> Consider the *relational theory of loneliness*.[1] Among other things, this theory distinguishes between *emotional loneliness* (utter loneliness created by the lack of a close emotional attachment to another person) and *social loneliness* (feelings of isolation and loneliness created by the absence of a close social network). This theory has important implications for many areas of social and behavioral research. For instance, this theory predicts that someone who is in bereavement due to the death of a spouse with whom he or she had a close *emotional* attachment will experience utter loneliness that cannot be moderated through *social* support.

Notice two things about the example given above. First, the prediction based on the theory runs counter to the commonsense notion that those who are lonely due to the loss of a significant other will feel less lonely with the social support of family and friends. The theory suggests that this notion is only partially true at best. Specifically, it suggests that family and friends will be able to lessen *social loneliness* but be ineffective in lessening the more deeply felt and potentially devastating *emotional loneliness*. Note that it is not uncommon for a theory to lead to predictions that run counter to common sense. In fact, this is a hallmark of theories that make important contributions to understanding human affairs and our physical world.

Second, the relational theory of loneliness can be tested with empirical research. A researcher can study those who have lost significant others, asking them about how lonely they feel and the types and strength of social support they receive. To be useful, a theory must be testable with empirical methods, which helps the scientific community to determine the extent of its validity.

Your job in reviewing literature will be made easier if you identify the major theories that apply to your topic of interest. Writers of empirical research reports often identify underlying theories and discuss whether their results are consistent with them. Following up on the leads they give you in their references to the theoretical literature will provide you with a framework for thinking about the bits and pieces of evidence you find in various reports about specific and often quite narrow research projects that are published in academic journals. In fact, you might choose to build your literature review around one or more theories. In other words, a topic for a literature review might be to review the research relating to a theory.

It is important to note that a literature review that contributes to a better understanding of one or more theories has the potential to make an important contribution to the writer's field because theories often have broad implications for many areas of concern in human affairs.

Literature Review Articles

Journals often carry literature review articles,[2] that is, articles that review the literature on specific topics—much like the literature review that you will write while using this book. Most journals that publish review articles set high standards for accepting such articles. Not only must they be well-written analytical narratives that bring readers up-to-date on what is known about a given topic, they must also provide fresh insights that advance knowledge. These insights may take many forms, including (a) resolving conflicts among studies that previously seemed to contradict each other, (b) identifying new ways to interpret research results on a topic, and (c) laying out a path for future research that has the potential to advance the field significantly. As a result, going through the process of preparing a literature review is not an easy way to get published in a journal. In fact, when you begin reviewing the literature on a topic, there is no guarantee that you will arrive at the level of insight required to pass the scrutiny of a journal's editorial board. However, if you follow the guidelines outlined in this book, which emphasize, first, *analyzing* (i.e., casting a critical eye on it; pulling it apart, sometimes into pieces) and, then, *synthesizing* (i.e., putting the pieces back together in a new form) literature, you stand a better chance than the average academic writer of producing a review suitable for publication.

It is worth noting that sometimes students are discouraged when they find that their topic has recently been reviewed in an academic journal. They may believe that if the topic was already reviewed, they should select a different topic. That is not necessarily a wise decision. Instead, these students should feel fortunate to have the advantage of considering someone else's labor and insights, that is, of having someone on whose work they can build or with whom they can agree or disagree. Writing is an individual process, so two individuals reviewing the same body of literature are likely to produce distinctly different but, potentially, equally worthy interpretations and reviews.[3]

Anecdotal Reports

As you review the literature on a specific topic, you may encounter articles built on anecdotal accounts of personal experiences. An *anecdote* is a description of an experience that happened to be noticed (as opposed to an observation based on research, in which there was considerable planning regarding whom and what to observe as well as when to observe a particular phenomenon in order to gather the best information). Anecdotal accounts are most common in journals aimed at practicing professionals such as clinical psychologists, social workers, and teachers. For instance, a teacher might write a journal article describing his or her experiences with a severely underachieving student who bloomed academically while in that teacher's classroom. Other teachers may find this interesting and worth reading as a source of potential ideas. But as a contribution to science, such anecdotes are seriously deficient. Without control and comparison, we do not know to what extent this teacher has contributed to the student's progress, if at all. Perhaps the student would have bloomed without the teacher's efforts because of improved conditions at home or because of a drug for hyperactivity prescribed by a physician without the teacher's knowledge. Given these limitations, anecdotal reports should be used very sparingly in literature reviews, and when they are cited, they should be clearly labeled as anecdotal.

Reports on Professional Practices and Standards

Some journals aimed at practicing professionals publish reports on practices and standards, such as newly adopted curriculum standards for mathematics instruction in a state or proposed legislation to allow clinical psychologists to prescribe drugs. When issues such as these are relevant to a topic being reviewed, they may merit discussion in a literature review.

The Writing Process

Now that we have considered the major types of materials you will be reviewing (i.e., reports of empirical research, theoretical articles, literature review articles, articles based on anecdotal evidence, and reports on professional practices and standards), we will briefly consider the process you will follow in this book and describe its organization.

The first consideration in planning to write a literature review is to recognize your reasons for writing the literature review as well as to acknowledge who your readers will be. This can range from writing a term paper for a class, to the literature review chapter of a doctoral dissertation, or even the literature review section of a journal article. These will be important considerations in deciding both the depth of your search for primary materials and the style of your review, sometimes referred to as the *writer's voice*. Also, an important but often overlooked distinction is made in this book between *conducting* a literature review (i.e., locating literature, reading it, and mentally analyzing it) and *writing* a literature review (i.e., deciding what you want to say to your readers about the literature and organizing it into a coherent narrative essay). In other words, writing a literature review involves a series of steps. In the field of composition and rhetoric, these steps collectively are referred to as the *writing process*. They include (a) managing the search for primary sources, (b) analyzing the information in those sources that is relevant to your area of interest, (c) synthesizing and organizing the information to address a specific topic on which you will focus and, then, producing the first draft of the review, and finally, (d) editing and preparing the final draft of the review. The process is much like the one you may have followed in your freshman English class when you were asked to write an analytical essay. We will begin with the first step, which is to recognize why you are writing the literature review and for whom.

Finding Your 'Writer's Voice': Writing for a Specific Purpose

Reviews of empirical research can serve several purposes. They can constitute the essence of a research paper in a class, which can vary in length and complexity depending on the professor's criteria. In a research report in a journal, the literature review is often brief and to the point, usually focusing on providing the rationale for specific research questions or hypotheses explored in the research. In contrast, the literature review in a thesis or dissertation is usually meant to establish that the writer has a thorough command of the literature on the topic being studied, typically resulting in a relatively long literature review. Obviously, these different purposes will result in literature reviews that vary in length and style. Consider the differences in the following types of literature reviews, each of which has a unique and specific purpose.

Although the guidelines given in the chapters that follow in this book can apply to any literature review, you will want to vary your approach to the writing task in accordance to your purpose for writing a review.

Writing a Literature Review as a Term Paper for a Class

Writing a literature review as a term paper assignment for a class can be somewhat frustrating because the task involves (a) selecting a topic in a field that may be new to you, (b) identifying and locating an appropriate number of research articles using databases that you may not be familiar with, and (c) writing and editing a well-developed essay, all in about three to four months. To compound matters, most instructors will expect you to prepare your review of literature outside of class time and with minimal guidance from them. Of course, they will also expect your literature review to be thoroughly researched and well written. Fortunately, this book was designed to help you to accomplish that.

With these difficulties in mind, it is necessary for you to plan your project carefully. First, you should make sure you understand the assignment and know as much as possible about your instructor's expectations near the beginning of the semester. This means that you should not hesitate to raise questions in class regarding the assignment. Keep in mind that if something is not clear to you, it may be unclear to other students, and they will benefit by hearing the answers to your questions.[4] Second, you will need to pace yourself as you undertake the writing process. Make sure that you allow sufficient time to follow the steps outlined in this book, including the process of selecting a topic; reading and evaluating the relevant research articles; synthesizing and organizing your notes; writing, redrafting, and revising your paper; and editing it for correctness and adherence to the required style manual.[5] It is helpful to map out the weeks of your school term and lay out a timeline. The following is a suggested timeline for a 15-week semester. Note that this timeline follows the organization of this book into its 4 parts.

Example 1.0.1

Suggested timeline for a 15-week semester

Stage 1	Preliminary library search and selection of topic
	Complete by the end of Week 3
Stage 2	Reading list and preliminary paper outline
	Complete by the end of Week 6
Stage 3	First draft of paper
	Complete by the end of Week 12
Stage 4	Revised final draft of paper
	Complete by the end of Week 15

Individual instructors' expectations regarding the length of a written review and the number of references cited may vary widely. For term papers written for introductory survey courses, instructors may require only a short review—perhaps as short as a few double-spaced typewritten pages with a minimum of 5 to 10 references. For such a review, you will need to be highly selective in identifying and citing references, perhaps limiting yourself to those that are the most important and/or most current. For upper-division courses, instructors may require longer reviews, which will entail reviewing larger numbers of references. Finally, for graduate-level classes in your academic major, your instructor may place no restrictions on length or the number of references, expecting you to review as many research reports as necessary to write a comprehensive literature review on your topic.

Given the limited time frame available for writing a term paper, your topic will, of necessity, be narrow. It will help you to look for an area that is well defined, especially if you are new to a field. A good way to select a topic is to examine the subheadings within the chapters of the textbook for your course. For instance, an educational psychology textbook might have a chapter on creativity with subsections on definitions of creativity, the measurement of creativity, and fostering creativity in the classroom. As an example, suppose you are especially interested in fostering creativity in the classroom. Reading this section, you might find that your textbook author mentions that there is some controversy regarding the effects of competition on promoting creativity (i.e., Can teachers foster creativity by offering rewards for its expression?). This sounds like a fairly narrow topic that you might start with as a tentative subject. As you search for journal articles on this topic,[6] you may find that there are more articles on it than you need for the term project assignment. If so, you can narrow the topic further by specifying that your review will deal with competition and creativity only in (a) elementary school samples and/or (b) the fine arts.

If you are not given a choice of topics but instead are assigned a topic by your instructor, begin your search for literature as soon as possible and promptly report any difficulties you encounter, such as finding that there is too little research on the assigned topic (perhaps the topic can be broadened or your instructor can point you to additional sources your literature search did not identify), or that there is too much research (perhaps the topic can be narrowed or your instructor can help you to identify other delimiters, such as reviewing only recent articles).

One consequence of having a short time frame for preparing a literature review as a term paper is that opportunities for feedback on your early drafts will be limited, so you will be responsible for doing much of the editing yourself. When you lay out your timeline, leave room for consulting with your instructor about your first draft, even if this has to be done during an office visit. Finally, the self-editing checklist at the end of the book will help you eliminate some common problems before you submit your paper in final form.

Writing a Literature Review Chapter for a Thesis or Dissertation

The review chapter for a thesis or dissertation is the most complex of the literature review types covered in this book because you will be expected to prepare the initial literature review as part of your research proposal, well before you begin your actual research. Conducting a literature review is one of the steps you will follow in the process of defining the research questions for your study, so you will probably have to redefine your topic and revise your research questions several times along the way.

Students writing a literature review chapter frequently ask, "How many research articles must I cite?" In addition, they ask, "How long should I make the review?" Some students are frustrated when they learn that there is no minimum either on the number of research articles to review or on the length of a review chapter. Often, standards regarding depth and length will vary, depending on the nature of the topic, the amount of literature on it, and the expectations of your thesis chair.

You should establish two main goals for your literature review. First, attempt to provide a *comprehensive* and *up-to-date* review of the topic. Second, try to demonstrate that you have a thorough command of the field you are studying. Keep in mind that the literature review will serve as the basic rationale for conducting your research, and the extent to which you accomplish these goals will contribute in large measure to how well your project will be received. Note that these goals reflect the seriousness of the task you have undertaken, which is to contribute to the body of knowledge in your field. Several traditions that have evolved through the years reflect how seriously academic departments view the writing of a thesis or dissertation. These include the defense of the research proposal, the defense of the finished thesis or dissertation, and the careful scrutiny of the final document by the university prior to its acceptance as a permanent addition to the library's holdings.

Some students procrastinate when it comes to writing a literature review chapter for a thesis or dissertation. After all, usually there are no set timelines. Therefore, it is important for you to set deadlines for yourself. Some students find it useful to plan an informal timeline in collaboration with the committee chair, perhaps by setting deadlines for completing the various steps involved in the overall process. The guidelines described in this book will be helpful in this regard. You should adopt a regular pattern of consultation with the professors on your committee to ensure that you remain focused and on track.

Finally, the level of accuracy expected in a thesis or dissertation project is quite high. This will require that you edit your writing to a level that far exceeds what may be expected in a term paper assignment. Not only must your writing conform to the particular style manual used in your field, but it should also be free of mechanical and grammatical errors. The guidelines in Chapter 12 and the self-editing checklist at the end of the book will help you to accomplish this. Make sure that you allow sufficient time to set your draft aside for a few days before editing your writing, and expect to use the self-editing guide several times before you give your adviser a draft of the review.

Writing a Literature Review for a Research Article

The literature review section of a research article published in a journal is the most straightforward of the three types of reviews covered in this book. These literature reviews are usually shorter and more focused than other types because their major purpose is to provide the background and rationale for specific and often very narrow research projects.

On the other hand, these reviews undergo a level of scrutiny that may exceed even that of a review for a thesis or dissertation. Research article submissions for refereed journals are routinely evaluated by two or three of the leading scholars in the area in which the research was conducted. This means that the literature review should not only reflect the current state of research on the topic, but it should also be error-free. Again, the self-editing checklist should be carefully applied.

Frequently, an author will write a journal article a year or more after the research was conducted. This often happens when students decide to write shorter, article-length versions of their theses or dissertations, or when they reframe a chapter or two into an article-length manuscript. If this applies to you, search the latest issues of the journals in your field to make sure that your literature review cites the latest work published on your topic.

Although there is some variation among journals, the literature review in a research article for a journal is usually expected to be combined with the introduction. In other words, the introduction to the research is framed as a short essay that introduces readers to both the topic and the purpose of the research while providing an overview of the relevant literature. Therefore, in preparing a research article, the emphasis of the review should be on establishing the scientific context in which a particular study was conducted and on the contributions it makes to the field. It should help to demonstrate the rationale for the original research reported in the article. As such, it is typically much more narrow and focused than a literature review chapter for a thesis or dissertation.

The Parts of this Text

Managing the Literature Search—Part I

As noted, this book is organized into four parts. Part I of this book describes how to manage the literature search. This is an essential part of the *planning-to-write* phase of the Writing Process. The current chapter provides an overview of the topic of academic literature reviews. Next, Chapter 2 guides you through the process of becoming familiar with the digital landscape of your university's library. Once you have mastered the digital search mechanics and have identified the principal digital databases for your field and topic, Chapter 3 assists you in conducting the process of surveying the totality of titles available in the databases you have targeted. Using a combination of keywords associated with each article, subject guides, and other resources available through your library, you will carefully refine your list of titles and use them in preparing a tentative written description of the topic of your review. The steps in Chapter 3 will assist you in refining your list of topics in order to identify the set of articles you plan to include in your review. Chapter 4 ends Part I with a description of how to organize your collection of articles in ways that will facilitate the collection of information from their contents. You will learn how to scan the articles and then group them according to a set of categories you develop, which will assist you in recording your notes in an orderly format that can be sorted and reorganized easily.

Analyzing the Relevant Literature—Part II

Part II of the book deals with the process of sifting through the information presented in the articles you have selected and organizing the information to address the specific topic that is the focus of your review. To begin the analysis of primary sources, you will need to read and gather specific information from each of the articles you have assembled, and Chapter 5 gives you step-by-step guidance in accomplishing this analysis. In other words, as you read, you separate the author's prose into its parts or elements. Because you will be analyzing a number of articles, you will need to prepare a systematic collection of notes. Part of the analysis process is sifting the elements on which you made notes, retaining the pertinent ones, and discarding those you do not need.

It is sometimes necessary to read and analyze the literature from a more specialized perspective. For instance, if your literature review is part of a research study you are planning to conduct, you will want to pay special attention to Chapter 6 (Analyzing Quantitative Research Literature) and Chapter 7 (Analyzing Qualitative Research Literature). These chapters provide brief overviews of more technical issues in analyzing these types of research.

The final step before you begin to write the first draft of your review is to organize your notes by assembling them into logical groupings. Chapter 8 describes a number of possible ways to arrange the information into formats that will facilitate greatly the actual writing of the draft that you are about to begin.

Writing the First Draft of Your Literature Review—Part III

Part III carries you through the steps leading to the writing of the first draft of your literature review. Having followed the steps in Part II, you are now able to begin creating a *synthesis* of the material you have read, which involves putting the parts from your notes back together into a new whole, a new organizational framework that supports your own point of view. Think of it like this: Each of the articles you read constitutes its own whole, but you must now create your own new whole made up of the parts or elements from the collection of articles you have read. That is the essence of Chapter 9. As part of this process, you need to describe your evaluation of the quality and importance of the research you have cited.

Now you are ready to write your first draft. With your audience in mind, decide whether you will write in a formal or less formal *voice*. An effective writer is aware of the reader's expectations and writes in ways that will meet those needs. For instance, a term paper written for a professor who is knowledgeable in a particular field is different from a literature review written for a thesis, which may be read by readers who are curious but not necessarily knowledgeable about a topic. A literature review in a thesis is different from a literature review in an article intended for publication in a journal or in a research paper written for a class. You should also identify the major subtopics and determine the patterns that have emerged from your notes, such as trends, similarities, contrasts, and generalizations. These steps are covered in Chapter 10. Once you have the first draft in hand, you need to make sure that your argument is clear, logical, and well supported, and that your draft is free of errors. Chapter 11 will help ensure that your argument makes sense to you and your readers.

Editing and Preparing the Final Draft of Your Review—Part IV

The final two chapters of this book, which comprise Part IV, coincide with the last two steps in the writing process: editing and redrafting your review. These steps are iterative (i.e., they are meant to be repeated). It is not uncommon for a professional writer to rewrite a draft three or more times, each time producing a refined, new and improved draft. Chapter 12 provides guidelines on how to approach the process of editing your essay and incorporating feedback from your readers, and Chapter 13 provides a detailed overview of how to prepare reference lists consistent with the principles outlined in the *Publication Manual of the American Psychological Association* (APA), which is the most frequently used style manual in the social and behavioral sciences. Once these steps are completed, you are ready to submit your finished product to its intended audience, be it your course instructor, your thesis chair, or the editor of the journal for which it was targeted. As noted, the editing and redrafting process is iterative, so you can expect to receive suggestions for changes, additions, and/or restructuring that will no doubt result in a new and improved final version of your review.

Activities for Chapter 1

1. Locate an original report of empirical research in your field, read it, and respond to the following questions. Note that your instructor may want to assign a particular research article for this activity. You will learn how to locate journal articles on specific topics by reading the remaining chapters in Part I of this book. At this point, however, your reference librarian or instructor can help you to identify specific journals in your field that are available in your college library.

Now, referring to the research article you have located or which your instructor has assigned, respond to the following questions.

A. Are there any obvious sampling problems? Explain. (Do not just read the section under the subheading "Sample" because researchers sometimes provide additional information about the sample throughout their reports, especially in the introduction, where they might point out how their sample is different from those used by other researchers, or near the end, where they might discuss the limitations of the sample in relation to the results.)
B. Are there any obvious measurement problems? Explain.
C. Has the researcher examined only a narrowly defined problem? Explain.
D. Did you notice any other flaws? Explain.
E. Overall, do you think the research makes an important contribution to advancing knowledge? Explain.

2. Read the first sample literature review (Review 1) near the end of this book and respond to the following questions. Note that you will want to read this review again after you have learned more about the process of writing a literature review. The questions below ask only for your first, general impressions. Later, you will be able to critique the review in greater detail.

A. Have the reviewers clearly identified the topic of the review? Have they indicated its delimitations? (For instance, is it limited to a certain type of individual or certain period of time? Does it deal only with certain aspects of the problem?)
B. Is the literature review written as a cohesive essay that guides you through the literature from subtopic to subtopic? Explain.
C. Have the reviewers interpreted and critiqued the literature, *or* have they merely summarized it? Give examples and discuss.
D. Overall, do you think the reviewers make an important contribution to knowledge through their synthesis of the literature? Explain.

Notes

1   This example is based on material in Stroebe, W., Stroebe, M., Abakoumkin, G., & Schut, H. (1996). The role of loneliness and social support in adjustment to loss: A test of attachment versus stress theory. *Journal of Personality and Social Psychology, 70,* 1241–1249. The relational theory of loneliness is based on and is an extension of *attachment theory*. For a detailed discussion of attachment theory, see Milyavskaya, M., McClure, M. J., Ma, D., Koestner, R., & Lydon, J. (2012). Attachment moderates the effects of autonomy-supportive and controlling interpersonal primes on intrinsic motivation. *Canadian Journal of Behavioural Science, 44,* 278–287.

2. Some journals also carry book reviews, test reviews, and reviews of other products and services. These will not be considered in this book. Hence, the term *review article* in this book refers only to a *literature review* article.
3. Keep in mind that empirical knowledge is an ever-evolving concept—not a fixed set of facts. Nothing is proven by empirical research; rather, research is used to arrive at varying degrees of confidence. Thus, researchers may differ in their interpretations even if they review the same literature on a given topic.
4. Idiosyncratic questions that other students may not find of interest generally should be raised with the instructor outside of class, perhaps during office hours. Examples: You are planning to go to graduate school and want to write a more extensive paper than required by the professor, or you have written a literature review for a previous class and would prefer to expand on it rather than write a new review.
5. The dominant style manual in the social and behavioral sciences is the *Publication Manual of the American Psychological Association* (now in its 6th edition). It is available for purchase from most college and university bookstores, and it can be purchased online at www.apastyle.org.
6. Searching electronic databases with an emphasis on how to narrow the search is discussed in detail in the next chapter.

Chapter 2

Learn to Navigate the Electronic Resources in Your University's Library

The majority of academic primary source literature is now available online. In fact, there is an increasing number of academic journals that exclusively publish their material in digital format. Academic research no longer requires that you conduct searches from within the stacks of a campus library, meaning that most preliminary library research must now be done online. As a result, you will most likely be conducting your research by using your own computer, probably from the comfort of your own home. In fact, it is very common for students to begin the research process well before they ever set foot in their university library. This means that familiarity and facility with online search tools is essential to conducting research in today's academic environment, and this chapter outlines some general approaches to searching and identifying online databases most relevant to your field of study.

Note that this chapter is written to assist novice researchers, some of whom are recent high school students. Upper-division and graduate students may not need the step-by-step guidance provided here for navigating online databases, but the overarching process of winnowing down references will apply to all students, both undergraduates and graduates.

✔ Step 1: Formalize Your Institutional Affiliation with Your University Library

Before you can access your library's online resources it is important that you first consult with a research librarian or your university's technology office to make sure that your institutional affiliation has been set up and is functional. In other words, you need to verify that the online login credentials that provide you with access to email, Wi-Fi, and other on-campus resources also include access to your library resources. Having this information readily available is necessary for you to begin the process of accessing your library's databases, either from on- or off-campus.

Navigating Electronic Resources

✔ Step 2: Set Up Your Online Access Credentials and/or Proxy Server

Your next task is to learn the specific steps you will need to follow in order to log into your library's online research services. Most universities do not require that you provide login credentials if you are simply accessing university resources from one of the library's computer stations, but you will still need to log into the network if you wish to print or otherwise save your results. Regardless of where you choose to conduct your research, at home or at the library, it is wise to have already acquired your access credentials so that you have the flexibility to login from either on- or off-campus.

Universities require that institutional affiliates (students, faculty, staff) have credentials to log into their various online resources and portals. University libraries often have their own login procedures for students who wish to access their resources from off-campus. Many academic institutions refer to this as setting up a *Proxy Server* or *Virtual Private Network (VPN)*, and in most cases they provide detailed guidelines for doing this on their library or Institutional Technology websites. A broad search of "Accessing Library Resources from Off-Campus" on your university's main webpage will help in locating this information.

Rather than requiring that you set up specialized *Proxy Servers* or *VPNs*, some university libraries require that you first visit their library homepage and use their hyperlinks to their online resources before redirecting you to the off-campus login pages. In many cases, you are required to visit your library's centralized online article database webpage first. When you click on the journal/database that you wish to access, you will be prompted to provide your institutional credentials, which will grant you access to the database. If you are able to set up a *Proxy Server* or *VPN* initially, you would in most cases bypass this process.

✔ Step 3: Inquire about University Library Research Workshops

Before beginning your own searches of online databases, it is strongly recommended that you inquire with your library about workshops tailored specifically to the library research process at your specific institution. Even if you have conducted online research before, these workshops are enormously helpful in walking you through the process and providing useful tips.

It is also recommended that you seek one-on-one assistance from a reference librarian that specializes in your field of study. Most university libraries have librarians assigned to specific disciplines (Education, Psychology, and so on) and/or departments. These librarians will have specialized knowledge of the databases and journals for your particular field, and they will save you valuable time by identifying the relevant online resources.

✔ Step 4: Select a Search Engine that Best Suits Your Needs

Learning to navigate a wide array of online databases can be intimidating. Each online database will have its own unique search engine, which you must learn to navigate as described in the steps that follow.

Generally speaking, it is best to begin with a database that casts as wide a net as possible for identifying potential research materials. Two search tools that are currently used at academic institutions are WorldCat and Google Scholar, and both provide free and unrestricted access to the public but also give you the option of linking directly to your university's library catalogs. It is recommended that you consult with a reference librarian to identify other databases specific to your discipline.

It is important to note that WorldCat searches a virtual database consisting of the catalogues of about 72,000 libraries in 170 countries and territories that participate in the Online Computer Library Center (OCLC) global cooperative. Almost all academic libraries in the U.S. participate in OCLC. By contrast, Google Scholar is a search engine that scours the web for academic texts found in online repositories, including journals and books, conference papers, theses and dissertations, abstracts, technical reports, and other scholarly literature. However, unless Google Scholar's settings are manipulated to search only the catalogs of particular databases or libraries, it can capture items that do not meet accepted peer-review academic standards. In other words, Google Scholar functions in the same way that a typical Google search operates, giving you any and all items posted on websites it locates, unless it is constrained using specific parameters that you must choose.

Most scholars that we consulted prefer to use WorldCat because they consider the search results to be more trustworthy and comprehensive. Still, some academics and university libraries have begun recommending that students use Google Scholar, which some describe as easier to use than WorldCat given its streamlined Google search box format. As noted, unless Google Scholar's settings are restricted it can capture items that do not meet accepted academic standards, so if you opt to use it make sure that you learn how to rein in its reach. Your research librarian can assist you with this.

We suggest that you consult with your instructor and your research librarian as you consider which databases to search for your project. Most university libraries offer online tutorials that will guide you in their use and provide accessibility information specific to your academic institution.

We have chosen to use WorldCat in this chapter to illustrate the search process, but it is recommended that you follow the general guidelines outlined here even if you choose to use other databases and/or search tools.

Navigating Electronic Resources

✔ Step 5: Familiarize Yourself with How Online Databases Function

As noted, regardless of which database you select for the search, it is important that you begin by learning how to navigate its website and that you plan to spend sufficient time for you to gain confidence in navigating the various parameters provided for you to conduct more structured and more targeted (i.e., narrower) searches. This will be especially important at times of the academic year when you may be under a great deal of pressure.

Whether you choose to use WorldCat or other databases, your first step will be to learn how to narrow your search parameters. The examples that follow illustrate the recommended procedures for manipulating the WorldCat parameters to narrow your search results.

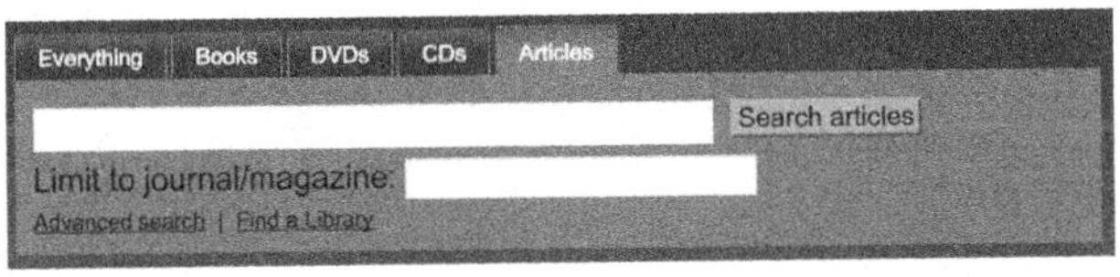

Figure 2.5.1 Limiting your search results to just "Articles"

When you first visit WorldCat.org (and most university library catalogs), you will find that the starting search page will have selected a default setting that will automatically search every record in its database. In WorldCat, this default setting is labeled "everything," and the search will bring up all titles (books, articles, reports, etc.) found within the database. Other databases may use various other labels for these type of all-inclusive searches, such as "OneSearch," "Multi-Search," etc.

Given that most literature reviews will emphasize journal articles as their primary source parameter, you will need to be sure that you select the "Articles" tab first, which will give you as output the entire list of journal article titles catalogued under the keyword(s) you have selected. You will notice that you also have the ability to limit your search results to a specific journal, which may be useful if your instructor has directed you in a particular direction. But first, consider how to identify the desired keyword(s), as demonstrated in the following example.

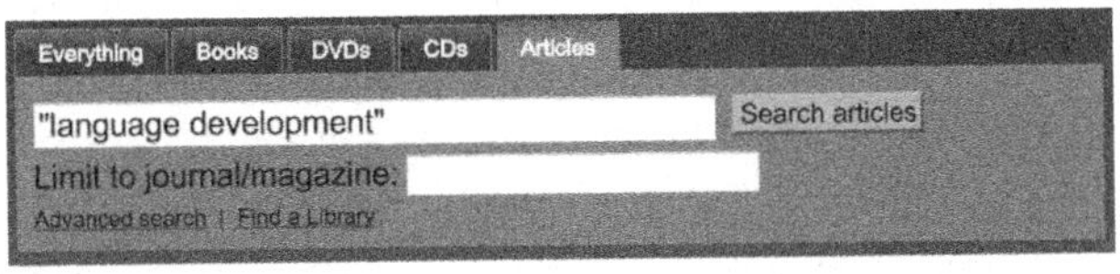

Figure 2.5.2 Input the relevant search keywords

Part I: Managing the Literature Search

Now that you have selected the "Articles" tab, you will need to input the relevant search keywords for your sample search. Obviously, this step requires that you have an idea of what you want to research. If your topic is still undetermined or if it is still very broad, Chapter 3 will provide detailed advice to help you through the process of narrowing the search keywords as well as for selecting a final topic.

For the purposes of these examples, we have entered the keyword "language development" (with quotations), and the WorldCat database returned 39,141 "hits" or specific published articles that it lists under this keyword.[1] The list is obviously impractical because of its size, and the following steps will illustrate the process of further narrowing down the results. Note that it is important that you enclose multi-word entries, such as "language development" in quotation marks. Otherwise, the search engine will look for all possible combinations of the individual words in your entry, including "language," "development," and "language development."

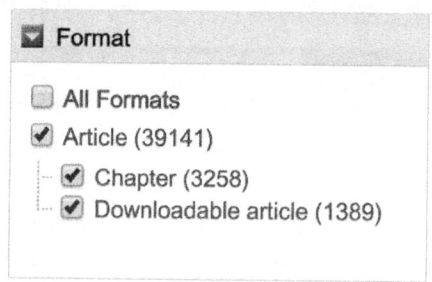

Figure 2.5.3 Scan your results as a first step in narrowing your search

As noted, your results using the keyword "language development" are much too broad. By scanning the results, however, you will quickly see several patterns evident in the listings given, including some that are specific to "children vs. adults" or "syntax vs. phonetics" or "first vs. second language acquisition." Suppose you select the still very broad topic "Second Language Acquisition." This topic will yield a narrower result, 20,657 hits, but even this list is much too large to be useful to you. Keep in mind that it is usually best to start with a general topic in order to be able to assess the amount of literature available for it, because this will help you to narrow it down to a more manageable result. But a result of more than 10,000 hits will need to be narrowed down, so by studying the parameters given in WorldCat, we now narrow the search to just "downloadable Articles" (the sidebar to the left of your search results, under the label "Format," permits you to delimit your search by the specific formats you select) and now our list numbers 754 articles. While this number is still too large for a term paper, it is probably a reasonable result if your objective is a thesis or dissertation.

Navigating Electronic Resources

In an actual assignment, you would continue to narrow your search parameters until you arrived at a more manageable and focused result. The lesson to be learned from these examples is that you should always remain open to modifying the keywords you use based on the results of your search.

In most cases, your library website will contain a "Databases" page that will arrange your university's online resources by subject. These are usually referred to as *Subject Guides*. Many institutions tailor their guides to the specific interests of their academic departments. This is an easy way to help identify journals that pertain to your given field of research and to which your institution provides access.

Note that depending on your library's subscriptions you may or may not have access to all the journals that you identify with outside search engines like WorldCat. Therefore, it is recommended that you discuss your results with a research librarian (who may be able to help identify additional resources), and also with your instructor.

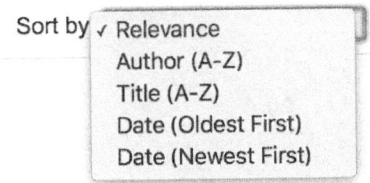

Figure 2.5.4 Locate the "Sort By" option on your search results page

As you scan the 754 titles generated in the above example, you will notice that the results are given in a somewhat random order, so you will need to use the "Sort By" option available in the WorldCat database. This is a pull-down menu located in the upper right-hand corner of the search results page, and it provides you the option of sorting the titles obtained either by Relevance (the default option) or by Author, Title, or Date (Oldest First or Newest First). Sorting by "Newest First" easily organizes your results in a manner that displays the most recently published research first. This can be helpful if you will be assessing the current-day state of research in a field. This option will provide an easy way of locating articles that will help you to refine your search.

Again, in an actual assignment, you would continue to narrow your search parameters to obtain more and more focused results. Continue this process by experimenting with the "Advanced Search" feature, which is described in Step 6.

✓ Step 6: Experiment with the "Advanced Search" Feature

"Advanced Search" features are available on most online databases. By clicking on "Advanced Search" you will be able to further manipulate the database's search parameters. This can prove quite useful if you are being asked to survey literature only for a specific time period (i.e. the last 10 years), or if you have already identified a scholar who has published widely on your topic.

Depending on how broad your search parameters are, your search may return a large number of results, as demonstrated in the examples above, and as you begin to specify more focused parameters you will derive a more focused result. One additional tool available to you for this process is illustrated in the screenshot that follows, which was found on WorldCat.org (see Figure 2.6.1). Notice that by using the Advanced Search page, you will have the option of narrowing your search further, by Year, Audience, Content, Format, and Language.

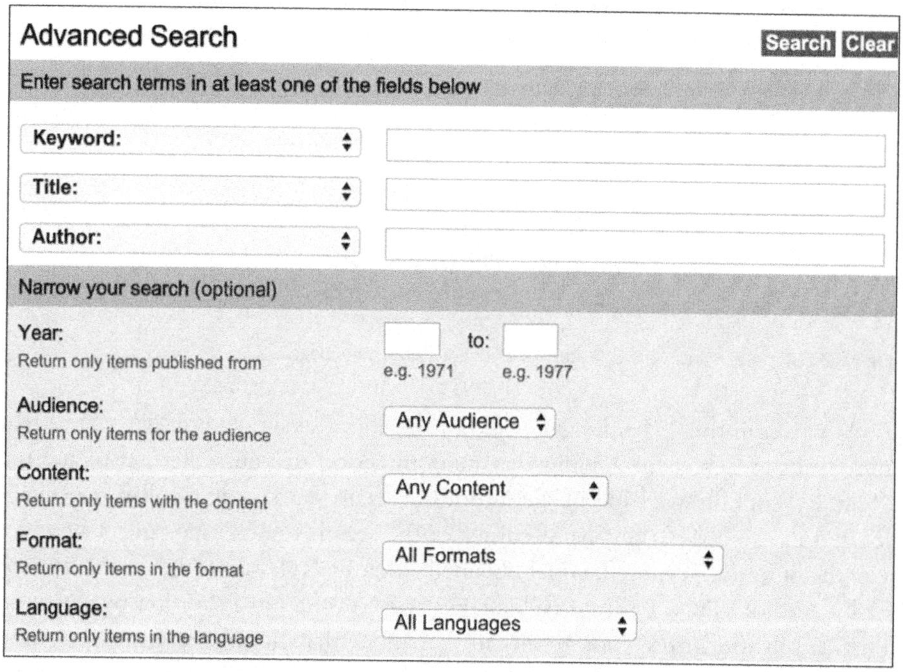

Figure 2.6.1 WorldCat's "Advanced Search" page

✔ Step 7: Identify an Array of Subject Keywords to Locate Your Sources

By clicking on each of the thousands of journal articles listed in these databases, you will retrieve an expanded set of information about the article. For instance, you will see the article's title, author, source journal, publication date, abstract, and *subject keywords* (i.e., descriptive terms and phrases that describe the article's contents). You are now able to narrow the scope of a search by manipulating one or more of these fields. If the subject keywords used in conducting your initial search prove to be too broad, as in our examples above, these fields will help you to refine the search. For example, one of the headings shown when you click on one of the articles will be "Subjects," and this will reveal additional possible keywords that can be used to identify articles with particular relevance to the one you have chosen. Once you have identified a list of new subject keywords, it is recommended that you initiate another search using the new term(s) to obtain even more results.

✔ Step 8: Learn How You Can Access the Articles You Choose

Following on from Step 7, after you have identified a relevant source, you must now learn how to obtain access to it. Depending on your library's database subscriptions and whether or not you have set up your *Proxy* or *VPN*, you may or may not be able to view the full text of the entries that you select.

Some articles will allow access by directly clicking on the "View Full Text" button. Depending on your computer's browser settings, WorldCat may already have determined your geographic location and may have listed nearby libraries that own the item. If you are logged in with a *Proxy* or *VPN*, another box may appear that will help you determine whether your library owns the item. Note that depending on your library's subscriptions you may not have access to all the journals that you identify, which may require that you use the Inter-Library Loan procedure. Your research librarian will guide you through this process.

✔ Step 9: Identify Additional Databases that May Be Useful for Your Field of Study

Every academic field has developed its own database services, which were designed to serve the needs of its students and scholars. Early in your search, you should identify the databases specific to your field of study, in consultation with your library's research librarian or your instructor. To emphasize, in addition to the information you receive in the library, you should ask your adviser or instructor about the preferred databases in your field. Then, you can find out where they are available and how to access them.

Once you have identified the databases that pertain most closely to your field of study, you should next make a list of databases to search once you have sufficiently narrowed your research topic. As an example, Figure 2.9.1 provides the library catalog OneSearch's suggestions for the "Most Useful" databases in "Linguistics/TESL." After you have identified a similar list for your field of study, you will be able to begin the research process for your topic.

> **Linguistics/TESL**
>
> **Most Useful**
>
> **Linguistics and Language Behavior Abstracts (LLBA)**
> Abstracts and indexes the international literature in linguistics and related disciplines in the language sciences. Covers all aspects of the study of language including phonetics, phonology, morphology, syntax and semantics. Documents indexed include journal articles, book reviews, books, book cha . . .
> More information
>
> **Communication & Mass Media Complete (EBSCO)**
> Indexing and abstracts for more than 600 journals and full text for over 500 journals in communication studies, speech, mass media, journalism, linguistics, and communicative disorders.
> More information
>
> **ERIC (ProQuest)**
> ERIC (Educational Resources Information Center) is sponsored by the U.S. Department of Education to provide extensive access to educational-related literature. ERIC provides coverage of journal articles, conferences, meetings, government documents, theses, dissertations, reports, audiovisual media, . . .
> More information
>
> **MLA International Bibliography (ProQuest)**
> Provides searchable access to more than 2 million bibliographic citations to journal articles, books, dissertations, and scholarly websites in academic disciplines such as language, literature, folklore, linguistics, literary theory and criticism, and the dramatic arts. Coverage includes literature . . .
> More information
>
> **Project MUSE**
> Full text of over 300 peer-reviewed journals published by university presses and scholarly societies with emphasis on humanities and social sciences.
> More information
>
> **JSTOR**
> Comprehensive archive of back issues of core scholarly journals in the arts, business, humanities, sciences and social sciences.
> More information

Figure 2.9.1 OneSearch online database subject guide for Linguistics/TESL

Keep in mind that if you have not set up your university access account, you will need to do so before searching these other databases (refer to Steps 1 and 2 earlier in this chapter). In fact, larger research libraries will have many more research services than are described here. If you are a student at a small university, it is recommended that you investigate whether your university's library maintains cooperative arrangements with larger institutions in your area. It is recommended that you discuss your results with a research librarian, who may be able to help identify further resources, and also with your instructor.

✔ Step 10: Repeat the Search Procedures with Other Databases

The Steps described above should have familiarized you with how to navigate and manipulate the search parameters of one major online database, WorldCat.org. Because the databases that you will consult will depend on your discipline, it is wise to repeat these steps with any other databases that you identify.

Activities for Chapter 2

1. Formalize your institutional affiliation with your university library. Consult with a reference librarian and/or your campus Institutional Technology office to determine the steps necessary to access library resources from off-campus.
2. Inquire about research workshops to learn how to navigate your university's library's online resources. These are usually scheduled by the university library. Also, identify the relevant research librarian for your field of study, and schedule an appointment to inquire about the library's available resources.
3. Conduct a sample search using WorldCat.org. Limit your search to specific types of sources (articles, books, etc.). Be sure that you experiment with both the "Advanced Search" and "Sort by" features.
4. Locate your library's online database *Subject Guides* for your field of study. Create a list of databases that you will need to search once you have identified your topic.

Note

1. Note that this particular search was conducted at 11:15 a.m. PST on June 24, 2016 and generated the results given in this and the following examples. The actual number of results you obtain will depend on when your search is conducted.

Chapter 3

Selecting a Topic for Your Review

"Where should I begin?" This may be the question most commonly asked by students preparing to write a literature review. While there is no easy answer, this chapter was designed to illustrate the process used by many professional writers and researchers in getting started. Keep in mind that writing is an individual process, so the procedures described here are intended as a roadmap rather than a prescription. By working through this chapter, you will be able to develop two important products that will help you to begin writing an effective literature review: a written description of your topic and a working draft of your reading list.

Obviously, the first step in any kind of academic writing is to decide what you will write about, but the specific path you follow in working through this step will vary depending on your purpose for writing a literature review. Chapter 1 described the three most common reasons for writing literature reviews.

✔ Step 1: Define Your General Topic

In any type of literature review you should narrowly define your topic. Example 3.1.1 presents a topic that is much too general. In fact, it is the title of a survey course taught at many major universities and represents a very extensive body of literature.

Example 3.1.1

Topic that is too general

General Topic: Child Language Acquisition

Obviously, the topic in Example 3.1.1 will have to be narrowed down considerably before it can be used as the basis for a literature review of manageable length. The steps that follow will guide you through a process that will result in better alternatives to this example.

Selecting a Topic

✔ Step 2: Familiarize Yourself with the Basic Organization of Your Selected Online Database

As noted in Chapter 2, before you begin to narrow down your research topic it is important that you familiarize yourself with the organization of the online databases that you wish to search. WorldCat.org and the vast majority of university library catalogs contain entries for a diverse body of sources, including journal articles, books, conference presentations, archival material, government documents, and so on. Because this book focuses on reviewing articles in academic journals, it is critical that you know how to manipulate your database search results to limit your results to these types of source materials. Thus, while narrowing down your overall topic is an important step, teaching yourself how to manage your search results so that they provide a manageable corpus of entries for you to consult is equally important.

✔ Step 3: Begin Your Search with a General Keyword, then Limit the Output

Unless you have previous knowledge of a particular topic, you should begin a database search with a general *keyword*. It is advised that you use a label or phrase that best describes the topic that you are investigating. Your keywords may be broader or narrower depending on how far along you are in the research process.

If this procedure results in too many references, you can limit the search by adding additional keywords with *Boolean operators* such as AND, OR, and NOT. For instance, if you search for *social* AND *phobia*, you will get only those entries that mention *both* of these terms.

Some databases, including *PsycARTICLES (EBSCO)* self-generate alternative search keywords and phrases as you are inputting your own. For instance, when you input *social phobia*, the database also suggests *social anxiety*. You should make note of these alternative subject keywords in case you would like to use them for further searches in other databases.

Here is one example of how Boolean operators helped to narrow down a search. Searching one major database in psychology, *PsycARTICLES (EBSCO)*, with the keyword *phobia*, from 2006 to 2016 yields 188 articles.[1] A search for *social* AND *phobia* yields 125 articles. Finally, a search for *children* AND *social* AND *phobia* yields only 22 articles. The specific steps that you will follow to limit your search outputs will vary depending on the database that you are searching. Chapter 2 presented a number of general strategies to help you familiarize yourself with search options in online databases.

Some online databases will automatically use your keywords to search titles, abstracts, and the *full text* of their articles. If searching in a database that does this

Part I: Managing the Literature Search

by default, such as *JSTOR*, you may need to implement further strategies to limit your search results. As described above, one effective technique for limiting the number of search results is to limit the search to keywords that only appear in the title AND abstract (summary of the article). Using these restrictions will help to eliminate articles in which the keyword is mentioned only in passing in the body of the article.

For example, the same search of *PsycARTICLES (EBSCO)* with the keyword *phobia* that includes a search of the full text of all articles yields 2,210 results. This is a much larger number than the 188 articles mentioned above and could be overwhelming to manage. Alternatively, if you offer even greater restriction with Boolean operators and limit the search to articles where *phobia* appears in BOTH the title AND the abstract (See Figure 3.3.1), 37 articles were obtained, which is a much smaller and more manageable number, depending on the scope and purpose of your literature review.

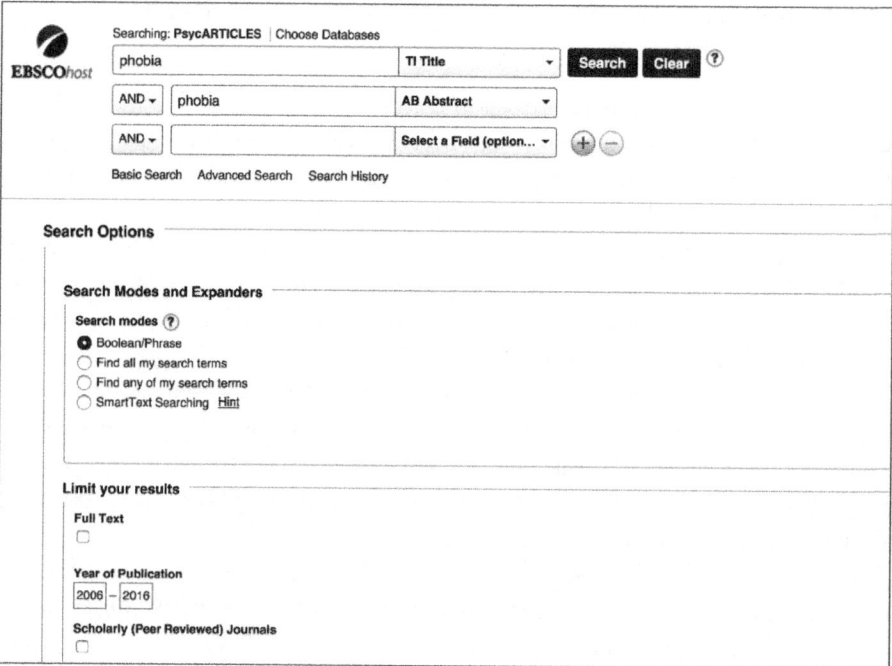

Figure 3.3.1 Sample database search with limited output criteria

Even though you may be in the early stages of experimenting with search keywords and their outputs, it is important that you save any results that appear to be of particular relevance to your topic. See Step 11 for more information about this process.

✔ Step 4: Identify Narrower Topic Areas If Your Initial List of Search Results Is Too Long

If the initial list of search results is too long, you should classify and clump recurring subtopics. Clumping search results into smaller topic areas will help facilitate the narrowing down of your overall topic. After having done this, you can then choose from one of the identified topic areas, according to your interest and the potential relevance to your course of study. Example 3.4.1 presents five possible revised topics that have been reclassified according to major themes discerned from a review of the titles and abstracts of the preliminary database search results of the broad topic, *Second Language Acquisition*.

Example 3.4.1

Identifying possible topic areas amongst initial search results

- Disorders Affecting Language Acquisition
- Role of Parents in Child Language Acquisition
- Language Acquisition Specifically Limited to Spanish-Speaking Children
- Acquisition of Grammatical Structures and Categories
- Language Acquisition in Infancy

These classifications are given merely to illustrate the process. In fact, search results could be reclassified into numerous other categories, and it is not necessary to sub-categorize them all. The objective here is to get a feel for the topics of interest or for methods of study represented within the broader spectrum of research articles suggested by your initial database search. It should be noted that some of the articles that you classify may appear in more than one topic area.

After classifying your results as shown in Example 3.4.1, examine them carefully for subsets that might serve as a topic for your literature review. For instance, a number of the articles for "Language Acquisition in Infancy" deal specifically with infant vocalization. If the number of articles identified for this identified subset is not sufficient for your purposes, proceed to Step 5 below. If not, you may choose to proceed to Step 6.

✔ Step 5: Increase the Size of Your Reference List, If Necessary

There are a number of ways to increase the number of search results once you have identified a manageable topic. First and foremost, if you have used date restrictions (i.e. 2006 to 2016) and do not have enough references for your literature review, you can, of course, expand your time frame.

Depending on the database you are searching, you might also find additional references by clicking on the author's name. You should do this with articles that you have identified as being particularly relevant to your topic. You can usually tell that a link is available if their name is underlined and/or in blue font. Clicking on the authors' names in co-authored articles may provide a number of additional references written by the same set of authors, including research reports and journal articles. Because academic scholars tend to conduct research and write on a given topic over an extended period of time, additional references that you identify may also prove to be relevant to the topic at hand.

In addition, as noted in Chapter 2, when examining an article entry, you may also choose to examine the list of hyperlink "Subject Keywords" for that article (see Figure 3.5.1 for an example of such a list). These descriptors may point you to related topics and other sources. By clicking on any one of these, you will conduct a new search of articles on whichever topic you select, potentially increasing the size of your reference list by identifying additional related articles.

Subjects: *Infant Development; *Language Development; *Learning; *Speech Perception; *Words (Phonetic Units); Statistics

---

Figure 3.5.1 Sample subject keywords in a *PsycARTICLES (EBSCO)* entry

It is also possible to search databases for other types of sources such as conference papers, curriculum guides, and theses and dissertations, which can be used to supplement the journal articles already identified. Refer to Chapter 2 for ways that you can expand or contract the type of entries displayed within your search results.

Note that for a report to be published in a journal, it usually must pass the scrutiny of one or more editors and editorial consultants or reviewers with special knowledge of the area. This is *not* the case, however, for many of the other types of sources included in online databases. Also, note that most databases do not attempt to judge the soundness or quality of the information in their entries. Thus, some nonjournal documents may be less useful than journal articles as sources of information.

✔ Step 6: Consider Searching for Unpublished Studies

Searching for *unpublished studies* is another way to increase the size of your reference list. In addition, you may want to search for studies not published in academic journals[2] because some of these unpublished studies may still prove to be relevant. Just because a study is not published in a journal does not mean it is not important. A potentially important study may not be published in a journal for the following reasons:

1. Some studies of potential importance are never even submitted to journals for possible publication. For instance, theses and dissertations tend to be too long to publish in an academic journal and must undergo extensive rewriting for publication. Many authors of theses and dissertations do not undertake this rewriting process. In addition, some researchers may become discouraged when the results of their studies are not consistent with their hypotheses. Instead of writing up such studies for submission to a journal, they may move on to conduct research in what they consider more fruitful areas using alternative research methods.
2. Some journal editors and expert reviewers may be biased against studies that show no significant difference or that fail to confirm the research hypotheses posed by the researchers.

One way to locate unpublished studies is to contact authors of published studies to ask them if they are aware of any unpublished studies on your topic.[3] For instance, they may have conducted studies that they decided not to submit for publication, or they may know of students or colleagues working on related topics. A second way is to expand your search to databases like ERIC (ProQuest) and *Dissertations & Theses* (ProQuest), that include such items.

✔ Step 7: Start with the Most Current Research, and Work Backward

As noted in Chapter 2, the most effective way to begin a search in a field that is new to you is to start with the most current journal articles. If you judge a recently published article to be relevant to your topic, the article's reference list or bibliography will provide useful clues about how to pursue your review of the literature. A good strategy would be to obtain articles relevant to your research topic, photocopy the reference lists at the end of each one, compare the lists for commonalities, and then locate any potential candidates for additional references. Keep in mind two important criteria for developing your reading list: The reading list should (1) represent the extent of knowledge about the topic and (2) provide a proper context for your own research if you are writing a literature review as part of an introduction to a research study you will be conducting.

✔ Step 8: Search for Theoretical Articles on Your Topic

As you learned in Chapter 1, theoretical articles that relate directly to your topic should be included in your literature review. However, a typical search of the literature in the social and behavioral sciences will yield primarily original reports of empirical research because these types of documents dominate academic journals. If you have difficulty locating theoretical articles on your topic, include *theory* as one of your search keywords. Example 3.8.1 is an article abstract that may be useful for someone planning to write about *theories* relating to social phobia.

> **Example 3.8.1**
>
> *An abstract of an article using the search keywords* **social, phobia,** *and* **theory**
>
> Martel (2013) proposed a metatheory, based on sexual selection theory and broad evolutionary psychological (EP) principles, to account for well-known sex differences in the emergence of common behavioral and certain internalizing disorders across childhood and adolescence, respectively. In this comment, I first enumerate several strengths and then offer 2 primary critiques about Martel's proposal. Martel provides an exceptional, integrative review that organizes several disparate literatures that hold promise to enhance understanding of such sex differences. At the same time, I raise critical questions regarding EP generally, and sexual selection theory specifically, as the metatheoretical framework chosen to bind together these different influences and mechanisms as drivers of the sex difference in different psychopathologies. Indeed, it is not clear that EP is necessary—nor does it provide unique explanatory power—to explicate the emergence of sex differences in internalizing and externalizing disorders among youth. Moreover, Martel's EP-based proposal pertains to adolescent-onset depression and social phobia but does not provide an explanation for known sex differences in other common childhood-onset and early adult-onset anxiety disorders.[4]

It is important to note that writers of empirical research reports will often discuss the relationship of their studies to theoretical literature and, of course, provide references to this literature. You should follow these leads by looking up the articles that they reference for yourself.

✔ Step 9: Look for Review Articles

A corollary to the search technique described in the previous step is to use the keyword *review* when searching databases for review articles.[5] Previously published review articles are very useful in planning a new literature review because they are helpful in identifying the breadth and scope of the literature in a field of study. They usually will include a much more comprehensive reference list than is typical in a research article.

Note that some journals publish only literature reviews, some emphasize original reports of empirical research but occasionally will publish literature review articles by leading researchers in a field, and other journals have editorial policies that prohibit publishing reviews. If you know the names of journals in your field that publish reviews, you might specify their names in a database search.[6] Because this will restrict your search to just those journals, this should be a separate search from your main one.

A search of *PsycARTICLES (EBSCO)* using the phrase *substance abuse* AND *treatment* as keywords in any field AND *literature review* in the "TI Title" field identified a number of useful articles that contain reviews on the treatment of substance abusers. Two are shown in Example 3.9.1.

Example 3.9.1

Two articles obtained through using **literature review** *in the search*

Bayles, C. (2014). Using mindfulness in a harm reduction approach to substance abuse treatment: A literature review. *International Journal of Behavioral Consultation and Therapy, 9,* 22–25.

Clifford, P.R., & Davis, C.M. (2012). Alcohol treatment research assessment exposure: A critical review of the literature. *Psychology of Addictive Behaviors, 26,* 773–781.

✔ Step 10: Identify the Landmark or Classic Studies and Theorists

Finally, it is important to identify the landmark studies and theorists on your topic (i.e., those of *historical importance* in developing an understanding of a topic or problem). Unfortunately, some students believe that this is an optional nicety. However, without at least a passing knowledge of landmark studies, you will not understand the present context for your chosen topic. If you are writing a thesis or dissertation, in which fairly exhaustive reviews are expected, a failure to reference the landmark studies might be regarded as a serious flaw.

It is not always easy to identify historically important studies at the very beginning of a literature search. However, authors of some journal articles explicitly note these, as is done in Example 3.10.1 (see next page).

While reading the articles you selected, you will often notice that certain authors' names are mentioned repeatedly. For instance, if you read extensively on how social factors affect learning, you will find that Albert Bandura's social-learning theory is cited by numerous authors of research articles. At this point, you would want to search the databases again using Bandura's first and last names, for two reasons: (1) to locate material he has written on his theory (keep in mind that you want it from the *original source* and not just someone else's paraphrasing of the theory) and (2) to try to locate any early studies that he may have conducted that led him to the theory,

Part I: Managing the Literature Search

> **Example 3.10.1[7]**
>
> *Excerpt from a research article that identifies a landmark theorist and related studies*
>
> Among the particularly influential theories of classical conditioning from the 20th century (e.g., Mackintosh, 1975; McLaren & Mackintosh, 2000; Pearce & Hall, 1980; Pearce, 1987; Rescorla & Wagner, 1972; Wagner & Rescorla, 1972), only Wagner (1981), Wagner and Brandon (2001), and the real-time model of Sutton and Barto (1981) offer any account of temporal contiguity. Disinterest among many major theorists has been accompanied by relatively little experimental attention to temporal contiguity, with the notable recent exception of research related to timing that is considered in the final section of this review. The last review of research on temporal contiguity in classical conditioning was published over 30 years ago (Gormezano & Kehoe, 1981).

or that he originally presented, to lend credence to the theory. Sorting search results by "Oldest First" or "Date Oldest" may help. Keep in mind that individuals who present theories very often conduct research and publish it in support of their theories. Their early studies that helped establish their theories are the ones that are most likely to be considered "landmark" or "classic." Note that when you conduct such a search of the database for this purpose, you should *not* restrict the search to only articles published in recent years. Searching all years of the PsycARTICLES database while restricting the search to the name *Albert Bandura*[8] as the author, AND *social* in the title, AND *learning* in all fields (Figure 3.10.1) yields five entries, including an early single-authored piece, which is shown in Example 3.10.2.

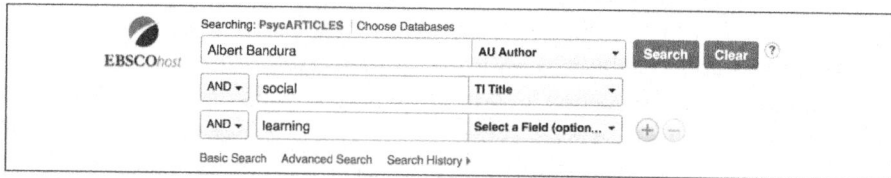

Figure 3.10.1 A PsycARTICLES search for landmark studies by Albert Bandura

> **Example 3.10.2**
>
> *An early study by a leading researcher and theoretician*
>
> Bandura, A. (1969). Social learning of moral judgments. *Journal of Personality and Social Psychology, 11,* 275–279.

Selecting a Topic

Finally, consult any relevant college textbooks. Textbook authors often briefly trace the history of thought on important topics and may well mention what they believe to be the classic studies on a particular topic.

✔ Step 11: Assemble the Collection of Sources You Plan to Include in Your Review

You will need to assemble the collection of sources that you have identified throughout your searches before you proceed to make a final selection of your topic. There are a number of ways that you can undertake this task, so it will be up to you how you choose to organize your data. Those already proficient in your campus's online citation tools (discussed in Chapter 13) may choose to utilize these programs to help save time compiling a formatted reference list later. Others may choose to use their computer's copy and paste features to create a separate Word document. It is really up to you how you choose to do this, but as noted, it is a prerequisite for you to identify which articles you will actually read closely for your review.

Most online databases offer the ability to save selected citations into their own folder. Given the fact that you probably have been experimenting with a number of different search keywords and criteria, this is a handy way for you to keep track of relevant articles. If you choose not to use these features, it is recommended that you adopt your system for saving citations early. Otherwise, it may prove very difficult to retrace your steps and locate articles that you have not already saved. See the arrow in Figure 3.11.1 for an example of where this option is located within the EBSCOhost database platform.

Figure 3.11.1 Locating EBSCOhost's "save citation to folder" feature

Once you have located the folder or save feature within your database you should familiarize yourself with the steps necessary to create a personalized repository of your articles. In EBSCOhost you simply click on the blue folder icon, which then turns yellow and a new dialog box appears noting that the reference has been placed in a pre-generated folder. See Figure 3.11.2 (on the following page). Please note that you may choose to go into the folder settings to create or rename different folders.

Part I: Managing the Literature Search

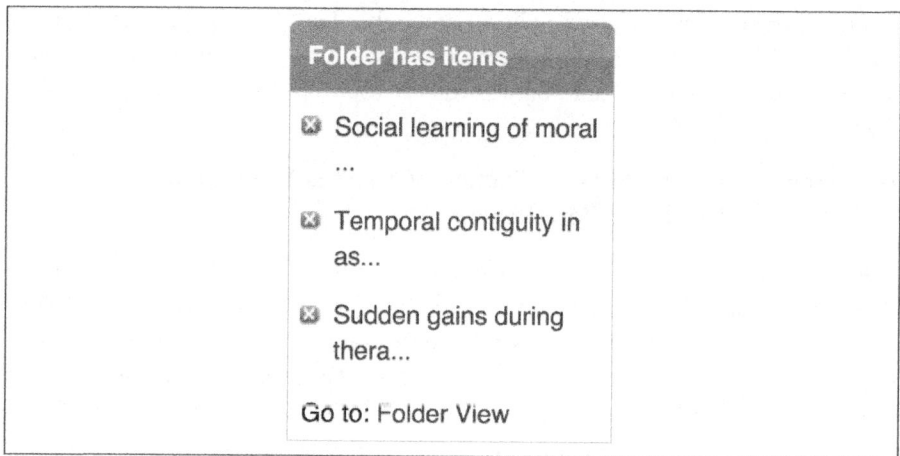

Figure 3.11.2 Saved to folder citations in EBSCOhost

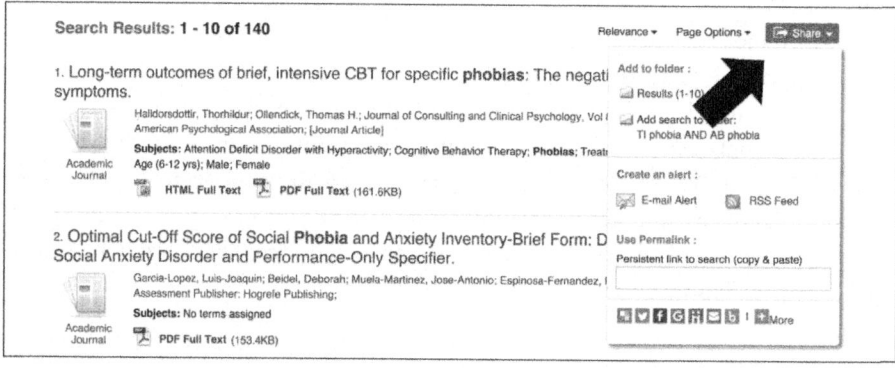

Figure 3.11.3 Export options in EBSCOhost

If you wish to save all results for a specific search, you can use the "Share" feature. This allows you to (1) export all entries into their own folder, (2) email yourself the list, (3) create a permalink that will allow you to easily access your search at a later time, or (4) share to a number of other online media platforms. See Figure 3.11.3 to see where to locate this information in EBSCOhost databases.

Regardless of how you choose to save this information, it is important that it be saved somewhere. You will be referring to this list at the beginning of Chapter 4, and it is necessary before you identify which articles you will actually be reading. If you chose to use the database's folder option, you may wish to print, save, or export the file to Word. See Figure 3.11.4 on the following page.

38

Selecting a Topic

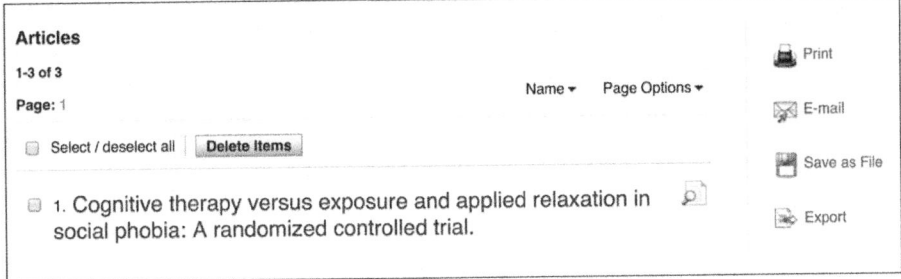

Figure 3.11.4 Further export options in EBSCOhost

At this point you should have compiled a list of possible sources that you intend to include in your literature review. The size of this list will depend on the scope of your literature review. Theses or doctoral students may have hundreds of potential sources. Students writing a literature review as a term paper for a specific course may choose to have a manageable corpus of closer to 50. The number of sources you consult may depend on the requirements of your specific instructor.

✔ Step 12: Write the First Draft of Your Topic Statement

Now that you have identified appropriate references, you can reexamine the list of articles you have generated and choose a more specific topic for your literature review.[9] The first draft of your topic statement should attempt to name the area you will investigate. Think of this statement as a descriptive phrase rather than as a paper or chapter title. Example 3.12.1 presents two statements: one for a literature review topic in the area of psychology and the other in linguistics. Note that these first drafts are still very general.

Example 3.12.1

Draft topic statements

Psychology:
Language Acquisition by Children with Speech Disorders

Linguistics:
Acquisition of Grammatical Structures and Categories

Each of the topics in Example 3.12.1 could be further narrowed by restricting it to a particular group, such as very young children (e.g., Language Acquisition by *Very Young Children* with Speech Disorders).

✔ Step 13: Redefine Your Topic More Narrowly

Selecting a reasonably narrow topic is essential if you are to defend your selection of a topic and write an effective review on it. Topics that are too broad will stretch the limits of your energy and time—especially if you are writing a review for a term project in a single-semester class. A review of a topic that is too broad very likely will lead to a review that is superficial, jumps from area to area within the topic, and fails to demonstrate to your reader that you have thoroughly mastered the literature on the topic. Thus, at this point, you should consider redefining your topic more narrowly.

Example 3.13.1 presents a topic that is much too broadly defined. Even though the writer has limited the review to English-speaking children as old as 4 years of age, it is still quite broad. Apparently, the writer has chosen to consider studies of children acquiring both the sound and the grammatical systems. If so, the finished review will either be a book-length manuscript (or two) or a shorter manuscript that presents a superficial treatment of the literature on this broad topic.

Example 3.13.1

A topic that is too broad for most purposes

This paper deals with child language acquisition. I will review the literature that deals with how children learn to speak in a naturalistic setting, starting with the earliest sounds and progressing to fully formed sentences. I will limit myself to English-speaking children, from birth to 4 years old.

Example 3.13.2 (see following page) is an improved version of the topic in Example 3.13.1. Note that the writer has narrowed the focus of the review to a specific aspect of language. The writer has stated clearly that the review has two main goals: (1) to catalog the range of verbal features that have been studied and (2) to describe what is known about the route children follow in acquiring them. Even though it is very likely that this topic will be modified several more times based on a careful reading of the studies found, it is sufficiently focused to provide the writer with a suitable initial statement of the topic for his or her literature review.

> **Example 3.13.2**
>
> *An improved, more specific version of Example 3.13.1*
>
> This paper describes what is known about how children acquire the ability to describe time and to make references to time, including the use of verbs and other features contained in the verb phrase. I will attempt, first, to describe the range of verb-phrase features that have been studied, and second, to describe the path children follow as they develop greater linguistic competence with reference to time.

✔ Step 14: Ask for Feedback from Your Instructor or Advisor

Before you begin to read the full texts of the articles that you have identified, it is always a good idea to consult with your instructor or advisor about your proposed topic. Not only would they possibly be able to offer feedback and validation of your topic, but they may also help you identify gaps within your references.

Activities for Chapter 3

1. First, become familiar with the electronic databases in your field. You can do so either by attending a workshop in your university library or by reading the documentation and practicing on your own. Note that many libraries now allow you to search their databases online from your home, but you will probably need to use a university computer account to do so. Once you are familiar with the databases, select one database to complete the rest of this exercise.

2. If your instructor has assigned a term paper on a specific topic, search the database using a simple phrase that describes this topic. If you are working on your own, select an area that interests you, and search the database using a simple phrase that describes your area of interest. How many citations for the literature did the search produce?

3. Retrieve two or three records from your search and locate the lists of descriptors. Compare the lists and note the areas of commonality as well as differences.

   - Write down the exact wording of three descriptors that relate to your intended topic. Choose descriptors that reflect your personal interest in the topic.
   - Compared to the simple phrase you used when you started, do you think these descriptors are more specific *or* more general? Why?

4. Now use the descriptors you just located to modify the search.

   - First, modify the search to select more records.
   - Then, modify the search to select fewer records.
   - If you used the connector AND, did it result in more *or* fewer sources? Why do you think this happened?
   - If you used the connector OR, did it result in more *or* fewer sources? Why do you think this happened?

5. If necessary, narrow the search further until you have between 50 and 150 sources, and print out the search results.

   - Carefully scan the printed list to identify several possible subcategories.
   - Compare the new categories with your original topic.
   - Redefine your topic more narrowly, and identify the articles that pertain to your new topic. Prepare a list of the references for these articles.

Notes

1. It is important to note that this database by default does not initially search the "full text" for these search terms. If your initial search presents too few results, you may wish to check the box "Also search within the full text of the articles."
2. Studies not published in journals are commonly referred to as "unpublished studies" even though they may be available in print form in certain academic libraries.
3. Contact information such as an email address is usually provided either as a footnote on the first page of a research article or near the end of an article—just before or after the reference list.
4. Hankin, B. L. (2013). Critical reflections on evolutionary psychology and sexual selection theory as explanatory account of emergence of sex differences in psychopathology: Comment on Martel (2013). *Psychological Bulletin, 139,* 1260–1264.
5. You should not limit yourself to just one iteration of the term. Some databases will allow you to search using multiple phrasings of the same general concept. For instance, if you type review in your search in PsycARTICLES, a dialog box will suggest that you search *review, literature review, a review of the literature,* among others.
6. In psychology, for instance, *Psychological Bulletin* is an important journal devoted to literature reviews. A premier review journal in education is the *Review of Educational Research.*
7. Kahn, E., & Rachman, A. W. (2000). Carl Rogers and Heinz Kohut: A historical perspective. *Psychoanalytic Psychology, 17,* 294–312.
8. When specifying an author's name, use both first and last names but do not enclose the full name with quotation marks, as this would exclude instances where the last name is listed first.
9. At this point, it is still premature for you to decide on a *final topic.* You should do this only after reading some of the articles you have located.

Chapter 4

Organizing Yourself to Begin the Selection of Relevant Titles

Now that you have identified the preliminary set of articles for your review, you should begin the process of analyzing them *prior to* writing your review. This chapter is designed to help you through this process. The end result will be a comprehensive compilation of notes that you will make as you read the articles, with specific, detailed information about each reference.

✔ Step 1: Scan the Articles to Get an Overview of Each One

Obviously, you have already read the titles of the articles when you selected them, and you probably also read the abstracts (i.e., summaries) that most journals place near the beginning of each article. Now you need to read the first few paragraphs of each article, where the author usually provides a general introduction to the problem area. This will give you a feel for the author's writing style as well as their general perspectives on the research problem. Then, jump to the paragraph that precedes the heading "Method," which is usually the first major heading in the text of a research article (sometimes labeled "Research Methods" or "Methodology"). This is the paragraph in which it is traditional for researchers to state their specific hypotheses, research questions, or research purposes. Next, scan the rest of the article, noting all headings and subheadings. Scan the text in each subsection, but do not allow yourself to get caught up in the details or any points that seem difficult or confusing. Your purpose at this point is to get an overview of the article.

Note that the process described in the paragraph above is what reading specialists call *prereading*. This is a technique widely recommended as the first step in reading technical reports. Because prereading gives you an overview of the purpose and contents of a report, it helps you to keep your eye on the big picture as you subsequently work through the details of a research report from beginning to end. The information you gain by prereading will also help you group the articles into categories, as suggested in the next guideline.

Example 4.1.1 shows in bold a typical set of major headings for a short research report in a journal.

Example 4.1.1

A typical set of major headings for a short research report in a journal

Title [followed by researchers' names and their institutional affiliations]

Abstract [a summary of the complete report]
[An introduction in which related literature is reviewed follows the abstract; typically, there is *no* heading called "Introduction."]

Method
    Participants [or Subjects]
    Measures [or Instrumentation]

Results and Discussion

Longer articles will often contain additional headings and subheadings, such as *Assumptions, Definitions, Experimental Treatments, Limitations,* and so on. Scanning each of these sections will help prepare you to navigate the article when you begin to read it in detail from beginning to end.

The last heading in a research article is usually "Discussion." This section is where researchers often reiterate or summarize their research purposes, research methods, and major findings, usually in the first few paragraphs. Reading this section of a report will help you when you read the results section in detail, which can be difficult if it contains numerous statistics.

✔ Step 2: Based on Your Prereading of the Articles, Group Them by Category

If your articles are in digital format, create folders to group them into the categories of studies you will describe. With printed copies, sort them into stacks that correspond roughly to these categories. You may choose to organize them in any number of ways, but the most common practice is to first organize them by topic and subtopic and then in chronological order within each subtopic. In Example 4.2.1, we show a possible grouping of articles into categories and subcategories for a review of research literature on the psychological effects of meditation. Note that this article is a meta-analysis that interprets data across a large number of research studies, and its organization is quite different than an empirical research report.

Also note that each sub-heading in 4.2.1 refers to the collection of articles reviewed by the authors that deal with the specific topic (the citations given are hypothetical and are provided just to illustrate this point).

Example 4.2.1[1]

Collection of articles reviewed by the authors that deal with the specific topic

I. **Theoretical Considerations about the Effects of Meditation**
   A. What Is Meditation? (Bach, 2005; Kunze, 2006)
   B. Meditation as a Means to Transformed Consciousness: Indian Theoretical Approaches
      1. Hindu approaches to meditation (Smith, 1999; Marks, 2000)
      2. Buddhist approaches to meditation (Elders, 1998, Prabhu, 2000)
   C. Meditation as a Means to Self-Regulation: Western Theoretical Approaches
      1. Cultivating mental balance (Adams, 2007)
      2. Specific effects of mindfulness practice
         a. Effects via attention control (Smith, 1999)
         b. Effects via a shift in perspective (Garza, 2003)
   D. What Could Have Been Predicted?
      1. Predictions of the Indian theoretical approaches (Prabhu, 2003)
      2. Predictions of the Western theoretical approaches (Prabhu, 2001)
      3. Common predictions (Smith, 1999)

II. **Studies, Dependent Measures, and Moderator Variables**
   A. Selection of Studies
   B. Categorization of Studies
      1. Classification of dependent measures
      2. Potential moderating variables
         a. Kind of control group
         b. Design of studies
         c. Randomization
         d. Publication outlet
         e. Year of publication
         f. Kind of meditation
         g. Amount of meditation practice

Part I: Managing the Literature Search

Example 4.2.2 shows a possible grouping of articles into categories and subcategories for a review article that examines the research literature on smoking cessation and menopause.

Example 4.2.2[2]

A possible grouping of articles into categories and subcategories

I. **Smoking, the Menopausal Transition, and Health**
   A. Hormone Therapy

II. **Weight Gain and Weight Concern in Peri- and Postmenopausal Women**
   A. Weight Gain During the Menopausal Transition
   B. Smoking Cessation-Related Weight Gain in Peri- and Postmenopausal Women
   C. Weight Concern in Peri- and Postmenopausal Women
   D. Interventions Targeting Weight Gain or Overconcern about Weight Gain

III. **Menopausal Symptoms and Smoking Cessation**
   A. Negative Affect
   B. Other Menopausal Symptoms

IV. **Estrogen Level, Nicotine Metabolism, and Nicotine Reinforcement**

V. **Smoking Cessation Outcomes in Peri- and Postmenopausal Women**

Organizing the articles into categories will facilitate your analysis if you read all the articles in each category or subcategory at about the same time. For instance, it will be easier to synthesize the literature on the effects of weight gain during the menopausal transition (see point II.A in Example 4.2.2) if all the articles on this topic are read together, starting with the most recent one.

✔ **Step 3: Conduct a More Focused Literature Search if Gaps Appear**

As you assess the collection of titles you have compiled, you may find that some areas of research are under-represented in your search results. This will necessitate that you return to the database and conduct additional and more focused searches.

Persistent gaps in the literature should be noted in your literature review, along with details of your unsuccessful attempts to identify any relevant studies.

It is important to note here that you will need to remain open to a return to the database throughout the writing process. Questions will inevitably arise as you continue your review of sources, and these should be followed up with focused attempts at resolving your questions. These may concern possible gaps, as noted, or they may involve other issues, such as a controversial interpretation of findings, patterns that appear implausible, or another as yet unforeseen issue.

The following is an example of a gap found in the literature regarding memory of auditory clues associated with the commission of a crime.

Example 4.3.1[3]

Noting a gap found in the literature review

Several gaps in the current research literature regarding auditory memory and earwitnesses are evident. Long retention intervals between encoding and questioning are described as a specific practical challenge in crime investigation (Deffenbacher, Bornstein, McGorty, & Penrod, 2008). Most previous studies test memory performance the same day as encoding, often only minutes after initial presentation of the stimuli. There are very few studies that have utilized longer delays of up to one week (Huss & Weaver, 1996; Lawrence et al., 1979).

✔ Step 4: Organize Yourself before Reading the Articles

It is important to organize yourself prior to beginning a detailed reading of the articles. Use the text-highlight feature in your word processing program to identify a notable section of your notes and insert a comment, or you can use the text-highlight feature to highlight the text in different colors corresponding to categories of items. If working with printed copies, you can use different-colored self-stick flags to mark different subtopics, different research methods, a review article or landmark study, or anything else that should be noted or might help you to organize your review.

✔ Step 5: Create a Spreadsheet or Table to Compile Your Notes

After you have organized the articles, you will now begin to read them and make notes as you read. The most efficient method for compiling your notes is to enter them into a spreadsheet or table on your computer. A spreadsheet will give you greater flexibility for inserting new categories that you may need to create, reordering the files into logical groupings, and copying-and-pasting elements across the span of the document. You can also accomplish some of these tasks with a table, though the steps may get more involved.

When you create the spreadsheet, begin with Column Headings that will ease the process of compiling your notes. Example 4.5.1 lists a common set of items that may be useful as a starting point. Note that the first four items are straightforward, and it is recommended that you begin by entering this information about all of the articles you have compiled. You may also wish to enter an identifier for the initial groupings of articles that you have compiled (Grouping Identifier). These groupings may relate to how you envision structuring your review—for example, using Example 4.2.1 above, it may be useful to group your articles by meditation approach, as in Indian vs. Western approach. Use your own judgment, based on the prereading you have done, in deciding how to group the articles in your collection.

Keep in mind that the notes you make in this spreadsheet can be very useful to you when you begin to structure your review, and especially so when you begin to write it. In making these notes, you are *analyzing* the contents of the articles in your collection (i.e., you are pulling out discrete elements from each source that you will later be able to combine with elements from other sources to construct your own original argument). For instance, the category Summary should contain a brief description of the main point(s) of the article, but in most cases it is less useful to simply copy-and-paste an entire Abstract because this avoids the task of analyzing its contents. The Methodology and Findings categories are more straightforward, but it is important to use descriptors that can help you sort through your material later (e.g., public vs. private school populations, confirming vs. contradictory findings, and so on). The Comments category is useful because it allows you to comment on what, in your opinion, makes a particular article notable. Is it a landmark study? Does it contain a table format that may help to display your own work? These are just some of the types of notes you can include under Comments.

These notes will also be helpful later if you decide to build tables that summarize groups of studies for presentation in your literature review. Guidelines for building such tables are presented in Chapter 8.

Example 4.5.1

A common set of items that may be useful as a starting point

Author's Name
Title of Article
Publication Year
Journal

> Grouping Identifier
> Summary
> Methodology
> Findings
> Comments

✔ Step 6: Remain Flexible as You Compile Your Notes

You will encounter considerable variation across studies, and your notes should be consistent and detailed enough for you to be able to describe both differences and similarities across them. You may need to expand on the categories given in Example 4.5.1 as you work through your sources, so it is important to remain flexible.

The categories in Example 4.5.1 are given as examples to guide you through this process. In an actual case, you may choose to disregard one or more of them, or you may decide that others are more appropriate. For example, it may be useful to add a category to record questions or concerns you have as you read through the material, or to note any conclusions you may reach about the validity of the research. Keep in mind that these notes can later be incorporated into your paper, perhaps in your discussion or conclusion, and using a separate category for this could save you valuable time later.

✔ Step 7: Take Extra Care When Copying an Author's Exact Words

Finally, remember that direct quotations should always be accompanied by page numbers, and it will save you considerable time later in the process if you already have the page numbers included in your notes. You should note the page numbers whenever you copy an author's words verbatim, and be sure to double-check your quotes for accuracy. For more information on the importance of avoiding plagiarism, see Chapter 12.

Activities for Chapter 4

1. Using your own search results developed at the end of Chapter 3, work through Steps 1 and 2 of this chapter. Then, exchange the results of your groupings with a fellow student, and critique each other's findings, especially with regard to the following points:

   - Categories identified for grouping the articles (Do they make sense? Are there alternative ways of grouping them? Etc.)
   - Do all of the articles on your list appear to be relevant for a review of your chosen topic?

Part I: Managing the Literature Search

2. Again working with a peer in your class, review the elements you have identified to include in your spreadsheet. Give each other feedback on the list of elements. Check for completeness, obvious gaps, duplications, and so on.

Notes

1 Based on Sedlmeier, P., Eberth, J., Schwarz, M., Zimmermann, D., Haarig, F., Jaeger, S., & Kunze, S. (2012). The psychological effects of meditation: A meta-analysis. *Psychological Bulletin, 138,* 1139–1171.
2 Based on McVay, M. A., & Copeland, A. L. (2011). Smoking cessation in peri- and postmenopausal women: A review. *Experimental and Clinical Psychopharmacology, 19,* 192–202.
3 Burrell, L. V., Johnson, M. S., & Melinder, A. (2016). Children as earwitnesses: Memory for emotional auditory events. *Applied Cognitive Psychology, 30,* 323–331.

PART II

Analyzing the Relevant Literature

Chapter 5

Conduct a Deep Analysis of the Articles

You have now completed the initial step in the analysis of the articles in your collection, and you have produced a comprehensive spreadsheet with detailed information about each source. Now you need to extend your analysis somewhat deeper by extracting more specific details from each article. This will help you to organize your material in more useful ways. This chapter will help you through this process.

✔ Guideline 1: Look for Explicit Definitions of Key Terms in the Literature

It should not surprise you that different researchers sometimes define key terms in different ways. If there are major differences of opinion on how the variables you will be writing about should be defined, you will want to make notes on the definitions. In fact, if several different definitions are offered, you might find it helpful to add a separate category in your spreadsheet to record just the definitions.

To see the importance of how a term is defined, consider definitions of *traditional bullying* and *cyberbullying* in Example 5.1.1 (Note: the example comes from one of the sample literature reviews in Appendix B). These definitions expand on the traditional understanding of bullying behavior, and the contrasting definitions allow the researcher to draw upon the earlier literature in order to investigate the behavior in the digital context. The authors go on to expand on varying categories of cyberbullying. As a reviewer, you will want to note such contrasts in definitions because they may help to explain discrepant results across studies.

Example 5.1.1[1]

Contrasting definitions of traditional bullying and cyberbullying

Olweus (1993) defined traditional bullying as repeated exposure to negative actions by one or more other people. Bullying can be direct, such as physically

---

> beating someone up, or indirect, which includes non-face-to-face methods like spreading rumors. This definition contains components that overlap with the current defition of cyberbullying. Cyberbulling is a repeated, intentional act done with the purpose of harming another person through technologies such as e-mail, cell phone messaging, social networking websites, chat rooms, and instant messaging (Beran & Li, 2005; Bhat, 2008; Campbell, 2005; Patchin & Hinduja, 2006), which can be perpetrated by a single individual or a group of people (Smith et al., 2008). Unlike traditional bullying, cyberbullying does not require a face-to-face confrontation or a physical location to convene and can be completely anonymous (Dehue, Bolman, & Vollink, 2008; Mason, 2008).

Make special note of authoritative definitions (i.e., definitions offered by experts), which you can quote or summarize. For instance, the author of Example 5.1.2 cites a definition used by a professional association in the literature review.

Example 5.1.2[2]

Definition cited by a professional association

> Throughout the article, I adopt the definition of *terrorism* used by the Department of Defense (2010a): "The calculated use of unlawful violence or threat of unlawful violence to inculcate fear, intended to coerce or to intimidate governments or societies in the pursuit of goals that are generally political, religious, or ideological."

Make note in your spreadsheet of definitions for related terms. For instance, consider Example 5.1.3, in which the term *sex differences* is defined separately from the term *gender differences*.

Example 5.1.3[3]

Related terms

> Although terminology in the field is not standardized, *sex differences* generally refers to biological differences or psychological differences stemming from biological origins, whereas *gender differences* generally refers to social-cultural differences, socially constructed differences, or differences in which the origin

is unknown. In this meta-analysis, we are unable to make claims about the causal origins of differences in self-conscious emotional experience between men and women. Thus, insofar as the origin of such differences remains unknown, we use the term *gender differences* to refer to differences in the emotional experience between men and women.

Note that it is usually a good idea to present definitions of key terms near the beginning of a literature review.

Also, consider pointing out contrasting terms when citing a definition, which is done in Example 5.1.4.

Example 5.1.4[4]

Contrasting terms

Collectivism, a concept that "emphasizes close, nurturing, and supportive interpersonal relationships," is valued in most Latino cultures over *individualism*, which is a more prominent value in mainstream U.S. culture (Mason et al., 1995, p. 7). Collectivism points to Latinos' tendency to think of collective well-being (that is, that of the family) over one's individual needs.

✔ Guideline 2: Look for Key Statistics to Use near the Beginning of Your Literature Review

You may wish to create a separate category in your spreadsheet for key statistics that you might want to cite near the beginning of your literature review. Example 5.2.1 shows the first sentence of a literature review on intimate-partner violence. Note that citing a specific percentage is a much stronger beginning than a general statement, such as "Many individuals in the United States are victimized by their partners," would be.

Example 5.2.1[5]

First sentence of a literature review on intimate-partner violence

Over 10% of women and men in a nationally representative United States sample have reported victimization by their partners within the prior 12 months (Straus & Gelles, 1990), reflecting the high prevalence of intimate partner violence in this country.

Part II: Analyzing the Relevant Literature

Citing statistics at the beginning of a literature review is optional, with some topics lending themselves more to the technique than others. However, if you plan to start with a reference to quantities (e.g., *Some* adolescents . . . ; *Frequently*, voters prefer . . . .), it is desirable to provide a specific estimate if it is available. For many topics in the social and behavioral sciences, relevant statistics can be found online at www.census.gov.

✔ Guideline 3: Pay Special Attention to Review Articles on Your Topic

If you find literature review articles (i.e., articles that consist solely of a literature review that is not just an introduction to a report of original research) on your topic or a closely related topic, read them carefully and make notes that will allow you to summarize them in your literature review. This was done by the authors of Examples 5.3.1 and 5.3.2, in which they briefly summarized a previous review in their review.

Example 5.3.1[6]

A summary of a previous review

A recent review of studies on the psychological health of cancer survivors reported that the prevalence of anxiety ranges by study from 6% to 23%, and the prevalence of depression from 0% to 58% (Andrykowski et al., 2008). The variance in these estimates can be explained by the diversity of the cancer survivor samples from which these prevalence estimates have been derived; samples differed with respect to time since diagnosis, type of cancer, stage of disease, and cancer treatment.

Example 5.3.2[7]

A summary of a previous review

For example, a recent review on adolescents' religiosity and mental health revealed that religious adolescents showed fewer internalizing and externalizing problems and had higher psychological well-being (Wong, Rew, & Slaikeu, 2006).

✔ Guideline 4: Make Note of Short but Important Quotations that Could Be Used Very Sparingly in Your Review

Direct quotations should be used very sparingly in literature reviews. This is because the use of too many quotations can interrupt the flow of the narrative. In addition, the writer of a review is usually able to summarize and paraphrase points more succinctly than the original author, who is obligated to provide more details on the research than the reviewer. Nevertheless, there are instances when an especially apt statement might be worthy of being quoted in a literature review. For instance, in Example 5.4.1, the writers are reviewing literature on attachment and parenting. The quoted material succinctly defines the term *attachment* in their review.

Example 5.4.1[8]

Direct quotation and definition

Bowlby (1969) described attachment as a "lasting psychological connectedness between human beings" (p. 194), defining it as an emotional bond established with someone who is perceived as a source of security and who provides a safe base from which individuals explore the world (Bowlby, 1988).

Another appropriate use of quotations is when citing legal matters, where the exact wording is important and even a small change in wording might change its legal meaning. Example 5.4.2 shows such a quotation of a federal law.

Example 5.4.2[9]

Direct quotation and definition

Almost a decade into the reform, [No Child Left Behind] is a large and complex piece of legislation that elicits a focus on public school education. However, the language of the federal NCLB is fairly straightforward. Section 111(b)(2)(K) of the Elementary and Secondary Education Act of 1965, as amended by NCLB, states:

> Accountability for Charter Schools—The accountability provisions under this Act shall be overseen for charter schools in accordance with State charter school law.

Note that the quotations in Examples 5.4.1 and 5.4.2 are quite short. It is almost always inappropriate to include long quotations (i.e., longer than a few sentences) in a literature review. After all, a review should be an original synthesis, not a repetition of already published materials.

✔ Guideline 5: Look for Methodological Strengths

It is unlikely that you will find a single research article with definitive results about any aspect of the human condition. Inevitably, some studies will be stronger than others, and these strengths should be noted in your review. Ask yourself how strong the evidence is, and keep in mind that in your role as the reviewer, you have the right and the responsibility to make these subjective evaluations.

The strength of a research article may come from the research methodology used. Do the research methods of one study improve on the data-gathering techniques of earlier studies? Does the article's strength derive from the size and generalizability of its subject pool? Does a set of studies demonstrate that the same conclusion can be reached through the use of a variety of methods? These and other similar questions will guide you in determining the strengths of particular studies. Identifying methodological strengths is considered in more detail in Chapters 6 (quantitative research) and 7 (qualitative research). The authors of Example 5.5.1 discuss the strength of one particular study on school-aged children.

Example 5.5.1[10]

Strength of a study

The Health Behavior in School-aged Children Study (HBSC) is perhaps the single best source of data on younger adolescents in multiple countries. Involving 42 countries in Europe and North America, the HBSC conducts school-based surveys every 4 years with national probability samples of youth with mean ages of 11.5, 13.5, and 15.5 years.

✔ Guideline 6: Look for Methodological Weaknesses

Remember that you should note any major weaknesses you encounter when reviewing research literature. The same process you used in identifying strengths should be used when you are identifying weaknesses. For instance, you should determine whether the author's research method has provided new insights into the research topic. Particularly, if an innovative methodology is used, does it seem appropriate, or does it raise the possibility of alternative explanations? Has an appropriate sample been used? Are the findings consistent with those of similar studies? Is enough evidence presented in the article for a reasonable person to judge whether the researcher's conclusions are valid?

Here again, it may be preferable to critique groups of studies together, especially if their flaws are similar. Generally, it is *inappropriate* to note each and every flaw in every study you review. Instead, note major weaknesses of individual studies, and keep your eye out for patterns of weaknesses across groups of studies. For instance, if all the research reports on a subtopic you are reviewing are based on very small samples, you might note this fact in your spreadsheet.

As an example, the author of Example 5.6.1 points out a weakness in the study of homework completion and accuracy rates with autistic children.

Example 5.6.1[11]

A weakness in a study

The study lacked the comparison of Student S's and Student J's homework completion and accuracy behavior with their class work completion and accuracy behavior. Additionally, duration for homework and class work completion could have provided additional information for analysis.

✔ Guideline 7: Distinguish between Assertion and Evidence

A common mistake made in literature reviews is to report an author's assertions as though they were findings. To avoid this mistake, make sure you have understood the author's evidence and its interpretation. A finding derives from the empirical evidence presented. An assertion is the author's opinion.

In Example 5.7.1, readers can easily distinguish between the assertions in the body of the paragraph and the evidence-based statements in the last sentence. Bold italics have been added for emphasis.

Example 5.7.1[12]

Distinction between evidence and assertions

The risk factor for binge eating that has received the most attention is dieting (Lowe, 1994). Dieting **is thought to** increase the risk that an individual will overeat to counteract the effects of caloric deprivation. Dieting **may** also promote binge eating because violating strict dietary rules can result in disinhibited eating (the abstinence–violation effect). Moreover, dieting entails a shift from a reliance on physiological cues to cognitive control over eating

Part II: Analyzing the Relevant Literature

> behaviors, which leaves the individual vulnerable to disinhibited eating when these cognitive processes are disrupted. In support of ***these assertions***, dieting predicted binge eating onset in adolescent girls (Stice & Agras, 1998; Stice, Killen, Hayward, & Taylor, 1998), and acute caloric deprivation resulted in elevated binge eating in adult women (Agras & Telch, 1998; Telch & Agras, 1996).

✔ Guideline 8: Identify the Major Trends or Patterns in the Results of Previous Studies

When you write your literature review, you will be responsible for pointing out major trends or patterns in the results reported in the research articles you review. This is done in Example 5.8.1.

> ### Example 5.8.1[13]
>
> *Trends in a study*
>
> A plethora of randomized clinical trials (RCTs) and recent meta analyses have indicated that cognitive behavioral therapy (CBT) is an efficacious treatment for youth with anxiety disorders (e.g., Bodden, Bögels, et al., 2008; Bodden, Dirksen, et al., 2008; Kendall, Hudson, Gosch, Flannery-Schroeder, & Suveg, 2008; Spielmans, Pasek, & McFall, 2007). While the earliest therapeutic interventions for childhood anxiety were merely downward extensions of adult treatment protocols, current interventions have since been appropriately modified to take into account relevant considerations in treating the child population—including such factors as developmental level, familial factors, and autonomy (Kendall et al., 2008).

Of course, you may not be as fortunate as the reviewer who wrote Example 5.8.1. There may be considerable inconsistencies in results from one research article to another. When this is the case, you should try to make sense of them for your readers. For instance, you might state a generalization based on a *majority* of the articles, or you might state a generalization based only on those articles you think have the strongest research methodology. Either option is acceptable as long as you clearly describe for your reader the basis for your generalization. Once again, careful note taking during the analysis stage will help you navigate through this process.

Conduct a Deep Analysis of the Articles

✔ Guideline 9: Identify Gaps in the Literature

It is every graduate student's dream to discover a significant gap in the literature, especially one that can form the crux of the student's thesis or dissertation study. In fact, gaps often exist because conducting research in some areas presents considerable obstacles for researchers. These gaps should be noted in a literature review, along with discussions of why they exist. If you identify a gap that you believe should be addressed, make note of it, and take it into consideration as you plan the organization of your review.

You will often find gaps mentioned in previous literature reviews, as in Example 5.9.1.

Example 5.9.1[14]

Points out gaps in the literature

The research discussed previously was mainly based on findings from Western literature conducted in the area of adolescent coping and the gender differences that existed in their coping styles. In comparison, there is a dearth of research in adolescent coping and the role of gender in predicting their choice of coping styles in Asian countries. Therefore, the aim of this study was to examine the coping behaviors of a sample of academically advanced students in an Asian context . . .

✔ Guideline 10: Identify Relationships among Studies

As you read additional articles from your list, make note of any relationships that may exist among studies. For instance, a landmark research article may have spawned a new approach subsequently explored in studies conducted by others, or two articles may explore the same or a similar question but with different age groups or language groups. It is important to point out these relationships in your review. When you write, you probably will want to discuss related ones together.

✔ Guideline 11: Note How Closely Each Article Relates to Your Topic

Try to keep your review focused on the topic you have chosen. It is inappropriate to include studies that have no relationship to the area of study in your literature review. Therefore, your notes should include explicit references to the specific aspects of a study that relate to your topic.

If you determine that there is no literature with a direct bearing on one or more aspects of your research topic, it is permissible to review peripheral research, but this should be done cautiously. Example 5.11.1 cites the example of year-round school schedules, implemented in Los Angeles as a curricular innovation.

Example 5.11.1[15]

Peripheral research cited

When Los Angeles first started implementing year-round school schedules, for example, there was no published research on the topic. There was research, however, on traditional school-year programs in which children attended school in shifts, on the effects of the length of the school year on achievement, and on the effectiveness of summer school programs. Students who were writing theses and dissertations on the Los Angeles program had to cite such peripheral literature in order to demonstrate their ability to conduct a search of the literature and write a comprehensive, well-organized review of literature.

Such examples are rare, and you are advised to consult with your instructor before you reach the conclusion that no studies have dealt with your specific research topic.

✔ Guideline 12: Evaluate Your Reference List for Currency and for Coverage

When you have finished reading the articles you have collected, you should reevaluate your entire reference list to ensure that it is complete and up-to-date. A literature review should demonstrate that it represents the latest work done in the subject area. As a rule of thumb, use a 5-year span from the present as a tentative limit of coverage, keeping in mind that you will extend your research further back when it is warranted. If your review is intended to present a historical overview of your topic, for instance, you may have to reach well beyond the 5-year span. However, remember that the reader of a literature review expects that you have reported on the most current research available. Thus, you should make explicit your reasons for including articles that are not current (e.g., Is it a landmark study? Does it present the only evidence available on a given topic? Does it help you to understand the evolution of a research technique?).

The question of how much literature is enough to include in a review is difficult to answer. In general, your first priority should be to establish that you have read the most current research available. Then, you should try to cover your topic as completely as necessary, not as completely as possible. Your instructor or faculty adviser can help you determine how much is enough.

Activities for Chapter 5

1. By now, you have scanned all of the articles you have identified up to now to include in your review. Go through each of these articles and make note of the following elements to include in the spreadsheet you developed in Chapter 4:

   - Definitions of terms (make note of which terms are especially important to a given study);
   - Key statistics that could be highlighted in your review; and
   - Features of the methodology, including sampling method, sample size, etc.

2. For each article, note any apparent strengths and/or weaknesses.

3. In each article, mark the places in the text that present important conclusions or that describe a point well. You should be looking for statements that may be used as direct quotations in your review.

4. Make notes of any gaps you have noticed in dealing with the topic you are pursuing, as well as any other patterns that you notice (e.g., similarities/differences among findings).

Notes

1 Schenk, A. M., & Fremouw, W. J. (2012). Prevalence, psychological impact, and coping of cyberbully victims among college students. *Journal of School Violence, 11*, 21–37.
2 Monahan, J. (2012). The individual risk assessment of terrorism. *Psychology, Public Policy, and Law, 18*, 167–205.
3 Else-Quest, N. M., Higgins, A., Allison, C., & Morton, L. C. (2012). Gender differences in self-conscious emotional experience: A meta-analysis. *Psychological Bulletin, 138*, 947–981.
4 Acevedo, V. (2008). Cultural competence in a group intervention designed for Latino patients living with HIV/AIDS. *Health & Social Work, 33*, 111–120.
5 Jose, A., Olino, T. M., & O'Leary, K. D. (2012). Item response theory analysis of intimate-partner violence in a community sample. *Journal of Family Psychology, 26*, 198–205.
6 Boehmer, U., Glickman, M., & Winter, M. (2012). Anxiety and depression in breast cancer survivors of different sexual orientations. *Journal of Consulting and Clinical Psychology, 80*, 382–395.
7 Seol, K. O., & Lee, R. M. (2012). The effects of religious socialization and religious identity on psychosocial functioning in Korean American adolescents from immigrant families. *Journal of Family Psychology, 26*, 371–380.
8 Vieira, J. M., Ávila, M., & Matos, P. M. (2012). Attachment and parenting: The mediating role of work-family balance in Portuguese parents of preschool children. *Family Relations, 61*, 31–50.

9. Gawlik, M. A. (2012). Moving beyond the rhetoric: Charter school reform and accountability. *The Journal of Educational Research, 105*, 210–219.
10. Farhat, T., Simons-Morton, B. G., Kokkevi, A., Van der Sluijs, W., Fotiou, A., & Kuntsche, E. (2012). Early adolescent and peer drinking homogeneity: Similarities and differences among European and North American Countries. *Journal of Early Adolescence, 32*, 81–103.
11. Gilic, L. (2016). Increasing homework completion and accuracy rates with parental participation for young children with Autism Spectrum Disorder. *Psychology, Society & Education, 8*, 173–186.
12. Stice, E., Presnell, K., & Spangler, D. (2002). Risk factors for binge eating onset in adolescent girls: A 2-year prospective investigation. *Health Psychology, 21*, 131–138.
13. Walker, J. V. III (2012). Parental factors that detract from the effectiveness of cognitive-behavioral treatment for childhood anxiety: Recommendations for practitioners. *Child & Family Behavior Therapy, 34*, 20–32.
14. Huan, V. S., Yeo, L. S., Ang, R. P., & Chong, W. H. (2012). Concerns and coping in Asian adolescents—gender as a moderator. *The Journal of Educational Research, 105*, 151–160.
15. Pyrczak, F., & Bruce, R. R. (2014). *Writing empirical research reports: A basic guide for students of the social and behavioral sciences* (8th ed.). Glendale, CA: Pyrczak Publishing.

Chapter 6

Analyzing Quantitative Research Literature

In the previous chapter, you were advised to make notes on important methodological strengths and weaknesses of the research articles you are reading prior to writing your literature review. This chapter will provide you with information on some points you may want to note regarding research methodology in quantitative studies. Those of you who have taken a course in research methods will recognize that this chapter contains only a very brief overview of some of the important issues.

✔ Guideline 1: Note Whether the Research Is Quantitative or Qualitative

Because quantitative researchers reduce information to statistics such as averages, percentages, and so on, their research articles are easy to spot. If an article has a results section devoted mainly to the presentation of statistical data, it is a safe bet that it is quantitative. The quantitative approach to research has dominated the social and behavioral sciences throughout the 1900s and into the present, so for most topics, you are likely to locate many more articles reporting quantitative than qualitative research.

The literature on how to conduct quantitative research emphasizes the following:

1. Start with one (or more) explicitly stated hypothesis that will remain unchanged throughout the study.[1] The validity of the hypothesis is evaluated only after the data have been analyzed (i.e., the hypothesis is not subject to change while the data are being collected).
2. Select an unbiased sample (such as a simple random sample obtained by drawing names out of a hat) from a particular population.
3. Use a relatively large sample of participants (typically at least 30 for an experiment and sometimes as many as 1,500 for a national survey).

4. Use measures that can be scored objectively, such as multiple-choice achievement tests and forced-choice questionnaires or attitude scales and personality scales with choices that participants mark.
5. Present results using statistics and make inferences to the population from which the sample was drawn (i.e., infer that what the researchers found by studying a sample is similar to what they would have found if they had studied the whole population from which the sample was drawn).

Qualitative research has a long tradition in the social and behavioral sciences, but it has gained a large following in many applied fields only in recent decades. It is sometimes easy to spot because the titles of the articles in this field often contain the word qualitative. In addition, qualitative researchers usually identify their research as qualitative in their introductions as well as in other parts of their reports.[2] You can also identify qualitative research because the results sections will be presented in a narrative describing themes and trends—often accompanied by quotations from the participants.

The literature on how to conduct qualitative research emphasizes the following:

1. Start with a general problem without imposing rigid, specific purposes and hypotheses to guide the study. As data are collected on the problem, hypotheses may emerge, but they are subject to change during the course of a study as additional data are collected.
2. Select a purposive sample—not a random one. For instance, a qualitative researcher may have access to some heroin addicts who attend a particular methadone clinic, and he or she may believe that the clients of this clinic might provide useful insights into the problems of recovering addicts. In other words, qualitative researchers use their *judgment* in selecting a sample instead of a mechanical, objective process such as drawing names from a hat at random.
3. Use a relatively small sample—sometimes as small as one exemplary case, such as a mathematics teacher who has received a national teaching award (once again, a purposive sample—selecting someone judged to be a potential source of important information).
4. Use relatively unstructured measures, such as semistructured interviews with open-ended questions (i.e., without "choices" for selection by participants), unstructured observations of behavior in natural contexts, and so on.
5. Measure intensively (e.g., spend extended periods of time with the participants to gain in-depth insights into the phenomena of interest).
6. Present results mainly or exclusively in words, with an emphasis on understanding the particular purposive sample studied and usually de-emphasizing or ignoring generalizations to larger populations.

Quantitative Research Literature

As you can see by comparing the previous two lists, the distinction between quantitative and qualitative research will be important when you evaluate studies for their strengths and weaknesses. The guidelines presented in this chapter are common ways recommended for evaluating quantitative research, which you should consider when evaluating and synthesizing in order to prepare a literature review. Guidelines for evaluating qualitative research are presented in the next chapter.

✔ Guideline 2: Note Whether a Study Is Experimental or Nonexperimental

An *experimental* study is one in which treatments are administered to participants *for the purposes of the study* and their effects are assessed. For instance, in an experiment, some hyperactive students might be given Ritalin® while others are given behavior therapy (such as a systematic application of one or another type of reward system) so that the relative effectiveness of the two treatments in reducing the number of classroom discipline problems may be assessed. (Note that almost all experiments are quantitative.) More generally, the purpose of an experimental study is to identify cause-and-effect relationships.

A *nonexperimental* study is one in which participants' traits are measured without attempting to change them. For instance, hyperactive students might be interviewed for an understanding of their perceptions of their own disruptive classroom behaviors without any attempt by the researcher to treat the students. Such a study might be quantitative (if the researcher uses highly structured interview questions with choices for students to select from and summarizes the results statistically) or qualitative (if a researcher uses semistructured or unstructured interview questions[3] and uses words to summarize the results in terms of themes, models, or theories).[4]

Here is an important caveat: Do not fall into the habit of referring to all research studies as experiments. For instance, if you are reviewing nonexperimental studies, refer to them as *studies*—not *experiments*. Use the term *experiment* only if treatments were administered to participants.

✔ Guideline 3: In an Experiment, Note Whether the Participants Were Assigned at Random to Treatment Conditions

An experiment in which participants are assigned at random to treatments is known as a *true experiment*. Random assignment to treatments is meant to eliminate bias in the assignment (e.g., with random assignment, there is no systematic bias that would assign the more disruptive students to the behavior therapy treatment while assigning the rest to treatment with Ritalin®). Other things being equal, more weight should be given to true experiments than to experiments employing other methods of assignment, such as designating the students in one school as the experimental group and the students in another school as the control group. Note that students are not normally assigned to schools at random. Hence, there may be important preexisting differences between the students in the two schools that may confound the interpretation of the results of such an experiment (e.g., socioeconomic status, language background, or self-selection, as occurs in magnet schools for the arts, the sciences, etc.).

✔ Guideline 4: Note Attempts to Examine Cause-and-Effect Issues in Nonexperimental Studies

The experimental method (with random assignment to treatment conditions) is widely regarded as the best quantitative method for investigating cause-and-effect issues. However, it is sometimes infeasible or impossible to treat participants in certain ways. For instance, if a researcher was exploring a possible causal link between the divorce of parents and their children dropping out of high school, it would obviously be impossible to force some parents to get divorced while forcing others to remain married for the purposes of the experiment. For this research problem, the best that can be done is to select some students who have dropped out and some who have not dropped out but who are very similar in other important respects (such as socioeconomic status, the quality of the schools they attended, and so on), and then investigate whether their parents' divorce rates differ in the hypothesized direction.[5] Suppose that the children of the divorced parents exhibited somewhat higher dropout rates than those of the children of nondivorced parents. Does this mean that divorce causes higher dropout rates? Not necessarily. The conclusion is debatable because the researchers may have overlooked a number of other possible causal variables. Here is just one: Perhaps parents who tend to get divorced have poorer interpersonal skills and relate less well to their children. It may be this deficit in the children's upbringing (and not the divorce *per se*) that contributed to their dropping out.[6]

The study we are considering is an example of a causal-comparative (or *ex post facto*) study. When using it, a researcher observes a current condition or outcome (such as dropping out) and searches the past for possible causal variables (such as divorce). Because causal-comparative studies are considered more prone to error than true experiments for examining causality, you should note when a conclusion is based on the causal-comparative method. In addition, you should consider whether there are other plausible causal interpretations the researcher may have overlooked.

✔ Guideline 5: Consider the Test-Retest Reliability of the Measure

Quantitative researchers refer to the tools they use (such as tests and questionnaires) as *measures*. Thus, the term *measurement* refers to the process by which quantitative researchers measure key variables.

Reliability refers to consistency of results. Here is an example: Suppose we administered a college admissions test one week and then readministered it to the same examinees the following week. The test would be considered reliable if the examinees who scored high the first week also tended to score high the second week.[7] By calculating a correlation coefficient, one can quantify the reliability of a test. Correlation coefficients can range from 0.00 to 1.00, with 1.00 indicating perfect reliability. Quantitative researchers generally regard a coefficient of 0.75 or higher to indicate adequate reliability. The type of reliability we are considering here is called *test-retest reliability*.[8]

When you analyze a quantitative study, examine the section on measurement to see if the researchers provide information on the reliability of the measures they used in their research. Typically, this information is very briefly presented, as in Example 6.5.1.

Example 6.5.1

A brief statement in a research report on test-retest reliability

The test-retest reliability of the measure with a 2-week interval between administrations was reported to be 0.81, which indicates adequate reliability (Doe, 2016).

While the statement in Example 6.5.1 is very brief, it assures you that the researcher whose research you are analyzing has considered the important issue of reliability. In addition, it provides you with a reference (i.e., Doe, 2016) that you could consult for more information on how reliability was determined.

✔ Guideline 6: Consider the Internal Consistency Reliability of the Measure

While test-retest reliability concerns the consistency of results over time (see Guideline 5), *internal consistency reliability* refers to consistency of results at one point in time. To understand this concept, consider a multiple-choice test with only two algebra test items. Suppose an examinee marked one item correctly and the other item incorrectly. This would indicate a *lack* of internal consistency because what we learned about the examinee's algebra knowledge varied from one item to the next (i.e., on one test item, the examinee earned one point, while on the other test item, the examinee earned zero points, which is the lowest possible score on a single item). Extending this concept to a test with a larger number of items and examinees, if those examinees who mark any one test item correctly *tend* to mark the other test items correctly (and if those examinees who mark any one test item *incorrectly tend* to mark the other test items *incorrectly*), the test would be said to have good internal consistency reliability.[9]

Failure to have internal consistency indicates that some of the items are not operating as indicated. There may be many reasons for this. One obvious reason is that some items may be ambiguous, causing examinees with much knowledge to mark incorrect answers. Of course, this would be undesirable.

Internal consistency reliability is almost universally examined by computing a statistic known as *Cronbach's alpha* (whose symbol is α). Like a correlation coefficient, α can range from 0.00 to 1.00, with values above 0.75 usually considered to indicate adequate internal consistency reliability for research purposes.[10] Example 6.6.1 shows how Cronbach's alpha might be reported in a research report.

Example 6.6.1[11]

A brief statement in a research report on internal consistency reliability

In the MASC (Multidimensional Anxiety Scale for Children), alpha was very high for total scores, as well as for the four subscale scores: .99 for Anxiety, .95 for PS, .88 for HA, .96 for SA, and .93 for SP.

While the statement in Example 6.6.1 is brief, it assures you that the researchers have considered internal consistency reliability.

✔ Guideline 7: Consider the Validity of the Measure

A measure (such as a college admissions test) is said to be *valid* to the extent that it measures what it is supposed to measure. For instance, to the extent that a college admissions test correctly predicts who will and who will not succeed in college, the test is said to be valid. In practice, it is safe to assume that no measure is perfectly valid. For instance, college admissions tests are at best only modestly valid.

In a *criterion-related validity* study, scores earned by examinees on a measure (such as a college admissions test) are correlated with scores earned on some other measure (such as freshmen GPAs earned in college). The extent of criterion-related validity is determined by calculating a correlation coefficient to describe the relationship. When this is done, the resulting correlation coefficient is called a *validity coefficient*.[12] Generally, coefficients above 0.30 indicate adequate validity for research purposes. Example 6.7.1 shows a brief statement regarding the *predictive criterion-related validity* of a college admissions test. It is called *predictive* because the admissions test was administered at one point in time, while the outcome (GPAs) was measured later, with the purpose being to determine how well the scores predict GPAs.

Example 6.7.1

A brief statement in a research report on predictive criterion-related validity

Using a sample of 240 examinees admitted to a small liberal arts college, Doe (2016) correlated scores on the XYZ College Admissions test with freshmen grades. The test was found to have adequate criterion-related validity ($r = .49$).

Example 6.7.2 shows a brief statement regarding *concurrent criterion-related validity*. The adjective *concurrent* refers to the fact that the two measures were administered at about the same time.

Example 6.7.2

A brief statement in a research report on concurrent criterion-related validity (predictive)

In a previous study, Doe (2016) correlated scores on the Smoking Cessation Questionnaire with data regarding smoking cessation gathered by trained and experienced interviewers. The questionnaire was administered to the participants on the same day that the participants were interviewed. Using the interview data as the criterion for judging the validity of the questionnaire, the questionnaire was found to have good criterion-related validity ($r = .68$). Thus, the Smoking Cessation Questionnaire is a reasonably valid substitute for the more expensive interview process for measuring smoking-cessation behaviors.

Another major type of validity is *construct validity*, which is the extent to which your test measures the theoretical concept that you assume it measures. This refers to any type of data-based study that sheds light on the validity of a measure. Construct validity studies can take many forms, most of which are beyond the scope of this book. However, to illustrate how such a study might be conducted, consider Example 6.7.3.

Example 6.7.3

A brief statement in a research report on construct validity

Scores on the new ABC Anxiety Scale were correlated with scores on the well-established Beck Depression Inventory, resulting in a correlation of .45. This result is consistent with major theories as well as previous studies (e.g., Doe, 2016) that indicate that individuals who are anxious have a moderate tendency to also be depressed. Thus, the correlation provides indirect evidence on the validity of the new anxiety scale.

The last major type of validity is *content validity*. Content validity is determined by having one or more experts evaluate the contents of a measure. It is especially important to determine the content validity of achievement tests. For instance, experts can be asked to compare the instructional objectives with the material covered by an achievement test in order to determine the extent to which they match. Content validity can also be determined for other types of measures, as illustrated in Example 6.7.4.

Example 6.7.4

A brief statement in a research report on content validity

The Infant Development Checklist was used as the measure of the outcome in this experiment. In a previous study, Doe (2016) reported that it had adequate content validity, as judged by three professors whose specialty is developmental psychology.

✔ Guideline 8: Consider Whether a Measure Is Valid For a Particular Research Purpose

A measure that has been shown to be reasonably valid in previous research may not be especially valid for use in all other studies. For instance, an attitude scale that has been shown to be valid for use with adolescents may have some unknown amount of validity for use with younger children in another study. Thus, if the purpose of the study is to study attitudes of younger children, the validity of the measure might be unknown. Put in more general terms, the validity of a measure is *relative* to the purposes of a study. It may be more valid in a study with one purpose (e.g., to determine attitudes of adolescents) than in another study with a different purpose (e.g., to determine attitudes of young children).

✔ Guideline 9: Note Differences in How a Variable Is Measured Across Studies

When you examine various published studies in which a variable of interest to you has been measured, you will often find that different researchers used different tools to measure the variable. For instance, one researcher may have measured attitude toward school with a forced-choice questionnaire (e.g., items for which participants respond to choices from "Strongly Agree" to "Strongly Disagree"), while another researcher might have used an observational checklist for classroom behaviors that indicate positive or negative attitudes (e.g., children working cooperatively on classroom projects). If similarities are found in results across studies using different measures, this lends support to the results. Obviously, differences in results among studies could be attributable to differences in the measurement.

Note that part of the measurement process is to determine the sources from which to collect data. For instance, to study violent juvenile delinquent behavior, one researcher might seek data from the participants' peers, while another might seek it from the participants themselves using essentially the same questions.[13] Differences in the sources with which the measure is used could also account for differences in results.

In light of the above, you should look for patterns across studies that might be attributable to measurement. For instance, do all the studies that support a certain conclusion use one method or type of measure while those that support a different conclusion use a different method? If your notes reveal this, you might consider making a statement such as the one in Example 6.9.1.

Example 6.9.1

A statement from a literature review that points out differences in measurement techniques (desirable)

While the two studies that used mailed questionnaires support the finding that inhalant use among adolescents is extremely rare (less than one-half of 1%), the three studies that used face-to-face interviews reported an incidence of more than 5%.

Note that Example 6.9.1 is much more informative than Example 6.9.2.

> **Example 6.9.2**
>
> *A statement from a literature review that fails to point out differences in measurement techniques (undesirable)*
>
> The research on the incidence of adolescent inhalant use has yielded mixed results, with two studies reporting that it is extremely rare and three others reporting an incidence of more than 5%.

✔ Guideline 10: Note How the Participants Were Sampled

Most quantitative researchers make inferences about populations based only on the samples studied. You should make notes on whether the samples studied seem likely to be representative of the populations to which one might wish to generalize. From a quantitative researcher's point of view, drawing a sample at random is best.

Unfortunately, most researchers cannot use random samples (at least not in their purest form). This is true for two reasons. First, many researchers work with limited funds and have limited cooperative contacts, which might be required for access to random samples. Because most researchers in the social and behavioral sciences are professors, it is not surprising that they often draw their samples from the student populations at the colleges or universities where they teach. Of course, what is true of college students might not generalize to other groups of individuals.

Second, even if a random sample of names is drawn, almost invariably, some of the individuals selected will refuse to participate. This is especially problematic in mailed surveys, for which response rates are notoriously low. It would not be surprising, for instance, to receive only a 25 percent response rate in a national survey that was mailed to a random sample of members of a professional association (e.g., an association of public school teachers).

Studies without random sampling and with low response rates should be interpreted with considerable caution. Such studies usually should be regarded as *suggestive* because they do not offer firm evidence.

✔ Guideline 11: Make Notes on the Demographics of the Participants

Making notes on the demographics[14] of the participants can also help you to identify patterns in the literature. For instance, have the researchers who studied the transition from welfare to work using urban samples obtained different results from researchers who have studied rural samples? Could the differences in the urban-rural status of the participants (a demographic characteristic) help to explain the differences in the findings? Note that you cannot answer such a question with certainty, but you could raise the possibility in your literature review. Other demographic characteristics often reported in research reports are gender, race, ethnicity, age, and socioeconomic status.

Research reports in which demographics are not reported in detail are generally less useful than ones in which demographics are reported in detail.

✔ Guideline 12: Note How Large a Difference Is—Not Just Whether It Is Statistically Significant

When a researcher says a difference is statistically significant, he or she is reporting that a statistical test has indicated that the difference is greater than might be created by chance alone. This does *not* mean that the difference is necessarily large. It would take several chapters of a statistics textbook to explain why this is true. However, the following analogy may help you to understand this point: Suppose there is a very tight race for the United States Senate, and Candidate A wins over Candidate B by 10 votes. This is indeed a very small difference, but it is quite significant (i.e., by counting all the votes systematically and carefully, we have identified a very small, nonchance, "real" difference).

Given that even a small difference is often statistically significant, you will want to make note of the sizes of the differences you find in the literature.[15] Suppose you read several studies that showed that computer-assisted instruction in English composition led to very slight but statistically significant increases in students' achievement. In fairness to your reader, you should point out the size of the differences, as illustrated in Example 6.12.1. You will be prepared to write such statements if you make appropriate notes as you read and analyze the literature.

Example 6.12.1

Differences in a study

In a series of true experiments at various colleges throughout the United States, the experimental groups receiving computer-assisted instruction in English composition consistently made very small but statistically significant gains as compared to the control groups in mathematics achievement. On average, the gains were only about one percentage point on multiple-choice tests. Despite their statistical significance, these very small gains make the use of the experimental treatment on a widespread basis problematic because of the greatly increased cost of using it instead of the conventional (control) treatment.

✔ Guideline 13: Presume That All Quantitative Studies Are Flawed

All quantitative studies are subject to errors of various kinds, so no one study should be taken as providing the definitive answer(s) to a given research problem. In fact, that is why you are combing through the evidence contained in original reports of research—to weigh the various pieces of evidence, all of which are subject to error—in order to arrive at some reasonable conclusions based on a body of literature. This brings us to an important point: Never use the word *prove* when discussing the results of empirical research. Empirical studies do not offer proof. Instead, they offer *degrees of evidence*, with some studies offering stronger evidence than others. While analyzing research articles, make notes on how convincing the evidence is in each article. Other things being equal, you should emphasize in your literature review the research articles that present the strongest evidence.

This guideline leads to another important principle. Namely, you will not be expected to dissect and discuss every flaw of every study you cite because flaws abound in studies. Instead, you should make notes on major flaws, especially in studies that you plan to emphasize in your review. In addition, you should critique the methodology of studies in groups whenever possible. For instance, you might point out that all of the studies in a particular group you are reviewing have common weaknesses. Good note-taking while you are reading the articles will help you to identify such commonalities.

Concluding Comment

This chapter briefly covers only some of the major methodological issues you might consider when you make notes on reports of quantitative research in preparation for writing a review of the literature. As you read the articles you have selected for your review, you will find additional information on these and other issues because researchers often critique their own research as well as that of others in their journal articles. Reading these critiques carefully will help you to comprehend more fully the research articles you will be reviewing.

Activities for Chapter 6

Directions: Locate an original report of quantitative research, preferably on a topic you are reviewing, and answer the following questions. For learning purposes, your instructor may choose to assign an article for all students in your class to read, and this activity may be structured as a group activity.

1. What characteristics of the report that you located led you to believe that it is an example of quantitative research?

Quantitative Research Literature

2. Is the study experimental *or* nonexperimental? On what basis did you decide?

3. If the study is experimental, were the participants assigned at random to treatment conditions? If not, how were they assigned?

4. If the study is nonexperimental, was the researcher attempting to examine cause-and-effect issues? If yes, did he or she use the causal-comparative method? Explain.

5. What types of measures (i.e., instruments) were used? Did the researcher provide enough information about them to allow you to make judgments on their adequacy for use in the research? If yes, do you believe they were adequate in light of the information provided? If no, what types of additional information about the measures should have been reported?

6. How did the researcher obtain a sample of participants? Was it at random from a population? If the study is a mailed survey, what was the response rate?

7. Has the researcher described the demographics of the participants in sufficient detail? Explain.

8. If the researchers reported statistically significant differences, did they discuss whether they were large differences? In your opinion, are the differences large enough to be of practical importance? Explain.

9. Did the researchers critique their own research by describing its limitations? Briefly describe any major flaws that you have identified in the research. Explain.

Notes

1 Quantitative researchers sometimes start with specific research questions or purposes instead of a hypothesis. As with hypotheses, the research questions or purposes remain unchanged throughout the study.
2 Note that quantitative researchers rarely explicitly state that their research is quantitative.
3 In addition, a qualitative researcher would be likely to conduct significantly longer interviews and possibly more than one interview.
4 Obviously, then, nonexperimental research can be quantitative or qualitative, while experimental research is almost always quantitative.
5 If the researcher had considerable resources and a long time frame, a study could be conducted in which children are tracked from the day they begin school until they graduate or drop out, noting which students drop out and which ones do not, as well as which students' parents get divorced. This longitudinal method is also inferior to

Part II: Analyzing the Relevant Literature

6. the experimental method for identifying cause-and-effect relationships because of possible confounding variables (i.e., many variables other than divorce may be responsible for the student's decision to drop out and the researchers may fail to control for all of them).
6. If this limitation is still not clear, consider the example further. Suppose that, based on the study in question, a dictatorial government made it illegal for parents to divorce in order to reduce the dropout rate. If the real cause of dropping out were parents' poor interpersonal skills, preventing divorce would not have the predicted effect because it was misidentified as a causal agent. Instead, the government should have mounted programs to assist parents in improving their interpersonal skills, especially in their dealings with their children.
7. Likewise, for high reliability, those examinees who scored low the first week would also score low the second week.
8. Other methods for determining reliability are beyond the scope of this book.
9. In other words, a measure with high internal consistency may be viewed as consisting of a set of homogenous items (i.e., all items tend to tap similar skills, attitudes, and so on).
10. If you have studied statistics, you know that correlation coefficients can also have negative values. In practice, however, when estimating reliability and internal consistency, they are always positive in value.
11. Rodriguez, A., Reise, S. P., & Haviland, M. G. (2016). Evaluating bifactor models: Calculating and interpreting statistical indices. *Psychological Methods, 21*, 137–150.
12. A *validity coefficient* is a correlation coefficient whose symbol is r.
13. Peers might be asked, "Has your friend John told you about any fights he has had in the past week?" while the participant might be asked, "Have you had any fights in the past week?"
14. *Demographics* are background characteristics of the participants.
15. Increasingly, quantitative researchers are reporting a relatively new statistic called *effect size*, which measures the size of differences between groups of participants relative to the differences among individual participants. While a discussion of this statistic is beyond the scope of this book, if you encounter this statistic while reviewing literature, use this rough guideline: Effect sizes of less than about .25 indicate a small difference, while effect sizes above .50 indicate a large difference.

Chapter 7

Analyzing Qualitative Research Literature

The major differences between qualitative and quantitative research are described in the first guideline of Chapter 6. Chapter 7 was written with the assumption that you have already carefully considered those differences.[1] In other words, while Chapter 6 deals with the analysis of quantitative research, this chapter deals with analyzing qualitative research.

✔ Guideline 1: Note Whether the Research Was Conducted By an Individual or By a Research Team

While both quantitative and qualitative research studies are frequently conducted by teams of researchers, the use of a team is more important in qualitative research than in quantitative research. For instance, if a quantitative researcher administers an objective attitude scale, scores it, and analyzes the data using a statistical software package, it is reasonable to expect that anyone else who uses care in scoring and entering the data would obtain the same results that the original researcher obtained. However, if a qualitative researcher conducts open-ended, semistructured interviews, the resulting raw data typically consist of many pages of transcripts of what the participants said in the interviews. It is possible that different researchers might analyze and interpret such data differently, calling into question the validity of the analysis of the data. However, if a team of researchers analyzes a set of qualitative data and arrives at a consensus on its meaning, consumers of research can have more confidence in the results of the research than if it were conducted by a single individual.

However, it is not necessary for all qualitative research to be conducted by a team. In fact, other qualified researchers may not be available to work with the researcher, or the requirements for a thesis or a dissertation might stipulate that the researcher work as an individual. When this is the case, it is especially important for consumers of qualitative research to ensure that the individual who conducted the qualitative research used at least one of the techniques described in Guidelines 3 and 4 presented later in this chapter.

✔ Guideline 2: When There Is a Research Team, Note Whether Analysis of the Data Was Initially Conducted Independently

Researchers who analyze a set of qualitative data should first analyze it independently (i.e., without consulting each other) in order to prevent one or more researchers from unduly influencing the others in the interpretation of the data. After the initial analysis, researchers then resolve any discrepancies, usually by discussing them until a consensus is reached. This process is described in Example 7.2.1.

Example 7.2.1[2]

Description of independent analysis followed by reaching a consensus

The judgments at termination and follow-up were based solely on patient interviews. We discussed every case of disagreement until a consensus solution could be reached, following the principles of consensual qualitative research (Hill et al., 2005). To deepen the picture of personality-related problems and the content of changes in anaclitic–introjective personality dimensions, verbal case formulations were compiled for each case and time point. During the consensus discussions, each case was compared with all the others, reviewed and reevaluated, and we commented on changes over time.

Other things being equal, qualitative research in which a team of researchers first analyze the data independently and then discuss their analyses to reach a consensus is stronger than research in which this is not done.

✔ Guideline 3: Note Whether Outside Experts Were Consulted

Consultation with one or more outside experts increases the confidence consumers of research can have in a qualitative study's research results. Consultation is especially important if an individual (and not a team) has conducted the research (see Guideline 1), but in either case it will result in increased confidence in the results.

Qualitative researchers usually refer to input on the adequacy of the results of data analysis from outside experts as a *peer review* process. In Example 7.3.1, the investigators assembled a group of cross-disciplinary experts to guide the interpretation of the results in the course of the data gathering. This process greatly enhances the reader's confidence in the results. By contrast, when the expert reviews the entire process of conducting the research as well as reviewing the results of the data analysis, the expert is usually referred to as an *auditor*.

> **Example 7.3.1**[3]
>
> *Description of ongoing analysis of results by a group of experts*
>
> The full investigator group, including consumer advocates, sociologists, psychologists, anthropologists, psychiatrists, and statisticians, met after each wave of interviews to review and discuss findings from each wave of interviews, questionnaires, and health-plan data. Such data and investigator triangulation enhance rigor (Patton, 1999). For analyses reported here, saturation (Miles & Huberman, 1994) was reached for each of the primary and cross-cutting themes.

✔ Guideline 4: Note Whether the Participants Were Consulted on the Interpretation of the Data

The literature on how to conduct qualitative research emphasizes conducting research in such a way that the results reflect the realities *as perceived by the participants*. In other words, the goal of qualitative research is to understand how participants perceive their own reality—not to establish a so-called objective reality. Thus, it is appropriate for qualitative researchers to prepare a tentative report of the results and to ask the participants (or a sample of them) to review the report and provide feedback on how well it reflects their perceptions. Qualitative researchers call this process *member checking*. This term has its origins in the idea that the participants in qualitative research are in fact *members* of the research team who are *checking* the results for accuracy. Example 7.4.1 illustrates how this might be described in a research report.

> **Example 7.4.1**[4]
>
> *Description of the use of member checking*
>
> Member checking is particularly important because it helps ensure that the meaning-making processes of the participants were represented well. It is critical in a constructivist study to stay as true to the participants' perceptions as possible (Crotty, 2003). The former students all indicated that the data analysis results fit with their experiences. For example, it was reported that learning to set limits and use child-centered attending skills as a unique way to relate to children were most relevant in the study findings. Members also agreed that their confidence in practicing and adherence to play therapy increased throughout their experiences.

Part II: Analyzing the Relevant Literature

While member checking is not essential for qualitative research to be judged adequate, it is especially helpful to an individual who is conducting research alone (as opposed to with a research team, whose members can reflect with each other on the accuracy of results).

✔ Guideline 5: Note Whether the Researchers Used a Purposive Sample or a Sample of Convenience

As you know from the material in Guideline 1 of Chapter 6, qualitative researchers strive to use *purposive samples*. Purposive samples are selected based on the careful judgment of the researchers regarding the types of individuals they consider to be especially good sources of data for a particular research topic. For instance, a qualitative researcher evaluating a clinical program might select for interviews several individuals who are just beginning the program and several who have been attending the program for more than a certain length of time. Selection criteria might also include gender (for instance, selecting some men and some women), age, and attendance (for instance, selecting only those who have attended regularly).

The authors of Example 7.5.1 indicate the criteria for their purposive sample.

Example 7.5.1[5]

Description of the use of purposive sampling

A nonprobabilistic purposive sampling strategy was used to recruit one-parent families, where fathers had been nonresident from early in the child's life and mothers had not entered into cohabiting relationships with subsequent partners. We sampled on the basis of the age of the child at which their father left the family home, rather than marital status of parents per se, as it has been suggested that living arrangements may be a better indicator of family structure than parental marital status (Bumpass & Raley, 1995; Sigle-Rushton & McLanahan, 2004). Families were excluded if fathers had left the home after the child was 2.5 years of age, in line with Weinraub and Wolf (1983) who used a similar cutoff age in their study of solo mother families. Families in which mothers had entered into cohabiting relationships with subsequent partners were also excluded, to avoid the confounding influence of substitute father figures on children's relationship with their nonresident father, as has been demonstrated by previous research (Amato et al., 2009; Juby, Billette, Laplante, & Le Bourdais, 2007). Finally, children who had no memory of contact with their fathers or did not know his identity were excluded.

In contrast, a *sample of convenience* is one in which the participants are selected solely or primarily on the basis that they are readily available (i.e., convenient to work with), as illustrated in Example 7.5.2.

Example 7.5.2[6]

Description of the use of a sample of convenience

Data were collected between 1997 and 2008 at the former Institute of Psychotherapy, Stockholm County Council, Sweden, and included 14 consecutive cases of publicly financed psychoanalyses (12 female and two male patients). Patients' sociodemographic characteristic are presented in more detail elsewhere (Werbart & Forsström, 2014) and summarized here. Mean age at the start of psychoanalysis was 33 years (SD = 6.9; range: 25–45). Patients were highly educated and had taken protracted sick leave before treatment (M = 106 days; SD = 131; range 4–330). All were referred to psychoanalysis from psychiatric outpatient clinics. Thirteen patients had undergone previous psychiatric treatment and 12 had been in psychotherapy prior to psychoanalysis.

Note that both qualitative and quantitative researchers regard samples of convenience as less desirable, but sometimes such a sample is the only type available to a researcher with limited contacts and resources. Nevertheless, research employing samples of convenience yields results that should be interpreted very cautiously.

✔ Guideline 6: Note Whether the Demographics of the Participants Are Described

As you will recall from Guideline 11 in Chapter 6, it is a good idea to make notes on the demographics of participants in preparation for analyzing research for inclusion in your literature review. By providing demographics relevant to the research topic, consumers of research are made aware of whom the participants are, which permits them to make judgments about the adequacy of the sample. For instance, the researchers who wrote the description of demographics in Example 7.6.1 were studying children's memory of auditory events. As you can see, the demographics they reported are relevant to the topic of their research.

Part II: Analyzing the Relevant Literature

Example 7.6.1[7]

Sample description of demographics in a study

Twenty-five first and second grade children (M = 7 years, 6 months, SD = 4.8 months, range: 6 years, 11 months – 8 years, 7 months, 9 males) and 35 third and fourth grade children (M – 10 years, 8 months, SD – 6.2 months, range: 9 years, 7 months – 11 years, 11 months, 15 males) participated in the study. Fifty-five children were of European ethnicity, two children were half European, and the ethnicity of three children was unknown. Participants were recruited by contacting elementary schools in a large city in Norway. The study was approved by the regional ethical committee (cf. The Helsinki declaration of 1964).

✔ Guideline 7: Consider Whether the Method of Qualitative Analysis Is Described in Sufficient Detail

To qualify as *research*, the method used to analyze the data must be carefully planned and systematic. In contrast, casual observation followed by a purely subjective discussion of it does not qualify as research.

To help consumers of research to determine whether a given report qualifies as *qualitative research*, qualitative researchers should describe in some detail how they analyzed the data. Note that it is insufficient for a researcher to say only that "the grounded-theory approach was used" or that "the analysis was based on a phenomenological approach." In Example 7.7.1, the researchers begin by naming *consensual qualitative research* (CQR) as the method of analysis and provide references where more information on the approach can be obtained. They follow this by summarizing the steps in CQR that they applied in the analysis.

Example 7.7.1[8]

Description of the use of Consensual Qualitative Research Methodology

The interview data were analyzed using the method suggested by Bogdan and Biklen (2007) and was performed by the authors. The researchers first immersed themselves in the data by reading and re-reading the transcriptions of the 26 individuals to get a sense of the totality of the data. The researchers together then developed coding categories that were reflective of the themes described by the participants. The coding was done by both

> researchers and was shared between the researchers. Throughout this process coding categories were sometimes collapsed and refined. The final coding categories were then used to code the data. When the researchers identified differences in the coding categories, they went back to the data and developed a consensus about which categories best reflected participants' responses. Quotes from the participants are identified in Results by number and gender.

✔ Guideline 8: Note Whether Quantities Are Provided When Qualitative Researchers Discuss Quantitative Matters

Just because research is qualitative does not mean that quantities should be ignored or left unreported. For instance, it is appropriate to use statistics when describing the demographics of participants in qualitative research, as in Example 7.6.1, in which the average age as well as a large number of percentages were provided.

When describing the results, it is usually undesirable to make statements such as "a few of the participants raised the issue of . . ." or "many of the participants perceived the issue as . . . ."

One approach to quantifying qualitative results is to use what qualitative researchers call *literal enumeration*, which merely means reporting specific numbers of participants for each statement of results. However, reporting many numbers can clutter up a report of qualitative research results. An alternative is to establish quantitative categories for otherwise vague terms such as *many*. This is illustrated in Example 7.8.1. Such a statement near the beginning of the results section helps to clarify how the terms were defined and used by the researchers.

> ### Example 7.8.1[9]
>
> *Definitions of otherwise vague terms that refer to quantities*
>
> Enumeration data were used in the results section that follows. Specifically, the word *many* indicates that more than 50% of the participants gave a particular type of response, the term *some* indicates that between 25% and 50% did so, while the term *a few* indicates that less than 25% did so.

Other things being equal, qualitative reports that provide guidance on quantities are more useful to consumers of research than those that do not.

Concluding Comment

This chapter briefly covers only some major methodological issues you might consider when you make notes on reports of qualitative research in preparation for writing your review of the literature. As you read the articles you have selected for your review, make notes about any other methodological issues and decisions made by the researchers that might affect the validity of the research results.

Activities for Chapter 7

Directions: Locate an original report of qualitative research, preferably on a topic you are reviewing, and answer the following questions. For learning purposes, your instructor may choose to assign an article for all students in your class to read, and this activity may be structured as a group activity.

1. What characteristics of the report that you have located led you to believe that it is an example of qualitative research?
2. Was the study conducted by an individual *or* by a research team?
3. Was the initial analysis of the results conducted *independently* or by more than one researcher?
4. Were outside experts consulted for peer review? For an audit? If yes, does this increase your confidence in the validity of the results?
5. Did researchers use *member checking*? If yes, does this increase your confidence in the validity of the results?
6. Is it clear whether a purposive *or* a convenience sample was used? Explain.
7. Has the researcher described the demographics of the participants in sufficient detail? Explain.
8. Did the researcher name a specific method of qualitative data analysis (e.g., consensual qualitative research)? Is it described in sufficient detail? Explain.
9. Did the researcher provide sufficiently specific qualitative information in the results section? Explain.
10. Briefly describe any major flaws in the research that you did not cover in your answers to Questions 1 through 9.

Notes

1 Students who are concentrating on reviewing qualitative research reports are *strongly* advised to review carefully the entirety of Chapter 6.

2   Werbart, A. & Levander, S. (2016). Fostering change in personality configurations: Anaclitic and introjective patients in psychoanalysis. *Psychoanalytic Psychology, 33,* 217–242.

3   Yarborough, B. J. H., Yarborough, M. T., Janoff, S. L., & Green, C. A. (2016). Getting by, getting back, and getting on: Matching mental health services to consumers' recovery goals. *Psychiatric Rehabilitation Journal, 39,* 97–104.

4   Smith-Adcock, S., Davis, E., Pereira, J., Allen, C., Socarras, K., Bodurtha, K., & Smith-Bonahue, T. (2012). Preparing to play: A qualitative study of graduate students' reflections on learning play therapy in an elementary school. *International Journal of Play Therapy, 21,* 100–115.

5   Nixon, E., Greene, S., & Hogan, D. (2012). "Like an uncle but more, but less than a father"—Irish children's relationships with nonresident fathers. *Journal of Family Psychology, 26,* 381–390.

6   Werbart, A. & Levander, S. (2016). Fostering change in personality configurations: Anaclitic and introjective patients in psychoanalysis. *Psychoanalytic Psychology, 33,* 217–242.

7   Burrell, L. V., Johnson, M. S., & Melinder, A. (2016). Children as earwitnesses: Memory for emotional auditory events. *Applied Cognitive Psychology, 30,* 323–331.

8   Brower, N., Skogrand, L., & Bradford, K. (2016). Measuring the effectiveness of experiential date nights: A qualitative study. *Marriage & Family Review, 52,* No. 6, 563–578.

9   This example is drawn from Orcher, L. T. (2014). *Conducting research: Social and behavioral science methods* (2nd ed.), p. 72. Glendale, CA: Pyrczak Publishing.

Chapter 8

Organizing Your Notes by Grouping the Results of Your Analysis

The guidelines in the previous chapters have helped you to select a topic, identify literature, and conduct a preliminary analysis of the articles on your list. Building tables that summarize literature is an effective way to help you get an overview of the literature you have considered. In addition, you may want to include in your literature review one or more of the tables you build, which will also help to provide an overview for the readers of your review.

✔ Guideline 1: Consider Building a Table of Definitions

Each of the variables you are considering should be defined early in your review. Building a table of definitions helps you and your readers under two circumstances. First, if there are a number of definitions of closely related variables, a table of definitions, such as the one in Example 8.1.1, makes it easy to scan the definitions in order to identify similarities and differences.

Example 8.1.1[1]

First table of definitions

Definitions of Psychological Empowerment Relevant to Tobacco Control Initiatives

Domain	Attributes	Definitions
Intrapersonal	Domain-specific efficacy	Beliefs in one's capabilities to organize and execute the courses of action required to produce specific changes related to tobacco control.
	Perceived sociopolitical control	Beliefs about one's capabilities and efficacy in social and political systems.
	Participatory competence	Perceived ability to participate in and contribute to the operations of the group or organization, through talking at meetings, working as a team member, and so on.
Interactional	Knowledge of resources	Awareness of whether resources exist to support the group and how to acquire them.
	Assertiveness	Ability to express your feelings, opinions, beliefs, and needs directly, openly, and honestly while not violating the personal rights of others.
	Advocacy	Pursuit of influencing outcomes, including public policy and resource allocation decisions within political, economic, and social systems and institutions that directly affect people's lives.

Grouping Your Results

Second, a table of definitions can be helpful if there are diverse definitions of a given variable. Consider arranging them chronologically by year to see if there are historical trends in how the variable has been defined across time. Example 8.1.2 illustrates the organization of such a table, using hypothetical entries.

Example 8.1.2

Second table of definitions

Definitions of Child Abuse Over Time (1945 to 2016)

Author	Definition	Notes
Doe (1945)	Defined as…	First published definition. Does not include psychological abuse.
Smith (1952)	Defined as…	
Jones (1966)	Defined as…	First definition to mention sexual abuse.
Lock (1978)	Defined as…	
Black & Clark (1989)	Defined as…	
Solis (2000)	Defined as…	Legal definition in Texas.
Ty (2003)	Defined as…	Most widely cited definition in recent literature.
Bart (2016)	Defined as…	

✔ Guideline 2: Consider Building a Table of Research Methods

Because different research methods can result in differences in the outcomes of studies, it is helpful to build a table that summarizes the methods employed, such as the one in Example 8.2.1. In addition to the methods described in this table for experiments (review Guidelines 2 and 3 in Chapter 6 for ways to describe differences between experiments), it is desirable to include a row indicating the type of experimental design that was used (e.g., randomized control group design) in each study.

Example 8.2.1[2]

Table of methods

Primary Study Characteristics (Methods)

Experimental design	Preyde (2010)	Galvan (2015)
Convenience sample	Undergraduate students in class	Undergraduate students in class
Convenience sample	Kindergarten class	First-grade class
Random selection	Parents	Parents
Not indicated	PTA members	Households in zip code area

✔ Guideline 3: Consider Including a Summary of Research Results in the Methods Table

Results can be summarized in a table showing the research methods (see Guideline 2) by adding an additional row or column to the table.

Instead of authors' names featured at the top of the columns, as in Example 8.2.1, they can be placed at the beginning of the rows, as in Example 8.3.1. In this example, the results of the studies are briefly summarized.

Example 8.3.1[3]

Summarized results

Longitudinal Studies Linking Religion and Adolescent Sexual Behavior

Publication date, authors	Location, year, SES; sample N	Age or grade; gender; ethnicity	Religiosity measures	Sexual behavior measures	Impact of religion on sex behavior
(1975) Jessor & Jessor	Small city in Rocky Mountain region, 1969 to 1971, middle class; $N = 424$	High school; M and F; White	Religiosity; church attendance	Ever had sexual intercourse at Time 1	High school females who initiated sexual intercourse between Time 1 and Time 2 were less religious and attended church less frequently.
(1983) Jessor, Costa, Jessor, & Donovan	Rocky Mountains, 1969 to 1972 and 1979; $N = 346$ virgins	Grades 7, 8, and 9 in 1969; M and F; White	Church attendance; religiosity[a]	Age at first coitus	Religiosity and more frequent attendance predicted later initiation of first coitus.
(1991) Beck, Cole, & Hammond[b]	United States, 1979, 1983; $N = 2,072$	14 to 17 years old; M and F; White virgins in 1979	Religious affiliation of adolescents and parents (Catholic, Baptist, mainline Protestant, institutional sect, Fundamentalist)	Coital experience (yes or no)	White adolescent females and males with institutionalized sect affiliation (e.g., Pentecostal, Mormon, Jehovah's Witness) were less likely than were mainline Protestants (e.g., Episcopalian, Lutheran, Methodist) to engage in first coitus between 1979 and 1983. Even when controlling for attendance, females with Baptist affiliation and males with Fundamentalist affiliation were less likely than were mainline Protestants to experience first coitus.
(1996) Crockett, Bingham, Chopack, & Vicary	Single rural school district in eastern United States, 1985, lower SES; $N = 289$	7th to 9th grades; M and F; White	Attendance	Age at first coitus	Females (but not males) who attended more frequently were more likely to be older (more than age 17) at first coitus.
(1996) Mott, Fondell, Hu, Kowaleski-Jones, & Menaghan[c]	United States, 1988, 1990, and 1992; $N = 451$	At least 14 years old in 1992; M and F; White (Black and Hispanic over-sampled)	Attendance; do friends attend same church?	Early initiation of first coitus (using age 14 as criterion for *early*)	Frequent attendees who also had peers attending the same church were less likely to be engaging in sexual intercourse at age 14.
(1996) Pleck, Sonenstein, Ku, & Burbridge[d]	United States, 1988 (Wave I, $N = 1,880$) 1990 to 1991 (Wave II, $N = 1,676$)	15 to 19 years old in 1988; males; 37% Black, 21% Hispanic, 3% other	Importance of religion; frequency of church attendance	Number of coital acts in past 12 months that did not include use of a condom	Males who attended church more frequently in mid-adolescence showed a decline (relative to predicted levels) in the frequency of unprotected sex in late adolescence.
(1997) Miller, Norton, Curtis, Hill, Schvaneveldt, & Young[e]	United States, 1976, 1981, and 1987; $N = 759$	7 to 11 years old in 1976; M and F; White and Black	Attendance (parent report); attitudes toward attending	Age at first coitus (reported retrospectively in Wave III)	Families who reported positive attitudes toward attending religious services were more likely to delay sexual debut.
(1999) Bearman & Bruckner[f]	United States, 1994 to 1996; $N = 5,070$	7th to 12th grades; females only; White, Black, Asian, Hispanic	Religious affiliation	First sexual intercourse (yes or no); age of first coitus; pregnancy risk (yes or no)	Beyond the effects of age on sexual debut, conservative Protestants and Catholics were less likely than were mainstream Protestants to experience first intercourse (sexual debut) between Time 1 and Time 2.
(1999) Whitbek, Yoder, Hoyt, & Conger	Midwestern state, 1989 to 1993, rural; $N = 457$	8th to 10th grades; M and F; White	Composite: attendance, importance (mother and adolescent)	Sexual intercourse (yes or no)	Mother's religiosity decreased likelihood of adolescent's sexual debut in 9th and 10th grades. Adolescent religiosity had strong negative effects on sexual debut.
(2001) Bearman & Bruckner	United States, 1994 to 1995 (Wave I), 1996 (Wave II); $N = 14,787$	7th to 12th grades; M and F; White, Hispanic, Asian, Black	Composite of attendance, perceived importance, and frequency of praying	Age at first coitus; contraceptive use at first coitus (yes or no); virginity pledger (yes or no)	Higher religiosity decreased the risk of sexual debut for White, Asian, and Hispanic adolescents of both genders. For Black adolescents, no relation between religiosity and risk of sexual debut was found. Religiosity delayed sexual debut in middle and late, but not early, adolescence. (Analyses conducted with non-Black respondents only.) Religiosity and contraceptive use at first coitus were unrelated.

Note: M = male; F = female.
a. The religiosity measure is not described for this article.
b. Data are from the National Longitudinal Survey of Youth (NLSY).
c. Data are from the National Longitudinal Survey of Youth (NLSY).
d. Data are from the National Survey of Adolescent Males (NSAM).
e. Data are from all three waves of the National Survey of Children (NSC).
f. Data are from Waves I and II of the National Longitudinal Study of Adolescent Health (Add Health).

Note that the summaries of results of the various studies in Example 8.3.1 are given in narrative descriptions (not described using statistics). Often, this is the best way to present the summaries of results. It is acceptable to present statistics, however, if they are straightforward and are comparable from study to study. For instance, if there are five studies that estimate the prevalence of inhalant use by high school students, and they all present results in terms of percentages, including the percentages would be appropriate in the summaries of results. On the other hand, if the statistics reported on a topic are diverse from study to study, it would be less desirable to present them statistically because they are not directly comparable from one study to another (e.g., one study presents percentages, one presents means and medians, another presents a frequency distribution, and so on). This is true because a reader should be able to scan columns and rows to note differences among studies. Scanning and comparing mixed statistics in a column can be confusing.

✔ Guideline 4: When There Is Much Literature on a Topic, Establish Criteria for Determining Which Literature to Summarize in a Table

Summary tables that will be inserted into a literature review do not necessarily need to include all studies on the topic of the review. However, if only some are included, you should describe the criteria used to determine whether or not to include an item. Examples 8.4.1 and 8.4.2 show sample statements that inform readers of such criteria.

Example 8.4.1

Description of criterion (i.e., only true experiments) for inclusion in a table

Table 1 summarizes characteristics of the participants, the treatments applied, and the outcome measures. This table includes only *true experiments* (i.e., experiments in which participants were assigned at random to experimental and control groups).

Example 8.4.2

Description of criterion (i.e., only recent surveys) for inclusion in a table

Table 2 summarizes the research methods and results of the five most recent surveys on the topic. Because the literature indicates that opinions on the issue vary over time, the most recent surveys provide the best indication of current public opinion on this issue.

Part II: Analyzing the Relevant Literature

✔ Guideline 5: When There Is Much Literature on a Topic, Consider Building Two or More Tables to Summarize It

Even after establishing criteria for inclusion of studies in a table (see Guideline 4), there may be too many studies to include in a single table. When this is the case, consider how the literature might be divided into groups so a different table may be built for each group of studies. For instance, one table might summarize the theories relevant to the topic, another might summarize the quantitative studies on a topic, and a third table might summarize the qualitative studies.

✔ Guideline 6: Present Tables in a Literature Review Only for Complex Material

During the early stages of synthesizing literature, there is no limit on the number of tables you may create to get an overview of the literature. However, you should include in your literature review only tables that deal with complex matters that might be difficult for your readers to follow in the text (i.e., items that may be difficult to follow in the narrative of the literature review).

Keep in mind that a literature review should *not* be a collection of tables. Instead, it should be primarily a narrative in which you summarize, synthesize, and interpret the literature on a given topic, with only a small number of tables inserted to assist readers in comprehending complex material.

✔ Guideline 7: Discuss Each Table Included in a Literature Review

All tables in a literature review should be introduced and discussed in the narrative of the literature review. Example 8.7.1 illustrates how this might be done.

Example 8.7.1

Discussion of a table in the literature review of an article

Table 1 summarizes the five studies in which the effectiveness of cognitive/behavioral therapy was examined using the Beck Depression Inventory as the outcome measure. Overall, the sample sizes were quite small, ranging from $n = 4$ to $n = 16$. Despite this limitation, the results show promise for use of cognitive/behavioral therapy because all the treated groups (i.e., experimental groups) showed statistically significant decreases in depression in comparison with the control groups.

While you should discuss each table, it is not necessary to describe every element in it. For instance, Example 8.7.1 discusses a table that summarizes five studies, yet the sample sizes used in only two of the studies ($n = 4$ and $n = 16$) are mentioned in the narrative.

✔ Guideline 8: Give Each Table a Number and Descriptive Title

All tables should have a number (e.g., Table 1, Table 2, and so on) as well as a descriptive title (i.e., a caption). Note that all tables in this chapter have table numbers and titles. Consult your discipline's style manual for guidance on how to format tables that you will use in your manuscript.

It is beyond the scope of this book to provide comprehensive directions for using a word processor to build tables. In programs such as Word, it is quite easy to learn how to modify tables, with only a little experimentation.

✔ Guideline 9: Insert *Continued* When Tables Split Across Pages

While it is desirable to fit each table on a single page, it is not always possible. When a table splits across pages, insert (*continued*) at the bottom of the table so that readers know to turn the page and continue reading the table. Note that the entry is enclosed within parentheses. Correspondingly, repeat the table number followed by (*continued*) at the top of the second part of the table on the next page.

Activities for Chapter 8

Directions: It is assumed that you have already read many of the articles that you will be evaluating and synthesizing in your literature review. Respond to the following questions to the extent that you can based on your preliminary reading of the literature.

1. Make a list of the definitions given in the articles you have read. Did you identify a sufficient number of definitions to warrant building a table of definitions? Explain.

2. Based on your readings, do you plan to build a table of research methods? Will it also include a row or column that summarizes the results of the studies?

3. What criteria can you use to distinguish among the studies you have read? If you are building a table of research methods, are these criteria useful in constructing the table? Explain.

4. Do you anticipate inserting more than one table in your literature review? Explain.

Notes

1. Holden, D. J., Evans, W. D., Hinnant, L. W., & Messeri, P. (2005). Modeling psychological empowerment among youth involved in local tobacco control efforts. *Health Education & Behavior, 32,* 264–278. Reprinted with permission.
2. Loosely based on Dryden, T., Baskwil, A., & Preyde, M. (2004). Massage therapy for the orthopaedic patient: A review. *Orthopaedic Nursing, 23,* 327–332.
3. Rostosky, S. S., Wilcox, B. L., Wright, M. L. C., & Randall, B. A. (2004). The impact of religiosity on adolescent sexual behavior: A review of the evidence. *Journal of Adolescent Research, 19,* 677–697. Reprinted with permission.

PART III

Writing the First Draft of Your Literature Review

Chapter 9

Synthesizing Trends and Patterns: Preparing to Write

At this point, you should have read and analyzed a collection of research articles and prepared detailed notes, possibly including summary tables as recommended in Chapter 8. You should now begin to synthesize these notes and tabled materials into a new whole, the sum of which will become your literature review. In other words, you are now ready to begin the process of *writing* your literature review. This chapter will help you to develop a detailed writing outline, which can save you valuable time and effort as you continue with the writing task.

✔ Guideline 1: Consider Your Purpose and Voice before Beginning to Write

Begin by asking yourself about your purpose in writing the literature review. Are you trying to convince your professor that you have expended sufficient effort in preparing a term paper for your class? Are you trying to demonstrate your command of a field of study in a thesis or dissertation? Or is your purpose to establish a context for a study you hope will be published in a journal? Each of these scenarios will result in a different type of final product, in part because of the differences in the writer's purpose, but also because of differences in the readers' expectations. Review the descriptions of the three types of literature reviews presented in Chapter 1.

After you establish your purpose and have considered your audience, decide on an appropriate *voice* (or style of writing) for your manuscript. A writer's voice in a literature review should be formal because that is what the academic context expects. The traditional voice in scientific writing requires that the writer de-emphasize himself or herself in order to focus the readers' attention on the content. In Example 9.1.1, the writer's *self* is too much in evidence. It distracts the reader from the content of the statement. Example 9.1.2 is superior because it focuses on the content.

Example 9.1.1[1]

Improper voice for academic writing

In this review, I will show that groups are often indispensable to many important life activities and have the potential for enhancing performance and productivity. However, I believe this potential is seldom fully realized. One well-documented limitation of groups I observed in the literature is the tendency for individuals to exert less effort when working in a group than when working individually, a phenomenon known as social loafing (Latané, Williams, & Harkins, 1979).

Example 9.1.2[2]

Suitable voice for academic writing

Groups are often indispensable to many important life activities and have the potential for enhancing performance and productivity. However, this potential is seldom fully realized. One well-documented limitation of groups is the tendency for individuals to exert less effort when working in a group than when working individually, a phenomenon known as social loafing (Latané, Williams, & Harkins, 1979).

Notice that academic writers tend to avoid using the first person. Instead, they let the material, including statistics and theories, speak for itself. This is not to say that the *first person* style of writing should never be used. However, it is traditional to use it sparingly.

✔ Guideline 2: Consider How to Reassemble Your Notes

Now that you have established the purpose for writing your review, identified your audience, and established your voice, you should reevaluate your notes to determine how the pieces you have described will be reassembled. At the outset, you should recognize that it is almost always unacceptable in writing a literature review to present only a series of annotations of research studies. In essence, that would be like describing individual trees when you really should be describing the forest. In a literature review, you are creating a unique new forest, which you will build by using the trees you found in the literature you read. In order to build this new whole, you should consider how the pieces relate to one another while preparing a topic outline, which is described in more detail in the next guideline.

Synthesizing Trends and Patterns

✔ Guideline 3: Create a Topic Outline That Traces Your Argument

Like any other kind of essay, the review should *first* establish for the reader the line of argumentation you will follow (this is called the *thesis*). This can be stated in the form of an assertion, a contention, or a proposition. *Then*, you should develop a traceable narrative that demonstrates that the line of argumentation is worthwhile and justified. This means that you should have formed judgments about the topic based on the analysis and synthesis of the literature you are reviewing.

The topic outline should be designed as a kind of road map of the argument, which is illustrated in Example 9.3.1. The outline given here is based on one of the sample literature reviews from Appendix B. Notice that it starts with descriptions of actual cases of cyberbullying and, then, moves right into a discussion of previous attempts at defining traditional bullying. Besides contrasting traditional bullying with cyberbullying, the authors flesh out other scholars' definitions of cyberbullying. It ends with a case for centering their study on college-age students.

Because the following outline will be referred to at various points throughout the rest of this chapter, please take a moment to examine it carefully. Place a flag on this page or bookmark it for easy reference to the outline when you are referred to it later.

Example 9.3.1[3]

Sample topic outline

Topic: How has bullying behavior changed in the digital age?

I. Introduction
   A. Introduce the topic of cyberbullying.
   B. Cite real-life examples.

II. Definitions of terms
   A. Contrasting definitions of traditional bullying and cyberbullying.
   B. Flesh out scholars' definition(s) of cyberbullying.
   C. Describe different forms/types of cyberbullying (e.g., harassment, stalking, "outing", etc.).

III. Review of previous research on rates of cyberbullying
   A. Varying rates have been reported—wide range (as low as 4.8%, as high as 55.3%).
   B. Studies of public school populations.
      1. Middle school students.
      2. Middle/high school students.

> C. Studies of college populations—relative little research available.
> D. Studies of workplace populations.
> E. Recap of the research on rates of cyberbullying.
>
> IV. How victims of cyberbullying are impacted
> A. Emotional impacts of cyberbullying.
> B. Behavioral consequences.
> C. Clinical symptoms.
> D. Suicidal behaviors.
> E. Other.
>
> V How victims cope after being cyberbullied
> A. Describe various coping strategies reported.
> B. Describe population groups studies for coping strategies.
>
> VI. This study will focus on college population
> A. Brief summary of the literature reviewed.
> B. Purpose now is to expand understanding of how cyberbullying impacts this group.
> C. And to add additional data on rates of cyberbullying among college-age students and to compare gender differences.

✔ Guideline 4: Reorganize Your Notes According to the Path of Your Argument

For your own literature review, the examples given in the previous guideline should guide you to create your own topic outline, which you should now have in hand, either in digital format or hard-copy. The topic outline described in the previous guideline describes the path of the authors' argument. For you, the next step should be to reorganize your notes according to your outline. You might begin by adding a column in your spreadsheet in which you add references to the appropriate places in the outline. For instance, in the example we are following (9.3.1) you would enter a "I" beside notations that describe actual instances of cyberbullying, a "II" beside notations that deal with definitions and forms or types of cyberbullying, a "III" beside notations that report statistics on bullying rates, and a "IV" beside notations that pertain to descriptions of the impact of bullying on the victims. Then, you would return to the topic outline and indicate the specific references to particular studies. For instance, write the names of references that discuss ways of defining cyberbullying directly to the right of Topic II on your outline.

✓ Guideline 5: Within Each Topic Heading, Note Differences among Studies

The next step is to note on your topic outline the differences in content among studies. Based on any differences, you may want to consider whether it is possible to group the articles into subtopics. For instance, the literature review on which Example 9.3.1 is based includes a figure to illustrate a sort of taxonomy of bullying behaviors, with two major divisions between "direct" and "indirect" bullying. This lends itself to a possible alternative organization of the discussion on how scholars have defined cyberbullying, as seen in Example 9.5.1.

Example 9.5.1

Possible alternative organization for point II in Example 9.3.1

1. Examples of direct bullying
   a. Harassment
   b. Stalking
   c. Other (e.g., threats, pranks, physical)

2. Examples of indirect bullying
   a. Cyberbullying
      (1) Flaming, Harassment, Denigration
      (2) Masquerade (Imposter)
      (3) Outing (e.g., rumors, private information)
      (4) Cyberstalking
   b. Other (e.g., word-of-mouth rumors)

You may also want to consider commenting about the consistency of results from study to study. For instance, refer back to Example 9.3.1. In the description of bullying rates, for each population group, various scholars report differences in their results. When you discuss such discrepancies, assist your reader by providing relevant information about the research, with an eye to identifying possible explanations for the differences. Were the first three articles older and the last one more current? Did the first three use a different methodology for collecting the data (e.g., were the statistics in one study based on official school records as opposed to data gathered using questionnaires)? Noting differences such as these may highlight important issues to discuss when you are writing your literature review.

Part III: Writing the First Draft

✔ Guideline 6: Within Each Topic Heading, Look for Obvious Gaps or Areas Needing Additional Research

In the full review based on the topic outline in Example 9.3.1, the reviewers noted that whereas much cross-cultural research has been conducted on school-age children, only two studies have focused on college students. Thus, any conclusions based on research on younger children may not apply to the older group. In addition, this points to an area that might become the focus for research in the current study, as was the case here.

✔ Guideline 7: Plan to Briefly Describe Relevant Theories

The importance of theoretical literature is discussed in Chapter 1. You should plan to briefly describe each theory that is relevant to the topic of your literature review. Example 9.7.1 illustrates this guideline with a description of objectification theory. Note that the authors start with a summary of the original theory and then summarize the research that supports the theory. Finally, they note that the theory has not been tested with men.

Example 9.7.1[4]

Definition of a relevant theory

Originally grounded in the experiences of women, objectification theory (Fredrickson & Roberts, 1997) posits that sexual objectification of women's bodies is omnipresent and can be internalized. Internalization of cultural standards of attractiveness occurs through constant exposure to socialization messages that promote compliance and identification with those messages. Such internalization can promote the adoption of an observer's perspective on one's own body, or self-objectification, which is manifested as persistent body surveillance. Body surveillance involves habitual monitoring and comparison of one's body against the internalized standard of attractiveness with a focus on how one's body looks rather than how it feels or functions. Body surveillance can, in turn, result in feelings of body shame for not meeting the (generally unattainable) cultural standards of attractiveness.

Research using cross-sectional and longitudinal data has supported a model of relations among these three objectification theory variables, such that internalization is related positively to body surveillance and body shame and body surveillance also has a unique positive relation with body shame. Body shame often mediates relations among objectification theory variables with outcomes variables, although both internalization and body surveillance often have unique additional relations with outcomes (for a review, see Moradi & Huang, 2008). This chain of relations is posited to underlie unhealthy efforts to alter one's appearance to comply with the internalized ideal; such efforts could include excessive dieting and exercise, eating disorders, and body-modifying surgery or drug use. An extensive body of literature has tested this model and extended its application to women of diverse racial and ethnic backgrounds, ability statuses, and sexual orientation identities, and aspects of the model are also gaining support in emerging research with men (Moradi & Huang, 2008). However, evaluation of the model's applicability to men's body image concerns is still needed.

✔ Guideline 8: Plan to Discuss How Individual Studies Relate to and Advance Theory

You should consider how individual studies, which are often narrow, help to define, illustrate, or advance theoretical notions. Often, researchers will point out how their studies relate to theory, which will help you in your considerations of this matter. For example, you would note in your topic outline if one or more theories will be discussed in your literature review, which will indicate to your reader that you will discuss the need for a well-developed theoretical model.

If there are competing theories in your area, plan to discuss the extent to which the literature you have reviewed supports each of them, keeping in mind that an inconsistency between the results of a study and a prediction based on theory may result from *either* imperfections in the theoretical model *or* imperfections in the research methodology used in the study.

✔ Guideline 9: Plan to Summarize Periodically and Again near the End of the Review

It is helpful to summarize the inferences, generalizations, and/or conclusions you have drawn from your review of the literature in stages. For instance, the outline in Example 9.3.1 calls for summaries at two points in the literature review (i.e., a summary of various results of rates of cyberbullying in II.E and an overall summary of the literature reviewed in VI.A). Long, complex topics within a literature review often deserve their own separate summaries. These summaries help readers to understand the direction the author is taking and invite readers to pause, think about, and internalize difficult material.

Part III: Writing the First Draft

As noted, the last main topic (Topic VI.) in Example 9.3.1 begins with a summary of all the material that preceded it. It is usually appropriate to start the last section of a long review with a summary of the main points already covered. This shows readers what the writer views as the major points of the review and sets the stage for a discussion of the writer's conclusions and any implications that may have been drawn. In a very short literature review, a summary may not be needed.

✔ Guideline 10: Plan to Present Conclusions and Implications

Note that a *conclusion* is an assertion about the present state of the knowledge on a topic. Example 9.10.1 illustrates a conclusion. It does not say that the conclusion has been proven. Reviewers should hedge and talk about degrees of evidence (e.g., "It seems safe to conclude that . . . ," "One conclusion might be that . . . ," "There is strong evidence that . . . ," or "The evidence overwhelmingly supports the conclusion that . . .").

Example 9.10.1

Statement of a conclusion

In light of the research on cultural differences in attitudes toward organ donation, *it seems safe to conclude that* (emphasis added) cultural groups differ substantially in their attitudes toward organ donation and that effective intervention strategies need to take account of these differences. Specifically . . .

If the weight of the evidence on a topic does not clearly favor one conclusion over the other, be prepared to say so. Example 9.10.2 illustrates this technique.

Example 9.10.2

Statement that a conclusion cannot be made

Although the majority of the studies indicate Method A is superior, several methodologically strong studies point to the superiority of Method B. In the absence of additional evidence, *it is difficult to conclude that* (emphasis added) . . .

An *implication* is usually a statement of what individuals or organizations should do in light of existing research. In other words, a reviewer usually should make suggestions as to what actions seem promising based on the review of the research. Thus, it is usually desirable to include the heading "Implications" near the end of a topic outline. Example 9.10.3 is an implication because it suggests that a particular intervention might be effectively used with a particular group.

Example 9.10.3

Statement of an implication

The body of evidence reviewed in this paper suggests that when working with Asian Americans, Intervention A seems most promising for increasing the number of organ donations made by this group.

At first, some novice writers assume that they should describe only "facts" from the published research and not attempt to offer their own conclusions or speculate about related implications. Keep in mind, however, that an individual who thoroughly and carefully reviewed the literature on a topic has, in fact, become an expert on it. For advice on the state of a knowledge base (conclusions) and what we should do to be more effective (implications), to whom else should we turn than an expert who has up-to-date knowledge of the research on a topic? Thus, it is appropriate to express your conclusions regarding the state of knowledge on a topic and the implications that follow from them.

✔ Guideline 11: Plan to Suggest Specific Directions for Future Research near the End of the Review

As you begin to think about what you want to say, keep in mind that it is inadequate to simply suggest that "more research is needed in the future." Instead, make specific suggestions. For instance, if all (or almost all) the researchers have used self-report questionnaires, you might call for future research using other means of data collection, such as direct observation of physical behavior and an examination of records kept by agencies that coordinate donations. If there are understudied groups such as Native Americans, you might call for more research on them. If almost all the studies are quantitative, you might call for additional qualitative studies. The list of possibilities is almost endless. Your job is to suggest those that you think are most promising for advancing knowledge in the area you are reviewing.

> ### Example 9.11.1[5]
>
> *Suggestion for future research*
>
> Although this review emphasized the role of expectations in ongoing relationships, expectations also seem important during the relationship initiation stage. For example, Oettingen and Mayer (2002) found that expectations of relationship formation predicted greater pursuit and incidence of relationship formation. In addition, expectations of rejection tend to result in reduced attempts at relationship initiation (Vorauer & Ratner, 1996). Furthermore, theories on mate preferences similarly suggest that people seek partners who are expected to be successful at reproduction and resource acquisition in the future (Buss, 1989; Fletcher, Simpson, Thomas, & Giles, 1999), which again demonstrates that expectations are important for relationship pursuit. Future research should examine mechanisms through which expectations impact relationship formation, as well as the effects of the features and contents of expectations.

✔ Guideline 12: Flesh out Your Outline with Details from Your Analysis

The final step before you begin to write your first draft is to review the topic outline you have created and to flesh it out with specific details from your analysis of the research literature. Make every effort, as you expand the outline, to include enough details to be able to write clearly about the studies you are including. Make sure to note the strengths and weaknesses of studies as well as the gaps, relationships, and major trends or patterns that have emerged in the literature. At the end of this step, your outline should be several pages long, and you will be ready to write your first draft.

Example 9.12.1 illustrates how a small portion of the topic outline in Example 9.3.1 (specifically, point II.B.) would look if it were fleshed out with additional details. Notice that several of the references in Example 9.12.1 appear in more than one place. For instance, Privitera & Campbell's 2009 report will be referred to under a discussion of both the repetition component and the power differential aspect because their article deals with both. You should avoid structuring your review as a series of summaries in which you summarize an article in one place and then drop it from the discussion. Instead, each source should be cited as many times as needed, as long as it bears on the points of your argument.

> **Example 9.12.1**
>
> *Part of a fleshed-out outline*
>
> II. Definitions of terms
>
>   B. Flesh out scholars' definition(s) of cyberbullying
>
>   1. As a "form of psychological cruelty" (Mason, 2008)
>   2. With or without the repetition component (Privitera & Campbell, 2009; Raskauskas & Stoltz, 2007; Slonje & Smith, 2008)
>   3. Include a power differential between perpetrator and victim (Hinduja & Patchin 2007; Mason, 2008; Privitera & Campbell, 2009)
>   4. Power imbalance criteria differences—physical strength, body build, age, technological ability (Vandebosch & Van Cleemput, 2008)

Activities for Chapter 9

Directions: For each of the model literature reviews that your instructor assigns, answer the following questions. The model literature reviews are near the end of this book.

1. These articles are all journal articles. Given the assumed audience for these manuscripts, did the authors use the appropriate academic voice in writing them? Explain why or why not.

2. Do the authors' arguments move logically from one topic to another? Explain.

3. Have the authors pointed out areas needing more research? Explain.

4. Do the articles help to define, illustrate, and/or advance theory? If so, explain. If not, why do you think they do not?

5. Are there summaries embedded in the articles? At the conclusion? Explain.

6. Are the conclusions and implications clearly described and discussed by the authors?

Notes

1. This is a hypothetical example based on Example 9.1.2.
2. Smart, D. L. & Karau, S. J. (2011). Protestant work ethic moderates social loafing. *Group Dynamics: Theory, Research, and Practice, 15,* 267–274.
3. The outline is based on the work of Schenk, A.M. & Fremouw, W. J. (2012). Prevalence, psychological impact, and coping of cyberbully victims among college students. *Journal of School Violence, 11,* 21–37.
4. Parent, M. C. & Moradi, B. (2011). His biceps become him: A test of objectification theory's application to drive for muscularity and propensity for steroid use in college men. *Journal of Counseling Psychology, 58,* 246–256.
5. Lemay, E. P. Jr. & Venaglia, R. B. (2016). Relationship expectations and relationship quality. *Review of General Psychology, 20,* 1, 57–70.

Chapter 10

Guidelines for Writing a First Draft

Up to this point, you have searched the databases for literature on the topic of your review, made careful notes on specific details of the literature, and analyzed these details to identify patterns, relationships among studies, gaps in the body of literature, as well as the strengths and weaknesses of particular research studies. Then, in Chapter 9, you reorganized your notes and developed a detailed writing outline in preparation for writing your literature review.

Actually, you have already completed the most difficult steps in the writing process: the analysis and synthesis of the literature and the charting of the course of your argument. These preliminary steps constitute the intellectual groundwork in preparing a literature review. The remaining steps—drafting, editing, and redrafting—will now require you to translate the results of your intellectual labor into a narrative account of what you have found.

The guidelines in this chapter will help you to produce a first draft of your literature review. The guidelines in Chapter 11 will help you to develop a coherent essay and avoid producing a series of annotations, and it presents additional standards that relate to style, mechanics, and language usage. But first, let's consider writing the first draft.

✔ Guideline 1: Begin by Identifying the Broad Problem Area, but Avoid Global Statements

Usually, the introduction of a literature review begins with the identification of the broad problem area under review. The rule of thumb is, "Go from the general to the specific." However, there are limits on how general one should be in the beginning. Consider Example 10.1.1. As the beginning of a literature review on a topic in higher education, it is much too broad. It fails to identify any particular area or topic. You should avoid starting your review with such global statements.

Example 10.1.1

Fails to identify particular area or topic

Higher education is important to both the economy of the United States and to the rest of the world. Without a college education, students will be unprepared for the many advances that will take place in this millennium.

Contrast Example 10.1.1 with Example 10.1.2, which is also on a topic in education but clearly relates to the specific topic that will be reviewed, bullying in schools.

Example 10.1.2[1]

Relates to the specific topic being reviewed

A significant proportion of children are involved in bullying across their school years. Children who are bullied report a range of problems, including anxiety and depression (Nansel, Overpeck, Pilla, Ruan, Simons-Morton, & Scheidt, 2001), low self-esteem (Egan & Perry, 1998), reduced academic performance (Juvonen, Nishina, & Graham, 2000), and school absenteeism (Eisenberg, Neumark-Sztainer, & Perry, 2003). Bullying may also be a significant stressor associated with suicidal behavior (Klomek, Marrocco, Kleinman, Schonfeld, & Gould, 2007).

✔ Guideline 2: Early in the Review, Indicate Why the Topic Being Reviewed Is Important

As early as the first paragraph in a literature review, it is desirable to indicate why the topic is important. The authors of Example 10.2.1 have done this by pointing out that their topic deals with a serious health issue.

Example 10.2.1[2]

Beginning of a literature review indicating the importance of the topic

Vitamin D insufficiency is increasing across all age groups (Looker et al., 2008). Recent research implicates vitamin D insufficiency as a risk factor for a variety of chronic diseases, including type 1 and 2 diabetes, osteoporosis, cardiovascular disease, hypertension, metabolic syndrome, and cancer (Heaney, 2008; Holick, 2006).

Of course, not all issues are of as much universal importance as the one in Example 10.2.1. Nevertheless, the topic of the review should be of importance to someone, and this should be pointed out, as in Example 10.2.2, which points to the wide use of the adjusted Rand index, or ARI, as the main reason for choosing to derive its variance as part of this study.

Example 10.2.2[3]

Beginning of a literature review indicating the importance of the topic

The measure of choice for determining the adequacy of a partition of observations into groups is the adjusted Rand index (ARI; Hubert & Arabie, 1985). The article introducing the ARI is the most highly cited paper ever published in the *Journal of Classification* with 2,756 citations, while a subsequent paper discussing properties of the ARI by Steinley (2004) is in the top 10% of cited papers published in *Psychological Methods* since 2004 with 144 citations. In this article, we derive the variance of the ARI, providing a critical component to the 30-year old measure. After the variance is derived, a simulation exploring the adequacy of using the normal approximation for inference is conducted.

✔ Guideline 3: Distinguish Between Research Findings and Other Sources of Information

If you describe points of view that are based on anecdotal evidence or personal opinions rather than on research, indicate the nature of the source. For instance, the three statements in Example 10.3.1 contain key words that indicate that the material is based on personal points of view (not research)—"speculated," "has been suggested that," and "personal experience."

Example 10.3.1

Beginnings of statements that indicate that the material that follows is based on personal points of view (not research)

"Doe (2016) speculated that . . . ."

"It has been suggested that. . . . (Smith, 2015)."

"Black (2014) related a personal experience, which indicated that. . . ."

Contrast the statements in Example 10.3.1 with those in Example 10.3.2, which are used to introduce research-based findings in a literature review.

Example 10.3.2

Beginnings of statements that indicate that the material that follows is based on research

"In a statewide survey, Jones (2016) found that. . . ."

"Hill's (2012) research in urban classrooms indicates that. . . ."

"Recent findings indicate that . . . (Barnes, 2014; Hanks, 2015)."

If there is little research on a topic, you may find it necessary to review primarily literature that expresses only opinions (without a research base). When this is the case, consider making a general statement to indicate this situation before discussing the literature in more detail in your review. This technique is indicated in Example 10.3.3.

Example 10.3.3

Statement indicating a lack of research

This database contains more than 50 documents, journal articles, and monographs devoted to the topic. However, none are reports of original research. Instead, they present anecdotal evidence, such as information on individual clients who have received therapeutic treatment.

✔ Guideline 4: Indicate Why Certain Studies Are Important

If a particular study has methodological strengths, mention them to indicate their importance, as was done in Example 10.4.1.

Example 10.4.1[4]

Indicates why a study is important (in this case, "a national survey" and "randomly selected")

The Pew Research Center (2007) recently conducted a national survey of 2,020 randomly selected adults and found that 21% of employed mothers

> preferred full-time work, 60% preferred part-time work, and 19% preferred no employment.

A study may also be important because it represents a pivotal point in the development of an area of research, such as a research article that indicates a reversal of a prominent researcher's position or one that launched a new methodology. These and other characteristics of a study may justify its status as important. When a study is especially important, make sure your review makes this clear to the reader.

✔ Guideline 5: If You Are Commenting on the Timeliness of a Topic, Be Specific in Describing the Time Frame

Avoid beginning your review with unspecific references to the timeliness of a topic, as in, "In recent years, there has been an increased interest in . . . ." This beginning would leave many questions unanswered for the reader, such as the following: What years are being referenced? How did the writer determine that the "interest" is increasing? Who has become more interested: the writer or others in the field? Is it possible that the writer became interested in the topic recently while others have been losing interest?

Likewise, an increase in a problem or an increase in the size of a population of interest should be specific in terms of numbers or percentages and the specific years being referenced. For instance, it is not very informative to state only that "The number of college students who cheat probably has increased" or that "There will be an increase in job growth." The authors of Examples 10.5.1 and 10.5.2 avoided this problem by being specific in citing percentages and time frames (italics and bold are added for emphasis).

> ### Example 10.5.1[5]
>
> *Names a specific time frame*
>
> Over the years, research in this area has documented a steady increase in cheating and unethical behavior among college students (Brown & Emmett, 2001). ***Going as far back as 1941, Baird (1980) reported that college cheating had increased from 23% in 1941 to 55% in 1970 to 75% in 1980. Moving forward, McCabe and Bowers (1994) reported that college cheating had increased from 63% in 1962 to 70% in 1993.***
>
> More recently, Burke, Polimeni, and Slavin (2007) stated that "various studies suggest that we may be at the precipice of a culture of academic

Part III: Writing the First Draft

malfeasance, where large numbers of students engage in various forms of cheating." The Center for Academic Integrity at Oklahoma State University (2009), conducted a large-scale survey of 1,901 students and 431 faculty members and found some very disturbing results, showing that 60% of college students engaged in at least one behavior that violated academic integrity and that 72% of undergraduate business majors reported doing this, versus 56% from other disciplines. **Brown, Weible, and Olmosk (2010) also reported that the percentage of cheating in undergraduate management classes in 2008 was close to 100%, which was an increase from the recorded 49% in 1988.**

Example 10.5.2[6]

Names a specific time frame

With the current economy showing signs of a sluggish recovery, employers are cautiously optimistic about what the future holds. Mixed indicators in the unemployment rate, depending on location, may mean an increase in job growth for certain industries. *A recent economic report released by* **USA Today** *shows the strongest 12-month national job growth* in Construction (3.9%), Leisure and Hospitality (3.4%), Education and Health Services (2.9%), and Professional and Business Services (2.9%) while traditionally strong and stable sectors such as Government (–0.3%) and Utilities (0.3%) are showing slower growth rates (Job Growth Forecast, 2011).

Most universities have writing centers that can be helpful by providing assistance to novice academic writers. Many of these centers maintain useful guides on their websites. One such site, which provides guidance to writers, can be found at: http://www.phrasebank.manchester.ac.uk. This site groups commonly used phrases found in academic writing into useful categories, such as Classifying and Listing, Describing Trends, Signaling Transition, Being Cautious, and so on.

✔ Guideline 6: If Citing a Classic or Landmark Study, Identify It as Such

Make sure that you identify the classic or landmark studies in your review. Such studies are often pivotal points in the historical development of the published literature. In addition, they are often responsible for framing a particular question or a research tradition, and they also may be the original source of key concepts or terminology used in the subsequent literature. Whatever their contribution, you should identify their status as classics or landmarks in the literature. Consider Example 10.6.1, in which a landmark study (one of the earliest investigations on the topic) is cited (emphasis added).

Example 10.6.1[7]

Identifies a landmark study

A few studies have examined the direct and indirect links between victimization and achievement in elementary school over time. **In one of the earliest investigations on this topic**, Kochenderfer and Ladd (1996) showed that peer victimization experiences served as a precursor of school adjustment problems (e.g., academic achievement, school avoidance, loneliness) across the kindergarten year.

✔ Guideline 7: If a Landmark Study Was Replicated, Mention That and Indicate the Results of the Replication

As noted in the previous guideline, landmark studies typically stimulate additional research. In fact, many are replicated a number of times, by using different groups of participants or by adjusting other research design variables. If you are citing a landmark study and it has been replicated, you should mention that fact and indicate whether the replications were successful. This is illustrated in Example 10.7.1 (italics and bold are added for emphasis).

Example 10.7.1[8]

Points at new evidence that questions prior hypothesis

In order to explain the difficulties experienced by children with the passive structure, Borer and Wexler (1987) put forward the A-chain maturation hypothesis, according to which children manage to master verbal passives at the age of 5 or 6. [...]

However, *the A-chain maturation approach is at odds with evidence coming from the acquisition of other A-movement constructions* where children behave adultlike, such as reflexive–clitic constructions (Snyder & Hyams, 2014) and subject-to-subject raising (Becker, 2006; Choe, 2012; Orfitelli, 2012).

✔ Guideline 8: Discuss Other Literature Reviews on Your Topic

If you find an earlier published review on your topic, it is important to discuss it in your review. Before doing so, consider the following questions:

How is the other review different from yours?

- Is yours substantially more current?
- Did you delimit the topic in a different way?
- Did you conduct a more comprehensive review?
- Did the earlier reviewer reach the same major conclusions that you have reached?

How worthy is the other review of your readers' attention?

- What will they gain, if anything, by reading your review?
- Will they encounter a different and potentially helpful perspective?
- What are its major strengths and weaknesses?

An honest assessment of your answers to these questions may either reaffirm your decision to select your current topic, or it may lead you to refine or redirect your focus in a more useful and productive direction.

✔ Guideline 9: Describe Your Reasons for Choosing Not to Discuss a Particular Issue

If you find it necessary to omit discussion of a *related issue*, it is appropriate to explain the reasons for your decision, as in Example 10.9.1. Needless to say, your review should completely cover the specific topic you have chosen, unless you provide a rationale for eliminating a particular issue. It is not acceptable to describe just a portion of the literature on your topic (as you defined it) and then refer the reader to another source for the remainder. However, the technique illustrated in Example 10.9.1 can be useful for pointing out the reasons for not reviewing an issue in detail in the review (italics and bold are added for emphasis).

Example 10.9.1[9]

Explains why an issue will not be discussed

To date, attempts to marry the generalized linear mixed model with chained equations imputation have met with limited success. For example, Zhao and Yucel (2009) examined chained equations imputation in a simple random

---

intercept model with one continuous and one binary variable. The method worked well when the intraclass correlation was very close to zero but produced unacceptable coverage rates in other conditions (coverage values ranged between .40 and .80). Performance aside, the procedure is computationally intensive and prone to convergence failures because the Gibbs sampler requires an iterative optimization step that fits a linear mixed model to the filled-in data. Zhao and Yucel (2009) reported that convergence failures were common as the intraclass correlation increased, and our own attempts to apply chained equations imputation to a random intercept model with a binary outcome produced convergence failures over 40% of the time. Collectively, these findings cast doubt on the use of generalized linear mixed models for categorical variable imputation; if the simplest random intercept models produce estimation failures and poor coverage rates, it is unlikely that the method will work in realistic scenarios involving random slopes or complex mixtures of categorical and continuous variables. *Given these difficulties, we provide no further discussion of this approach.*

✔ Guideline 10: Justify Comments Such As "No Studies Were Found"

If you find a gap in the literature that deserves mention in your literature review, explain how you arrived at the conclusion that there is a gap. At the very least, explain how you conducted the literature search, which databases you searched, and the dates and other parameters you used. You do not need to be overly specific, but the reader will expect you to justify your statement about the gap.

To avoid misleading your reader, it is a good idea early in your review to make statements such as the one shown in Example 10.10.1. This will protect you from criticism if you point out a gap when one does not actually exist. In other words, you are telling your reader that there is a gap as determined by the use of *a particular search strategy*.

Example 10.10.1[10]

Describes the strategy for searching literature

We systematically searched for relevant studies until February 2011. We started with an initial set of reports on children with incarcerated parents collected in our previous research on this topic. Four methods were used to search for additional studies. First, keywords were entered into 23 electronic

> databases and Internet search engines. The keywords entered were (*prison**
> or *jail** or *penitentiary* or *imprison** or *incarcerat** or *detention*) and (*child** or *son**
> or *daughter** or *parent** or *mother** or *father**) and (*antisocial** or *delinquen** or
> *crim** or *offend** or *violen** or *aggressi** or *mental health* or *mental illness* or
> *internaliz** or *depress** or *anxiety* or *anxious* or *psychological** or *drug** or *alcohol**
> or *drink** or *tobacco* or *smok** or *substance* or *education** or *school* or *grade** or
> *achievement*).
>
> Second, bibliographies of prior reviews were examined (Dallaire, 2007; S. Gabel, 2003; Hagan & Dinovitzer, 1999; Johnston, 1995; Murray, 2005; Murray & Farrington, 2008a; Myers et al., 1999; Nijnatten, 1998) as well as edited books on children of incarcerated parents (Eddy & Poehlmann, 2010; K. Gabel & Johnston, 1995; Harris & Miller, 2002; Harris, Graham, & Carpenter, 2010; Shaw, 1992b; Travis & Waul, 2003). Third, experts in the field were contacted to request information about any other studies that we might not have located. The first group of experts contacted consisted of about 65 researchers and practitioners who we knew were professionals with an interest in children with incarcerated parents. The second group consisted of about 30 directors of major longitudinal studies in criminology . . . .

✔ Guideline 11: Avoid Long Lists of Nonspecific References

In academic writing, references are used in the text of a written document for at least two purposes. First, they are used to give proper credit to an author for an idea or, in the case of a direct quotation, for a specific set of words. A failure to do so would constitute plagiarism. Second, references are used to demonstrate the breadth of coverage given in a manuscript. In an introductory paragraph, for instance, it may be desirable to include references to several key studies that will be discussed in more detail in the body of the review. However, it is inadvisable to use long lists of references that do not specifically relate to the point being expressed. For instance, in Example 10.11.1, the long list of nonspecific references in the first sentence is probably inappropriate. Are these all empirical studies? Do they report their authors' speculations on the issue? Are some of the references more important than others? It would have been better for the author to refer the reader to a few key studies, which themselves would contain references to additional examples of research in that particular area, as illustrated in Example 10.11.2.

Example 10.11.1

First sentence in a literature review (too many nonspecific references)

Numerous writers have indicated that children in single-parent households are at greater risk for academic underachievement than children from two-parent households (Adams, 2015; Block, 2014; Doe, 2013; Edgar, 2015; Hampton, 2009; Jones, 2015; Klinger, 2008; Long, 2011; Livingston, 2010; Macy, 2011; Norton, 2012; Pearl, 2012; Smith, 2009; Travers, 2010; Vincent, 2011; West, 2008; Westerly, 2009; Yardley, 2011).

Example 10.11.2

An improved version of Example 10.11.1

Numerous writers have suggested that children in single-parent households are at greater risk for academic underachievement than children from two-parent households (e.g., see Adams, 2015, and Block, 2014). Three recent studies have provided strong empirical support for this contention (Doe, 2013; Edgar, 2015; Jones, 2015). Of these, the study by Jones (2015) is the strongest, employing a national sample with rigorous controls for. . . .

Notice the use of "e.g., see . . . ," which indicates that only some of the possible references are cited for the point that the writers have suggested. You may also use the Latin abbreviation *cf.* (which means *compare*).

✔ Guideline 12: If the Results of Previous Studies Are Inconsistent or Widely Varying, Cite Them Separately

It is not uncommon for studies on the same topic to produce inconsistent or widely varying results. If so, it is important to cite the studies separately in order for the reader to interpret your review correctly. The following two examples illustrate the potential problem. Example 10.12.1 is misleading because it fails to note that the previous studies are grouped according to the two extremes of the percentage range given. Example 10.12.2 illustrates a better way to cite inconsistent findings.

Part III: Writing the First Draft

Example 10.12.1

Inconsistent results cited as a single finding (undesirable)

In previous studies (Doe, 2013; Jones, 2015), parental support for requiring students to wear school uniforms in public schools varied considerably, ranging from only 19% to 52%.

Example 10.12.2

Improved version of Example 10.12.1

In previous studies, parental support for requiring students to wear school uniforms has varied considerably. Support from rural parents varied from only 19% to 28% (Doe, 2013), while support from suburban parents varied from 35% to 52% (Jones, 2015).

✔ **Guideline 13: Speculate on the Reasons for Inconsistent Findings in Previous Research**

The authors of Example 10.13.1 speculate on inconsistent findings regarding shame about in-group moral failure (italics and bold are added for emphasis).

Example 10.13.1[11]

Speculation of inconsistent findings of previous research (desirable)

We **think** that the inconsistent findings regarding shame about in-group moral failure **may result** from the rather broad conceptualization of shame in past work. As Gausel and Leach (2011) recently pointed out, different studies of shame have conceptualized the emotion as involving quite different combinations of appraisal and feeling. Some previous work conceptualizes shame as a combination of the appraisal of *concern for condemnation* and an attendant *feeling of rejection*. Most previous work conceptualizes shame as a combination of the appraisal that the self *suffers a defect* and an attendant *feeling of inferiority*.

✔ Guideline 14: Cite All Relevant References in the Review Section of a Thesis, Dissertation, or Journal Article

When writing a thesis, dissertation, or an article for publication in which the literature review precedes a report of original research, typically you should first cite all the relevant references in the literature review of your document. Avoid introducing new references to literature in later sections, such as the results or discussion sections. Make sure you have checked your entire document to ensure that the literature review section or chapter is comprehensive. You may refer back to a previous discussion of a pertinent study when discussing your conclusions, but the study should have been referenced first in the literature review at the beginning of the thesis, dissertation, or article.

✔ Guideline 15: Emphasize the Need for Your Study in the Literature Review Section or Chapter

When writing a thesis, a dissertation, or an article for publication in which the literature review precedes a report of original research, you should use the review to help justify your study. You can do this in a variety of ways, such as pointing out that your study (a) closes a gap in the literature, (b) tests an important aspect of a current theory, (c) replicates an important study, (d) retests a hypothesis using new or improved methodological procedures, (e) is designed to resolve conflicts in the literature, and so on.

Example 10.15.1 was included in the literature review portion of a research report designed to examine the variables linked to success in adult continuing education learners of British Sign Language in the UK. In their review, the authors point out gaps in the literature and indicate how their study addresses these gaps and adds to the understanding of this population. This is a strong justification for the study.

Example 10.15.1[12]

Justifies a study

The study contained several unique elements. First, data were collected from three colleges of further education in the UK that differed in some aspects of their mode of delivery. Further education in the UK is similar to continuing education in the United States. It is education that follows compulsory post-16 secondary education, but which usually is not at degree level. Two centers offered provision that was typical of the UK. A third center included several atypical initiatives in its provision, such as additional weekly conversational

> classes, which had the potential to enhance the student experience. Comparison of the centers' success rates offered the prospect of evaluating the impact of these differences on success. Second, this article investigates variables that might be important for success in UK Level 1 and 2 courses. The levels are equivalent to the first and second years of a UK General Certificate of Secondary Education qualification. [...] Third, information was collected on several variables that had not been tested before in L2 sign language learning context (e.g., self-reported visual thinking style).

Activities for Chapter 10

Directions: For each of the model literature reviews that your instructor assigns, answer the following questions. The model literature reviews are presented near the end of this book.

1. Describe the broad problem area addressed by each of the model reviews. Did each of the authors adequately explain this broad problem at the start of their reviews? Explain your answer.

2. Did the authors make clear for the reader the importance of the topic being reviewed? How? Was this effective, in your opinion?

3. Did the authors distinguish between research findings and other sources of information by using appropriate wording? Explain how this was done.

4. Was a landmark study cited? If yes, was it described as such? What relationship exists, if any, between the landmark study and the study presented in the review?

5. Are there references to other reviews on related issues that are not discussed in detail in the model literature review? Explain why they are referenced.

6. If an author stated that "no studies were found" on some aspect of the topic, was this statement justified (as indicated in this chapter)?

Notes

1 Hunt, C., Peters, L., & Rapee, R. M. (2012). Development of a measure of the experience of being bullied in youth. *Psychological Assessment, 24*, 156–165.
2 Lukaszuk, J. M., Prawitz, A. D., Johnson, K. N., Umoren, J., & Bugno, T. J. (2012). Development of a noninvasive vitamin D screening tool. *Family & Consumer Sciences Research Journal, 40*, 229–240.

3   Steinley D., Brusco, M. J., & Hubert, L. (2016). The variance of the adjusted Rand index. *Psychological Methods, 21*, 261–272.
4   Buehler, C., O'Brien, M., & Walls, J. K. (2011). Mothers' part-time employment: Child, parent, and family outcomes. *Journal of Family Theory & Review, 3*, 256–272.
5   Burton, J. H., Talpade, S., & Haynes, J. (2011). Religiosity and test-taking ethics among business school students. *Journal of Academic and Business Ethics, 4*, 1–8.
6   Butler, T. H. & Berret, B. A. (2012). A generation lost: The reality of age discrimination in today's hiring practices. *Journal of Management and Marketing Research, 9*, 1–11.
7   Juvonen, J., Wang, Y., & Espinoza, G. (2011). Bullying experiences and compromised academic performance across middle school grades. *Journal of Early Adolescence, 31*, 152–173.
8   Volpato, F., Verin, L., & Cardinaletti, A. (2016). The comprehension and production of verbal passives by Italian preschool-age children. *Applied Psycholinguistics, 37*, 901–931.
9   Enders, C. K., Mistler, S. A., & Keller, B. T. (2016). Multilevel multiple imputation: A review and evaluation of joint modeling and chained equations imputation. *Psychological Methods, 21*, 222–240.
10 Murray, J., Farrington, D. P., & Sekol, I. (2012). Children's antisocial behavior, mental health, drug use, and educational performance after parental incarceration: A systematic review and meta-analysis. *Psychological Bulletin, 138*, 175–210.
11 Gausel, N., Leach, C. W., Vignoles, V. L., & Brown, R. (2012). Defend or repair? Explaining responses to in-group moral failure by disentangling feelings of shame, rejection, and inferiority. *Journal of Personality and Social Psychology, 102*, 941–960.
12 Allbutt, J. & Ling, J. (2016). Adult college learners of British Sign Language: Educational provision and learner self-report variables associated with exam success. *Sign Language Studies, 16*, 330–360.

Chapter 11

Guidelines for Developing a Coherent Essay

This chapter is designed to help you refine your first draft by guiding you in developing a coherent essay. Remember that a literature review should not be written as a series of connected summaries (or annotations) of the literature you have read. Instead, it should have a clearly stated argument, and it should be developed in such a way that all of its elements work together to communicate a well-reasoned account of that argument. Recall that this was a principal concern in preparing the detailed outline discussed in Chapter 9, but especially important here is for you to revisit Guidelines 3 and 4 in that chapter. In other words, the topic outline was designed to trace the path of your argument, and your notes should now have been rearranged to fit this path. If you have not done this, it is important that you go back and accomplish these tasks.

✔ Guideline 1: If Your Review Is Long, Provide an Overview near the Beginning of the Review

When writing a long literature review, it is important to provide readers with an explicit road map of your argument. This is usually done in the introductory section of the review, which should include an overview of what will be covered in the rest of the document. Example 11.1.1 illustrates this.

Example 11.1.1[1]

An effective road map at the beginning of a review

The major purpose of the present . . . review is to provide a comprehensive analysis of three broad questions. First, do incentives to cooperate promote and sustain cooperation in small group social dilemmas? Second, what variables might influence the effectiveness of incentives? Finally, do reward and

> punishment differ in their ability to promote and sustain cooperation? As we discuss shortly, we adopt an interdependence-theoretical analysis for understanding whether incentives might promote cooperation and when these incentives might be especially effective.

✔ Guideline 2: Near the Beginning of a Review, State Explicitly What Will and Will Not Be Covered

Some topics are so broad that it will not be possible to cover the research completely in your review. This is especially true if you are writing a term paper, which may have page-length restrictions imposed by your instructor, or if you are preparing an article for publication, in which reviews traditionally are relatively short. In such cases, you should state explicitly, near the beginning of your review, what will and will not be covered (i.e., the delimitations of your review). The excerpt in Example 11.2.1 illustrates application of this guideline. In this example, the authors report that the current report is part of a larger data-gathering research project, though the current study deals with just a portion of the data.

Example 11.2.1[2]

A statement of the delimitations of a review

This study was part of a larger project where children were presented different stimuli. Participants watched a short movie clip and a live theater scene, performed an experiment involving baking powder and water, and identified sounds by pointing to the picture. Additionally, participants were exposed to olfactory and tactile stimuli, as well as auditory stimuli in the form of the two sound events. Approximately 2 weeks later children were interviewed about the stimuli with either a standard interview or a cognitive interview before performing a recall and recognition task for the sound events. The present study will only comprise data concerning recall and recognition of the two sound events.

✔ Guideline 3: Specify Your Point of View Early in the Review

As has been emphasized previously, your literature review should be written in the form of an essay that has a particular point of view that reflects your review of the research. This point of view is instrumental in your construction of the thesis statement of your essay (the assertion or proposition that is supported in the remainder of the essay).

Part III: Writing the First Draft

The expression of your point of view does not need to be elaborate or detailed (although it can be). In Example 11.3.1, the reviewers briefly indicate their point of view (that while social scientists and engineers have developed quite differently within their respective disciplines, there is some benefit to be gained from sharing data across disciplinary lines). This informs readers very early in the review that this overarching point of view guides the interpretation and synthesis of the literature.

Of course, you should settle on a point of view *only after* you have read and considered the body of literature as a whole. In other words, this guideline indicates when you should *express* your point of view (early in the review), not when you should *develop* it.

Example 11.3.1[3]

Early summary of the path of an argument

The common view of trading zones is that they equally benefit each participating domain—so computer scientists benefit from engaging with social scientists as much as vice versa. But is this really so? Do these fields share a common research culture, and an overlapping set of research interests, so as to make exchange possible? Or do they have incommensurable views that will make exchange difficult? Can we expect their shared focus on big data to result in equal, reciprocal forms of exchange where theoretical perspectives and research frameworks are exported in either direction? Or is it more likely that some domains will take more of a lead—colonizing those who follow?

In the following sections, we describe how these domains—social science, on the one hand, and engineering/industry (we collapse the two for simplicity's sake), on the other—adopt very different frameworks and cultures of research. [...]

✔ Guideline 4: Aim for a Clear and Cohesive Essay and Avoid Annotations

It has been emphasized several times thus far that an effective literature review should be written in the form of an essay. Perhaps the single most reported problem for novice academic writers is their difficulty in abandoning the use of annotations in the body of a literature review.

Annotations are brief summaries of the contents of articles. Stringing together several annotations in the body of a review may describe what research is available on a topic, but it fails to organize the material for the reader. An effective review of literature is organized to make a point. The writer needs to describe how the individual studies relate to one another. What are their relative strengths and weaknesses? Where are the gaps, and why do they exist? All these details and more need to support the author's main purpose for writing the review. The detailed outline developed in Chapter 9 describes the path of the argument, but it is up to the writer to translate this into a prose account that integrates the important details of the research literature into an essay that communicates a unique point of view.

Example 11.4.1 shows how a number of studies can be cited together as part of a single paragraph. Clearly, then, the organization of the paragraph is topical—not around the reports of individual authors.

> **Example 11.4.1**[4]
>
> *A single paragraph with multiple sources*
>
> Fanon had little clinical or theoretical experience of psychoanalysis (though see Burman, under review c, for an account of his practice). Most authoritative accounts portray him as much more influenced by phenomenology and especially existentialism, in particular by Sartre (Macey, 2012; Desai, 2014). The designation 'psychoanalyst of culture' (Gates, 1991: 248), as offering an account of racialized sociogenesis or the social construction of blackness and, in particular, black masculinity as 'phobogenic' (generating phobia), is much more convincing. Gates (1991) and Macey (2012) are both scathing of efforts to portray Fanon as a proto-Lacanian, notwithstanding the privileged focus he accords visual (mis)recognition in the constitution of the separation between self and other. This focus on the visual is indeed vital and suggestive, and clearly invites a Lacanian narration as disrupting the line of the Imaginary by the installing of a racist symbolic order (see also Vergès, 1997).

✔ Guideline 5: Use Subheadings, Especially in Long Reviews

Because long reviews, especially those written for theses and dissertations, often deal with articles from more than one discipline area, it is advisable to use subheadings in order to distinguish the areas from each other. If you decide to use subheadings, place them strategically to help advance your argument and allow the reader to follow your discussion more easily. The topic outline you prepared in Chapter 9 can help you to determine where they should be placed, though you may need to recast some of the topic headings as labels rather than statements.

Part III: Writing the First Draft

✔ Guideline 6: Use Transitions to Help Trace Your Argument

Strategically placed transitional phrases can help readers to follow your argument. For instance, you can use transitions to provide readers with textual clues that mark the progression of a discussion, such as when you begin paragraphs with *First*, *Second*, and *Third* or *Finally* to mark the development of three related points. Of course, any standard writing manual will contain lists of transitional expressions commonly used in formal writing.

These transitions should not be overused, however. Especially in a short review, it may not be necessary to use such phrases to label the development of three related points when each is described in three adjacent paragraphs. Another problem often found in short reviews is the overuse of what Bem (1995) calls "meta-comments," which are comments about the review *itself* (as opposed to comments about the literature being reviewed).[5] For instance, in Example 11.6.1, the writers restate the organization of the review (i.e., this is an example of a meta-comment) partway through the document. While there is nothing inherently wrong with making meta-comments, you should avoid frequent restatements that rehash what you have already stated.

Example 11.6.1[6]

Example of the use of meta-comments

This complex use of time will be illustrated with Hannah's diaries. The next section of the paper provides an introduction to Hannah and a description of her diaries. This is followed by a discussion of the theoretical context of time and relational space, including cultural space. The multidirectional nature of time, space, affect, and symbolization will be explored. Then the three entries will be presented and used to illustrate these ideas of creating and gathering time as a foundational process of affect emergence, recognition, regulation, and the creation of symbolization and subjectivity.

✔ Guideline 7: If Your Topic Spans Two or More Disciplines, Consider Reviewing Studies from Each Discipline Separately

Some topics naturally transcend disciplinary boundaries. For instance, if you were writing about diabetes management among teenage girls, you would find relevant sources in several discipline areas, including health care, nutrition, and psychology. The health care literature, for instance, might deal with variations in insulin therapies (such as variations in types of insulin used or the use of insulin pumps versus syringes). The nutrition journals, on the other hand, might include studies on alternative methods for managing food intake in the search for more effective methods to control episodes of insulin shock. Finally, the psychological literature might offer insights into the nature of the stressors common to adolescent girls, especially with respect to how these stressors may interfere with the girls' decision-making processes concerning self-monitoring, nutrition choices, and value orientations. While these examples are hypothetical, it is easy to see how such a review might benefit from being divided into three sections, with the findings from each discipline area reviewed separately.

✔ Guideline 8: Write a Conclusion for the End of the Review

The end of your literature review should provide closure for the reader. That is, the path of the argument should end with a conclusion of some kind. How you end a literature review, however, will depend on your reasons for writing it. If the review was written to stand alone, as in the case of a term paper or a review article for publication, the conclusion needs to make clear how the material in the body of the review has supported the assertion or proposition presented in the introduction. On the other hand, a review in a thesis, dissertation, or journal article presenting original research usually leads to the research questions that will be addressed.

If your review is long and complex, you should briefly summarize the main threads of your argument, then present your conclusion. Otherwise, you may cause your reader to pause in order to try to reconstruct the case you have made. Shorter reviews usually do not require a summary, but this judgment will depend on the complexity of the argument you have presented. You may need feedback from your faculty adviser or a colleague to help you determine how much you will need to restate at the end. Example 11.8.1 presents a brief summary and conclusion section that appeared at the end of a long literature review. In most cases, for very long reviews, a more detailed summary would be desirable.

Example 11.8.1[7]

A summary and conclusion section at the end of a long review

There is a general belief in society that frequent exposure to print has a long-lasting impact on academic success, as if practicing reading is the miracle drug for the prevention and treatment of reading problems (for reviews, see Dickinson & McCabe, 2001; Phillips, Norris, & Anderson, 2008). This comprehensive meta-analysis of print exposure provides some scientific support

Part III: Writing the First Draft

> for this belief. Our findings are consistent with the theory that reading development starts before formal instruction, with book sharing as one of the facets of a stimulating home literacy environment. Books provide a meaningful context for learning to read, not only as a way of stimulating reading comprehension but also as a means of developing technical reading skills even in early childhood. In preconventional readers, we found that print exposure was associated moderately with oral language and basic knowledge about reading. Reading books remained important for children in school who were conventional readers . . . .

✔ Guideline 9: Check the Flow of Your Argument for Coherence

One of the most difficult skills to learn in academic writing is how to evaluate one's own writing for coherence. Coherence refers to how well a manuscript holds together as a unified argument. It is important to ask yourself how well the various elements of your review connect with one another. This requires that you carefully evaluate the effectiveness of the rhetorical elements of your document that tell the reader about its structure and about the relationships among its elements. Subheadings often go a long way in identifying a manuscript's structure. Transitional expressions and other kinds of rhetorical markers also help to identify relationships among sections, as in "the next example," "in a related study," "a counterexample," and "the most recent (or relevant) study." Obviously, there are many more such examples. Remember, these kinds of rhetorical devices are useful navigational tools for your reader, especially if the details of the review are complex.

Activities for Chapter 11

Directions: Working with a peer from your class, exchange papers and independently respond to the following questions. Then, together, share each other's feedback and discuss.

1. If the review is long, did the author provide an overview of the review near its beginning? Explain.

2. Did the author explicitly state what would and would not be covered in the review? Explain.

3. Is the review a clear and cohesive essay? Explain.

4. Did the author avoid annotations? Explain.

5. If the review is long, did the author use subheadings? Explain.

6. Did the author use transitions to help trace his or her argument? Explain.
7. If the topic reaches across disciplines, did the author review studies from each discipline separately?
8. Did the author write a conclusion for the end of the review?
9. Is the flow of the argument coherent?

Notes

1. Balliet, D., Mulder, L. B., & Van Lange, P. A. M. (2011). Reward, punishment, and cooperation: A meta-analysis. *Psychological Bulletin, 137,* 594–615.
2. Burrell, L. V., Johnson, M. S., & Melinder, A. (2016). *Applied Cognitive Psychology, 30,* 323–331.
3. McFarland, D. A., Lewis, K., & Goldberg, A. (2016). Sociology in the era of Big Data: The ascent of forensic social science. *The American Sociologist, 47,* 1, 12–35.
4. Burman, E. (2016). Fanon's Lacan and the traumatogenic child: Psychoanalytic reflections on the dynamics of colonialism and racism. *Theory, Culture & Society, 33,* 77–101.
5. Bem, D. J. (1995). Writing a review article for *Psychological Bulletin. Psychological Bulletin, 118,* 172–177.
6. Gentile, K. (2016). Generating subjectivity through the creation of time. *Psychoanalytic Psychology, 33,* 264–283.
7. Mol, S. E., & Bus, A. G. (2011). To read or not to read: A meta-analysis of print exposure from infancy to early adulthood. *Psychological Bulletin, 137,* 267–296.

PART IV

Editing and Preparing the Final Draft of Your Review

Chapter 12

Guidelines for Editing Your Essay and Incorporating Feedback

At this point in the writing process, you have completed the major portion of your critical review of the literature. However, your work is not yet done. You should now undertake the important final steps in the writing process—redrafting your review.

New writers often experience frustration at this stage because they are now expected to take an impartial view of a piece of writing in which they have had a very personal role. In the earlier stages, as the writer, you were the one analyzing, evaluating, and synthesizing other writers' work. Now, your draft is the subject of your own and your readers' analysis and evaluation. This is not an easy task, but it is a critical *and* necessary next step in writing an *effective* literature review.

The first step in accomplishing this role reversal is to put the manuscript aside for a period of time, thereby creating some distance from the work and from your role as the writer. Second, remind yourself that the writing process is an ongoing negotiation between a writer and the intended audience. This is why the role reversal is so important. You should now approach your draft from the perspective of someone who is trying to read and understand the argument being communicated.

The redrafting process typically involves evaluating and incorporating feedback. That feedback may come from an instructor and your peers, or it may come from your own attempts to refine and revise your own draft. If you are writing a literature review as a term paper, solicit feedback from your professor at key points during the writing process, either by discussing your ideas during an office hours visit or, if your professor is willing, by submitting a first draft for comments. If it is for a thesis or dissertation, your earliest feedback will be from your faculty adviser, although you should also consider asking fellow students and colleagues for comments. If the review is for an article intended for publication, you should seek feedback from instructors, fellow students, and colleagues. The more feedback you are able to receive, the better.

As the writer, you should determine which comments you will incorporate and which you will discard, but the feedback you receive from these various sources will give you valuable information on how to improve the communication of your ideas to your audience. The following guidelines are designed to help you through this process.

✔ Guideline 1: The Reader Is Always Right

This guideline is deliberately overstated to draw your attention to it because it is the most important one in the redrafting process. If an educated reader does not understand one of your points, the communication process has not worked. Therefore, you should almost always seriously consider changing the draft to make it clearer for the reader. It will usually be counterproductive to defend the draft manuscript. Instead, you should try to determine why the reader did not understand it. Did you err in your analysis? Did you provide insufficient background information? Would the addition of more explicit transitions between sections make it clearer? These are only a few of the possible problems with the manuscript. Plan to spend enough time discussing the misunderstandings with your reader so you will fully understand the source of the difficulty.

✔ Guideline 2: Expect Your Instructor to Comment on the Content

It is important for you to obtain your instructor's feedback on the *content* of your manuscript early in the redrafting process. If your first draft contained many stylistic and mechanical errors, such as misspellings or misplaced headings, your instructor may feel compelled to focus on these matters and defer the comments on the content until the manuscript is easier to read.

✔ Guideline 3: Concentrate First on Comments about Your Ideas

As the previous two guidelines suggest, your first priority at this stage should be to make sure that your ideas have come across as you intended. Of course, you should note comments about stylistic matters and eventually attend to them, but your first order of business should be to ensure that you have communicated the argument you have developed. Thus, you need to carefully evaluate the feedback you receive from all your sources—your fellow students as well as your instructor—because at this stage you need to concentrate your efforts on making sure that your paper communicates your ideas effectively and correctly. (Some important matters concerning style and language use are covered later in this chapter.)

✔ Guideline 4: Reconcile Contradictory Feedback by Seeking Clarification

You may encounter differences of opinion among those who review your draft document. For instance, it is not unusual for members of a thesis or dissertation committee to give you contradictory feedback. One member may ask that you provide additional details about a study, while another member may want you to de-emphasize it. If you encounter such differences of opinion, it is your responsibility to seek further clarification from both sources and negotiate a resolution. First, make sure that the different opinions were not due to one person's failure to comprehend your argument. Second, discuss the matter with both individuals and arrive at a compromise.

✔ Guideline 5: Reconcile Comments about Style with Your Style Manual

Make sure that you have carefully reviewed the particular style manual that is required for your writing task. If your earliest experience with academic writing was in an English department course, you may have been trained to use the Modern Language Association's *MLA Handbook*.[1] Many university libraries advise that theses and dissertations follow *The Chicago Manual of Style*.[2] However, the most widely used manual in the social and behavioral sciences is the *Publication Manual of the American Psychological Association*.[3] If you are preparing a paper for publication, check the specific periodical or with the publisher for guidelines on style before submitting the paper. Finally, many academic departments and schools will have their own policies with respect to style. Regardless of which style manual pertains to your writing task, remember that you are expected to adhere to it meticulously. As you consider incorporating any feedback you receive, make sure that it conforms to the required style manual.

✔ Guideline 6: Allow Sufficient Time for the Feedback and Redrafting Process

Students often experience frustration when they are faced with major structural or content revisions and have an imminent deadline. You can expect to have to prepare at least one major redraft of your literature review, so you should allow yourself plenty of time for it. Professional writers often go through three or more drafts before they consider a document to be a final draft. While you may not have quite so many drafts, you should allow enough time to comfortably go through at least several revisions of your document.

✔ Guideline 7: Compare Your Draft with Your Topic Outline

The topic outline you prepared after reading Chapter 9 traced the path of the argument for the literature review. Now that your first draft is completed, compare what you have written with the topic outline to make sure you have properly fleshed out the path of the argument.

✔ Guideline 8: Check the Structure of Your Review for Parallelism

The reader of a literature review, especially a long, complex review, needs to be able to follow the structure of the manuscript while internalizing the details of the analysis and synthesis. A topic outline will typically involve parallel structural elements. For instance, a discussion of weaknesses will be balanced by a discussion of strengths, arguments for a position will be balanced by arguments against, and so on. These expectations on the part of the reader stem from long-standing rhetorical traditions in academic writing. Therefore, you need to check your manuscript to make sure that your descriptions are balanced properly. This may require that you explain a particular lack of parallelism, perhaps by stating explicitly that no studies were found that contradict a specific point (see Guideline 10 in Chapter 10 if this applies to your review).

✔ Guideline 9: Avoid Overusing Direct Quotations, Especially Long Ones

One of the most stubborn problems for novice academic writers in the social and behavioral sciences is the overuse of quotations. This is understandable, given the heavy emphasis placed in college writing classes on the correct use of the conventions for citing others' words. In fact, there is nothing inherently wrong with using direct quotations. However, problems arise when they are used inappropriately or indiscriminately.

A direct quotation presented out of context may not convey the full meaning of the author's intent. When a reader struggles to understand the function of a quotation in a review, the communication of the message of the review is interrupted. Explaining the full context of a quotation can further confuse the reader with details that are not essential for the purpose of the review at hand. By contrast, paraphrasing the main ideas of an author is usually more efficient and makes it easier to avoid extraneous details. In addition, paraphrasing eliminates the potential for disruptions in the flow of a review due to the different writing styles of various authors. In both cases, you are still required to cite your sources.

Finally, it is seldom acceptable to begin a literature review with a quotation. Some students find it hard to resist doing this. Remember that it is usually very difficult for the reader to experience the intended impact of the quotation when it is presented before the author of the literature review has established the proper context.

✔ Guideline 10: Avoid Using Synonyms for Recurring Words

The focus of a review of empirical research should be on presenting, interpreting, and synthesizing other writers' ideas and research findings as clearly and precisely as possible. This may require you to repeat words that describe routine aspects of several studies. Students who are new to academic writing sometimes approach the task as though it were a creative writing exercise. *It is not!* Literature reviews should include information about many studies (and other types of literature), all of which readers should be able to internalize quickly. Therefore, it is important to adhere to the use of conventional terms, even if they should recur. Clarity is best achieved when the writer consistently uses conventional terms throughout, especially when referring to details about a study's methodology or some other technical aspect of the research.

In general, it is best not to vary the use of labels. For instance, if a study deals with two groups of participants, and the researcher has labeled them Groups 1 and 2, you should usually avoid substituting more creative phrases (e.g., "the Phoenix cohort" or "the original group of youngsters"). On the other hand, if alternative labels help to clarify a study's design (e.g., when Group 1 is the control group and Group 2 the experimental group), use the substitute expressions instead, but remain consistent throughout your discussion. Example 12.10.1 illustrates how the use of synonyms and "creative" sentence construction can confuse readers. At various points, the first group is referred to as the "Phoenix cohort," as "Group I," and as the "experimental group," which is bound to cause confusion. Example 12.10.2 is an improved version in which the writer consistently uses the terms *experimental group* and *control group* to identify the two groups.

Example 12.10.1

Inconsistent use of identifying terms

The Phoenix cohort, which was taught to correctly identify the various toy animals by name, was brought back to be studied by the researchers twice, once after 6 months and again at the end of the year. The other group of youngsters was asked to answer the set of questions only once, after 6 months, but they had been taught to label the animals by color rather than by name. The performance of Group I was superior to the performance of Group II. The superior performance of the experimental group was attributed to. . . .

Part IV: Edit and Prepare the Final Draft

> **Example 12.10.2**
>
> *Improved version of Example 12.10.1*
>
> The experimental group was taught to identify toy animals by color and was retested twice at 6-month intervals. The control group, which was taught to identify the toys by name, was retested only once after 6 months. The performance of the experimental group was superior to the performance of the control group. The superior performance of the experimental group was attributed to . . . .

✔ **Guideline 11: Spell Out All Acronyms When You First Use Them, and Avoid Using Too Many**

So many acronyms have become part of our everyday lexicon that it is easy to overlook them during the editing process. Some examples are school acronyms, such as UCLA and USC; professional acronyms, such as APA and MLA; and acronyms from our everyday lives, such as FBI, FDA, and GPA. As obvious as this guideline may seem, it is quite common to find these and other examples of acronyms that are never spelled out. Make sure you check your document carefully for acronyms and spell them out the first time that you use them.

Sometimes, it is useful to refer to something by its acronym, especially if its full title is long and you intend to refer to it several times. For instance, the Graduation Writing Assessment Requirement for students in the California State University system is commonly referred to as the GWAR. In general, you should avoid using too many acronyms, especially ones that are not commonly recognized, like GWAR. In a complex literature review, using a few acronyms may be helpful, but using too many may be confusing.

✔ **Guideline 12: Avoid the Use of Contractions—They Are Inappropriate in Formal Academic Writing**

Contractions are a natural part of language use. They are one example of the natural process of linguistic simplification that accounts for how all languages change, slowly but surely, over time. Many instructors, even some English composition instructors, tolerate the use of contractions on the assumption that their use reflects the changing standards of acceptability in modern-day American English. In spite of such attitudes, however, it is almost always *inappropriate* to use contractions in formal academic writing.

> ### Example 12.12.1
>
> *Inappropriate contraction use*
>
> The experimental group **wasn't** instructed to identify their toy animals by color and **didn't** respond to prompts correctly.

> ### Example 12.12.2
>
> *Improved version of Example 12.12.1*
>
> The experimental group **was not** instructed to identify their toy animals by color and **did not** respond to prompts correctly.

✔ Guideline 13: When Used, Coined Terms Should Be Set Off by Quotations

It is sometimes useful to coin a term to describe something in one or two words that would otherwise require a sentence or more. Coined terms frequently become part of common usage, as with the noun "Google," which is now commonly used as a verb (e.g., Can you please *google* her address?). However, coined terms should be used sparingly in formal academic writing. If you decide to coin a term, set it off with quotation marks the first time it is used to indicate that its meaning cannot be found in a standard dictionary.

✔ Guideline 14: Avoid Slang Expressions, Colloquialisms, and Idioms

Remember that academic writing is *formal* writing. Therefore, slang, colloquialisms, and idioms are not appropriate in a literature review. While many slang terms such as *cool* (meaning "good") and *ain't* are becoming part of our conversational language repertoire, they should be avoided altogether in formal writing. Colloquialisms, such as *thing* and *stuff*, should be replaced with appropriate noncolloquial terms (e.g., *item, feature,* and *characteristic*). Similarly, idioms, such as "to rise to the occasion" and "to demolish the opposing theories," should be replaced by more formal expressions, such as *to address the need* or *to disprove the other theories.*

Part IV: Edit and Prepare the Final Draft

✔ Guideline 15: Use Latin Abbreviations in Parenthetic Material—Elsewhere, Use English Translations

The Latin abbreviations shown below with their English translations are commonly used in formal academic writing. With the exception of et al., these abbreviations are limited to parenthetic material. For instance, the Latin abbreviation in parentheses at the end of this sentence is proper: (i.e., this is a correct example). If the word or phrase is not in parentheses, you should use the English translation: That is, this is also a correct example. In addition, note the punctuation required for each of these abbreviations. Note especially that there is no period after *et* in "et al."

cf.	compare	e.g.,	for example	et al.	and others
etc.	and so forth	i.e.,	that is	vs.	versus, against

✔ Guideline 16: Check Your Draft for Common Writing Conventions

There are a number of additional writing conventions that all academic disciplines require. Check your draft to ensure you have applied all the following items before you give it to your instructor to read.

a. Make sure you have used complete sentences. One technique that students may find useful is reading the draft aloud to themselves. If you pause while reading a sentence, this generally signals that a sentence requires clarification and should be revised.
b. It is sometimes acceptable to write a literature review in the first person. However, you should avoid excessive use of the first person in formal academic writing.
c. It is inappropriate to use gendered language in academic writing. For instance, it is incorrect to always use masculine or feminine pronouns (he, him, his vs. she, her, hers) to refer to a person when you are not sure of the person's gender (as in, "the teacher left her classroom . . . ," when the teacher's gender is not known). Often, gendered language can be avoided through use of the plural form ("the teachers left their classrooms . . ."). If you must use singular forms, alternate between masculine and feminine forms or use *he or she*.
d. You should strive for clarity in your writing. Thus, you should avoid indirect sentence constructions and passive voice, such as, "In Smith's study, it was found . . . ." An improved version would be, "Smith found that . . . ."
e. In general, the numbers zero through nine are spelled out (e.g., one, two, and so forth), but numbers 10 and above are written as numerals (e.g., 25, 1995, etc.). Two exceptions to this rule are numbers assigned to a table or figure and measurements expressed in decimals or in metric units.

f. Always capitalize nouns followed by numerals or letters when they denote a specific place in a numbered series. For instance, this is Item f under Guideline 16 in Chapter 12. (Note that *I*, *G*, and *C* are capped.)
g. Always spell out a number when it is the first word or phrase in a sentence, as in, "Seventy-five participants were interviewed. . . ." Sometimes a sentence can be rewritten so that the number is not at the beginning, as in "Researchers interviewed 75 participants. . . . "

✔ Guideline 17: Write a Concise and Descriptive Title for the Review

The title of a literature review should identify the field of study you have investigated as well as tell the reader your point of view. However, it should also be concise and describe what you have written. In general, the title should not draw attention to itself. Rather, it should help the reader to adopt a proper frame of reference with which to read your paper. The following suggestions will help you to avoid some common problems with titles.

a. **Identify the field but do not describe it fully.** Especially with long and complex reviews, it is not advisable that you try to describe every aspect of your argument. If you do, the result will be an excessively long and detailed title. Your title should provide your reader with an easy entry into your paper. It should not force the reader to pause in order to decipher it.

b. **Consider specifying your bias, orientation, or delimitations.** If your review is written with an identifiable bias, orientation, or delimitation, it may be desirable to specify it in the title. For instance, if you are critical of some aspect of the literature, consider using a phrase such as, *A Critique of* . . . or *A Critical Evaluation of* . . . as part of your title. Subtitles often can be used effectively for this purpose. For instance, "The Politics of Abortion: A Review of the Qualitative Research" has a subtitle indicating that the review is delimited to qualitative research.

c. **Avoid "cute" titles.** Avoid the use of puns, alliteration, or other literary devices that detract from the content of the title. While a title such as "Phonics vs. 'Hole' Language" may seem clever if your review is critical of the whole language approach to reading instruction, it will probably distract readers. A more descriptive title, such as "Reading as a Natural or Unnatural Outgrowth of Spoken Language," will give the reader of your review a better start in comprehending your paper.

d. **Keep it short.** Titles should be short and to the point. Professional conference organizers will often limit titles of submissions to about nine words in order to facilitate the printing of hundreds of titles in their program books. While such printing constraints are not at play with a term paper or a chapter heading, it is still advisable to try to keep your review title as simple and short as possible. A good rule of thumb is to aim for a title of about 10 words, plus or minus three.

✔ Guideline 18: Strive for a User-friendly Draft

You should view your first draft as a work in progress. As such, it should be formatted in a way that invites comments from your readers. Thus, it should be legible and laid out in a way that allows the reader to react easily to your ideas. The following list contains some suggestions for ensuring that your draft is user-friendly. Ask your faculty adviser to review this list and add additional items as appropriate.

a. **Spell-check, proofread, and edit your manuscript.** Word-processing programs have spell-check functions. Use the spell-check feature before asking anyone to read your paper. However, there is no substitute for editing your own manuscript carefully, especially because the spell-check function can overlook some of your mistakes (e.g., *see* and *sea* are both correctly spelled, but the spell-check function will not highlight them as errors if you type the wrong one). Remember that your goal should be an error-free document that communicates the content easily and does not distract the reader with careless mechanical errors.

b. **Number all pages.** Professors sometimes write general comments in the body of an email message or as a memo in addition to their annotated notes on your paper. Unnumbered pages make such comments more difficult to write because professors do not have specific page numbers to reference.

c. **Double-space the draft.** Single-spaced documents make it difficult for the reader to write specific comments or suggest alternate phrasing. They also often times do not meet proper discipline-specific guidelines. For example, the APA manual guidelines specify that all papers should be double-spaced.

d. **Use standard one-inch margins.** Narrower margins may save paper, but they restrict the amount of space available for your instructor's comments.

e. **Use a stapler or a strong binder clip to secure the draft.** Your draft is one of many papers your instructor will read. Securing the document with a stapler or a strong clip will make it easier to keep your paper together. If you use a folder or a binder to hold your draft, make sure that it opens flat. Plastic folders that do not open flat make it difficult for your professor (or editor) to write comments in the margins between pages.

f. **Include a title page.** Because your draft is one of many papers your instructor will read, it is important to identify yourself as the author. Always include a properly formatted title page.

- **APA papers require a title page and should be centered and double-spaced**. The full title of your paper should not be underlined.

- APA guidelines do not require that you list the course instructor's name and date, however this is often required by your university or professor.
- **Each page should have a header with a shortened version of your title and page number.** This shortened title should be no more than 50 characters, including spaces.

Example 12.18.1

Sample APA title page

Running head: SHORTENED TITLE IN CAPS   1

                                    Title
                            First Name Last Name
                                Course Title
                              Instructor's Name
                              Date Submitted

g. **Keep at least one backup of your paper file.** You should back up your files in multiple places and always keep a hard copy for your records! Many students choose to use online cloud services such as *Dropbox* or *Google Docs* to ensure that even if one's computer hard drive crashes or is stolen, a copy of the file will still exist.
h. **If submitting a hard copy of your paper, make sure the draft is printed clearly.** While many instructors now prefer or require electronic submissions, if you are planning to turn in a hard-copy version of your paper, you should make sure the print is dark enough to be read comfortably. You should be sure to review your assignment guidelines/syllabi and/or check with your instructor about their submission preferences.
i. **Avoid "cute" touches.** In general, you should avoid using color text for highlighted words (use italics instead), mixing different size fonts (use a uniform font size throughout except for the title), or using clip art or any other special touches that may distract the reader by calling attention to the physical appearance of your paper instead of its content.

✔ **Guideline 19: Make Sure That You Have Enclosed in Quotation Marks and/or Cited All Words and Ideas That Are Not Your Own**

One of the dangers inherent in accessing research materials in digital format is how easy it has become to incorporate exact phrases (and more) into one's writing. It is important that you take extra care to use only your own words to describe ideas and concepts that come from the works you have reviewed in the literature. If you choose to use words, phrases, or entire passages from such sources, make sure that you have cited them in accordance with the APA's guidelines, or with your field's citation guidelines if you are following another style manual.

You may formally cite a reference in your narrative in one of several ways. Regardless, the APA style handbook adheres to the author-date method of in-text citation. This means that when quoting directly from another author's work, you reference the author's last name and the year of publication for the source in the text. It is important that any exact words and phrases that are not your own also be placed within quotation marks. See Examples 12.19.1 and 12.19.2 below.

Example 12.19.1

Direct quotation with author as part of the narrative

According to Galvan and Galvan (2016), "under no circumstances should you forget to correctly cite your source's words directly" (p. 101).

> **Example 12.19.2**
>
> *Direct quotation with parenthetical citation*
>
> President Harrison's speech spoke openly to the idea that "under no circumstances should you forget to correctly cite your source's words directly" (Galvan & Galvan, 2016, p. 101).
>
> Note: When you cite two authors' names in parentheses, use the ampersand (&) instead of the word *and*. If the citation is in the narrative, use the word *and*. You should use semicolons to separate more than two citations in parentheses, as in this example: (Black, 2014; Brown, 2015; Green, 2016).

If you are paraphrasing an idea but not directly quoting another author's words, your in-text citations will only need to make reference to the author and year of publication. In such cases, it is not customary to include the page numbers. See Example 12.19.3. You should also apply this rule when citing a book, journal article, or other source in its entirety (and not a specific page or set of pages). See Example 12.19.4.

> **Example 12.19.3**
>
> *Indirect quotation with parenthetical citation*
>
> University policies are generally very strict in administering punishment for plagiarism offenses (Galvan & Galvan, 2016).

> **Example 12.19.4**
>
> *Indirect quotation with parenthetical citation*
>
> Galvan and Galvan (2016) utilized a three-part process to describe the mechanics of completing a literature review.

When you cite a secondary source, be sure you have made it clear:

> **Example 12.19.5**
>
> *Citing a secondary source with in-text citations*
>
> (Doe, as cited in Smith, 2016).

Note that only Smith (2016) should be placed in the reference list (guidelines for which are included in Chapter 13). All sources directly cited in the body of your essay *must* appear in your reference list at the end of your paper.

✔ Guideline 20: Use Great Care to Avoid Plagiarism

As noted, our professional style manuals, including APA, give specific guidelines for how one is to credit another author's words in our own writing. Plagiarism is the act of knowingly representing as our own the words, ideas, or work of another author or person. Given the widespread use of online resources and information, it is important to exercise caution when citing published works and others' ideas.

If you are uncertain about what constitutes plagiarism, it is recommended that you consult your university's Code of Student Conduct or policy on Academic Dishonesty. These documents are usually found in your university's main catalog and reprinted in other places that are readily available to students.

University library websites and University Writing Centers often have their own plagiarism guides for students to consult. Online plagiarism materials are frequently located in the same space as library style manuals and citation guides (see Chapter 13). The California State University, Los Angeles library's website is one example of an accessible repository of information about plagiarism. It links to a video tutorial and other helpful online plagiarism guides: http://calstatela.libguides.com/style. Click on the "About Plagiarism" tab on the main page or the blue "plagiarism" hyperlink to be redirected to this information.

The University of Washington's Psychology Writing Center provides a downloadable writing guide titled *How and When to Cite* (http://web.psych.washington.edu/writingcenter/). On the main page, click the "Writing Guides" link, which will take you to a list of handouts in PDF format. Under the "Avoiding Plagiarism" heading, you will find a statement on academic responsibility prepared by the university's Committee on Academic Conduct (1994),[4] which discusses six types of plagiarism, listed below, along with examples of (a) the original text, (b) a possible plagiarized text, and (c) a proper non-plagiarized version.

(1) Using another writer's words without proper citation;

— **Original Text**: The cheating methods spurred by new technology have been met in kind with the development of sophisticated cheating detection software.

— **Plagiarized Text**: The cheating methods spurred by new technology have been met in kind with the development of sophisticated cheating detection software. [Note: this example takes the authors' words directly without using quotation marks or adding a citation.]

— **Proper Version**: According to researchers, "The cheating methods spurred by new technology have been met in kind with the development of sophisticated cheating detection software" (Paulhus & Dubois, 2015, p. 183).[5]

(2) Using another writer's ideas without proper citation;

— **Original Text**: In the past, clever students may have been well aware of traditional detection methods and exerted caution.
— **Plagiarized Text**: Clever students in the past may have exerted caution because they were aware of traditional detection methods. [Note: in this example, the points were reordered and some words were changed, but the writer uses the authors' ideas without referencing their work.]
— **Proper Version**: Paulhus and Dubois (2015) suggest that historically, "clever students may have been well aware of traditional detection methods and exerted caution" (p. 187).

(3) Citing a source but reproducing the exact words of a printed source without quotation marks;

— **Original Text**: In the past, clever students may have been well aware of traditional detection methods and exerted caution.
— **Plagiarized Text**: In the past, clever students may have been well aware of traditional detection methods and exerted caution (Paulhus & Dubois, 2015, p. 187). [Note: Even when you include a citation, using the authors' exact words without quotation marks is considered plagiarism.]
— **Proper Version**: According to Paulhus and Dubois (2015), "[i]n the past, clever students may have been well aware of traditional detection methods and exerted caution" (p. 187).

(4) Borrowing the structure of another author's phrases or sentences without crediting the author from whom it came:

— **Original Text**: In the past, clever students may have been well aware of traditional detection methods and exerted caution.
— **Plagiarized Text**: Previously, clever students may have exerted caution due to their knowledge of traditional detection methods. [Note: The writer changes order and rewords parts of the original text, but does not cite the original source at all.]
— **Proper Version**: Previously, clever students may have exerted caution due to their being aware of traditional detection methods (Paulhus & Dubois, 2015, p. 187).

Part IV: Edit and Prepare the Final Draft

(5) Borrowing all or part of another student's paper or using someone else's outline to write your own paper; and

(6) Using a paper-writing service or having a friend write the paper for you.

As an institutional defense against plagiarism, many universities subscribe to online software that assists instructors in identifying plagiarized materials in their students' written assignments. *Turnitin* is an online tool that generates reports that directly identify phrases, sentences, and entire passages that appear to have been copied from other sources (both online and in print). Depending on the instructor, students may or may not have access to their own *Originality Reports*. See Figure 12.20.1 for a sample of what instructors can see when accessing student Originality Reports. In other words, by using such tools, it is fairly easy for an instructor to identify uncredited or improperly cited material. It is extremely important that students exercise great caution when incorporating ideas from outside sources and that they ensure that all such ideas are properly cited.

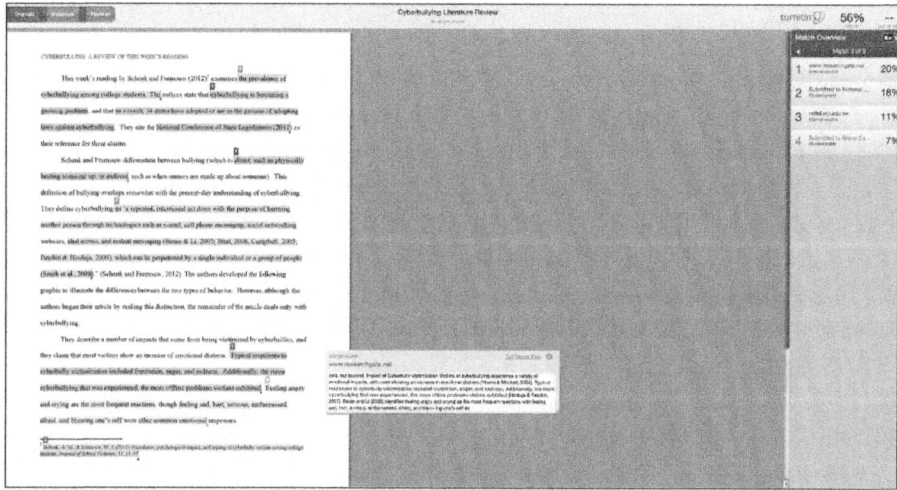

Figure 12.20.1 Sample *Turnitin* instructor originality report

Note: This paper was written for illustrative purposes. It was based on the model literature review by Schenk & Fremouw (2012) reprinted in Appendix B.

It is easy to quarrel about whether borrowing even one or two words would constitute plagiarism or whether an idea is really owned by an author. However, plagiarism is easily avoided simply by making sure that you cite your sources properly. If you have any doubt about this issue with respect to your own writing, talk with your instructor. It should also be noted that plagiarism detectors will often flag literature reviews, particularly short ones with many cited sources, as having a high probability of plagiarism due to the student's reference list. If using a standard format, such as APA style, the references will show up as "copied" because the citations appear as similar content. If using Turnitin, it may be possible for you to exclude reference lists and, if appropriate, quoted material from the analysis. This may be a good exercise for you to help identify your use (or perhaps overuse) of quotations (even if properly cited) within your literature review. If this becomes an issue for you, we suggest that you discuss this with your instructor.

To emphasize, plagiarism is a very serious matter that in most cases results in failing an assignment, an entire class, or even expulsion from a university. Further, plagiarism in theses and dissertations may result in the invalidation of the entire work, permanent expulsion from a graduate program and/or the tarnishing of one's academic reputation and career.

✔ Guideline 21: Get Help If You Need It

It should be obvious from the content of this chapter that the expectations of correctness and accuracy in academic writing are high. If you feel that you are unable to meet these demands at your current level of writing proficiency, you may need to get help. International students are often advised to hire proofreaders to help them meet their instructors' expectations. Most universities offer writing classes, either through the English department or in other disciplines. Some offer workshops for students struggling with the demands of thesis or dissertation requirements, and many universities have writing centers that provide a variety of services for students. If you feel you need help, talk with your instructor about the services available at your university. You should not expect your instructor to edit your work for style and mechanics.

Activities for Chapter 12

1. Examine the titles of the model literature reviews in Appendix B.

   - How well does each title serve to identify the field of the review?
   - Do the titles of the literature reviews specify the authors' points of view?

2. Now consider the first draft of your own literature review.

   - Compare your first draft with the topic outline you prepared. Do they match? If not, where does your draft differ from the outline? Does this variation affect the path of the argument of your review?
   - Find two or three places in your review where your discussion jumps to the next major category of your topic outline. How will the reader know

that you have changed to a new category (i.e., did you use subheadings or transitions to signal the switch)?

3. Ask two of your fellow students, or peers outside of class, to read the draft of your literature review and comment on the content. Compare their comments.

- On which points did your peers agree?
- On which points did they disagree? Which of the two opinions will you follow? Why?
- Consider the places in your review that your peers found hard to follow. Rewrite these passages, keeping in mind that you want your points to be accessible to any reader.

4. Write five questions designed to guide your instructor or your peers in giving you feedback on the content of your review.

- Reread your review draft, and respond to your own questions by pretending you are the instructor.
- Revise your draft according to your own feedback.
- Reconsider the five questions you wrote for your instructor or your peers. Which questions would you leave on your list? What questions would you add?

Notes

1. Modern Language Association of America. (2016). *MLA handbook* (8th ed.). New York, NY: Modern Language Association of America.
2. University of Chicago Press. (2014). *The Chicago manual of style* (16th ed.). Chicago: University of Chicago Press.
3. American Psychological Association. (2010). *Publication manual of the American Psychological Association* (6th ed.). Washington, DC.: American Psychological Association.
4. Committee on Academic Conduct. (1994). *Bachelor's degree handbook*. University of Washington.
5. Paulhus, D.L., & Dubois, P.J. (2015). The link between cognitive ability and scholastic cheating: A meta-analysis. *Review of General Psychology, 19*, 183–190.

Chapter 13

Preparing a Reference List[1]

The guidelines in this chapter for preparing reference lists are consistent with the principles in the *Publication Manual of the American Psychological Association* (APA), which is the most frequently used style manual in the social and behavioral sciences. The APA Manual, which can be found in most university libraries' Reference area, can be purchased at most college and university bookstores and online at www.apastyle.org. In addition, many university libraries offer their own easy-to-access and discipline-specific citation guides on their websites. It is recommended that you check with your library's reference desk for further information.

✔ Guideline 1: Consider Using Bibliographic Software to Help Manage the Details of Your References

The development of software to help manage bibliographies has profoundly changed the ways in which writers can approach their literature searches. Proprietary bibliographic software such as EasyBib, EndNote Web, and RefWorks, and open source (free) software such as Zotero, were developed to help researchers collect and manage bibliographic information for their sources. Many university libraries offer free subscriptions to select online citation formatting tools, and it is recommended that you check with your university's reference librarian for the bibliographic tools that may be available to you at no cost.

Should you choose to use them, reference managers offer the ability to create and store a repository of potential sources while you conduct your research, saving you the extra steps of trying to assemble a complete list of referenced sources after-the-fact. This eliminates the tedious extra steps of copying-and-pasting potential citations into a separate document, and/or printing large numbers of pages in order to not lose track of the bibliographic details for your citations. It is a personal decision whether you elect to incorporate this new technology into your research process, but it should be noted that they offer useful features, including, but not limited to, the ability to store PDFs of entire articles and screenshots of relevant websites, or the option of organizing references by keywords. More importantly, they can help you accomplish the objectives of producing a complete and properly formatted bibliography with the click of a button. The guidelines that follow address formatting issues that you will need to address regardless of whether you choose to use bibliographic software or not.

✔ Guideline 2: Place the Reference List at the End of the Review under the Main Heading "References"

The main heading "References" should be centered. Do not underline, use boldface, italics, or quotation marks. It is the last element in a review except for author contact information or appendices, if any.

✔ Guideline 3: A Reference List Should Refer Only to Sources Cited in the Literature Review

Writers often have some sources that, for one reason or another, were not cited in their reviews. References for these uncited materials should *not* be included in the reference list at the end of a literature review. Remember, a reference list includes *only* the items that were cited in the actual literature review you have written.

✔ Guideline 4: List References Alphabetically by Author's Surname

For sources with multiple authors, use the surname of the first author (i.e., the first author mentioned at the beginning of the source).

Note: If using bibliographic software to organize your literature searches, you may be given an option to "Export to Word" when you are ready to compile your reference list. Upon exporting your references to your word processing software, citations should already be listed in alphabetical order with hanging indents (see Guideline 6 below). You should make sure that the font style and size are consistent with the rest of your document.

✔ Guideline 5: Double-Space All Entries

All text contained within your reference list should be double-spaced.

✔ Guideline 6: Use Hanging Indents for the Second and Subsequent Lines of References

A hanging indent is created when the first line is *not* indented but the subsequent ones are indented, as in Example 13.6.1, where the surnames of the authors stand out in the left margin of the list.

> **Example 13.6.1**
>
> *Three references in alphabetical order with hanging indents*
>
> Apple, D. W. (2016). Experimental evidence of the XYZ phenomenon. *The Journal of New Developments, 55,* 99–104.
>
> Boy, C. C. (2014). New evidence on the validity of the XYZ phenomenon. *Journal of Psychological Renderings, 44,* 454–499.
>
> Catty, F. B., & Jones, C. M. (2015). The XYZ phenomenon reexamined. *Journal of Social and Economic Justice, 167,* 19–26.

✔ Guideline 7: Learn How to Create Hanging Indents Using a Word Processing Program

Word-processing programs make it easy to create hanging indents. For instance, to create a hanging indent using Microsoft Word:

1. Type a reference as a paragraph without any indents.
2. Right-click on the reference, and then select "Paragraph." A dialog box will appear.
3. Within the dialog box, click on the down-arrowhead below "Special," then click on the word "Hanging." (Note that at this point, Word will suggest a size for the indent under the word "By." The standard size is one-half inch.)
4. Click OK.[2]

✔ Guideline 8: Italicize the Titles of Journals and Their Volume Numbers

As most students know from basic composition classes, the titles of books should be italicized. Likewise, journal names should also be italicized.

Typically, all issues of a journal for a given year constitute a volume. Volume 1 consists of all issues the first year a journal was published, Volume 2 consists of all issues the second year, and so on. Within each volume, all page numbers are sequential. In other words, the first page of the first issue of a year is page 1. For the next issue of the same year, the page numbers pick up where the previous issue left off. For instance, if the first issue of the year ends on page 98, the second issue of the year begins with page 99.

In light of the above, it is clear that all a reader needs in order to locate an article is the title of the journal as well as the volume number and page numbers. Issue numbers are not essential for this purpose.

Part IV: Edit and Prepare the Final Draft

Volume numbers should be italicized. (Issue numbers do not need to be included in a reference.)

Example 13.8.1 has both the title of the journal (*Applied Cognitive Psychology*) and its volume number (*30*) italicized.

Example 13.8.1

A reference with the journal title and volume number italicized

Burrell, L. V., Johnson, M. S., & Melinder, A. (2016). Children as earwitnesses: Memory for emotional auditory events. *Applied Cognitive Psychology, 30,* 323–331.

Note: Many newer library search engines provide already-generated citations on a source's catalog entry page. While these can help save time, one should be careful to double-check that the provided citations are in the proper format and contain all the necessary information. You may notice that the suggested entries include issue numbers, which as noted, are not necessary. The following illustration was produced using the OneSearch library databases tool.

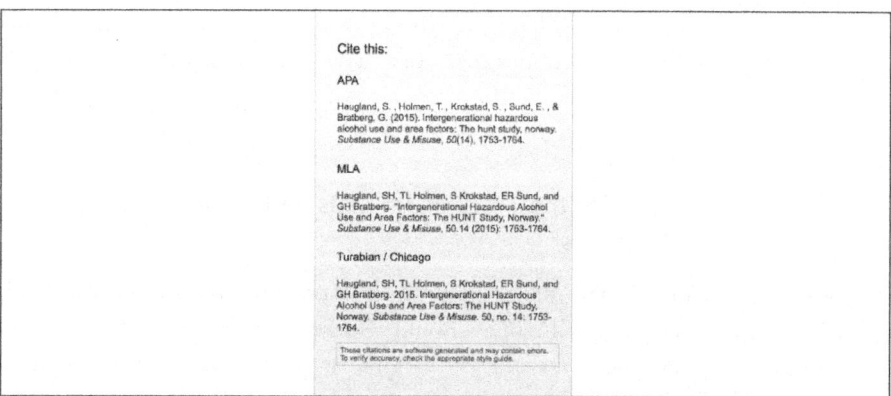

Figure 13.8.1 Dialogue box that appears after clicking 'Cite This' in OneSearch

✔ Guideline 9: Pay Particular Attention to Capitalization

Style manuals specify when to capitalize in reference lists. For instance, in APA style, only the first letter of the first word in the main title (and subtitle, if any) of an article title is capitalized. This is true even though all important words in the titles of articles

Preparing a Reference List

in the journals themselves are capitalized. This illustrates that some matters of style cannot be logically deduced. Attention to details in a style manual is required.

✔ Guideline 10: Pay Particular Attention to Punctuation

Failure to use proper punctuation in a reference list could lead to corrections on a student's review. In APA style for print journals, for instance, there should always be a period after the close of the parentheses around the year of publication and at the end of the reference.

✔ Guideline 11: Do Not Add Extraneous Material Such As Abbreviations for Page Numbers

Page numbers in APA style for journals are the last two numbers in a reference. APA style does not use abbreviations such as "p." or "pp." for page numbers in reference lists. Refer to Guideline 19 in Chapter 12 for guidelines on in-text citation formatting.

✔ Guideline 12: Journal Articles Accessed through Online Database Repositories Should Be Cited as if They Were Accessed in their Print Form

Do not cite journal articles accessed through online databases as websites. Journal articles accessed through online article repositories such as JSTOR must cite the source as if it were viewed in print form (Example 13.12.1). Online databases should provide the relevant citation information either in the search results or as an option to "Cite This Item" (Example 13.12.2). You may then choose to copy and paste the citation into your reference list (by clicking on the clipboard icon to its right), or export to other bibliographic citation tools (by clicking on the appropriate hyperlink).

Example 13.12.1

A sample JSTOR search listing with journal publication information

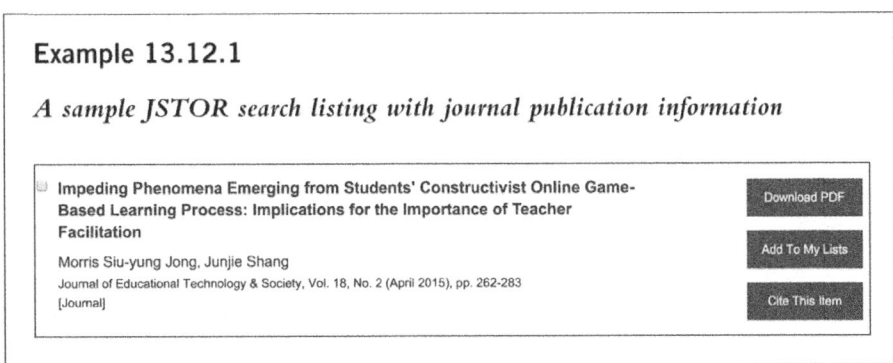

Part IV: Edit and Prepare the Final Draft

Example 13.12.2

Dialogue box that appears after clicking "Cite This Item" in JSTOR

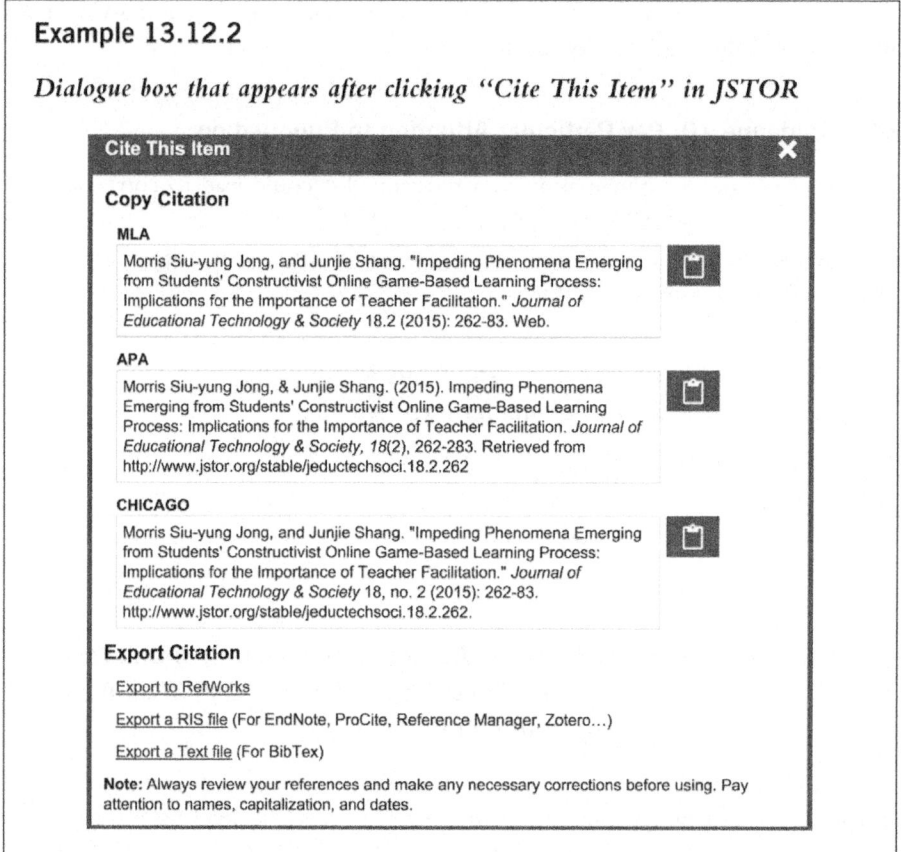

✔ **Guideline 13: Provide the Date and URL in References for Material Published Online**

Because material published online may be modified periodically, it is important to indicate the date on which online material was retrieved. Your listing may vary depending on the level of information about the source's author and publication available to you. Regardless, it is important that you provide a full and complete URL (such as www.example.com/retrieve) as well as any other identifying information, such as the name of the author, if known.

Example 13.13.1

A reference to material retrieved online with a publication date

Jones, A. A. (2016, July 15). *Some new thoughts on material evidence in the XYZ matter*. Retrieved August 5, 2016, from www.newexample.org/specimen

Example 13.13.2

A reference to material retrieved online where no publication date for the content is identified

Jones, A. A. (n.d.). *Some new thoughts on material evidence in the XYZ matter.* Retrieved August 5, 2016, from www.newexample.org/specimen

Example 13.13.3

A reference to material retrieved online where no author or date is listed

Sample Research Society. (n.d.). Some new thoughts on material evidence in the XYZ matter. Retrieved August 5, 2016, from www.newexample.org/specimen

✔ **Guideline 14: Format References to Books in Accordance with a Style Manual**

Example 13.14.1 shows a reference to a book formatted in APA style.

Example 13.14.1

A reference to a book in APA style

Martocci, Laura. (2015). *Bullying: The social destruction of self.* Philadelphia, PA: Temple University Press.

✔ **Guideline 15: If Using Online Bibliographic Tools, Make Sure That Generated Citations Are Listed in Correct Format**

Although you may choose to use online citation formatting tools to help aid in the preparation of your reference list, it is important to make sure that the generated citations are in the correct format. For instance, Example 13.12.2 provides a suggested APA citation that includes a hyperlink. Depending on how you are citing the source (footnote, in-text citation, reference list, etc.), this information would need to be adjusted to reflect the conventions of the format. It is recommended that you crosscheck your generated list with Guidelines 1–14 above.

Part IV: Edit and Prepare the Final Draft

✔ Guideline 16: Double-Check the Reference List against the Citations in the Body of the Review

In addition to checking that all cited material is referenced in the reference list, check that the spelling of the authors' names is the same in both places. Also, check to see that the years of publication in the citations and in the reference list are consistent.

Concluding Comment

To cite a type of source not covered in this chapter, consult a comprehensive style manual, such as the *Publication Manual of the American Psychological Association*, which specifies how to cite many types of specialized sources, such as a newsletter article, an unpublished paper presented at a professional meeting, a published technical report, and so on.

Activities for Chapter 13

1. Create a sample reference list entry and apply the hanging indentation formatting.

2. Check with your university's library to see which free bibliographic tools are available for your use. Generate and export a sample reference list to your word processing software. Do not forget to make sure that all the formatting guidelines outlined in this chapter have been applied to your sample.

3. Have you referenced any types of sources not covered in this chapter (e.g., a newsletter or conference paper)? If so, consult the appropriate online and/or printed citation guides to determine how to prepare proper citations for them.

Notes

1. The original version of this chapter was adapted from Pan, M. L. (2008). *Preparing literature reviews: Qualitative and quantitative approaches* (3rd ed.). Glendale, CA: Pyrczak Publishing. It has since been updated and has undergone significant revision.
2. If the default size suggested by Word is too large or small, right-click again on the reference, click on "Paragraph" again, and change the number of inches under "By."

Appendix A

Comprehensive Self-editing Checklist for Refining the Final Draft

The final draft should be as accurate and error-free as possible in terms of both its content and its mechanics and style. After you have carefully considered the feedback you received from your peers and academic advisers, and after you have revised the manuscript in light of their input, you should carefully edit your manuscript a final time. The purpose for this final review is accuracy.

The items in the following checklist are grouped according to some of the major criteria instructors use in evaluating student writing. Most of these criteria are absolutely critical when one is writing a thesis or dissertation. However, your instructor may relax some of them in the case of term papers written during a single semester.

You will find that most of the items on the checklist were presented in the earlier chapters as guidelines, but many additional ones have been added in an attempt to cover common problems that are sometimes overlooked by student writers. You should show this checklist to your instructors and ask that they add or eliminate items according to their own preferences.

Keep in mind that the checklist is designed to help you to refine the manuscript. Ultimately, the extent of perfection you achieve will depend on how meticulously you edit your own work.

Adherence to the Writing Process for Editing and Redrafting

___ 1. Have you asked your instructors to review this checklist and to add or delete items according to their preferences?
___ 2. After finishing your last draft, did you set your manuscript aside for several days before you began to revise it (i.e., did you create an appropriate distance from your manuscript before changing roles from "writer" to "reader")?
___ 3. Did you ask one or more persons to review your manuscript?
___ 4. Have you addressed all the questions raised by your reviewers?
___ 5. Did you reconcile all differences of opinion among your reviewers?

Appendix A

Importance or Significance of the Topic

___ 6. Is your topic important, from either a theoretical or a practical perspective?
___ 7. Does it present a fresh perspective or identify a gap in the literature (i.e., does it address a question not previously addressed)?
___ 8. Is your topic's significance or importance demonstrated and justified?
___ 9. Is this an appropriate topic for your field of study?
___ 10. Is the topic timely in terms of what is being reported in the research literature?
___ 11. Does the title of your manuscript adequately describe the subject of your review?

Organization and Other Global Considerations

___ 12. Does your review include an introduction along with a discussion and conclusions section?
___ 13. Did you include a reference list?
___ 14. Does the length and organization of your review follow the criteria set forth by (a) your instructor, if you are writing a term paper; (b) your committee chair, if you are writing a thesis or dissertation; or (c) the publication guidelines of the journal you have targeted, if you are writing for publication?

Effectiveness of the Introduction

___ 15. Does your introduction describe the scope of the literature you have reviewed and why the topic is important?
___ 16. Did you describe in your introduction the general structure of your paper?
___ 17. Does your introduction identify the line of argumentation you have followed in your manuscript?
___ 18. Does the introduction state what will and will not be covered, if this is appropriate?
___ 19. Does the introduction specify your thesis statement or point of view, if this is relevant?

Currency and Relevance of the Literature Cited

___ 20. Did you review the most current articles on the topic?
___ 21. Are the studies you reviewed current?
___ 22. If you have included older articles, did you have a good reason for including them?

___ 23. Have you explained why you have described some findings as being strong?
___ 24. Have you explained why you have described other findings as being weak?
___ 25. Did you identify the major patterns or trends in the literature?
___ 26. Have you identified in your manuscript the classic or landmark studies you cited?
___ 27. Did you specify the relationship of these classic studies to subsequent studies they may have influenced?

Thoroughness and Accuracy of the Literature Reviewed

___ 28. Is the coverage of your review adequate?
___ 29. Have you noted and explained the gaps in the literature?
___ 30. Have you described any pertinent controversies in the field?
___ 31. If you answered "yes" to Item 30, did you make clear which studies fall on either side of the controversy?
___ 32. Have you checked the draft for parallelism?
___ 33. Have you noted and explained the relationships among studies, such as which ones came first? Which ones share similarities? Which ones have differences?
___ 34. Did you indicate the source of key terms or concepts?
___ 35. Are there gaps in the body of your manuscript?

Coherence and Flow of the Path of the Argument

___ 36. Does each study you reviewed correspond with a specific part of your topic outline?
___ 37. Have you deleted citations to studies you decided not to include in your review because they do not relate to the path of your argument?
___ 38. Is the path of your argument made clear throughout the manuscript?
___ 39. Does each part of your review flow logically from the preceding part?
___ 40. If you have used "meta-comments" (see Chapter 10, Guideline 6), are they essential?
___ 41. If you have used subheadings, do they help to advance your argument?
___ 42. If you have not used subheadings, would adding them help to advance your argument?
___ 43. Is your manuscript coherent, or would additional transitional devices help to clarify how it holds together?

Appendix A

Effectiveness of the Conclusion

___ 44. Does your conclusion provide closure for the reader?
___ 45. Does your conclusion make reference to the line of argumentation you specified in the introduction?

Accuracy of Citations and the Reference List

___ 46. Have you checked your style manual's guidelines for citing references in the narrative (e.g., when to use parentheses, how to cite multiple authors, and how to cite a secondary source)?
___ 47. Have you checked each citation in the manuscript to make sure that it appears on your reference list?
___ 48. Have you checked all entries on the reference list to make sure that each one is cited in your manuscript?
___ 49. Have you eliminated all entries from your reference list that are not cited in the manuscript?
___ 50. Are most of the dates of the studies included in the reference list within the recent past?
___ 51. Have you checked for accuracy and consistency between the dates in your manuscript and the dates in your reference list?
___ 52. Have you checked the accuracy of the spelling of the authors' names in your manuscript and in your reference list?

Mechanics and Overall Accuracy of the Manuscript

___ 53. Did you read and edit your manuscript carefully?
___ 54. Did you perform a final spell-check of the entire manuscript?
___ 55. Are your margins set appropriately?
___ 56. Did you number all the pages?
___ 57. Is your manuscript double-spaced?
___ 58. Did you include your full name (and, for theses and dissertations, your telephone number or email address)?

Appropriateness of Style and Language Usage

___ 59. Have you carefully reviewed the appropriate style manual for your field?
___ 60. Have you checked your manuscript for consistency with your style manual?
___ 61. Are your headings formatted in accordance with the guidelines specified in the appropriate style manual?

Comprehensive Self-editing Checklist

___ 62. If you used Latin abbreviations (such as i.e., e.g., etc.), are they in parentheses, and have you checked for the required punctuation?
___ 63. If you have used long quotations, are they absolutely necessary?
___ 64. Does each quotation contribute significantly to the review?
___ 65. Can any of these quotations be paraphrased?
___ 66. Did you avoid the use of synonyms for important key terms and concepts?
___ 67. If you have coined a new term, is it set off in quotations the first time it is used?
___ 68. Have you avoided slang terms, colloquialisms, and idioms?
___ 69. Have you avoided contractions?
___ 70. Have you included any annotations that are not linked to the path of the argument of your review?
___ 71. Have you avoided using a series of annotations?
___ 72. Have you spelled all acronyms in full on first mention?
___ 73. If you have used the first person, is it appropriate?
___ 74. Have you avoided using sexist language?
___ 75. If you used numbers in the narrative of your review, did you ensure that you spelled the numbers zero through nine in full?
___ 76. If you used a noun followed by a number to denote a specific place in a sequence, did you capitalize the noun (as in "Item 76" of this checklist)?
___ 77. If you used a number to begin a sentence, did you spell it in full?

Grammatical Accuracy

___ 78. Did you check your manuscript for grammatical correctness?
___ 79. Is every sentence of your manuscript a complete sentence?
___ 80. Have you avoided using indirect sentence constructions (as in, "In Galvan's study, it was found ....")?
___ 81. Have you been consistent in your use of tenses (e.g., if you use the present tense in describing one study's findings, do you use this tense throughout, unless you are commenting on the historical relationship among studies)?
___ 82. Have you checked for the proper use of commas and other punctuation marks?
___ 83. Have you attempted to avoid complicated sentence structures?
___ 84. If you have any long sentences (e.g., several lines), have you attempted to break them down into two or more sentences?
___ 85. If you have any long paragraphs (e.g., a page or longer), have you attempted to break them down into two or more paragraphs?

Appendix A

Additional Editing Steps for Non-native English Speakers and Students with Serious Writing Difficulties

___ 86. If your proficiency in English is not at a high level, have you asked a proofreader for assistance?
___ 87. Have you checked the entire manuscript for the proper article usage (e.g., a, an, the)?
___ 88. Have you checked the manuscript for proper use of prepositions?
___ 89. Have you checked each sentence for proper subject–verb agreement?
___ 90. Have you checked the manuscript for proper use of idiomatic expressions?

Additional Guidelines Suggested by Your Instructor

___ 91. _____
___ 92. _____
___ 93. _____
___ 94. _____
___ 95. _____

Appendix B

Sample Literature Reviews

1) Balderrama-Durbin, C.M., Allen, E.S. & Rhoades, G.K. (2012). **Demand and withdraw behaviors in couples with a history of infidelity.** *Journal of Family Psychology, 26*(1), 11–17.

Although most Americans (up to 97%) believe that engaging in extramarital sex is wrong (Johnson et al., 2002), prevalence rates of infidelity remain high with approximately 22%–25% of men and 11%–15% of women admitting to engaging in extramarital sex (for a review of rates and correlates of extradyadic involvement [EDI] see Allen et al., 2005). EDI—that is, sexual involvement with a person outside the primary dyad—typically is associated with problems for partners and their relationship. Many negative emotional and behavioral correlates of EDI have been documented including partner violence, acute anxiety, depression, suicidal ideation, and symptoms similar to those of posttraumatic stress disorder (Cano & O'Leary, 2000; Gordon, Baucom, & Snyder, 2004). Relationship distress and dissolution are also commonly associated with EDI, with infidelity being the most frequently cited cause of divorce (Amato & Previti, 2003).

While prior literature has examined a broad range of correlates of infidelity, studies examining specific characteristics of communication related to EDI are rare. In a recent observational longitudinal study (Allen et al., 2008), women's infidelity was predicted by lower levels of their own premarital positive communication and by higher levels of negative communication and invalidation by both partners. Men's infidelity was predicted by their own lower levels of premarital positive communication and by higher invalidation communication by their partner. Thus, findings suggest that problems in communication are a significant risk factor for engaging in infidelity (as well as for general marital distress; Fincham & Beach, 1999; Markman, Rhoades, Stanley, Ragan, & Whitton, 2010). Indeed, existing infidelity interventions incorporate communication skill building as a core treatment component (Baucom, Snyder, & Gordon, 2009).

Appendix B

Conflict communication serves as an important indicator of both current and future relationship functioning (Markman et al., 2010). Dissatisfied couples are more likely to engage in negative conflict communication behaviors including criticism, defensiveness, contempt, and withdrawal (Gottman, 1993). One of the most widely studied and well-documented negative communication patterns is the demand/withdraw pattern in conflict communication. During conflict interactions, distressed couples often display a dyadic conflict pattern in which one spouse blames, nags, criticizes, or pressures the other for change, while the other spouse withdraws or avoids conflict (Christensen & Heavey, 1990). This demand/withdraw pattern correlates strongly with relationship dissatisfaction (Eldridge, Sevier, Jones, Atkins, & Christensen, 2007; Ridley, Wilhelm, & Surra, 2001), and is seen more often during problem discussions among couples seeking marital therapy and divorcing couples compared with nondistressed couples (Christensen & Shenk, 1991).

Gender differences in demand and withdraw conflict behaviors have been demonstrated in multiple studies. As a group, dissatisfied wives tend to demand change from their husbands, whereas dissatisfied husbands tend to withdraw from conflict with their wives (Caughlin & Vangelisti, 2000; Christensen & Heavey, 1990; Christensen & Shenk, 1991; Eldridge et al., 2007). Several theoretical perspectives have been proposed to account for this gender difference in conflict behavior including power differences, intimacy regulation, and gender roles (Caughlin & Vangelisti, 2000; Christensen & Heavey, 1990; Nichols & Rohrbaugh, 1997). However, recent empirical evidence suggests that demand and withdraw behavior is often dependent on the context in which it occurs (Holley, Sturm & Levenson, 2010; Vogel, Murphy, Werner Wilson, Cutrona, & Seeman, 2007) and that one omnibus theoretical model may not adequately explain variations in demand and withdraw behavior. With this in mind, it is important to evaluate not only gender differences but contextual factors that might influence individual demand and withdraw behavior in couple conflict discussions.

The present study examined demand and withdraw behaviors in conflict discussions among couples with and without a history of sexual EDI. Based on the existing literature on EDI and relationship distress, it could generally be predicted that couples with a history of EDI would have higher demand and withdraw behaviors compared with those couples without such history of EDI in their relationship. However, the current article sought to examine demand and withdraw behaviors for couples without EDI and two types of couples with a history of EDI: those with and without partner knowledge of EDI ("known" and "unknown" EDI, respectively). Making specific hypotheses based on factors, such as EDI knowledge, is difficult. Being aware of a partner's EDI may exacerbate distress and negative conflict behaviors. However, previous research has suggested that couples with infidelity that remains unknown throughout marital therapy may have more relationship distress relative to couples with infidelity that is known (Atkins,

Eldridge, Baucom, & Christensen, 2005); thus, there instead may be higher levels of demand and withdraw behaviors in relationships where there is unknown infidelity if these behaviors serve as a marker for more distress or other problems in the relationship. Therefore, no specific hypotheses based on EDI knowledge were made—we pose the evaluation of relative levels of demand and withdraw behaviors for these groups of couples as exploratory research questions. Additionally, because demand and withdraw behaviors in couples with a history of EDI may vary by the role of the partner in the EDI (i.e., the individual who engaged in the EDI compared with the partner who did not), we conducted further exploratory analyses examining demand and withdraw behaviors as a function of participation in an EDI for couples with known and unknown EDI. Specific hypotheses based on role in the EDI were also not formulated given the novelty of examining this specific context and the multitude of theoretical possibilities.

Method

Participants

To be included, couples needed to be in a "serious and steady" relationship that had lasted a minimum of one year. The sample consisted of 74 married couples and 96 committed heterosexual dating couples.[1] Participants ranged in age from 18 to 67 years ($M = 34.8$, $SD = 11.7$), with men being slightly older ($M = 36.0$, $SD = 11.9$) than women ($M = 33.5$, $SD = 11.6$). The average education for participants was 14.3 years ($SD = 2.4$, range = 8 –20), with women being slightly more educated ($M = 14.5$, $SD = 2.4$) than men ($M = 14.0$, $SD = 2.5$). The median annual income for men fell in the range of $20,000 –$29,000 and $15,000 –$19,000 for women. The median length of the couple's relationship was 3.5 years. Approximately 49% of couples had at least one child. Of the couples with children, the mean number of children was 2.4 ($SD = 1.6$). The largest representation of participants were White Non-Hispanic (43.8%), Hispanic participants constituted the next largest representation (22.1%), followed by African American (19.1%). There was a small representation of Asian American participants (2.1%) and Native American participants (2.4%). The remaining (10.5%) were multiracial or other.

This article was published Online First December 26, 2011.

Christina M. Balderrama-Durbin and Elizabeth S. Allen, Department of Psychology, University of Colorado Denver; Galena K. Rhoades, Department of Psychology, University of Denver.

Christina M. Balderrama-Durbin is now at the Department of Psychology, Texas A&M University.

This study was funded Elizabeth S. Allen's start-up funds, provided by the University of Colorado Denver.

Appendix B

Correspondence concerning this article should be addressed to Christina M. Balderrama-Durbin, Department of Psychology – Mailstop 4235, College Station, TX 77843-4235. E-mail: balderrama-durbin@tamu.edu

Notes

1. Married and dating couples differed significantly in terms of age and length of relationship ($ps < .05$). Effect sizes for these differences were $d = .33$ and $d = .74$, respectively. Data from both groups were pooled for analyses to preserve adequate statistical power. Primary analyses controlled for the length of the relationship; moreover, all analyses were reanalyzed using relationship status (married vs. dating) as a between subjects factor and the overall pattern of results was retained. (While females in a dating relationship withdrew significantly more than females in a married relationship, $F(1, 154) = 5.92$, $p < .05$, the patterns based on EDI group held across married and dating samples.)

References

Allen, E. S., Atkins, D., Baucom, D. H., Snyder, D. K., Gordon, K. C., & Glass, S. P. (2005). Intrapersonal, interpersonal, and contextual factors in engaging in and responding to extramarital involvement. *Clinical Psychology: Science and Practice, 12*, 101–130. doi:10.1093/ clipsy.bpi014

Allen, E. S., Rhoades, G. K., Stanley, S. M., Markman, H. J., Williams, T., Melton, J., & Clements, M. L. (2008). Premarital precursors of marital infidelity. *Family Process, 47*, 243–259. doi:10.1111/j.15455300.2008.00251.x

Allen, E. S., & Rhoades, G. K. (2008). Not all affairs are created equal: Emotional involvement with an extradyadic partner. *Journal of Sex & Marital Therapy, 34*, 51–65. doi:10.1080/00926230701620878

Allen, E. S. (2001). *Attachment styles and their relation to patterns of extradyadic and extramarital involvement* (Unpublished doctoral dissertation). University of North Carolina, Chapel Hill, NC.

Amato, P. R., & Previti, D. (2003). People's reasons for divorcing: Gender, social class, the life course, and adjustment. *Journal of Family Issues, 24*, 602–626. doi:10.1177/0192513X03024005002

Atkins, D. C., Eldridge, K. E., Baucom, D. H., & Christensen, A. (2005). Infidelity and behavioral couple therapy: Optimism in the face of betrayal. *Journal of Consulting and Clinical Psychology, 73*, 144 –150. doi:10.1037/0022-006X.73.1.144

Baucom, B. R., Atkins, D. C., Eldridge, K., McFarland, P., Sevier, M., & Christensen, A. (2011). The language of demand/withdraw: Verbal and vocal expression in dyadic interactions. *Journal of Family Psychology*. Advance online publication. doi:10.1037/a0024064

Baucom, D. H., Snyder, D. K., & Gordon, K. C. (2009). *Helping couples get past the affair: A clinician's guide.* New York, NY: Guilford Press. Cano, A., & O'Leary, K. D. (2000). Infidelity and separations precipitate major depressive episodes and symptoms of nonspecific depression and anxiety. *Journal of Consulting and Clinical Psychology, 68*, 774–781. doi:10.1037/0022-006X.68.5.774

Caughlin, J. P., & Vangelisti, A. L. (2000). An individual difference explanation of why married couples engage in the demand/withdraw pattern of conflict. *Journal of Social and Personal Relationships, 17,* 523–551. doi:10.1177/0265407500174004

Christensen, A., & Heavey, C. L. (1990). Gender and social structure in the demand/withdraw pattern of marital conflict. *Journal of Personality and Social Psychology, 59,* 73–81. doi:10.1037/0022-3514.59.1.73

Christensen, A., & Shenk, J. L. (1991). Communication, conflict, and psychological distance in nondistressed, clinic, and divorcing couples. *Journal of Consulting and Clinical Psychology, 59,* 459–463. doi: 10.1037/0022-006X.59.3.458

Eldridge, K. A., & Christensen, A. (2002). Demand–withdraw communication during couple conflict: A review and analysis. In P. Noller & J. A. Feeney (Eds.), *Understanding marriage: Developments in the study of couple interaction* (pp. 289–322). Cambridge, UK: Cambridge University Press. doi:10.1017/CBO9780511500077.016

Eldridge, K. A., Sevier, M., Jones, J., Atkins, D. C., & Christensen, A. (2007). Demand-withdraw communication in severely distressed, moderately distressed, and nondistressed couples: Rigidity and polarity during relationship and personal problem discussions. *Journal of Family Psychology, 21,* 218–226. doi:10.1037/0893-3200.21.2.218

Fincham, F. D., & Beach, S. R. H. (1999). Conflict in marriage: Implication for working with couples. *Annual Review of Psychology, 50,* 47–77. doi:10.1146/annurev.psych.50.1.47

Gordon, K. C., Baucom, D. H., & Snyder, D. K. (2004). An integrative intervention for promoting recovery from extramarital affairs. *Journal of Marital and Family Therapy, 30,* 1–12. doi:10.1111/j.17520606.2004.tb01235.x

Gottman, J. M. (1993). The roles of conflict engagement, escalation, and avoidance in marital interaction: A longitudinal view of five types of couples. *Journal of Consulting and Clinical Psychology, 61,* 6–15. doi:10.1037/0022-006X.61.1.6

Holley, S. R., Sturm, V. E., & Levenson, R. W. (2010). Exploring the basis of gender differences in the demand-withdraw pattern. *Journal of Homosexuality, 57,* 666–684. doi:10.1080/00918361003712145

Johnson, C. A., Stanley, S. M., Glenn, N. D., Amato, P. A., Nock, S. L., Markman, H. J., & Dion, M. R. (2002). *Marriage in Oklahoma: 2001 baseline statewide survey on marriage and divorce.* Oklahoma City, OK: Oklahoma Department of Human Services.

Karney, B. R., Kreitz, M. A., & Sweeney, K. E. (2004). Obstacles to ethnic diversity in marital research: On the failure of good intentions. *Journal of Social and Personal Relationships, 21,* 509–526. doi:10.1177/0265407504044845

Markman, H. J., Rhoades, G. K., Stanley, S. M., Ragan, E. P., & Whitton, S. W. (2010). The premarital communication roots of marital distress and divorce: The first five years of marriage. *Journal of Family Psychology, 24,* 289–298. doi:10.1037/a0019481

Nichols, M. P., & Rohrbaugh, M. J. (1997). Why do women demand and men withdraw? The role outside the career and family involvements. *The Family Journal: Counseling and Therapy for Couples and Families, 5,* 111–119. doi:10.1177/1066480797052004

Notarius, C. I., & Vanzetti, N. (1983). Marital agendas protocol. In E. Filsinger (Ed.), *Marriage and family assessment: A sourcebook for family therapy* (pp. 209–227). Beverly Hills, CA: Sage.

Ridley, C. A., Wilhelm, M. S., & Surra, C. A. (2001). Married couples' conflict responses and marital quality. *Journal of Social and Personal Relationships, 18,* 517–534. doi:10.1177/0265407501184005

Appendix B

Sevier, M., Simpson, L. E., & Christensen, A. (2004). Observational coding of demand-withdraw interactions in couples. In P. K. Kerig & D. H. Baucom (Eds.), *Couple observational coding systems* (pp. 159–171). Mahwah, NJ: Erlbaum, Inc.

Shrout, P. E., & Fleiss, J. L. (1979). Intraclass correlations: Uses in assessing rater reliability. *Psychological Bulletin, 86,* 420–428. doi: 10.1037/0033-2909.86.2.420

Vogel, D. L., Murphy, M. J., Werner-Wilson, R. J., Cutrona, C. E., & Seeman, J. (2007). Sex differences in the use of demand and withdraw behavior in marriage: Examining the social structure hypothesis. *Journal of Counseling Psychology, 54,* 165–177. doi:10.1037/0022-0167.54.2.165

2) **Burrell, L.V., Johnson, M.S. & Melinder, A. (2016). Children as earwitnesses: Memory for emotional auditory events.** *Applied Cognitive Psychology***, 30, 323–331.**

Witnesses to crimes may in some cases be unable to perceive visual information, for instance because the witness is blindfolded, the event occurs in darkness, or the event is shielded from view. In such instances, memory for auditory information can play a vital role in police investigations and criminal proceedings. Despite the potential importance of earwitness testimonies, relatively few studies have investigated the performance of earwitnesses as opposed to eyewitnesses (Wilding, Cook, & Davis, 2000; Yarmey, Yarmey, & Todd, 2008). The majority of research regarding earwitnesses has focused on person identification based on vocal information (Hollien, 1990; Öhman, Eriksson, & Granhag, 2011). Memory for environmental sounds and sound events has on the other hand been minimally investigated (Marcell, Malatanos, Leahy, & Comeaux, 2007), even though memory for environmental sounds has been of great importance in several well-known criminal cases, such as the kidnapping of millionaire Fabian Bengtsson (Brink, 2005) and the Bladerunner shooting in 2013 (Laing, 2014).

Auditory memory

Environmental sounds are naturally occurring non-speech, non-musical sounds (Gygi & Shafiro, 2007), such as a ball bouncing, a glass braking, or a barking dog. Environmental sounds comprise a broad range of semantic and acoustic complexity, and are often highly familiar (Gygi & Shafiro, 2007; Marcell et al., 2007). In authentic sound environments, the acoustic stimuli encompass several intermixed sounds (Gygi & Shafiro, 2007). Such auditory scenes are called environmental sound events, and are defined as sequences of closely grouped and temporally related environmental sounds that tell a story or establish a sense of place (McAdams & Bigand, 1993). Previous research has indicated that listeners perceive environmental sound events as familiar events or situations, that the course of events is understandable, and that emotional sound events elicit emotional reactions (Marcell et al., 2007).

Studies exploring memory abilities generally report that recall and recognition performance differs between modalities (Lawrence, Cobb, & Beard, 1979). Memory for pictures has been reported to be extraordinary accurate and robust (Cohen, Horowitz, & Wolfe, 2009), while memory for auditory stimuli has repeatedly been reported to be well below memory for pictures (Cohen et al., 2009; Snyder & Gregg, 2011). When asked to distinguish between pairs of pictures where one had been previously presented, participants were very accurate in identifying the previously presented pictures compared to the same task performed with environmental sounds (Cohen et al., 2009). In addition to modality differences in memory, Cohen et al. (2009) and Miller and Tanis (1971) reported differing memory performance within the auditory modality: spoken language was recognized more accurately than environmental sounds.

Studies utilizing recall tasks report that the amount of recalled sounds range from 23% (Crutcher & Beer, 2011) to 95% (Paivio, Philipchalk, & Rowe, 1975) of all presented environmental sounds. Percentage of recalled items depends on the duration of delay, the number of stimuli, the individual task, and whether the encoding was incidental or intentional. Most studies generally report around a 50% recall among adult participants (Bartlett, 1977; Ferrara, Puff, Gioia, & Richards, 1978; Philipchalk & Rowe, 1971; Thompson & Paivio, 1994). Recognition tests have also reported an array of results, ranging from a hit rate of 0.38 (Clark, Stamm, Sussman, & Weitz, 1974) to 0.89 (Zucco, 2003), with an average rate of 0.70 in adults (Cycowicz & Friedman, 1999; Lawrence & Banks, 1973; Lawrence et al., 1979; Opitz, Mecklinger, & Friederici, 2000; Röder & Rösler, 2003; Schulze, Vargha-Khadem, & Mishkin, 2012).

Several gaps in the current research literature regarding auditory memory and earwitnesses are evident. Long retention intervals between encoding and questioning are described as a specific practical challenge in crime investigation (Deffenbacher, Bornstein, McGorty, & Penrod, 2008). Most previous studies test memory performance the same day as encoding, often only minutes after initial presentation of the stimuli. There are very few studies that have utilized longer delays of up to one week (Huss & Weaver, 1996; Lawrence et al., 1979). These studies report declining memory performance with increased duration, and this problem may be greater for young children than for older children and adults (Goodman & Melinder, 2007). According to the Norwegian Criminal Regulation, penal code 239 § 4, interviews of witnesses should be conducted within two weeks after a criminal incident has been reported. The interviewing of the witnesses in the present study was hence conducted after two weeks in order to investigate memorability for sounds in accordance with the Norwegian regulations. Furthermore, cognitive psychology has informed us that memory retention markedly decreases the first period after encoding, followed by stabilization the next weeks (Murre & Dros, 2015). The present study therefore utilized a two-week delay in order to investigate children's stable memory performance over time.

Furthermore, only a single study by Marcell et al. (2007) report the use of environmental sound events as opposed to individual and incoherent environmental sounds. Logically, one would assume that the use of environmental sound events instead of individual environmental sounds has higher ecological validity and ability to generalize to criminal incidents. Encoding, organization, and memories for individual and incoherent environmental sounds might be different than memories for coherent, cohesive, and informative environmental sound events.

Last, another gap in the current research literature is the evident lack of child participants. A small number of studies have utilized child participants and compared the proficiency of different age groups for remembering voices and conversations (Ling & Coombe, 2005; Öhman et al., 2011; Öhman, Eriksson, & Granhag, 2013a; Öhman, Eriksson, & Granhag, 2013b). Because very few previous studies have utilized child participants, a two-week delay, and environmental sound events, the present study aims to investigate children's memory for environmental sound events after a two-week delay.

The influence of emotions on memory

In a witness context, the stimuli to be remembered are often highly emotional in nature, rendering it important to investigate how earwitness testimonies of neutral material compare to the memory of emotional stimuli. Numerous studies have yielded robust results indicating that emotional memories are more detailed and more resilient to forgetting than neutral memories (Bradley & Lang, 2000; Mirandola, Toffalini, Grassano, Cornoldi, & Melinder, 2014; Putman, van Honk, Kessels, Mulder, & Koppeschaar, 2004). This is especially true for central aspects of an event, compared to more peripheral information (Baugerud & Melinder, 2012; Kim, Vossel, & Gamer, 2013; for a review see Christianson, 1992). When asked to either recall or recognize previously presented pictures, arousing pictures are remembered better than neutral pictures after both short delays (Bradley, Greenwald, Petry, & Lang, 1992; Kensinger & Schacter, 2006) and long delays of up to one year (Bradley et al., 1992; Bywaters, Andrade, & Turpin, 2004). The advantage of arousing material has also been found when participants were asked to recognize previously presented words (Bayer, Sommer, & Schacht, 2011). Interestingly, in a study by Bradley and Lang (2000), the memory advantage of emotional stimuli was also reported for auditory material. After listening to 60 environmental sounds, participants performed an incidental recall task following a short delay. Sounds categorized as highly emotional were recalled significantly better than neutral sounds (Bradley & Lang, 2000). There are few studies that examine the relation between emotional sounds and memory, and no previous studies have investigated the effect of emotionality on memory for environmental sound events.

Emotional material is arousing in nature and can both have a positive and negative valence, distinguishing it from neutral or non-emotional material (Brainerd, Holliday, Reyna, Yang, & Toglia, 2010). Memory tests comparing positive and negative material seldom report a differing memory performance (Bayer et al., 2011; Bradley et al., 1992; Bradley & Lang, 2000; Kensinger & Schacter, 2006). Evidently, it is not stimuli valence, but degree of arousal that mainly influences memorability. Traumatic events seem to be the most vivid, detailed, and clear memories of all, probably because these events elicit the greatest degree of arousal. This superior memorability of traumatic events is also evident in children (Peterson & Whalen, 2001).

Development of episodic memory

A multitude of studies have reported increased long-term memory abilities with increased age (Eysenck, 2009b; Fivush, 2002). These results have been confirmed both in and outside of the laboratory setting (Gathercole, 1998; Hanten et al., 2007; Howe, 2006). When studying interviews for medical emergencies, younger children performed poorer than older children (Peterson & Whalen, 2001). Similar results have been reported when interviewing alleged sex abuse victims (Lamb, Sternberg, & Esplin, 2000). There are several differences between memory abilities of young preschool-aged children compared to older school-aged children (Bruck, Ceci, & Hembrooke, 1998; Goodman & Melinder, 2007). In general, older children report more information and more details than younger children (Hanten et al., 2007; Howe, 2006; Lamb et al., 2000), older children recount more accurate narratives of previous experiences (Nelson & Fivush, 2004; Peterson & Whalen, 2001), and forgetting proceeds more rapidly in younger compared to older children (Lamb et al., 2000). When asked to recall a previous experience, older children's testimonies are more complete and consist of the core components: who, when, where, and what (Qin, Quas, Redlich, & Goodman, 2002; Reese, 2009).

In the present study, participants were divided into two age groups: 7–8 years and 9–11 years. The rationale behind this specific divide is based on research indicating that the memory of children younger than approximately 7 years is qualitatively different from the memory of adults, while the memory of children older than 7 years is roughly similar to adult's memory (Howe, 2006; Lamb et al., 2000; Peterson & Whalen, 2001). Because memory for sounds is evidently poorer than memory for pictures (Cohen et al., 2009; Snyder & Gregg, 2011), we assumed that this general divide in memory around 7 years of age would be somewhat postponed to later ages. The average 6-year-old would for example have major difficulty recalling even a single sound even though the same child would be proficient at recalling pictures. We hence minimally increased the age of the youngest age group, resulting in one group aged 7–8 years and one group aged 9–11 years.

ACKNOWLEDGEMENTS

We thank Svein Magnussen for valuable help with the manuscript. The study was supported by grants from the Norwegian Directorate for Children, Youth, and Family Affairs (13/60525).

REFERENCES

Augusti, E. M., & Melinder, A. (2013). The effect of neutral and negative colour photographs on children's item directed forgetting. *European Journal of Developmental Psychology, 10*, 378–391.

Bartlett, J. C. (1977). Remembering environmental sounds: The role of verbalization at input. *Memory & Cognition, 5*, 404–414.

Baugerud, G. A., & Melinder, A. (2012). Maltreated children's memory of stressful removals from their biological parents. *Applied Cognitive Psychology, 26*, 261–270.

Bayer, M., Sommer, W., & Schacht, A. (2011). Emotional words impact the mind but not the body: Evidence from pupillary responses. *Psychophysiology, 48*, 1553–1561.

Bernstein, D. A., Penner, L. A., Clarke-Stewart, A., & Roy, E. J. (2006). *Psychology* (7 edn). Boston, NY: Houghton Mifflin Company.

Bradley, M. M., Greenwald, M. K., Petry, M. C., & Lang, P. J. (1992). Remembering pictures: Pleasure and arousal in memory. *Journal of Experimental Psychology-Learning Memory and Cognition, 18*, 379–390.

Bradley, M. M., & Lang, P. J. (2000). Affective reactions to acoustic stimuli. *Psychophysiology, 37*, 204–215.

Brainerd, C. J., Holliday, R. E., Reyna, V. F., Yang, Y., & Toglia, M. P. (2010). Developmental reversals in false memory: Effects of emotional valence and arousal. *Journal of Experimental Child Psychology, 107*, 137–154.

Breslin, C. W., & Safer, M. A. (2011). Effects of event valence on long-term memory for two baseball championship games. *Psychological Science, 22*, 1408–1412.

Brink, B. (2005). Glassbilens melodi avslöjade misstänkt kidnappargömma [The ice cream truck's melody revealed suspected kidnapper-hideout]. SvD Nyheter. Retrieved from http://www.svd.se/nyheter/inrikes/ glassbilens-melodi-avslojade-misstankt-kidnappargomma_394847.svd Accessed 15 September 2014.

Brown, R., & Kulik, J. (1977). Flashbulb memories. *Cognition, 5*, 73–99.

Bruck, M., Ceci, S. J., & Hembrooke, H. (1998). Reliability and credibility of young children's reports: From research to policy and practice. *American Psychologist, 53*, 136–151.

Bywaters, M., Andrade, J., & Turpin, G. (2004). Determinants of the vividness of visual imagery: The effects of delayed recall, stimulus affect and individual differences. *Memory, 12*, 479–488.

Christianson, S. A. (1992). Emotional stress and eyewitness memory: A critical review. *Psychological Bulletin, 112*, 284–309.

Clark, M., Stamm, S., Sussman, R., & Weitz, S. (1974). Encoding of auditory stimuli in recognition memory tasks. *Bulletin of the Psychonomic Society, 3*, 177–178.

Cohen, M. A., Horowitz, T. S., & Wolfe, J. M. (2009). Auditory recognition memory is inferior to visual recognition memory. *Proceedings of the National Academy of Sciences of the United States of America, 106*, 6008–6010.

Crutcher, R. J., & Beer, J. M. (2011). An auditory analog of the picture superiority effect. *Memory & Cognition, 39*, 63–74.

Cycowicz, Y. M., & Friedman, D. (1999). The effect of intention to learn novel, environmental sounds on the novelty P3 and old new recognition memory. *Biological Psychology, 50*, 35–60.

Deffenbacher, K. A., Bornstein, B. H., McGorty, E. K., & Penrod, S. D. (2008). Forgetting the once-seen face: Estimating the strength of an eyewitness's memory representation. *Journal of Experimental Psychology, 14*, 139–150.

Eysenck, M. W. (2009a). Eyewitness testimony. In A. Baddeley, M. W. Eysenck, & M. C. Anderson (Eds.), *Memory* (pp. 317–342). Hove, England: Psychology Press.

Eysenck, M. W. (2009b). Memory in childhood. In A. Baddeley, M. W. Eysenck, & M. C. Anderson (Eds.), *Memory* (pp. 267–291). Hove, England: Psychology Press.

Ferrara, R. A., Puff, C. R., Gioia, G. A., & Richards, J. M. (1978). Effects of incidental and intentional learning instructions on the free recall of naturalistic sounds. *Bulletin of the Psychonomic Society, 11*, 353–355.

Fivush, R. (2002). Event memory in early childhood. In N. Cowan (Ed.), *The development of memory in childhood* (pp. 139–161). Hove, England: Psychology Press.

Gathercole, S. E. (1998). The development of memory. *Journal of Child Psychology and Psychiatry, and Allied Disciplines, 39*, 3–27.

Goodman, G. S., & Melinder, A. (2007). Child witness research and forensic interviews of young children: A review. *Legal and Criminological Psychology, 12*, 1–19.

Gygi, B., & Shafiro, V. (2007). General functions and specific applications of environmental sound research. *Frontiers in Bioscience, 12*, 3152–3166.

Hamann, S. (2001). Cognitive and neural mechanisms of emotional memory. *Trends in Cognitive Sciences, 5*, 394–400.

Hanten, G., Li, X. Q., Chapman, S. B., Swank, P., Gamino, J., Roberson, G., & Levin, H. S. (2007). Development of verbal selective learning. *Developmental Neuropsychology, 32*, 585–596.

Hollien, H. F. (1990). *The acoustics of crime: The new science of forensic phonetics*. New York, NY: Plenum Press.

Howe, M. L. (2006). Developmentally invariant dissociations in children's true and false memories: Not all relatedness is created equal. *Child Development, 77*, 1112–1123.

Howe, M. L. (2007). Children's emotional false memories. *Psychological Science, 18*, 856–860.

Hudson, J. A., & Fivush, R. (1991). As time goes by: Sixth graders remember a kindergarten experience. *Applied Cognitive Psychology, 5*, 347–360.

Huss, M. T., & Weaver, K. A. (1996). Effect of modality in earwitness identification: Memory for verbal and nonverbal auditory stimuli presented in two contexts. *Journal of General Psychology, 123*, 277–287.

Ihlebæk, C., Løve, T., Eilertsen, D. E., & Magnussen, S. (2003). Memory for a staged criminal event witnessed live and on video. *Memory, 11*, 319–327. Kensinger, E. A., Garoff-Eaton, R. J., & Schacter, D. L. (2007). Effects of emotion on memory specificity: Memory trade-offs elicited by negative visually arousing stimuli. *Journal of Memory and Language, 56*, 575–591.

Kensinger, E. A., & Schacter, D. L. (2006). Amygdala activity is associated with the successful encoding of item, but not source, information for positive and negative stimuli. *Journal of Neuroscience, 26*, 2564–2570.

Kim, J. S.-C., Vossel, G., & Gamer, M. (2013). Effects of emotional context on memory for details: The role of attention. *Plos One, 8*, 1–16.

Kleinsmith, L. J., & Kaplan, S. (1963). Paired-associate learning as a function of arousal and interpolated interval. *Journal of Experimental Psychology, 65*, 190–193.

Laing, A. (2014). Oscar Pistorius murder trial: Witness heard argument before shots. The Telegraph. Retrieved from http://www.telegraph.co.uk/news/worldnews/oscar-pistorius/10675289/Oscar-Pistorius-murder-trial-Witness-heard-argument-before-shots.html

Lamb, M. E., Sternberg, K. J., & Esplin, P. W. (2000). Effects of age and delay on the amount of information provided by alleged sex abuse victims in investigative interviews. Child Development, 71, 1586–1596.

Lang, P. J. (1980). Behavioral treatment and bio-behavioral assessment. In J. B. Sidowski, J. H. Johnson, & T. A. Williams (Eds.), *Technology in mental health care delivery systems* (pp. 119–167). Norwood, NY: Ablex.

Lawrence, D. M., & Banks, W. P. (1973). Accuracy of recognition memory for common sounds. *Bulletin of the Psychonomic Society, 1*, 298–300. Lawrence, D. M., Cobb, N. J., & Beard, J. I. (1979). Comparison of accuracy in auditory and tactile recognition memory for environmental stimuli. *Perceptual and Motor Skills, 48*, 63–66.

Ling, J., & Coombe, A. (2005). Age effects in earwitness recall of a novel conversation. *Perceptual and Motor Skills, 100*, 774–776.

List, J. A. (1986). Age and schematic differences in the reliability of eyewitness testimony. *Developmental Psychology, 22*, 50–57.

Marcell, M., Malatanos, M., Leahy, C., & Comeaux, C. (2007). Identifying, rating, and remembering environmental sound events. *Behavior Research Methods, 39*, 561–569.

McAdams, S., & Bigand, E. (1993). Introduction to auditory cognition. In S. McAdams, & E. Bigand (Eds.), *Thinking in sound: The cognitive psychology of human audition* (pp. 1–8). Oxford, England: Oxford University Press.

Miller, J. D., & Tanis, D. C. (1971). Recognition memory for common sounds. *Psychonomic Science, 23*, 307–308.

Mirandola, C., Toffalini, E., Grassano, M., Cornoldi, C., & Melinder, A. (2014). Inferential false memories of events: Negative consequences protect from distortions when the events are free from further elaboration. *Memory, 22*, 451–461.

Murre, J. M. J., & Dros, J. (2015). Replication and analysis of Ebbinghaus' forgetting curve. *Plos One, 10*, 1–23.

Music Technology Group of Universitat Pompeu Fabra (2012). [Online database]. Retrieved from freesound.org.

Nelson, K., & Fivush, R. (2004). The emergence of autobiographical memory: A social cultural developmental theory. *Psychological Review, 111*, 486–511. Öhman, L., Eriksson, A., & Granhag, P. A. (2011). Overhearing the planning of a crime: Do adults outperform children as earwitnesses? *Journal of Police and Criminal Psychology, 26*, 118–127.

Öhman, L., Eriksson, A., & Granhag, P. A. (2013a). Enhancing adult's and children's earwitness memory: Examining three types of interviews. *Psychiatry, Psychology and Law, 20*, 216–229.

Öhman, L., Eriksson, A., & Granhag, P. A. (2013b). Angry voices from the past and present: Effects on adult's and children's earwitness memory. *Journal of Investigative Psychology and Offender Profiling, 10*, 57–70.

Opitz, B., Mecklinger, A., & Friederici, A. D. (2000). Functional asymmetry of human prefrontal cortex: Encoding and retrieval of verbally and nonverbally coded information. *Learning & Memory, 7*, 85–96.

Paivio, A., Philipchalk, R., & Rowe, E. J. (1975). Free and serial recall of pictures, sounds, and words. *Memory & Cognition, 3*, 586–590.

Parkin, A. J. (2002). The development of procedural and declarative memory. In N. Cowan (Ed.), *The development of memory in childhood* (pp. 113–137). Hove, England: Psychology Press.

Peterson, C., & Whalen, N. (2001). Five years later: Children's memory for medical emergencies. *Applied Cognitive Psychology, 15*, 7–24.

Philipchalk, R. P., & Rowe, E. J. (1971). Sequential and nonsequential memory for verbal and nonverbal auditory stimuli. *Journal of Experimental Psychology, 91*, 341–343.

Putman, P., van Honk, J., Kessels, R. P. C., Mulder, M., & Koppeschaar, H. P. F. (2004). Salivary cortisol and short and long-term memory for emotional faces in healthy young women. *Psychoneuroendocrinology, 29*, 953–960.

Qin, J., Quas, J. A., Redlich, A. D., & Goodman, G. S. (2002). Children's eyewitness testimony: Memory development in the legal context. In N. Cowan (Ed.), *The development of memory in childhood* (pp. 301–341). Hove, England: Psychology Press.

Reese, E. (2009). The development of autobiographical memory: Origins and consequences. In P. Bauer (Ed.), *Advances in child development and behavior* (pp. 145–200). San Diego, CA: Elsevier Academic Press Inc.

Röder, B., & Rösler, F. (2003). Memory for environmental sounds in sighted, congenitally blind and late blind adults: Evidence for crossmodal compensation. *International Journal of Psychophysiology, 50*, 27–39.

Schulze, K., Vargha-Khadem, F., & Mishkin, M. (2012). Test of a motor theory of long-term auditory memory. *Proceedings of the National Academy of Sciences of the United States of America, 109*, 7121–7125.

Siegler, R. S. (1991). *Children's thinking*. Upper Saddle River, NJ: Prentice Hall. Snyder, J. S., & Gregg, M. K. (2011). Memory for sound, with an ear toward hearing in complex auditory scenes. *Attention, Perception, & Psycho-physics*, 1993–2007. Thompson, V. A., & Paivio, A. (1994). Memory for pictures and sounds: Independence of auditory and visual codes. *Canadian Journal of Experimental Psychology, 48*, 380–398.

Wilding, J., Cook, S., & Davis, J. (2000). Sound familiar? *The Psychologist, 13*, 558–562.

Yarmey, A. D., Yarmey, M. J., & Todd, L. (2008). Frances McGehee (1912–2004): The first earwitness researcher. *Perceptual and Motor Skills, 106*, 387–394.

Zucco, G. M. (2003). Anomalies in cognition: Olfactory memory. *European Psychologist, 8*, 77–86.

Correspondence to: Annika Melinder, Cognitive Developmental Research Unit (EKUP), Department of Psychology, University of Oslo, Norway.
E-mail: a.m.d.melinder@psykologi.uio.no

Appendix B

3) Grekin E.R. & Ayna, D. (2012). Waterpipe smoking among college students in the United States: A review of the literature. *Journal of American College Health,* **60(3), 244-249.**

Abstract

Objective: To review the literature on college student waterpipe use with a focus on undergraduates in the United States.

Participants: Undergraduate students.

Methods: Studies were accessed using the databases PubMed, MEDLINE, PsycINFO, and Academic Search Premier. Searches included combinations of the following keywords: "waterpipe," "hookah," "shisha," "nargila," "argileh," "hubble bubble," "college," "university," and "student."

Results: Results demonstrate that approximately 1 in 5 American college students report past-year waterpipe use. Results also suggest that there are a number of established correlates of waterpipe smoking, including male gender, Arab ethnicity, cigarette smoking, and the belief that waterpipe smoking is less harmful than cigarette smoking.

Conclusions: Despite its harmful health effects, waterpipe smoking is quite common among college students. Future research with better methodologies and theoretical frameworks are needed to advance the field.

Keywords: *college, hookah, review, student, university, waterpipe*

Dr Grekin and Ms Ayna are with the Department of Psychology at Wayne State University in Detroit, Michigan.

Waterpipe use (alternatively called hookah, shisha, nargila, argileh, or hubble bubble) is a 400year-old form of smoking in which tobacco is heated with charcoal and its smoke is passed through water prior to inhalation. The typical waterpipe contains a "head" filled with tobacco, a glass bowl filled with water, and a hose for inhaling or "puffing." The waterpipe has traditionally been associated with Middle Eastern cultures; however, in recent years, its use has spread to North America and Europe. Like all forms of tobacco use, waterpipe smoking increases the risk for a variety of adverse health outcomes. More specifically, its use has been associated with esophageal cancer,[1,2] chromosomal aberrations,[3] decreased pulmonary and cardiovascular function,[4,5] low birth weight,[6] infertility,[7] dental problems,[8,9] and infectious diseases.[10,11] Waterpipe smokers have also been known to report symptoms of tobacco dependence, including craving,[12,13] and repeated quit attempts.[14] However, despite these harmful health outcomes, there has been a distinct increase in the popularity of waterpipe use, particularly in the Middle East where, in some cultures, lifetime prevalence rates are as high as 70%.[12,15]

Waterpipe smoking is particularly prevalent among university students and other young adults.[16,17] There are several factors that could account for this. First, waterpipe tobacco is relatively inexpensive, a fact touted by many waterpipe forums and Web sites. Second, unlike other tobacco products, waterpipe tobacco can be purchased online, making it particularly accessible to university students, who are likely to have easy Internet access. Moreover, many waterpipe Web sites do not verify age, a fact that may attract underage smokers. Third, waterpipe smoking has become integrated into the "social scene" on many university campuses. There has been a notable rise in the number "hookah bars" and "waterpipe cafes" near college campuses,[18] and many students cite socialization as a primary motivation for their waterpipe use.[19] Fourth, in the 1990s, a new form of sweetened waterpipe tobacco called Maassel was introduced. Maassel is produced in a variety of flavors (fruit, toffee, coffee, etc) and tends to be more appealing to young adults than the unflavored tobacco traditionally used in the waterpipe.[12] Finally, many young adults mistakenly believe that waterpipes are safer than cigarettes (ie, that waterpipes contain less nicotine, are not addictive, etc) and that their use does not constitute "smoking."[20]

Although a number of individual studies have documented the prevalence and correlates of waterpipe use among university students, there have been no systematic reviews of this literature. The present article aims to fill this gap by examining (1) the prevalence of waterpipe smoking among college students, (2) demographic correlates of waterpipe smoking, (3) beliefs about waterpipe smoking, and (4) relationships between waterpipe smoking and cigarette smoking. We will also review methodological limitations of existing waterpipe studies and suggest directions for future research.

Methods

Identification of Studies

We conducted a literature search using the databases PubMed, MEDLINE, PsycINFO, and Academic Search Premier. Searches included combinations of the following keywords: "waterpipe," "hookah," "shisha," "nargila," "argileh," "hubble bubble," "college," "university," and "student." Studies that combined data from college students and non–college students in analyses (eg, Maziak et al[21]) were excluded from this review. Studies that focused on graduate or professional students, rather than undergraduates, were also excluded. This review primarily focuses on college students in the United States; however, data from Middle Eastern students are also presented throughout the article for comparison purposes.

We identified 16 studies of college student waterpipe smoking that used 14 different samples. All 16 studies had been published since 2001. Seven of the 16 studies examined waterpipe smoking among college students in the United States or Europe[16,17,22–26] (Table 1). The remaining 9 studies examined waterpipe smoking among college students in the Middle East[27–35] (Table 2).

Appendix B

TABLE 1. Studies Examining Waterpipe Use Among College Students in the United States or Europe

Authors	Sample	Study design	% Reporting lifetime smoking	% Reporting past-year smoking	% Reporting past-month smoking
Primack et al[22]	8,745 students at 8 universities	Online survey	29.5	—	7.2
Eissenberg et al[23]	744 freshmen in introductory psychology courses	Online survey	—	—	20.0
Grekin and Ayna[16]	602 students in psychology courses	Online survey	15.1	12.4	—
Jackson and Aveyard[17]	937 students in randomly selected courses	Paper-and-pencil survey	37.9	—	21.1
Primack et al[24]	3,600 randomly selected students	Online survey	41.0	30.6	9.5
Smith-Simone et al[25*]	411 freshmen at a private university	Online survey	28.0	—	15.3
Smith et al[26*]	411 freshmen at a private university	Online survey	28.0	—	15.3

Note. Studies marked with an asterisk (*) use the same sample.

TABLE 2. Studies Examining Waterpipe Use Among College Students in the Middle East

Authors	Sample	Study design	% Reporting lifetime smoking	% Reporting past-year smoking	% Reporting past-month smoking
Azab et al[28]	548 students at 4 universities in Jordan	Interviewer-administered questionnaire	61.1	—	42.7
Roohafza et al[35]	233 university students in Iran	Interviewer-administered questionnaire	—	—	19.2
Mandil et al[34]	1,057 university students in the United Arab Emirates	Paper-and-pencil survey	—	—	5.6
Chaaya et al[33]	416 students at American University of Beirut	Interviewer-administered questionnaire	43.0	—	28.3
Maziak et al[19*]	587 university students in Syria	Interviewer-administered questionnaire	45.3	—	14.7
Maziak et al[21*]	587 university students in Syria	Interviewer-administered questionnaire	45.3	—	14.7
Tamim et al[29]	1,964 students attending 5 universities in Lebanon	Paper-and-pencil survey	—	—	32.4
Tamim et al[27]	553 students attending 4 universities in Lebanon	Paper-and-pencil survey	—	—	43.3

Note. Studies marked with an asterisk (*) use the same sample. One study cited in the review (Labib et al[32]) did not include a comparison group of nonsmokers and, therefore, prevalence rates from this sample could not be included in the table.

Results

Prevalence of Waterpipe Use

Among studies conducted in the United States or Europe, *lifetime* waterpipe smoking rates ranged from 15.1% to 41.0% ($M = 30.3\%$, $SD = 10.1\%$), *past-year* smoking rates ranged from 12.4% to 30.6% ($M = 21.5\%$, $SD = 12.9\%$), and *past-month* smoking rates ranged from 7.2% to 21.1% ($M = 14.6\%$, $SD = 6.2\%$; Table 1). Of the 9 studies examining waterpipe use among Middle Eastern college students, *lifetime* smoking rates ranged from 43.0% to 61.1% ($M = 49.8\%$, $SD = 9.9\%$). None of the Middle Eastern studies reported *past year* smoking rates. *Past-month* or *current* smoking rates ranged from 5.6% to 43.3% ($M = 26.6\%$, $SD = 14.2\%$; Table 2).

Several conclusions can be drawn from these prevalence data. First, rates of waterpipe use in the United States and Europe are quite high, with approximately 1 in 5 college students reporting past-year waterpipe smoking. In comparison, approximately 30% of college students report past-year cigarette smoking,[36] suggesting that although cigarette smoking remains the most popular form of tobacco use among American college students, waterpipe smoking is a close second. Second, the limited data that are available suggest that rates of waterpipe smoking among Middle Eastern college students are substantially higher than rates among Western samples, with approximately 1 in 4 Middle Eastern college students reporting waterpipe use during the past month.

Gender Differences in Waterpipe Use

With the exception of Primack et al,[24] all of the studies in this review found that males were more likely than females to report waterpipe use.[16,17,22,23,25-35] These gender differences were particularly pronounced when examining current, as opposed to lifetime, use. For example, Smith-Simone et al[25] conducted a cross-sectional Internet survey of 411 college freshmen and found that, among females, 77.4% were never smokers, 13.6% were ever smokers, and 9.0% were current smokers. In contrast, among males, 67.0% were never smokers, 11.8% were ever smokers, and 21.2% were current smokers. Similarly, Maziak et al[30] conducted interviews with 587 randomly selected university students in Syria and found that 62.6% of men and 29.8% of women reported lifetime waterpipe use, whereas 25.5% of men and 4.9% of women reported past-month waterpipe use. It should be noted that, in the United States, there are few reported gender differences in cigarette smoking among college samples.[37] Thus, the factors that make waterpipe use more popular among males than females cannot be generalized to all tobacco products.

Ethnic/Racial Differences in Waterpipe Use

Two of the studies in this review found that students of Arab descent, attending college in the United States or Europe, were significantly more likely than their non-Arab peers to report waterpipe use. Specifically, Grekin and Ayna[16] found that 62% of Arab students, as opposed to 11% of nonArab students, had used a waterpipe in their lifetime. Similarly, Jackson and Aveyard[17] found that 81.3% of Arab students had tried a waterpipe, as compared with 38.1% of white students, 26.1% of black students, and 40.9% of Asian students. No other studies have compared waterpipe use among Arab versus non-Arab students outside of the Middle East.

All of the remaining American studies found that black students were less likely than students of other races to use a waterpipe.[22-26] For example, Primack et al[22] found that 13.3% of black students had smoked a waterpipe as compared with 31.4% of white students, 23.2% of Asian students, and 33.2% of students who identified as "other" or "mixed." Similarly, Eissenberg et al[23] found that 35.5% of white

Appendix B

students, 9.1% of black students, and 33.7% of students identifying as "other" reported past-30-day waterpipe use. These data are consistent with the broader literature on race and substance use, which suggests that black college students are less likely than their white counterparts to smoke cigarettes or to use alcohol.[37,38]

Beliefs About Waterpipe Smoking

Five studies have examined beliefs about waterpipe smoking among American and European college students.[17,23–26] Overall, these studies suggest that college students perceive waterpipe use to be less harmful and more socially acceptable than cigarette use. For example, Smith-Simone et al[25] conducted a cross-sectional Internet survey of 411 freshmen at a private university and found that students believed waterpipe smoking to be less addicting and more socially acceptable than cigarette smoking. Students also believed that they were more likely to be influenced by friends to use waterpipe as opposed to cigarettes in the next year and that friends looked "cooler" when using waterpipes versus cigarettes. Using the same sample, Smith et al[26] found that 37% of participants perceived waterpipe use to be less harmful than cigarette use. In addition, current (odds ratio [OR] = 6.77) and lifetime (OR = 3.19) waterpipe smokers were more likely than never smokers to perceive waterpipe use as less harmful than cigarette use, suggesting that beliefs about waterpipe harmfulness may play a role in the initiation and/or maintenance of smoking.

Primack et al[24] sent an online survey to 3,600 randomly selected university students as part of the National College Health Assessment (the researchers paid to have waterpipe questions added to their university's version of the survey). Data from the 647 students who responded indicated that more than half of the sample (52%) believed waterpipe smoking to be less addictive than cigarette smoking. In addition, multivariate models revealed associations between past-year waterpipe use (yes/no) and (1) low perceived harm (believing waterpipe smoking is less harmful than cigarette smoking; OR = 2.54), (2) low perceived addictiveness (believing waterpipe smoking is less addictive than cigarette smoking; OR = 4.64), (3) perception of high social acceptability (believing that waterpipe smoking is socially acceptable among peers; OR = 20.00), and (4) high perception of popularity (believing that a large percentage of college students have smoked a waterpipe; OR = 4.72).

Eissenberg et al[23] conducted an online survey of waterpipe use among 744 college freshmen enrolled in introductory psychology courses. Compared with never smokers, those who had smoked in the past month were more likely to believe that (1) waterpipe smoking is socially acceptable among peers (OR = 3.71), (2) waterpipe smoking makes peers look "cool" (OR = 2.47), (3) waterpipes are less harmful than cigarettes (OR = .31), and (4) waterpipes are less addicting than cigarettes (OR = .65).

Finally, Jackson and Aveyard administered a crosssectional paper-and-pencil questionnaire to 937 students in randomly selected courses at Birmingham University in the United Kingdom. They then sent a follow-up survey to the 75 students who reported at least monthly waterpipe use. Twenty-one of the 75 heavy users responded to the follow-up survey. All but 1 of these heavy users considered waterpipe smoking to be socially acceptable, and 68.4% thought that waterpipe smoking was less harmful than cigarette smoking.

Associations Between Waterpipe Smoking and Cigarette Smoking

Four studies have examined relationships between waterpipe smoking and cigarette smoking among American and European college students, and all 4 have found significant associations between the 2 forms of tobacco use.[16,17,23,24] For example, Eissenberg et al[23] found that past-month waterpipe use was associated with a greater likelihood of having smoked cigarettes (OR = 10.44) and cigars/cigarillos (OR = 6.31). Similarly, Grekin and Ayna[16] found that cigarette users were twice as likely as non–cigarette users to report lifetime waterpipe use. Strong cigarette/waterpipe associations have also been found in studies of Middle Eastern college students.[29–31]

To date, however, no studies have longitudinally assessed cigarette versus waterpipe trajectories. Thus, it is unclear whether cigarette use typically precedes or follows waterpipe use or whether waterpipe use is more frequent or intense among students who simultaneously use cigarettes.

It is also important to note that, although cigarette smoking is a robust correlate of waterpipe use, a substantial proportion of waterpipe users do not smoke cigarettes. For example, Primack et al[24] found that 35.4% of students who had smoked a waterpipe in the past year had never smoked a cigarette. Similarly, Jackson and Aveyard[17] found that 65% of regular (at least monthly) waterpipe smokers had never smoked cigarettes. It is not clear what factors are associated with the exclusive use of waterpipe (ie, waterpipe use in the absence of cigarette smoking). However, preliminary data suggest that the 2 forms of tobacco have different correlates. For example, male gender seems to be predictive of waterpipe, but not cigarette use.[37] Similarly, club and intramural athletic participation appears to protect against cigarette smoking, but not waterpipe smoking.[22] These data suggest that waterpipes and cigarettes are viewed differently by different groups of people; however, more data are needed to delineate common and unique risk factors for the 2 types of tobacco products.

Comment

Future Directions/Limitations

The literature on waterpipe smoking among college students has grown rapidly over the past 10 years. However, there are still relatively few studies in this area and many potential waterpipe smoking predictors have not been examined (eg, peer smoking, smoking expectancies, smoking motives, alcohol/drug use comorbidity, anxiety/depression/stress, etc). In addition, there are several methodological limitations that limit our ability to draw conclusions about college student waterpipe use. First, most existing waterpipe studies use data from convenience (eg, introductory psychology students), rather than representative samples. In addition, the few studies that attempt to recruit representative samples suffer from low response rates. For example, Primack et al[24] sent an online survey to 3,600 randomly selected university students as part of the National College Health Assessment; however, only 18.6% of recruited students completed the survey. Notably, there are often important differences between survey responders and nonresponders, and it is, therefore, difficult to generalize from existing data to the broader population of college student waterpipe smokers. Nationally representative studies and representative single campus studies are needed to accurately examine the prevalence and correlates of waterpipe smoking.

Second, all existing student waterpipe studies are crosssectional, rather than longitudinal or prospective. As a result, it is unclear which variables precede and predict the development of waterpipe use. In addition, it is impossible to draw conclusions about typical trajectories of watepipe use (eg, does waterpipe use tend to peak during adolescence and decline throughout the third decade of life, like alcohol and drug use?).

Third, most student waterpipe smoking data are based on online surveys, rather than interviews or laboratory tasks. Although online surveys are ideal for assessing certain, standardized, correlates of waterpipe use (eg, personality, beliefs, attitudes, demographic information), there are many substance use correlates that cannot be adequately measured with surveys, such as neuropsychological functioning, laboratory based impulsivity, and *Diagnostic and Statistical Manual of Mental Disorder* diagnoses.

Fourth, no college student waterpipe studies have examined waterpipe dependence, as opposed to simple quantity and frequency of use. Waterpipe dependence is a fuzzy concept that is difficult to define due to the social/intermittent nature of waterpipe smoking and its high comorbidity with cigarette use. However, several researchers have proposed methods of characterizing waterpipe dependence[39] and at least 1 factor-analyzed scale has been published.[40] Thus, it would be useful for future studies to explore characteristics of waterpipe dependence among student populations.

Fifth, very few college student studies have examined interactions between potential predictors of waterpipe use. It would be useful to know whether relationships between independent variables and waterpipe use differ depending on gender, ethnicity, age, personality, and a variety of other variables.

Sixth, no studies have explored the role of culture in the initiation and maintenance of waterpipe use. More specifically, although one set of studies has examined waterpipe smoking among Middle Eastern students and another set of studies has examined smoking among Western students, no studies have explored differential predictors and correlates of waterpipe smoking among students in Middle Eastern versus Western cultures. This type of international data would provide information about the unique cultural contexts that support or inhibit waterpipe use.

Finally, the literature on college student watepipe smoking is decidedly atheoretical. Theoretical frameworks that explain current empirical findings and suggest directions for future research would add greatly to the field.

Despite these limitations, the existing literature points to a variety of potential waterpipe smoking interventions for college students. For example, it is clear that college students as a whole, and waterpipe smokers in particular, believe that waterpipe use is less harmful than cigarette use. Providing information about the harmful health effects of waterpipe tobacco (eg, through college counseling centers, peer mentors, student orientation sessions, etc) may help to decrease its use. It may also be useful to develop targeted prevention/intervention programs for those most likely to smoke waterpipe (ie, males, cigarette smokers, Arab students in the United States, etc). Finally, at the societal level, efforts are needed to decrease the accessibility of waterpipe tobacco to underage smokers by monitoring online waterpipe tobacco availability and waterpipe sales to underage smokers.

Conclusions

Despite its associated health risks, the prevalence of waterpipe smoking among college students is quite high, with approximately 1 in 5 students reporting past-year use. There are also a number of established correlates of waterpipe smoking, including male gender, Arab ethnicity, cigarette smoking, and the belief that waterpipe smoking is less harmful than cigarette smoking. Though intriguing, the existing literature on college student waterpipe smoking is small and future studies using different methodologies and better theoretical frameworks are needed to advance our knowledge in this area.

Note

For comments and further information, address correspondence to Emily R. Grekin, PhD, Department of Psychology, Wayne State University, 5057 Woodward Avenue, 7th floor, Detroit, MI 48202, USA (e-mail: grekine@wayne.edu).

References

1. Gunaid AA, Sumairi AA, Shidrawi RG, et al. Oesophageal and gastric carcinoma in the Republic of Yemen. *Br J Cancer.* 1995;71:409–410.
2. Nasrollahzadeh D, Kamangar F, Aghcheli K, et al. Opium, tobacco, and alcohol use in relation to oesophageal squamous cell carcinoma in a high-risk area of Iran. *Br J Cancer.* 2008;98:1857–1963.

3. Yadav JS, Thakur S. Genetic risk assessment in hookah smokers. *Cytobios.* 2000;101:101–113.
4. Kiter G, Ucan ES, Ceylan E, Kilinc O. Water-pipe smoking and pulmonary functions. *Respir Med.* 2000;94:891–894.
5. Mutairi SS, Shihab-Eldeen AA, Mojiminiyi OA, Anwar AA. Comparative analysis of the effects of hubble-bubble (sheesha) and cigarette smoking on respiratory and metabolic parameters in hubble-bubble and cigarette smokers. *Respirology.* 2006;11:449–455.
6. Nuwayhid IA, Yamout B, Azar G, Al Kouatly Kambris M. Narghile (hubble-bubble) smoking, low birth weight, and other pregnancy outcomes. *Am J Epidemiol.* 1998;148:375–383.
7. Inhorn MC, Buss KA. Ethnography, epidemiology, and infertility in Egypt. *Soc Sci Med.* 1994;3:671 686.
8. Dar-Odeh NS, Abu-Hammad OA. Narghile smoking and its adverse health consequences: a literature review. *Br Dent J.* 2009;206:571–573.
9. Natto S, Baljoon M, Bergstrom J. Tobacco smoking and periodontal health in a Saudi Arabian population. *J Periodontol.* 2005;76:1919–1926.
10. Munckhof WJ, Konstantinos A, Wamsley M, Mortlock M, Gilpin CA. A cluster of tuberculosis associated with use of marijuana water pipe. *Int J Tuberc Lung Dis.* 2003;7:860–865.
11. Steentoft J, Wittendorf J, Andersen JR. Tuberculosis and water pipes as source of infection. *Ugeskr Laeger.* 2006;198:904–907.
12. Maziak W, Eissenberg T, Ward KD. Patterns of waterpipe use and dependence: implications for intervention development. *Pharmacol Biochem Behav.* 2005;80:173–179.
13. Maziak W, Rastam S, Ibrahim I, Ward K, Shihadeh A, Eissenberg T. CO exposure, puff topography, and subjective effects in waterpipe tobacco smokers. *Nicotine Tob Res.* 2009;11: 806–811.
14. Ward K, Hammal F, VanderWeg M, et al. Are waterpipe users interested in quitting? *Nicotine Tob Res.* 2005;7:149–156.
15. Knishkowy B, Amitai Y. Water-pipe (waterpipe) smoking: an emerging health risk behavior. *Pediatrics.* 2005;116:e113–e119.
16. Grekin ER, Ayna D. Argileh use among college students in the United States: an emerging trend. *J Stud Alcohol Drugs.* 2008;69:472–475.
17. Jackson DJ, Aveyard P. Waterpipe smoking in students: prevalence, risk factors, symptoms of addiction, and smoke intake. Evidence from one British university. *BMC Public Health.* 2008;8:174. doi:10.1186/1471-2458-8-174.
18. Cobb C, Ward K, Maziak W, Shihadeh A, Eissenberg T. Waterpipe tobacco smoking: an emerging health crisis in the United States. *Am J Health Behav.* 2010;34:275–285.
19. Maziak W, Eissenberg T, Rastam S, et al. Beliefs and attitudes related to waterpipe smoking among university students in Syria. *Ann Epidemiol.* 2004;14:646–654.
20. Ward KD, Eissenberg T, Gray JN, Srinivas V, Wilson N, Maziak W. Characteristics of U.S. waterpipe users: a preliminary report. *Nicotine Tob Res.* 2007;9:1339–1346.
21. Maziak W, Rastam S, Eissenberg T, et al. Gender and smoking status based analyses of views regarding waterpipe and cigarette smoking in Aleppo, Syria. *Prev Med.* 2004;38:479–484.
22. Primack BA, Fertman CI, Rice KR, Adachi-Mejia AM, Fine MJ. Waterpipe and cigarette smoking among college athletes in the United States. *J Adolesc Health.* 2010;46:45–51.

23. Eissenberg T, Ward KD, Smith-Simone S, Maziak W. Waterpipe tobacco smoking on a U.S. college campus: prevalence and correlates. *J Adolesc Health.* 2008;42:526–529.
24. Primack BA, Sidani J, Agarwal AA, Shadel WG, Donny EF, Eissenbert TE. Prevalence and associations with waterpipe tobacco smoking among U.S. university students. *Ann Behav Med.* 2008;36:81–86.
25. Smith-Simone SY, Curbow BA, Stillman FA. Differing psychosocial risk profiles of college freshmen waterpipe, cigar and cigarette smokers. *Addict Behav.* 2008;33:1619–1624.
26. Smith SY, Curbow B, Stillman FA. Harm perceptoin of nicotine products in college freshmen. *Nicotine Tob Res.* 2007;9:977–982.
27. Tamim H, Musharrafieh U, Almawi WY. Smoking among adolescents in a developing country. *Aust N Z J Public Health.* 2001;25:185–186.
28. Azab M, Khabour OF, Alkaraki AK, Eissenberg T, Alzoubi KH, Primack BA. Waterpipe tobacco smoking among university students in Jordan. *Nicotine Tob Res.* 2010;12:606–612.
29. Tamim H, Terro A, Kassem H, et al. Tobacco use by university students in Lebanon, 2001. *Addiction.* 2003;98:933–939.
30. Maziak W, Fouad MF, Asfar T, et al. Prevalence and characteristics of narghile smoking among university students in Syria. *Int J Tuberc Lung Dis.* 2004;8:882–889.
31. Maziak W, Hammal F, Rastam S, et al. Characteristics of cigarette smoking and quitting among university students in Syria. *Prev Med.* 2004;39:330–336.
32. Labib N, Radwan G, Makhail N, et al. Comparison of cigarette and waterpipe smoking among female university students in Egypt. *Nicotine Tob Res.* 2006;9:591–596.
33. Chaaya M, El-Roueiheb Z, Chemaitelly H, Azar G, Nasr J, Al-Sahab B. Argileh smoking among university students: a new tobacco epidemic. *Nicotine Tob Res.* 2004;6:457–463.
34. Mandil A, Hussein A, Omer H, Turki G, Gaber I. Characteristics and risk factors of tobacco consumption among University of Sharjah students, 2005. *East Mediterr Health J.* 2007;13:1449–1458.
35. Roohafza H, Sadeghi M, Shahnam M, Bahonar A, Sarafzadegan N. Perceived factors related to cigarette and waterpipe (ghelyan) initiation and maintenance in university students of Iran. *Int J Public Health.* 2011;56:175–180.
36. Johnston LD, O'Malley PM, Bachman JG, Schulenberg JE. *Monitoring the Future: National Survey Results on Drug Use, 1975–2007. Volume II: College Students and Adults Ages 19–45.* Bethesda, MD: National Institute on Drug Abuse; 2008. NIH publication 08–6418B.
37. Johnston LD, O'Malley PM, Bachman JG, Schulenberg J.E. *Monitoring the Future National Survey Results on Drug Use, 1975–2009. Volume II: College Students and Adults Ages 19–50.* Bethesda, MD: National Institute on Drug Abuse. 2010. NIH publication 10-7585.
38. Grant BF, Dawson DA, Stinson FS, Chou SP, Dufour MC, Pickering RP. The 12-month prevalence and trends in DSMIV alcohol abuse and dependence. *Alcohol Res Health.* 2006;29: 79–91.
39. Asfar T, Ward KD, Eissenberg T, Maziak W. Comparison of patterns of use, beliefs, and attitudes related to waterpipe between beginning and established smokers. *BMC Public Health.* 2005;5: 19. doi:10.1186/1471-2458-5-19.
40. Salameh P, Waked M, Aoun Z. Waterpipe smoking: construction and validation of the Lebanon Waterpipe Dependence Scale (LWDS-11). *Nicotine Tob Res.* 2008;10:149–158.

Appendix B

4) Gulbrandsen, C. (2016). Measuring older women's resilience: Evaluating the suitability of the Connor-Davidson Resilience Scale and the Resilience Scale. *Journal of Women & Aging*, *28*(3), 225–237.

MEASURING OLDER WOMEN'S RESILIENCE

Introduction

The aim of this article is to evaluate the psychometric properties of two measurement tools that have been used to measure resilience and to discuss how the tools can be used in future studies to advance understanding of resilience in women age 60 and over. A review of studies that have evaluated the psychometric properties of the Connor-Davidson Resilience Scale (CD-RISC) (Connor & Davidson, 2003) and the Resilience Scale (Wagnild & Young, 1993) will be provided. Since the measurement tools were developed, researchers who have used and evaluated the tools have focused primarily on evaluating the reliability and validity of the instruments. Several authors have provided substantial support for their reliability and validity for use across age groups. Although researchers have examined age differences in resilience and the association between resilience and other related constructs, there is scant research that has used the CD-RISC or the Resilience Scale to examine gender differences in resilience in older adults' resilience. The purpose of reviewing researchers' evaluations of the psychometric properties of the CDRISC and the Resilience Scale is to describe the implications the evaluative studies have for future research on resilience in women 60 years of age and over.

Why Examine Older Women's Resilience?

Although older women have been represented as frequently as older men in studies of older adults' resilience, very few studies have examined gender differences in older adults' resilience. In contrast, several studies have highlighted distinct gender differences in older adults according to numerous other health and psychosocial factors. According to researchers who have studied older women's aging, older women contend with greater longevity than older men, have a greater likelihood of being widowed, endure higher rates of poverty at older ages, and have a greater likelihood of experiencing chronic health conditions (Cornwell, 2011; Felten, 2000; Hamid, Momtaz, & Rashid, 2010; Iecovich & Cwikel, 2010; Malatesta, 2007; Martin-Matthews, 2011; Quail, Wolfson, & Lippman, 2011). The findings of these studies strongly suggest that there are distinct gender differences in age-related adversity. Further research is necessary to determine the effect of the gender differences in adversity on older women's resilience.

Although other instruments for measuring resilience are available, the CD-RISC (Connor & Davidson, 2003) and the Resilience Scale (Wagnild & Young, 1993) were chosen for consideration in this article because several researchers have confirmed the reliability and validity of both instruments and have also provided support for the suitability of both instruments for use with adult and older adult populations (Connor & Davidson, 2003; Lamond et al., 2008; Lundman, Strandberg, Eisemann, Gustafson, & Brulin, 2007; Resnick & Inguito, 2011; Wells, 2009). Researchers have introduced other instruments, such as the Resilience Scale for Adults (Friborg, Hjemdal, Rosenvinge, & Martinussen, 2003) and the Brief Resilience Coping Scale (Sinclair & Wallston, 2004). However, since fewer researchers have examined the psychometric properties of these instruments, there is presently less support for their reliability and validity and considerably less documentation of their use with older adults (Ahern, Kiehl, Lou Sole, & Byers, 2006). Future researchers who use the CD-RISC and the Resilience Scale to examine resilience in older women can proceed on the basis of the favorable psychometric properties of the instruments to explore the directions resilience scholars have recommended to glean more nuanced understandings of older women's resilience. Although research on gender differences in older adults' resilience has been scant, researchers who have examined resilience using the CD-RISC and the Resilience Scale have identified promising directions for examining the complexity of resilience according to age, gender differences, and other identity differences such as ethnicity, health, and geographic location (Lamond et al., 2008; Nygren, Randström, Lejonklou, & Lundman, 2004; Resnick & Inguito, 2011; Wagnild & Young, 1990; Wells, 2009; Yu & Zhang, 2007).

Both Connor and Davidson (2003) and Wagnild and Young (1993) have acknowledged the need to further test their instruments with more heterogenous samples. Researchers who have tested the CD-RISC (Connor & Davidson, 2003) and the Resilience Scale (Wagnild & Young, 1993) have highlighted selection bias as a limitation to their research. They have acknowledged that the generalizability of their research findings is limited by the homogeneity of their samples according to gender, age, ethnicity, language, income, and education (Lamond et al., 2008; Nygren et al., 2005; Resnick & Inguito, 2011; Wagnild & Young, 1993). Studies that have examined older adults' resilience have included samples that consist primarily of White, middle-class men and women. Several researchers who have tested the CD-RISC and the Resilience Scale have recommended future research to examine resilience in samples that vary according to gender, age, ethnicity, education, health, income, and geographic location (Nygren et al., 2005; Smith, 2009; Wagnild, 2009). Based on the psychometric properties outlined in this article, the authors propose that the CD-RISC or Resilience Scale could be used as a basis for further examining older women's resilience.

Appendix B

Defining Resilience

The conceptual definitions of resilience that form the basis for the CD-RISC (Connor & Davidson, 2003) and the Resilience Scale (Wagnild & Young, 1993) are considered in the context of diverse, competing definitions of resilience. Researchers have commented on the vague nature of conceptual definitions featured in literature that fail to distinguish resilience from other closely related constructs such as well-being and self-efficacy (Hengudomsub, 2007; Lightsey, 2006). Other authors have underscored the lack of agreement in the literature regarding conceptual definitions of resilience (Bonanno, 2012; Damásio, Borsa, & da Silva, 2011; Hengudomsub, 2007; Herrman et al., 2012).

Connor and Davidson (2003) and Wagnild and Young (1993) prefaced their investigations of resilience and the testing of their instruments with conceptual definitions of resilience, defining resilience as a dispositional characteristic or trait that is comprised of personal qualities such as inner strength, competence, optimism, and flexibility that contribute to one's ability to cope effectively when faced with adversity. The authors' definitions identified specific dimensions of resilience that are represented by the items included in their instruments.

The Resilience Scale (Wagnild & Young, 1993) and the Connor-Davidson Resilience Scale (Connor & Davidson, 2003) have both been subject to rigorous psychometric testing by their developers. The development of CD-RISC and the Resilience Scale yielded operational definitions that identified specific, measurable components of resilience. These researchers constructed operational definitions of resilience by identifying distinct components of resilience and then measuring the extent to which their interrelationships clustered around resilience as an overarching construct. Both Connor and Davidson (2003) and Wagnild and Young (1993) constructed items on their instruments in order to measure the components of resilience and the extent to which the components, individually and collectively, accounted for the variance in resilience scores.

Gerontology researchers have articulated conceptual definitions of resilience that pertain specifically to older adults. Fuller-Iglesias, Sellars, and Antonucci (2008) proposed that, "older adults who actively adapt to environmental and biological challenges related to aging are reflecting the process of resilience" (p. 184). Other researchers have defined older adults' resilience as a complex construct that is related to a breadth of risk and protective factors (Dorfman, Méndez, & Osterhaus, 2009; Gooding, Hurst, Johnson, & Tarrier, 2012; Wagnild, 2009). Researchers have measured older adults' resilience in order to understand the relationship between resilience and potentially protective factors such as self-efficacy, optimism, self-rated successful aging, self-rated mental and physical health, social support; self-esteem, and risk factors such as depression and cognitive impairment (Lamond et al., 2008; Lundman et al., 2007; Nygren, Alex, Jonsen, Gustafson, Norberg, & Lundman,

2005; Resnick & Inguito, 2011; Wells, 2009). Authors have proposed that measuring resilience can identify older adults with low levels of resilience, quantify the effects of interventions directed at increasing resilience, and detect changes in resilience over time (Connor & Davidson, 2003; Lamond et al., 2008; Nygren et al., 2005; Resnick & Inguito, 2011; Wells, 2009).

Felten (2000) suggested that operational definitions of resilience proposed in reference to younger populations are not necessarily relevant to older women's resilience. Based on researchers' suggestions, further research is needed to construct and test operational definitions of resilience that pertain specifically to older women and that discern age and gender differences.

Measuring Resilience

Researchers who have used the Resilience Scale (Wagnild & Young, 1993) and the CD-RISC (Connor & Davidson, 2003) have evaluated each instrument's capacity to measure resilience. Some of the researchers who have evaluated the Resilience Scale with older adult samples (Nygren et al., 2005, Resnick & Inguito, 2011) and the CD-RISC (Lamond et al., 2008) have supported the reliability of the instruments by providing correlation coefficients for internal consistency and test-retest reliability respectively.

The validity of each measure has been examined by conducting factor analyses with the CD-RISC (Lamond et al., 2008; Yu & Zhang, 2007) and Rasch analyses with the Resilience Scale (Resnick & Inguito, 2011). These tests of validity have confirmed the fit of items in order to support instrument validity and have concluded that the tools measure what they claim to measure: the construct of resilience.

Connor-Davidson Resilience Scale

The Connor-Davidson Resilience Scale has been recognized as a reliable and valid instrument (Ahern et al., 2006; Clauss-Ehlers, 2008). It is a brief self-rated instrument that aims to quantify resilience and consists of 25 items, each with a 5-point response where 0 = *not true at all*, 1 = *rarely true*, 2 = *sometimes true*, 3 = *often true*, and 4 = *true nearly all of the time*. Connor and Davidson (2003) provided descriptions of items on the scale, including "Able to adapt to change," "Thinking of self as a strong person," "Knowing where to turn for help," and "Strong sense of self." Scores on the CD-RISC can range from 0 to 100. Although higher scores indicate higher resilience, Connor and Davidson did not propose a cut-off score between high and low resilience.

Kathryn Connor, MD, and Jonathan Davidson, MD, both faculty from Duke University Department of Psychiatry and Behavioral Sciences, explained their research interests in examining the relationship between resilience and outcomes for the treatment of anxiety, depression, and posttraumatic stress disorder. At the

Appendix B

time they developed the CD-RISC, Connor and Davidson (2003) noted that there was no widely accepted measure of resilience for use in psychiatric practice. Their aims in developing the scale were to develop a reliable, valid measure of resilience, to identify reference values for psychiatric populations and the general population, and to examine how resilience is affected by pharmalogical treatment. They noted that their study was the first to examine the association between resilience and pharmalogical intervention. Their original study on the development and testing of the CD-RISC provided support for resilience as a construct that can be measured and quantified.

Their initial study tested the CD-RISC with a sample of adults (n = 806) consisting of 77% Caucasian, 65% female participants, with a mean age of 43.8. Their sample consisted of the following subsamples: primary care outpatients, participants from a study on generalized anxiety disorders, participants from two clinical trials for posttraumatic stress disorder, and psychiatric outpatients in private practice.

Reliability. The developers' own evaluation of the CD-RISC provided strong support for the instruments' internal consistency (Cronbach's alpha = 0.89) and with the general population sample and test-retest reliability with the generalized anxiety disorder and post-traumatic stress disorder samples (0.87). Other researchers have supported the internal consistency of the CD-RISC, with Cronbach's alpha = 0.923 (Lamond et al., 2008) and 0.92 (Smith, 2009).

Convergent validity. In Connor and Davidson's (2003) initial psychometric testing of the CD-RISC, convergent validity was supported by a statistically significant positive correlation in the psychiatric outpatient subsample with hardiness (n = 30) (r = 0.83), as measured by the Kobasa's Hardiness Measure (Kobasa, 1979), statistically significant positive correlations for the majority of subjects between resilience and social support scores (r = 0.36) as measured by the Sheehan Social Support Scale and negative correlations between resilience and perceived stress scores (r = –0.32) as measured by the Sheehan Stress Vulnerability Scale. Other researchers have indicated support for convergent validity of the CD-RISC with measures of correlates of resilience (Lamond et al., 2008; Smith, 2009; Yu & Zhang, 2007), reporting positive correlations with constructs such as self-esteem (0.49) and life satisfaction (0.48) (Yu & Zhang, 2007), emotional health and well-being (0.494), optimism (0.438), self-rated successful aging (0.425), physical functioning (0.116) (Lamond et al., 2008), and willingness to seek help for depressive symptoms (r = 0.39) (Smith, 2009). Additionally, Lamond et al. (2008) reported a negative correlation between resilience scores and cognitive functioning (–0.403).

Construct validity. To determine construct validity of the CD-RISC, Connor and Davidson (2003) conducted an exploratory factor analysis, which yielded a five-component structure: Factor 1 represented personal competence, high standards, and tenacity; Factor 2 represented trust in one's instincts, tolerance of negative affect, and strengthening effects of stress; Factor 3 represented acceptance of change and secure relationships; Factor 4 represented personal control; and Factor 5 represented spiritual influences.

Other researchers have conducted further factor analyses (Lamond et al., 2008; Smith, 2009; Yu & Zhang, 2007) and confirmed the five-factor structure originally proposed by Connor and Davidson (2003), which further supported the construct validity of the measure. The varying factor structures found in relation to specific populations strongly suggests that the nature of resilience differs across populations.

Of particular relevance to the discussion of older women's resilience is how Lamond et al. (2008) identified a distinct factor structure in a sample of older women that consisted of the following factors: personal control and goal orientation, adaption and tolerance for negative affect, leadership and trust in instincts, and spiritual coping. This factor structure diverged from the different five-factor structure originally identified by Connor and Davidson (2003). Although older men were not included in their study sample, the factor analysis conducted by Lamond et al. (2008) suggests that resilience in older women is comprised of a different factor structure than the factor structure Connor and Davidson described.

Other researchers have reported differing factor structures according to other aspects of difference, such as ethnicity. Yu and Zhang (2007) noted that the CD-RISC had only been tested with Western samples and suggested that the definition of resilience is likely to vary because the nature of and perspective on adversity varies considerably across cultures and geographic regions. Their research tested the CD-RISC on a sample of Chinese adults aged 18 to over 60. To determine if there was a different factor structure for their Chinese sample than Connor and Davidson (2003) identified, Yu and Zhang conducted factor analyses on a Chinese sample. They identified a three-factor structure consisting of tenacity, strength, and optimism, and based on their findings, they suggested that the factor structure of resilience is culturally dependent.

Connor and Davidson (2003) supported the utility of the CD-RISC in a clinical setting, highlighting its capacity for identifying individuals with low resilience and to measure the effect of interventions. The authors' initial testing of the instrument supported the responsiveness of resilience scores to treatment and the positive correlation between resilience scores global improvement in individuals with depression and anxiety.

CD-RISC 2

Other researchers have developed abbreviated versions of the CD-RISC that could be used more easily in clinical settings. As an example, Vaishnavi, Connor, and Davidson (2007) constructed a two-item scale, designated as the CD-RISC 2, for use in clinical populations with mental health diagnoses of anxiety, depression, and posttraumatic stress disorder. They proposed that items #1 (able to adapt to change) and #8 (tend to bounce back after illness or hardship) adequately captured the essence of resilience as a construct and accordingly suggested that the CD-RISC-2 is suitable as a screening tool to measure improvements in clinical populations following treatment. Vaishnavi et al. (2007) suggested that the instrument had comparable reliability and validity to the CD-RISC.

The Connor Davidson Resilience Scale has been used to measure resilience in different age groups, including older adults. However, very few investigators have focused exclusively on its use with older women (Lamond et al., 2008; Smith, 2009). Considering that aging involves the emergence of new risk factors and that resilience in older women has been associated with a unique factor structure, examining correlates of resilience and continuing to explore the interrelationships among various risk and protective factors that arise as women age is a viable avenue of future research.

The Resilience Scale

The Resilience Scale was originally developed by Gail Wagnild, an assistant professor of nursing, and Heather Young, a doctoral student in nursing, both at the University of Washington in Seattle in 1993. Wagnild (2009) described how the Resilience scale was developed from an earlier qualitative study conducted by Wagnild and Young (1990) with 24 female participants, ranging in age from 67 to 92. The themes identified in their qualitative study informed the development of the items on the Resilience Scale. Wagnild (2009) outlined five distinct characteristics of resilience that were derived from the thematic analysis in the qualitative study and provided the conceptual foundation for the Resilience Scale: *perseverance* in contending with adversity; *equanimity*, an approach to life that involves taking what comes one's way; *meaningfulness*, having a purpose for living; self-reliance, a belief in the value of one's personal strengths and capacities; and *existential aloneness*, an acceptance of one's uniqueness and the reality that one faces many experiences alone.

The original 50 items of the first version of the scale were verbatim statements from the women in the study. Wagnild and Young's (1993) further refinement and development of the scale reduced the tool to 25 items. Examples of items on the scale include, "I usually manage one way or another," "I am determined," "I take things one day at a time," and "My life has meaning." The items are scored on a 7-point scale ranging from 1 (*disagree*) to 7 (*agree*) (Wagnild & Young, 1993). Individual scores are obtained by summing the responses to each item. According to Wagnild (2009), a score of 145 or more indicates high resilience, between 125 and 145 indicates moderate resilience, and below 120 indicates low resilience. In a later assessment of the Resilience Scale, Wagnild (2009) indicated that results tend to be negatively skewed and speculated on the potential for bias due to social desirability. Wagnild (2009) suggested that social desirability and acquiescence explained the tendency toward higher scores. She recommended further development of the instrument to respond to this criticism.

Reliability. Wagnild and Young (1993) conducted a rigorous psychometric evaluation of the Resilience Scale. Their initial testing (Wagnild & Young, 1993) provided strong support for the scale's internal consistency (Cronbach's alpha = 0.91). Researchers (Nygren et al., 2004; Resnick & Inguito, 2011; Wells, 2009) have provided additional support for the internal consistency of the Resilience Scale, reporting Cronbach's alpha values ranging from 0.85 to 0.94. Researchers have also reported test-retest reliability coefficients from 0.67 to 0.84 (Lundman et al., 2007; Nygren et al., 2004; Wagnild, 1993). However, Lundman et al. (2007) commented that there is insufficient support for test-retest reliability of the instrument between longer durations of time than 1 year.

Convergent validity. Several authors have focused their psychometric testing on convergent validity with measures of other constructs that have been associated with resilience (Wagnild, 2003; Wells, 2009). Wells (2009) examined resilience in a sample of rural older adults (n = 106, mean age 75 years) and focused on the relationship between resilience and protective factors. Self-rated mental health was identified as the factor with the most significant correlation with resilience (r = 0.58), followed by self-rated physical health (r = 0.24). Researchers who have focused on convergent validity of the Resilience Scale with older adult samples have examined the positive correlations between resilience and risk and protective factors such as sense of coherence (0.35), purpose in life (0.53), self-transcendence (0.49), self-rated physical (0.24) and mental health (0.58) (Nygren et al., 2005; Wagnild, 2003; Resnick & Inguito, 2011; Wells, 2009), and a negative correlation with suicidal ideation (Lau, Morse, & MacFarlane, 2010).

Construct validity. In their initial testing of the Resilience Scale, Wagnild and Young (1993) expected to derive five factors that corresponded to the five themes they identified in their qualitative analysis. Instead, they discovered that a two-component structure accounted for 44% of the variance in resilience scores. The two components they identified were acceptance of life and individual competence (Nygren et al., 2004; Wagnild & Young, 1993). This factor structure was found to distinguish the items on the scale with the exception of four items, which were double loaded. Other researchers found double loading between the two factors, acceptance of life and individual competence, which called the construct validity of the scale into question (Lundman et al., 2007; Resnick & Inguito, 2011).

Resnick and Inguito (2011) focused their critique of the Resilience Scale on its construct validity. To test construct validity and to determine the effectiveness of each item in measuring resilience, they employed a Rasch analysis to examine the fit of items to the measurement instrument and to determine if any of the items compromised the validity of the measure. The findings from the Rasch analysis suggested a fair fit of the items to the model and identified items that compromised validity. Two items (5: "I can be on my own if I have to," and 11: "I seldom wonder what the point of it all is") were identified as poor fits with the model.

Appendix B

They also reported significant measurement error on the scale's items. They speculated that the high measurement error on each item could be attributed to participants' inconsistent use of response options. In order to perform the Rasch analysis, Resnick and Inguito remedied the disordered response patterns by changing the response options to a modified forced-choice format, with responses between 1 and 3 coded as *agree* and responses between 4 and 7 coded as *disagree*.

Translated versions of the Resilience Scale. The Resilience Scale (Wagnild & Young, 1993) has been translated into other languages. Psychometric testing of Swedish (Nygren et al., 2004), Dutch (Portzky, Wagnild, De Bacquer, & Audenaert, 2010), Spanish (Heilemann, Frutos, Lee, & Kury, 2004), and Japanese (Nishi, Uehara, Kondo, & Matsuoka, 2010) versions of the Resilience Scale has revealed comparable reliability and validity with the original English version.

The reliability testing of the Swedish version conducted by Nygren et al. (2004) with a sample of 19–85-year-old adults ($n = 142$) reported internal consistency (Cronbach's alpha = 0.88) for the initial test administration and test-retest reliability ($r = 0.78$). Nygren et al. (2004) reported a lower mean score on the test and retest of 141 and 139 respectively with the Swedish-language version, compared to the mean score of 148 reported by Wagnild and Young (1993) in their study with older adults ($n = 810$).

Authors also described how they modified the original instrument to create reliable and valid versions of the Resilience Scale in other languages. In a study using the Dutch version of the Resilience Scale, Portzky et al. (2010) described how the 7-point Likert scale in the English version was changed to a 4-point response system in the Dutch version and explained that a 4-point response system would require participants to choose positive or negative responses. The Dutch version resulted in a new range of scores between 25 and 100. Portzky et al. (2010) reported internal consistency (Cronbach's alpha = 0.85) and test-retest reliability ($r = 0.90$ over 3 months) for the Dutch version, which are comparable with the English version.

Heilemann et al. (2004) noted that for the Spanish version of the Resilience Scale, two items were omitted from data analysis on the "acceptance of life" subscale in a study involving female participants aged 21–40 ($n = 315$). Although there was adequate support for internal consistency (Cronbach's alpha = 0.90) for the Spanish version of the "personal competence" 17-item item subscale, the support for internal consistency (Cronbach's alpha = 0.69) was not as strong for the Spanish version of the "acceptance of self and life" six-item subscale.

In a study with adults aged 18–51 ($n = 497$) using the Japanese-language version of the Resilience Scale, Nishi et al. (2010) reported high internal consistency (Cronbach's alpha = 0.90) and high test-retest reliability ($r = 0.83$). However, the authors suggested low concurrent validity of the Japanese version of the Resilience Scale, based on the low mean score of 111.19, the positive correlation between scores on the Resilience Scale and the Perceived Stress Scale (Cohen,

Kamarck, & Mermelstein, 1983), and the low correlation between resilience scores and depressive symptoms.

Measuring gender differences using the Resilience Scale. Only three studies were found in which investigators explored gender differences in older adults' scores on the Resilience Scale (Lundman et al., 2007; Nygren et al., 2005; Wells, 2009), and of these, only two reported statistically significant findings with respect to gender differences. Lundman et al. (2007) examined the psychometric properties of the Swedish version of the Resilience Scale in a study that included subsamples from several other health studies. Two of the subsamples included older adults 60 and older and 85 and older. Lundman et al. examined gender differences and reported statistically significant gender differences in mean resilience scores only in adults 50–59 ($p = .023$). Nygren et al. (2005) conducted a study with Swedish older adults age 85 and older ($n = 125$) and reported statistically significant correlations for women only between resilience scores and scores on measures of self-transcendence, sense of coherence, purpose in life, and self-rated mental health. In a study looking at factors associated with resilience in community-dwelling rural older adults, Wells (2009) examined gender differences in resilience scores but did not report any significant findings. The very limited and inconsistent findings related to gender differences in older adults' resilience suggests that further research is needed to discern and more closely examine gender differences in resilience in this age group.

Based on research that supported the reliability and validity of the Resilience Scale, Ahern et al. (2006) contended that the Resilience Scale (Wagnild & Young, 1993) is suitable for all age groups. Authors have reported that the Resilience Scale differentiates resilience according to age, with older adults generally scoring higher on the measure than younger adults and adolescents (Nygren et al., 2005).

References

Ahern, N., Kiehl, E., Lou Sole, M., & Byers, J. (2006). A review of instruments measuring resilience. *Issues in Comprehensive Pediatric Nursing, 29*(2), 103–125. doi:10.1080/0146 0860600677643

Bonanno, G. (2012). Uses and abuses of the resilience construct: Loss, trauma, and health-related adversities. *Social Science and Medicine, 74,* 753–756. doi:10.1016/j.socscimed. 2011.11.022

Clauss-Ehlers, C. (2008). Sociocultural factors, resilience, and coping: Support for a culturally sensitive measure of resilience. *Journal of Applied Developmental Psychology, 29,* 197–212. doi:10.1016/j.appdev.2008.02.004

Cohen, S., Kamarck, T., & Mermelstein, R. (1983). A global measure of perceived stress. *Journal of Health and Social Behavior, 24*(4), 385–396. doi:10.2307/2136404

Connor, K., & Davidson, J. (2003). Development of a new resilience scale: The Connor-Davidson Resilience Scale (CD-RISC). *Depression and Anxiety, 18,* 76–82. doi:10.1002/da.10113

Appendix B

Cornwell, B. (2011). Independence through social networks: Bridging potential among older women and men. The Journals of Gerontology Series B: *Psychological Sciences and Social Sciences, 66B*(6), 782–794. doi:10.1093/geronb/gbr111

Damásio, B., Borsa, J., & da Silva, J. (2011). 14-item resilience scale (RS-14): Psychometric properties of the Brazilian version. *Journal of Nursing Measurement, 19*(3), 131–145. doi:10.1891/1061-3749.19.3.131

Dorfman, L., Méndez, E., & Osterhaus, J. (2009). Stress and resilience in the oral histories of rural older women. *Journal of Women and Aging, 21,* 303–316. doi:10.1080/08952840903285237

Felten, B. (2000). Resilience in a multicultural sample of community-dwelling women older than age 85. *Clinical Nursing Research, 9*(2), 102–123. doi:10.1177/10547738000090020200202

Friborg, O., Hjemdal, O., Rosenvinge, J., & Martinussen, M. (2003). A new rating scale for adult resilience: What are the central protective resources behind healthy adjustment? *International Journal of Methods in Psychiatric Research, 12*(2), 65–76. doi:10.1002/mpr.143

Fuller-Iglesias, H., Sellars, B., & Antonucci, T. (2008). Resilience in old age: Social relations as a protective factor. *Research in Human Development, 5*(3), 181–193. doi:10.1080/15427600802274043

Gooding, P., Hurst, A., Johnson, J., & Tarrier, N. (2012). Psychological resilience in young and older adults. *International Journal of Geriatric Psychiatry, 27,* 262–270. doi:10.1002/gps.2712

Hamid, T., Momtaz, Y. A., & Rashid, S. (2010). Older women and lower self-rated health. *Educational Gerontology, 36,* 521–528. doi:10.1080/03601270903534606

Heilemann, M., Frutos, L., Lee, K., & Kury, F. (2004). Protective strength factors, resources, and risks in relation to depressive symptoms among childbearing women of Mexican descent. *Health Care for Women International, 25*(1), 88–106. doi:10.1080/07399330490253265

Hengudomsub, P. (2007). Resilience in later life. *Thai Pharmalogical Health Science Journal, 2*(1), 115–123.

Herrman, H., Stewart, D., Diaz-Granados, N., Berger, E., Jackson, B., & Yuen, T. (2012). What is resilience? *Canadian Journal of Psychiatry, 56*(5), 258–265.

Iecovich, E., & Cwikel, J. (2010). The relationship between well-being and self-rated health among middle-aged and older women in Israel. *Clinical Gerontologist, 33,* 255–269. doi:10.1080/07317115.2010.502103

Kobasa, S. (1979). Stressful life events, personality and health: An inquiry into hardiness. *Journal of Personality and Social Psychology, 37*(1), 1–11. doi:10.1037/0022-3514.37.1.1

Lamond, A., Depp, C., Allison, M., Langer, R., Reichstadt, J., Moore, D., . . . Jeste, D. (2008). Measurement and predictors of resilience among community-dwelling older women. *Journal of Psychiatric Research, 43,* 148–154. doi:10.1016/j.jpsychires.2008.03.007

Lau, R., Morse, C., & MacFarlane, S. (2010). Psychological factors among elderly women with suicidal intentions or attempts to suicide: A controlled comparison. *Journal of Women and Aging, 22,* 3–14. doi:10.1080/08952840903488831

Lightsey, O. R. (2006). Resilience, meaning, and well-being. *The Counseling Psychologist, 34*(1), 96–107. doi:10.1177/0011000005282369

Lundman, B., Strandberg, G., Eisemann, M., Gustafson, Y., & Brulin, C. (2007). Psychometric properties of the Swedish version of the Resilience Scale. *Scandinavian Journal of Caring Sciences, 21,* 229–237. doi:10.1111/j.1471-6712.2007.00461.x

Malatesta, V. (2007). Introduction: The need to address older women's mental health issues. *Journal of Women and Aging, 19*(1–2), 1–12. doi:10.1300/J074v19n01_01

Martin-Matthews, A. (2011). Revisiting widowhood in later life: Changes in patterns and profiles, advances in research and understanding. *Canadian Journal on Aging, 30*(3), 339–354. doi:10.1017/S0714980811000201

Nishi, D., Uehara, R., Kondo, M., & Matsuoka, Y. (2010). Reliability and validity of the Japanese version of the Resilience Scale and its short version. *BMC Research Notes, 3*(1), 310. doi:10.1186/1756-0500-3-310

Nygren, B., Aléx, L., Jonsén, E., Gustafson, Y., Norberg, A., & Lundman, B. (2005). Resilience, sense of coherence, purpose in life and self-transcendence in relation to perceived physical and mental health among the oldest old. *Aging & Mental Health, 9*(4), 354–362. doi:10.1080/1360500114415

Nygren, B., Randström, K. B., Lejonklou, A. K., & Lundman, B. (2004). Reliability and validity of a Swedish language version of the Resilience Scale. *Journal of Nursing Measurement, 12*(3), 169–178. doi:10.1891/jnum.12.3.169

Portzky, M., Wagnild, G., De Bacquer, D., & Audenaert, K. (2010). Psychometric evaluation of the Dutch Resilience Scale RS-nl on 3265 healthy participants: A confirmation of the association between age and resilience found with the Swedish version. *Scandinavian Journal of Caring Sciences, 24*(1), 86–92. doi:10.1111/j.1471-6712.2010.00841.x

Quail, J., Wolfson, C., & Lippman, A. (2011). Unmet need for assistance to perform activities of daily living and psychological distress in community dwelling elderly women. *Canadian Journal on Aging, 30*(4), 591–602. doi:10.1017/S0714980811000493

Resnick, B., & Inguito, P. (2011). The Resilience Scale: Psychometric properties and clinical applicability in older adults. *Archives of Psychiatric Nursing, 25*(1), 11–20. doi:10.1016/j.apnu.2010.05.001

Sinclair, V., & Wallston, K. (2004). The development and psychometric evaluation of the brief resilient coping scale. *Assessment, 11*(1), 94–101. doi:10.1177/1073191103258144

Smith, P. (2009). Resilience: Resistance factor for depressive symptoms. *Journal of Psychiatric and Mental Health Nursing, 16*, 829–837. doi:10.1111/j.1365-2850.2009.01463.x

Vaishnavi, S., Connor, K., & Davidson, J. (2007). An abbreviated version of the Connor-Davidson Resilience Scale (CD-RISC), the CD-RISC2: Psychometric properties and applications in psychopharmacological trials. *Psychiatry Research, 152*, 293–297. doi:10.1016/j.psychres.2007.01.006

Wagnild, G. (2009). A review of the Resilience Scale. *Journal of Nursing Measurement, 17*(2), 105–113. doi:10.1891/1061-3749.17.2.105

Wagnild, G., & Young, H. (1990). Resilience among older women. *Image: Journal of Nursing Scholarship, 22*, 252–255.

Wagnild, G., & Young, H. (1993). Development and psychometric evaluation of the Resilience Scale. *Journal of Nursing Measurement, 1*(2), 165–178.

Wells, M. (2009). Resilience in rural community-dwelling older adults. *The Journal of Rural Health, 25*(4), 415–419. doi:10.1111/j.1748-0361.2009.00253.x

Yu, X., & Zhang, J. (2007). Factor analysis and psychometric evaluation of the Connor Davidson Resilience Scale (CDRISC) with Chinese people. *Social Behavior and Personality: An International Journal, 35*(1), 19–30. doi:10.2224/sbp.2007.35.1.19

Appendix B

5) Kosko, K.W. & Miyazaki, Y. (2012). **The effect of student discussion frequency on fifth-grade students' mathematics achievement in U.S. schools.** *The Journal of Experimental Education, 80*(2), 173–195.

Mathematical discourse in the form of classroom discussion is considered an effective strategy for increasing student mathematics achievement. Sharing ideas through discussion allows students to organize their reasoning and encourages them to justify their solution strategies (D'Ambrosio, Johnson, & Hobbs, 1995; Silver, Kilpatrick, & Schlesinger, 1990). The act of putting thought into words helps students to structure and clarify their reasoning. Talking about mathematics communicates the concept(s) to others but also helps communicate the concept(s) to the individual speaking (Pimm, 1987; Silver et al., 1990). This act of reflection allows individuals to further clarify their own thinking and restructure it when appropriate.

It seems acceptable that an understanding of mathematical concepts should translate into higher achievement in mathematics itself. A deepened understanding of mathematical concepts is an advocated benefit of peer discussion. Therefore, having students discuss mathematics with one another should increase mathematical achievement. Yet, this seemingly obvious logical consequence does not appear to be fully supported in the empirical literature. That is, although some studies show higher achievement for students who discuss mathematics more frequently (e.g., Hiebert & Wearne, 1993; Mercer & Sams, 2006), literature exists that shows frequent student discussion of mathematics has a negative effect on achievement (i.e., Shouse, 2001). Such a discrepancy in the literature pressed us to question what the true effect of student discussion was, whether such an effect was positive or negative, and why the results in the various studies differed. Finding answers to such questions is the goal of the present study. To achieve this goal, we used a large-scale dataset collected in the United States (Early Childhood Longitudinal Study) to investigate the general effect of discussion on mathematics achievement as well as differences of such effect between different classrooms/schools.

Benefits of Mathematical Discussion

Mathematics education literature has strongly supported the academic benefits of mathematical classroom discussion (hereafter referred to as *mathematical discussion*). Describing results from Stigler and Hiebert (1997), Grouws (2004) cited the Trends in International Mathematics and Science Study (TIMSS) as evidence that having students share solution methods and solve problems together increases mathematics achievement. Stigler and Hiebert (1997) evaluated video collected from 231 classrooms, including 100 in Germany, 50 in Japan, and 81 in the United States, with one lesson videotaped in eighth-grade each classroom. Qualitative findings suggested that students in the U.S. classrooms engaged in mathematics at a lower average grade level, which concur with the quantitative findings. However, teachers in the United States were observed to be much less likely to have students develop mathematical concepts (about 22% in the United States compared with 78% in Germany and 82% in Japan) and much more likely to simply state mathematical concepts (78% in the United States compared with 22% in Germany and 18% in Japan). It is notable that engaging students in discussing math concepts was considered a part of developing mathematical concepts. However, Grouws (2004) identified a separate finding in the study that focused on a particular distinction made in Japanese mathematics classrooms. Japanese students were identified as being more likely than their American counterparts to discuss mathematical solution strategies with one another. In concordance with Grouws (2004), D'Ambrosio et al. (1995) suggested that mathematical discussion is a means of increasing mathematics achievement. By observing more frequent math discussion in classrooms where more advanced mathematics were done by students, the results provided by Stiger and Hiebert (1997), and described by Grouws (2004), suggests that more frequent discussion may be related to higher achievement.

Observing 6 different second-grade U.S. classrooms, Hiebert and Wearne (1993) found that 2 of 6 teachers observed asked students to explain and justify their mathematics significantly more than the other teachers in the study. In addition, students of these two teachers had higher gains in content knowledge than the students of the other four teachers. In comparing one of the classrooms to three of similar beginning achievement, Hiebert and Wearne (1993) noted:

> Compared to A, B, and C, Classroom D students worked fewer place-value and computation problems, spent more time on each problem, engaged in more whole-class discussion, and shared more of the discourse by describing their solution strategies and explaining their responses (p. 419).

A similar distinction was noted between classrooms E and F, in which students were recognized as higher achieving, but students in class E engaged in more frequent discussion and saw higher achievement gains.

A more recent study, conducted by Mercer and Sams (2006) in Britain, compared achievement for fifth-grade students of teachers who received training in conducting math discussion and teachers who did not receive such training. Mercer and Sams (2006) found that the prior set of students discussed math more frequently than did the latter group and also had statistically significant higher gains in mathematics achievement. Although Mercer and Sams (2006) and Hiebert and Wearne (1993) focused on the quality of discussion and frequency, in both studies more frequent math discussion resulted in higher gains in math achievement.

Appendix B

Koichu, Berman, and Moore (2007) found evidence that incorporating language related to heuristic literacy, the use of heuristics in problem solving and appropriate heuristic language in mathematical discourse, into classroom dialogue increased achievement scores. In their experiment Koichu et al. (2007) engaged eighth-grade students in two Israeli classrooms in problem solving. Students solved problems in groups before discussing them as a class, similar to what Grouws (2004) described of successful peer discussions in Japanese mathematics classrooms. Koichu et al. (2007) found that incorporating heuristics into student dialogue significantly increased mathematics achievement scores.

Evaluating data from the 1988 National Education Longitudinal Study (NELS), Shouse (2001) used a regression analysis and found that more frequent 10th-grade student discussion in mathematics had a slightly negative effect on mathematics achievement. Although small in magnitude, the findings were statistically significant. Tenth-grade students were asked how often they participated in student discussions about mathematics. As stated, results showed that more frequent student discussion had a small negative effect on mathematics achievement. This result contradicts much of what reform-oriented mathematics advocates in relation to student discussion as well as the aforementioned studies.

The NELS data is a national data set collected by the U.S. Department of Education and is very reliable. Therefore, at first glance the results found by Shouse (2001) seem counterintuitive. Yet, there is a specific weakness in Shouse's (2001) analysis that the present study seeks to address, with a more recent set of data. Shouse's (2001) study used regression analysis, which does not take into account the nested structure of student data. Hierarchical linear modeling (HLM), however, does take into account the groups that students are in and accounts for this statistically. For example, if weekly discussion is more effective in some classrooms than others, HLM will allow for this between-classrooms difference to be examined statistically while such differences would not be addressed in regression analysis.

The other studies mentioned regarding the relation between math achievement and frequency of mathematical discussion are mainly qualitative in nature. Whereas some studies conduct statistical analysis (e.g., Mercer & Sams, 2006), others do not. Even with the statistical analysis included, these studies hold a similar weakness to Shouse (2001) in that they do not fully investigate the differences in the effect of math discussion frequency by classroom. This provides further need for a large-scale analysis of such an effect, as is proposed by the present study.

Implementation of Mathematical Discussion

The previous section aimed to describe the background of literature linking the frequency of mathematical discussion to higher mathematics achievement. However, the studies supporting a positive relation between frequent math discussion and math achievement (e.g., Mercer & Sams, 2006; Stigler & Hiebert, 1997) also articulate the quality of the more frequently occurring discussions of mathematics. There are also several other qualitative studies that describe teacher practices in implementing effective mathematical discourse (e.g., Truxaw & DeFranco, 2007; Wood, 1999; Yackel & Cobb, 1996). Contrasting these studies are other qualitative investigations that observed teachers engaging students in more frequent discussion, but discussion that was not deemed effective in engaging students in deep mathematical thinking.

One such study was conducted by Manouchehri and St. John (2006), who, in describing some of their findings, compared two episodes of classroom talk where there was a large degree of student participation. The teachers in each classroom actively engaged students in the discussion, and on the surface, the two classrooms appeared similar. However, in one classroom the teacher explained and justified mathematical positions where in the other classroom the students did so. More specifically, although students in both classrooms engaged in the discussions frequently, students in one classroom took more ownership of the discussion than students in the other classroom.

Kazemi and Stipek (2001) observed students in fourth- and fifth-grade classrooms and found that while all observed teachers had similar levels of mathematical discussion, some teachers were more likely to require students to explain and justify their mathematics than other teachers. All teachers asked their students to describe how they solved problems, but one group of teachers asked students to discuss such descriptions and other teachers asked students whether they agreed with the descriptions or not.

The two studies presented in the preceding paragraphs highlight the fact that more frequent mathematical discussion does not necessarily equate with more effective or higher quality mathematical discussion. Yet, what is not clear is the degree to which the two do not equate. As stated earlier in the literature review, it is logical that more effective mathematical discussion should occur in accord with higher frequencies of mathematical discussion. Many of the studies describing the link between higher math achievement and mathematical discussion suggest this is the case. Yet, the studies presented in this section suggest that it is not always the case. The slightly negative effect of frequent math discussion found by Shouse (2001) may be evidence of this, or it may simply be evidence of an incomplete analysis of the problem.

Other Factors That Benefit Mathematics Achievement

Despite the results found by Shouse (2001), much of the literature suggests that more frequent mathematical discussion can result in improved student achievement

Appendix B

in mathematics. Yet, there are many other factors that contribute to mathematics achievement of students. Factors such as socioeconomic status (SES), race/ethnicity, and gender have been prevalent historically in educational research, and we discuss these briefly in this section. Other factors have also been identified in the literature, but we discuss only a few here, for simplicity.

Two factors that have historically affected mathematics achievement have also been intertwined in their effect are SES and race/ethnicity (Kohr, Coldiron, Skiffington, Masters, & Blust, 1987).

Tate (1997) conducted a review of the literature in which he found that between 1973 and 1992, the achievement gap attributable to race closed in Grades 4, 8, and 12. In addition, the achievement gap attributable to SES also closed. Even though the achievement gap was reduced, it was still present. Lubienski (2002) examined National Assessment of Educational Progress (NAEP) data from 1990, 1996, and 2000 in regards to how SES and race/ethnicity interacted with mathematics achievement of students in Grades 4, 8, and 12. She found that the achievement gap increased from 1990 to 2000 for Black students in Grade 8 and remained the same for Grades 4 and 12. In addition, SES did not adequately explain the achievement gaps. However, differences in achievement as a result of SES were still observed. Georges and Pallas (2010) examined Kindergarten and Grade 1 data from the Early Childhood Longitudinal Study (ECLS) and found that Black and Hispanic students generally entered school with fewer basic mathematics skills. As the students caught up to White students in basic mathematics skills, Whites "made progress in the more advanced mathematics skills . . ." (p. 286). A similar gap related to SES was also reported. Georges and Pallas (2010) examined this data to determine the degree to which the gap closed or grew over the school year and summer breaks, but the results still indicate an ever present gap related to race/ethnicity and SES.

Another historic achievement gap in regards to mathematics achievement is related to gender. Fennema and Sherman (1977) found that although there were few gender-related cognitive differences in Grades 9–12 high school students, many sociocultural beliefs and factors did appear to affect math achievement in regards to gender. In particular, a cultural belief more prevalent at the time of the study was that female students had less aptitude for mathematics, whereas Fennema and Sherman (1977) found this achievement gap was due mostly to the belief rather than any innate cognitive ability. A decade following Fennema and Sherman's (1977) study, Doolittle and Cleary (1987) found that the gender gap was still present for high school seniors, even when accounting for mathematics background of students. Tate's (1997) review of literature another decade later indicated that the achievement gap between male and female students was present but getting smaller in magnitude. Recently, McGraw, Lubienski, and Strutchens (2006) examined data on gender and mathematics achievement from 1990 to 2003 for students in Grades 8 to 12 and they found that the gender gap was relatively small but consistently present. In sum, the literature described here suggests that gender is and has consistently been a factor affecting mathematics achievement.

There are additional factors which have been consistently identified in the literature and have significant effect on mathematics achievement. Weiner (1985) reviewed several studies regarding varying factors of emotion and motivation affect student achievement. In examining the varying results of these studies, he found that

> ... research investigations made use of a variety of types of subjects judging a variety of achievement situations, and involving the self or another. A virtually infinite number of causal ascriptions are available in memory. However, within the achievement domain, a relatively small number from the vast array tend to be salient. The most dominant of these causes are ability and effort (p. 549).

Weiner's (1972) attribution theory combined ability and effort as predictors of student achievement. In studying how various aspects of motivation influenced the mathematics achievement of 11- and 12-year-olds, Seegers and Boekaerts (1993) confirmed the positive effect of effort on mathematics achievement. Van de gaer, Pustjens, Van Damme, and De Munter (2008) found that effort in the form of participation explained gender differences in mathematics achievement for primary grades students. Similarly, Lloyd, Walsh, and Yailagh (2005) examined the mathematics achievement of fourth- and seventh-grade students and found that students with a positive disposition toward effort had higher mathematics achievement. Further, reviewing literature concerning mathematics achievement, Middleton and Spanias (1999) confirmed that effort is among the more influential predictors to consider. These various sources suggest that effort is a consistent predictor of mathematics achievement.

The factors affecting students' mathematics achievement thus far described have been consistently shown to predict or explain mathematics achievement, whereas there is only limited research on the effect of mathematical discussion on mathematics achievement. Therefore, it is important to consider these factors in exploring how mathematical discussion affects students' achievement. However, there are additional factors to consider that can affect mathematical achievement and possibly affect the effectiveness of mathematical discussion. Pimm (1987) suggested that while mathematical discussion is often advocated, it is rarely implemented. Since Pimm's statement, however, two influential documents from the National Council of Teachers of Mathematics (NCTM, 1989; NCTM, 2000) have provided far reaching support for mathematical discussion in the classroom. These documents have influenced how teacher educators teach future teachers, as well as how practicing teachers engage in their practice. Therefore, it stands to

Appendix B

reason that two factors could be interrelated with how effective discussion is in increasing students mathematical understanding. The first is the number of years teachers have been in the classroom, and the second is the number of math methods courses they have taken.

Clotfelter, Ladd, and Vigdor (2007) found that, in general, the more years of experience a teacher has, the higher were the mathematics achievement scores of their students. However, they also found that teachers who stay beyond 2–3 years are less effective in producing higher mathematics achievement than are those teachers who leave the classroom. Croninger, Rice, Rathbun, and Nishio (2007) examined elementary school data from ECLS and found that of the varying teacher qualifications that predict student achievement, years experience, the number of undergraduate methods coursework, and the highest earned degree are factors that have a significant effect.

Some logical conclusions can be drawn concerning teachers' experience in years and in methods courses. The longer teachers are in the classroom, the more refined their teaching becomes, and, therefore, the more effective mathematical discussions in such classrooms should be. In addition, since mathematical discussion has been increasingly advocated in recent years (NCTM, 1989; NCTM, 2000), teacher educators have likely encouraged this practice in their methods courses. Thus, the more of these methods courses a teacher has taken, it is logical that such teachers would engage their students in better quality mathematical discussion.

Overview

What seems apparent from the review of literature is that there are two issues that need to be addressed in analysis. The first is whether there is a positive relation between more frequent math discussion and math achievement on average. The second is whether this effect varies between classrooms, which would be evidence of the different quality of frequent math discussions observed by qualitative studies (i.e., Kazemi & Stipek, 2001; Manouchehri & St. John, 2006).

Therefore, the primary research question in this study is whether frequency of student discussion about mathematics has a significant positive effect on mathematics achievement on average across classrooms and schools. In addition to this primary research question, it is prudent to investigate whether there are differences in the effectiveness of discussion in some classrooms as compared with others, because this may help explain conflicting results in the literature. Thus, a secondary research question is to determine whether there is significant variability of the effect of discussion on mathematics achievement across teachers, classrooms, or schools, and if it is found, to identify the characteristics of these constituents that can explain such variability.

References

Alro, H., & Skovsmose, O. (2002). *Dialogue and learning in mathematics education: Intention, reflection, critique.* Boston, MA: Kluwer Academic Publishers.

Borenson, H. (1986). Teaching students to think in mathematics and to make conjectures. In M. Driscoll & J. Confrey (Eds.), *Teaching mathematics: Strategies that work K–12* (pp. 63–70). Portsmouth, NH: Heinemann.

Boyd, D., Lankford, H., Loeb, S., Rockoff, J. E., & Wyckoff, J. (2008). *The narrowing gap in New York City teacher qualifications and its implications for students in high-poverty schools.* National Center for Analysis of Longitudinal Data in Education Research. Retrieved from http://tpcprod.urban.org/UploadedPDF/1001268 narowinggapinnewyork.pdf

Clotfelter, C. T., Ladd, H. F., & Vigdor, J. L. (2007). Teacher credentials and student achievement: Longitudinal analysis with student fixed effects. *Economics of Education Review, 26,* 673–682.

Croninger, R. G., Rice, J. K., Rathbun, A., & Nishio, M. (2007). Teacher qualifications and early learning: Effects of certification, degree, and experience on first-grade student achievement. *Economics and Education Review, 26,* 312–324.

D'Ambrosio, B., Johnson, H., & Hobbs, L. (1995). Strategies for increasing achievement in mathematics. In R. W. Cole (Ed.), *Educating everybody's children: Diverse teaching strategies for diverse learners* (pp. 121–137). Alexandria, VA: Association for Supervision and Curriculum Development.

Doolittle, A. E., & Cleary, T. A. (1987). Gender-based differential item performance in mathematics achievement items. *Journal of Educational Measurement, 24,* 157–166.

Fennema, E., & Sherman, J. (1977). Sex-related differences in mathematics achievement, spatial visualization and affective factors. *American Educational Research Journal, 14*(1), 51–71.

Georges, A., & Pallas, A. M. (2010). New look at a persistent problem: Inequality, mathematics achievement, and teaching. *The Journal of Educational Research, 103,* 274–290.

Grouws, D. A. (2004). Mathematics. In G. Cawelti (Ed.), *Handbook of research on improving student achievement* (3rd ed., pp. 160–178). Arlington, VA: Education Research Service.

Hancewicz, E. (2005). Discourse in the mathematics classroom. In J. M. Kenney (Ed.), *Literacy strategies for improving mathematics instruction* (pp. 72–86). Alexandria, VA: Association for Supervision and Curriculum Development.

Hiebert, J., & Wearne, D. (1993). Instructional tasks, classroom discourse, and students' learning in second-grade arithmetic. *American Educational Research Journal, 30,* 393–425.

Kazemi, E., & Stipek, D. (2001). Promoting conceptual thinking in four upper-elementary mathematics classrooms. *The Elementary School Journal, 102*(1), 59–80.

Kohr, R. L., Coldiron, J. R., Skiffington, E. W., Masters, J. R., & Blust, R. S. (1987). *The influence of race, class and gender on mathematics achievement and self-esteem for fifth, eight and eleventh grade students in Pennsylvania schools* (Research report). Harrisburg: Pennsylvania State Department of Education.

Koichu, B., Berman, A., & Moore, M. (2007). The effect of promoting heuristic literacy on the mathematical aptitude of middle-school students. *International Journal of Mathematical Education in Science and Technology, 38*(1), 1–17.

Appendix B

Liu, X., Spybrook, J., Congdon, R., Martinez, A., & Raudenbush, S. W. (2009). *Optimal Design software for multi-level and longitudinal research* (Version 2.0) [Computer software]. Retrieved from http://sitemaker.umich.edu/group-based

Lloyd, J. E. V., Walsh, J., & Yailagh, M. S. (2005). Sex differences in performance attributions, self-efficacy, and achievement in mathematics: If I'm so smart, why don't I know it? *Canadian Journal of Education, 28,* 384–408.

Lubienski, S. T. (2002). A closer look at Black–White mathematics gaps: Intersections of race and SES in NAEP achievement and instructional practices data. *The Journal of Negro Education, 71,* 269–287.

Manouchehri, A., & St. John, D. (2006) From classroom discussions to group discourse. *Mathematics Teacher, 99,* 544–551.

McGraw, R., Lubienski, S. T., & Strutchens, M. E. (2006). A closer look at gender in NAEP mathematics achievement and affect data: Intersections with achievement, race/ethnicity, and socioeconomic status. *Journal for Research in Mathematics Education, 37,* 129–150.

Mercer, N., & Sams, C. (2006). Teaching children how to use language to solve math problems. *Language and Education, 20,* 507–528.

Middleton, J. A., & Spanias, P. A. (1999). Motivation for achievement in mathematics: Findings, generalizations and criticisms of the research. *Journal for Research in Mathematics Education, 30*(1), 65–88.

National Center for Education Statistics. (2004). *Spring 2004 fifth-grade child-level questionnaire: Mathematics teacher.* Retrieved from http://nces.ed.gov/ecls/pdf/fifthgrade/teacherMath.pdf

National Center for Education Statistics. (2006a). *Early Childhood Longitudinal Study, kindergarten class of 1998–1999 (ECLS-K): Combined users' manual for the ECLS-K fifth-grade data files and electronic codebooks (2006–032).* Washington, DC: Author.

National Center for Education Statistics. (2006b). *ECLS-K longitudinal kindergarten-fifth grade public-use data file, fifth grade cross-section.* Washington, DC: Author.

National Council of Teachers of Mathematics. (1989). *Curriculum standards for school mathematics.* Retrieved from http://www.nctm.org/fullstandards/previous/CurrEvStds/intro.asp

National Council of Teachers of Mathematics. (2000). *Principles and standards for school mathematics.* Reston, VA: Author.

Pimm, D. (1987). *Speaking mathematically: Communication in mathematics classrooms.* New York, NY: Routledge & Kegan Paul.

Raudenbush, S. W., & Bryk, A. S. (2002). *Hierarchical linear models: Applications and data analysis methods* (2nd ed.). Thousand Oaks, CA: Sage.

Raudenbush, S. W., Bryk, A. S., & Congdon, R. (2005). *HLM-6: Hierarchical linear and nonlinear modeling.* Lincolnwood, IL: Scientific Software International.

Seegers, G., & Boekaerts, M. (1993). Task motivation and mathematics achievement in actual task situations. *Learning and Instruction, 3,* 133–150.

Sfard, A. (2007). When the rules of discourse change, but nobody tells you: Making sense of mathematics learning from a commognitive standpoint. *Journal of the Learning Sciences, 16,* 565–613.

Shouse, R. (2001). The impact of traditional and reform-style practices on students mathematical achievement. In T. Loveless (Ed.), *The great curriculum debate: How should we teach reading and math?* Washington, DC: Brookings Institution Press.

Silver, E. A., Kilpatrick, J., & Schlesinger, B. (1990). *Thinking through mathematics: Fostering inquiry and communication in mathematics classrooms*. New York, NY: College Entrance Examination Board.

Snijders, T. A. B., & Bosker, R. J. (1999). *Multilevel analysis*. Thousand Oaks, CA: Sage.

Stigler, J. W., & Hiebert, J. (1997). Understanding and improving classroom mathematics instruction. *Phi Delta Kappa, 79*(1), 14–21.

Tate, W. F. (1997). Race-ethnicity, SES, gender, and language proficiency trends in mathematics achievement: An update. *Journal for Research in Mathematics Education, 28,* 652–679.

Tobin, K. (1986). Effects of teacher wait time on discourse characteristics in mathematics and language arts classes. *American Educational Research Journal, 23,* 191–200.

Truxaw, M. P., & DeFranco, T. C. (2007). Lessons from Mr. Larson: An inductive model of teaching for orchestrating discourse. *Mathematics Teacher, 101,* 268–272.

Van de gaer, E., Pustjens, H., Van Damme, J., & De Munter, A. (2008). Mathematics participation and mathematics achievement across school: The role of gender. *Sex Roles, 59,* 568–585.

Weiner, B. (1972). Attribution theory, achievement motivation, and educational process. *Review of Educational Research, 42,* 203–215.

Weiner, B. (1985). An attributional theory of achievement motivation and emotion. *Psychological Review, 92,* 548–573.

Wood, T. (1999). Creating a context for argument in mathematics class. *Journal for Research in Mathematics Education, 30,* 171–191.

Yackel, E., & Cobb, P. (1996). Sociomathematical norms, argumentation, and autonomy in mathematics. *Journal for Research in Mathematics Education, 27,* 458–477.

Address correspondence to Karl W. Kosko, School of Education, University of Michigan, 610 East University Avenue, Rm 2404, Ann Arbor, MI 48109, USA. E-mail: kwkosko@umich.edu

6) **Mason, O.J. & Holt, R. (2012). Mental health and physical activity interventions: A review of the qualitative literature.** *Journal of Mental Health,* **21(3), 274–284.**

Abstract

Background: Interventions based on physical activity are of proven efficacy as adjunctive interventions in mental health, but less is known about how these benefits come about.

Aims: This review summarises the qualitative research on the perspectives of service users so as to shed light on possible psychological and social mechanisms of therapeutic change.

Method: Thirteen published studies were identified by a detailed search of the peer-reviewed literature employing a variety of methodologies across a range of physical

activity contexts for participants with severe and enduring mental health difficulties. The results are grouped thematically, and the studies were compared and contrasted with respect to methodology and findings.
Findings: There was a high degree of congruence in support of the themes of social interaction and social support; feeling safe; improved symptoms; a sense of meaning, purpose and achievement; identity and the role of the facilitating personnel.
Conclusions: Exercise interventions deserve greater emphasis both theoretically and clinically, as many service users experience them as socially inclusive, non-stigmatising and, above all, effective in aiding recovery.

Keywords: *qualitative data, physical activity intervention*

Introduction

Despite a wealth of quantitative research regarding the psychological benefits of physical activity, there is limited agreement regarding the possible mechanisms that may lead to improved mental health outcomes. Commonly, outcome studies focus on symptomatic improvement, rather than on how and why change occurs (Fox, 2000). This review examines studies that explore the experiences of mental health service users participating in physical activity programmes. Following a brief summary of the quantitative literature, the main part of the review examines 13 qualitative studies. Following several methodological observations, we examine the role that such interventions can have from a recovery perspective.

Some, but not all, evidence suggests a relationship between physical activity and positive mental health (Biddle et al., 2000). Several meta-analyses have found exercise to have therapeutic benefits similar to those observed in psychotherapeutic interventions. For instance, Stathopolou et al. (2006) found a large effect across 11 randomised controlled trials (RCTs), with the best evidence for depression. They also found preliminary evidence for efficacy in anxiety and eating and substance-use disorders. A recent Cochrane review (Mead et al., 2009) of 25 trials in depression found that the best trials yield only moderate effect sizes that are not statistically significant, and even this association does not necessarily imply that physical activity *per se* is responsible. Epidemiological evidence has been cited by some as supportive of a causal link (e.g. Mutrie, 2000) and by others as not (e.g. O'Neal et al., 2000). Far fewer studies have investigated schizophrenia: both Faulkner's (2005) and Ellis et al.'s (2007) reviews were tentative about the degree to which physical activity is associated with a reduction of both positive and negative symptoms of schizophrenia. The accumulation of positive evidence has led to recommendations that exercise should be an integral part of both mental health promotion and management of mental health problems (Biddle & Mutrie, 2001; Grant, 2000). For example, the National Institute for Health and Clinical Excellence (2007) depression guidelines recommend structured, exercise programmes.

Mediators of the relationship between physical activity and symptomatic outcome have not been studied extensively. Evidence about who is helped and how is valued by clinicians in making choices about patient care. Semi-structured qualitative interviewing of clinical psychologists about their perceptions of exercise (Faulkner & Biddle, 2001) revealed that though favoured as a lifestyle option, the lack of an explanation for clinical change reduced their willingness to consider it as a treatment. Within the literature, mechanisms fall broadly into psychological or physiological categories. Potential physiological mechanisms include changes in neurotransmitter function (e.g. Brocks et al., 2003) and reductions in stress hormones relating to mood and arousal (e.g. cortisol; Duclos et al., 2003).

The psychological mechanisms that have received some attention are those of self-efficacy, distraction and self-esteem. Linking physical activity to self-efficacy theory, Craft (2005) found that having and monitoring exercise goals as well as utilising the social support of others may contribute to increased self-efficacy and thus recovery from depression. Bodin and Martinsen's (2004) RCT on depression compared martial arts with the use of a stationary exercise bike. While the bike was ineffective, martial arts practice led to greater self-efficacy and reduced symptoms. It is less clear that exercise acts as a distraction from more negative rumination. Craft (2005) measured levels of rumination and distraction, in addition to self-efficacy, among a group of women diagnosed with clinical depression attending an exercise group. Those in the exercise group used more distraction techniques than controls, although this was not significantly associated with a reduction in depression. The most studied theoretical approach to self-esteem (Sonstroem & Morgan, 1989) suggests that activity helps enhance perceived physical competencies (e.g. physical endurance), which then lead to greater global self-esteem. Mutrie (1997, p. 307) has suggested that qualitative methods may "hold the key to a better understanding of the mechanisms underlying the effect of exercise on life quality".

The importance of understanding participation from a service user perspective is receiving increasing support (e.g. Chadwick, 1997). Repper and Perkins (2003) have argued that this process must involve the "voice of first-hand experience". If we are to move towards a culture of promoting positive mental health within mental health services, then we need to focus more on the positive contribution that exercise can make to a person's life and his or her recovery from mental illness. The qualitative literature concerning this has not been reviewed to date beyond several minor observations within Stathopolou et al.'s (2006) largely quantitative review restricted to the trial literature. Qualitative studies can potentially contribute to a greater depth of understanding of how and why exercise can aid recovery, and it is timely to review a literature that has burgeoned in recent years. We hope to understand and highlight those aspects of participation that participants see as important in the recovery process.

Appendix B

Method

Included study characteristics

For inclusion, the following criteria were followed:

(1) use of an exercise/sport intervention ("sport*"/exercis*);
(2) participants to include mental health service users (mental health/psychiatr*);
(3) a qualitative methodology (qualitative*/phenomenol*/grounded/discourse) and
(4) focus of study on the service users' experience.

In order to search the entire range of possible areas (sport, exercise, psychology and health), PubMed, PsychInfo, Cochrane Library and Cinahl were thoroughly searched using the combination of terms from criteria 1 to 3. Further references of related reviews and articles were searched by hand to identify any additional studies. Thirteen published reports were identified (Table I); however, five of these papers relate to the participants of one original study (Carless & Douglas, 2008a), each focusing on a different aspect of the participants' experiences. The data across these studies were synthesised by one author so as to conduct an analysis based on their thematic content (RH using Braun & Clarke's, 2006, methodology). Six themes were identified where similar content was seen in two or more studies and where this was deemed important by at least some of them. As Braun and Clarke (2006, p. 82) pointed out, the assessment of "keyness" is necessarily subjective, and we were keen to be inclusive as the contexts, participants and methods were highly diverse so that unanimity could not be expected. The themes were then checked against the original results of the studies for validity by the other author (OM). We did not aim to test a particular theory but rather to represent the content of the papers in a brief accessible form that can aid theoretical thinking. The authors (both clinical psychologists working with adults with severe and enduring mental health problems) were concurrently conducting an evaluation of a physical activity-based intervention in secondary mental health care, though not in its delivery.

Methodology: a critical appraisal

While in general the samples were well situated (depth of detail about the participants and contexts), researchers varied widely in disclosing their backgrounds, roles and perspectives. One author (Guy from Crone & Guy, 2008) named himself as a service user, while the other is unidentified. They suggested that the shared experiences between the participants and the interviewer put interviewees at ease, but did not consider what influence this might have had on their interpretation of the data. Faulkner (of Faulkner & Sparks, 1999) reflected on how his role as a locum worker who set up the exercise programme in the hostel may have influenced the research

Sample Literature Reviews

Table I. Summary of studies.

Study and sample	Methodology/analysis	Intervention	Findings
Carless (2008): Single case study	PO, participant/ professional interviews and medical records; content/narrative analysis	Running	Exercise was found to be a meaningful activity which reinforces identity and sense of self
Carless and Douglas (2004): Seven men with severe and enduring mental health problems and four professionals	PO and FG; interviews	Nine-week golf programme (weekly sessions)	Themes were categorised according to factors that encouraged attendance and those factors that threatened attendance
Carless and Douglas (2008a): As for Carless and Douglas (2004)	PO and interviews; narrative analysis	Various sports and exercise groups	The following narratives were identified: "action", "achievement" and "relationship"
Carless and Douglas (2008b): Two men from Carless and Douglas (2004)	Case-study ethnographic research PO, analysis of records and interviews	Sports and exercise groups at a day centre	For one participant, sport was central to his identity. For another, sport and exercise represented a return to meaningful activities
Carless and Douglas (2008c): As for Carless and Douglas (2004)	Ethnography including PO, interviews and FG	Golf, football, gym, badminton, tennis, swimming and running	Evidence for informational, tangible, esteem and emotional support were offered and received by participants through exercise
Carless and Sparkes (2008): Three patients from Carless and Douglas (2004)	Interpretative case-study approach	Swimming, gym use and a walking group	A narrative account of each patient's story is given for the reader to reflect on
Carter-Morris and Faulkner (2003): Five males with enduring mental health problems. Carers of service users (n not stated)	Interviews; some GT methods used	Football project. No further details given	Themes: (1) Normalisation and a personally meaningful opportunity for social interaction; (2) participation helped to challenge auditory hallucinations and delusional beliefs; (3) barriers to participation related to side effects of medication
Crone (2007): Mental health service users. N=4. Two males and two females	Semi-structured interviews; methods from GT	A walking project	Themes: (1) Attitudes regarding the project; (2) factors affecting participation; (3) attitudes and opinions of the project; (4) perceived benefits and outcomes of participation; (5) experiences
Crone and Guy (2008): 11 mental health service users (10 males and 1 female)	FG, GT	Activities including badminton, gym, water aerobics and bowling	Themes: Taking part, reasons for participation, previous experiences, role of sports therapy, attitudes/opinions, factors affecting participation, perceived benefits and future improvements

Appendix B

Table I. (continued)

Study	Method	Intervention	Findings
Faulkner and Sparkes (1999): One male and one female, both with schizophrenia diagnosed	Ethnography, 10 weeks, participants and key worker interviews	Walking and swimming twice 30 min/week	A positive change in psychological well-being, sleeping patterns, social interactions, hygiene, coping strategy and distraction
Faulkner and Biddle (2004): Two males and one female with depression	Repeated semi-structured interviews and narrative analysis	Gym-on-prescription scheme	Three varying narratives presented. Results discussed in terms of benefits and problems
Priest (2007): Mental health day service users. N= 14. 10 males and 4 females	PO, interviews, group discussion and GT	Weekly walking group	Categories: Closer to what is more natural, feeling safe, being part, striving, getting away, being me and finding meaning
Raine et al. (2002): 20 stakeholders involved in a gym set up for people with mental health problems. This included gym users (8 females and 12 males)	Interviews and FGs; data analysis not stated	Community gym facility	The gym's non-institutional appearance, community location, and perceived (psychological) and physical distance from health services Activities are meaningful and socially valued. The importance of fostering positive relationships

Note: FG, focus group; PO, participant observation; GT, grounded theory.

process. He explicitly stated that his aim is to see whether the programme is beneficial and described friendships developing over time in his key worker role. Others did not describe their values, interests or roles in any detail beyond profession (Carter-Morris, a community psychiatric nurse; Priest, a clinical psychologist; Crone, no details given).

There is some explicit evidence of researchers thinking about their own contribution to the process, but of course unless this is made explicit, it is difficult to judge its extent. Priest gave excerpts of field notes integrated into category descriptions. While we learn, more by detective work than explicit self-description, that Douglas (of Carless & Douglas, 2008a) is a golf coach, we learn nothing about how her interests impact on data interpretation. Sparkes (of Carless & Sparkes, 2008) served as a "critical friend" and "theoretical sounding board" to encourage self-critique by Carless.

Credibility (whether the participants view the results as representative) was approached and discussed in a variety of ways. Priest conducted a data analysis seminar with her colleagues to explore the meaning of categories and also returned to the walking group to represent her interpretations for their feedback. Crone (2007) stated that credibility was addressed by the researcher attending the walks before and after data collection, but no details were given about how this constituted a reliability check or enabled the participants to respond; rather the study seems to be driven by the researcher's interest in perceived benefits. Helpfully, several studies compared results from the participants with interviews with the carers (Carter-Morris & Faulkner, 2003) or gym staff and referrers (Carless & Douglas, 2008b; Raine et al., 2002).

Many of the studies have very small samples and several studies are subsets of a single group. A necessary consequence of this is that the entire data corpus is made up of fewer than 70 participants, only 17 of whom are female. Negative reports may well be lacking due to selection bias. In the interests of greater representativeness, diversity and generalisability, further sampling is critical in this context. Overall, we had the impression that the researchers tended to be enthusiasts for the interventions under study and sometimes had explicit agendas and roles in evaluating them, but took great care to attend to the meanings of the accounts provided by the participants and to offer back their results for further comment and/or compare them with those of other stakeholders. In many cases, few details of the analytic approach taken were given.

Findings

Types of mental health problems and interventions

Although some studies were very specific about the nature of the mental illness and diagnoses were stated (e.g. schizophrenia; Carter-Morris & Faulkner, 2003; Faulkner & Sparkes, 1999), others simply stated that the participants had a "serious mental illness" (e.g. Carless & Douglas, 2008a). Still others stated that the participants were service users within the mental health service but that specific diagnosis was not known (Crone, 2007; Crone & Guy, 2008; Raine et al., 2002). Priest (2007) gave examples of the problems experienced by the group including hearing voices and trauma. Table I illustrates the range of interventions, with some providing a specific physical activity, while others offered a wide range.

Types of qualitative methodologies

Three studies employed grounded theory and four used a form of content analysis (Table I). Priest (2007), however, combined methods from grounded theory and ethnography. Faulkner and Sparkes (1999) described an ethnographic method in which they used a combination of participant observation and interviews with the participants and their key workers. Raine et al. (2002) described their methodology as a participatory model in which they used focus groups and semi-structured interviews with gym users, gym staff and referral agencies. Faulkner and Biddle (2004) interviewed three participants attending (or failing to attend) a local leisure centre over the course of a year, taking a narrative approach to their unfolding accounts.

Carless and Douglas (2008a) employed a narrative approach arguing that the social constructionist position may be a helpful way of unpicking some of the mechanisms by which physical activity can help with people with mental health

Appendix B

difficulties. They adopted three methods of data collection including interviews and focus groups with mental health professionals, semi-structured interviews with the participants and participant observation. In a development of the original wider study of 11 men, Carless and Sparkes (2008) offered an interpretative case-study approach to explore experiences of three men in greater depth. Three stories were presented and, unusually, the authors invited the readers to make their own conclusions about the stories, rather than interpreting the data themselves.

Theme 1: an opportunity for social interaction and social support

Nine studies explicitly reported the importance of social interaction and inclusion as part of their involvement in physical activity. In her evaluation of a walking project for users of secondary mental health care, Crone (2007) reported how one of the main benefits perceived by the participants was the opportunity to meet and be with others. In Carter-Morris and Faulkner's (2003) evaluation of a football project for mental health service users, a main theme was "a personally meaningful opportunity for social interaction". The participants reported that their involvement in the project offered a safe opportunity for interaction, where their diagnosis did not matter; participation in the football project had led to a widening of their social worlds. The gym-on-prescription scheme studied by Faulkner and Biddle (2004) was seen as normalising and promoting social interaction by a participant whom they termed a "slow starter".

In an ethnographic study of a mental health day service walking group, an important identified theme was the experience of "being part" of something (Priest, 2007). This was in stark contrast to isolation that people had described in their lives previously. Linked to this idea was the way in which people were able to connect with those who were in a similar situation like themselves.

Again, Crone and Guy (2008) found that opportunities for social interaction led to greater confidence, echoing quantitative studies of self-esteem discussed earlier. There was a sense that it was easier to socialise with others in the same situation, where the pressures were very different from those of other social situations. Carless and Douglas (2008a) identified a relationship narrative whereby the main motivation of the participants was to be able to share their experiences with others.

Going beyond a mere reference to the concept, Carless and Douglas (2008c) made the first attempt to explore and operationalise the nature of social support in a physical activity context for people with serious mental illness. In a development of their earlier work, Carless and Douglas (2008c) analysed the content of their interviews for evidence to support Rees and Hardy's (2000) multi-dimensional model of social support. Support for each of the following dimensions of social support was found: informational support, tangible support and emotional support. As they recognised, however, the findings simply illuminate some of the social support processes operating, rather than offering a definitive view.

Theme 2: a sense of meaning, purpose and achievement

Mentioned in five studies, this theme necessarily covers a breadth of gains and satisfactions as the activities are highly varied. The participants in the walking project visited selected areas of Somerset such as "areas of outstanding natural beauty" or bird reserves and often featured educational talks about flora and fauna (Crone, 2007). They described their experience in terms of purposeful activity and a sense of doing something to keep them busy. Greater mastery also led to a sense of achievement. Similarly, Crone and Guy (2008) found that people also gained a sense of achievement and satisfaction from purposive activity. Priest's (2007) theme of "striving" (physical exertion leading to a sense of feeling better) conveyed that people acknowledged the process of physical activity and that there was an intrinsic sense of reward and achievement.

In a narrative case study of two men, Carless and Douglas (2008b) highlighted how for both men, sports offered an opportunity to achieve something and develop a personal competence. In the larger narrative study, Carless and Douglas (2008a) discussed the emergence of both an action narrative and an achievement narrative. The action narrative referred to a physical process such as "going places and doing stuff" and contrasted with a narrative of serious mental illness involving inactivity. The achievement narrative was derived from accounts where the participants spoke about learning sports-related skills and developing a sense of improvement. They noted how achieving in the present led the participants to develop confidence regarding future activity. Carless and Douglas (2000a) suggested that by telling their stories, the participants were able to incorporate these achievements in relation to sports into their identities and sense of self.

Theme 3: the role of facilitating personnel

Six studies made reference to the valued role of the personnel who facilitated the projects, and for other studies, this was admittedly not substantially within their remit. Crone (2007) found that "being approachable and being responsive to the diverse needs of the client group" were important. In the community gym, non-mental health professionals were viewed positively by users, as they were able to talk openly, without any fear of repercussions (Raine et al., 2002). In contrast, for others, a lack of a mental health trained professional was the source of some anxiety. Overall, staff were perceived as non-judgemental, supportive, interested and caring. Related to the feelings of safety, Priest (2007) described how important it seemed for participants to know that staff were taking overall responsibility for the walking group. The role of staff in motivating the participants to attend was identified as important in the study of sport as therapy by Crone and Guy (2007). This was also an important factor identified by Carless and Douglas (2004), where supportive phone calls from staff promoted attendance.

Appendix B

The role of staff in providing "esteem" was highlighted by Carless and Douglas (2008a) – substantiating what Rees and Hardy (2000) described as "the bolstering of a person's sense of competence or self-esteem by others". This support was found to promote an individual's sense of competence and confidence as well as a sense of pleasure and pride.

Theme 4: feeling safe

The title "Feeling safe" from Priest's (2007) study of a walking group is explicitly reflected in four studies. This sense of safety is associated by participants with being in a group with other people also experiencing distress as well as being in a physical or emotional "place" in which they did not feel threatened. Instead of feeling threatened and insecure, participants felt accepted and secure. Interestingly, "being outdoors" or "in nature" also contributed to the feelings of safety in this study.

The concept of "psychological safety" was heavily represented in data from the community gym facility (Raine et al., 2002). For example, participants were concerned that they might experience stigma if they were to go to a community gym, though its connection to wider society was valued. Related to this idea of feeling safe, two studies highlighted the importance of a caring and non-competitive environment stressing how this enabled shared talk about experiences of mental illness and treatment (Carless & Douglas, 2004; Raine et al., 2002).

Theme 5: improved symptoms

Consistent with quantitative measures, nine studies explicitly reported a positive effect on participants' symptoms. Four of five participants with psychotic experiences (Carter, Morris & Faulkner, 2003) suggested that their experiences helped them challenge voices and distressing beliefs and also redirect their attention away from their symptoms to reinforce "a more positive sense of reality". This echoed previous research by Faulkner and Sparkes (1999), who found that exercise helped to reduce participants' perception of their auditory hallucinations. Crone and Guy (2008) also found evidence of the distraction response style discussed earlier, as participants described the participation in sports therapy as a time away from thinking about their illness. Carless and Douglas' (2008b) participants described improved mood and concentration as a result of their involvement in physical activity. Priest's (2007) walking group found an opportunity to "escape from things that were difficult in their life" and alleviated the experience of "oppression and emotional pain" (p. 49) as well as better sleep. Interestingly, Carless and Douglas (2008a) found that participants' narratives focused on achievement, relationships and actions, as opposed to symptoms or illness.

Theme 6: identity

Most prominently of the four studies with identity-related themes, Carless and Douglas (2008a) argued that physical activity experiences enhance the quality of life for men with serious mental illness by enabling them to reconstruct a more positive and meaningful identity. In a later case study of one young man who had re-engaged with running, Carless (2008) argued that the young man's previous athletic identity was removed by the impact of serious mental illness and that his re-engagement in exercise was a way of regaining and rebuilding his sense of self and his identity. Echoing this, one participant attending a football project described regaining his identity as "a footballer", allowing him to "escape from his identity as someone with a mental illness" (Carter-Morris & Faulkner, 2003, p. 27). The "slow starter" using gym on prescription (Faulkner & Biddle, 2004) reported albeit subtle benefits to body image. Though the concept of self-identity is broader than those of self-efficacy and self-esteem, it probably encompasses the self-esteem variables highlighted earlier in the quantitative literature.

Conclusions

Although there was repeated, albeit anecdotal, evidence of improvement in symptoms, most interviews were conducted by health professionals sometimes with a focus on describing health benefits. Nevertheless, symptom-based improvements formed only one of six areas of impact, and the results are certainly in tune with the recent shift to a broader understanding of recovery by services and their users alike. Rather the participants across many studies tended to highlight both the positive social interaction and relationships and the sense of meaning, purpose and achievement opportunity that participation in physical activity provided the opportunity for. Interestingly, these elements are key factors identified by social psychologists as being important for positive mental well-being (Ryff, 1989).

Not only do the results contextualise exercise interviews as going beyond purely physical health-related factors, but they also extend beyond "classic" psychological factors such as self-efficacy and self-esteem. It is not that these concepts do not apply or are irrelevant, rather that in participants' experience they are part of a much wider picture of their social role, relationships and identity. The intervention context seems to enable broader psychosocial changes to occur based on the relationships that develop with both professionals and participants; these may then generalise to other aspects of participants' lives. Whatever be the activity-based intervention provided, it was the relationships formed and the participants' place in the group that seemed to be important to the changes that took place. These broader psychosocial processes are deserving of both qualitative and quantitative attention.

Facilitators (project personnel) were highlighted as having a very important role, described by participants as key to providing a sense of safety and support and

Appendix B

thus helping build their confidence and esteem. Facilitators' commitment to provision and belief in participants' capacity to reconstruct a more positive self-identity are very likely contributors to this aspect of intervention. However, it is rare that health professionals include physical activity as a treatment option in mental health or have the commitment to an area frequently seen as lying outside their professional remit. For example, a recent survey of GP referrers (The Mental Health Foundation, 2009) found that nearly half did not perceive an accessible referral route and concluded that this, as well as unawareness about availability, means that many people are being denied exercise referral as a treatment option. Benefits were seen both to having facilitators from outside the formal mental health context and to having mental health professionals involved. Tentatively, it seems that both have much to contribute to programmes contributing in very different ways. Given the value placed by service users on mental health professionals stepping out of the traditional clinic-based role, clinicians should feel encouraged to come alongside in such activities – a role perhaps generally seen as restricted to occupational therapy.

The barriers for clinicians to refer or encourage physical activity may be manifold depending on the service context, but at the very least many have "gym-on-prescription" or other schemes available to them. With greater understanding of the possible benefits of exercise participation, clinicians would be more likely to consider physical activity as a treatment option integral to care planning and refer accordingly. There will, of course, also be barriers for service users and it is very possible that forms of activity outside the confines of the gym or sports field, such as dancing and cycling, would have similar benefits with likely implications for self-efficacy and self-esteem. The stress that participants placed on non-specific factors having an important role in clinical change supports this extrapolation. Many variants of dance may be more acceptable to traditionally non-sporting groups such as some Asian women for whom sports/gym options may not be as relevant.

As provision of mental health services moves further away from traditional treatments to a broader recovery model (Davidson & Roe, 2007; Repper & Perkins, 2003), there will be even greater potential for physical activity participation. The studies reviewed here are highly supportive of Repper and Perkins' (2003, p. ix) contention that it is the "recovering of the social roles and relationships that give life value and meaning" for service users. Likewise, Davidson and Roe (2007), in their recent conceptualisation of recovery, suggested that a central part of the recovery process comprises the rebuilding of the sense of self and one's social identity. Participation in physical activity interventions can play an important role for many more in the future.

Declaration of Interests: The authors report no conflicts of interest. The authors alone are responsible for the content and writing of the paper.

References

Biddle, S., & Mutrie, N. (2001). *Psychology of physical activity: Determinants, well-being and interventions.* London: Routledge.

Biddle, S., Fox, K., & Boucher, S. (Eds.). (2000). *Physical activity and psychological well-being.* London: Routledge.

Bodin, T., & Martinsen, E.W. (2004). Mood and self-efficacy during acute exercise in clinical depression: A randomized, controlled study. *Journal of Sport & Exercise Psychology, 26,* 623–633.

Braun, V., & Clarke, V. (2006). Using thematic analysis in psychology. *Qualitative Research in Psychology, 3,* 77–101.

Brocks, A., Meyer, T., Opitz, M., Bartmann, U., Hillmer-Vogel, U., & George, A. (2003). 5-HT1A responsivity in patients with panic disorder before and after treatment with aerobic exercise, clomipramine or placebo. *European Neuropsychopharmacology, 13,* 153–164.

Carless, D. (2008). Narrative, identity, and recovery from serious mental illness: A life history of a runner. *Qualitative Research in Psychology, 5*(4), 233–248.

Carless, D., & Douglas, K. (2004). A golf programme for people with severe and enduring mental health problems. *Journal of Mental Health Promotion, 3*(4), 26–39.

Carless, D., & Douglas, K. (2008a). Narrative, identity and mental health: How men with serious mental illness re-story their lives through physical activity. *Psychology of Sport and Exercise, 9*(5), 576–594.

Carless, D., & Douglas, K. (2008b). The role of sport and exercise in recovery from mental illness: Two case studies. *International Journal of Men's Health, 7*(2), 139–158.

Carless, D., & Douglas, K. (2008c). Social support for and through exercise and sport in a sample of men with serious mental illness. *Issues in Mental Health Nursing, 29*(11), 1179–1199.

Carless, D., & Sparkes, A. (2008). The physical activity experiences of men with serious mental illness: Three short stories. *Psychology of Sport and Exercise, 9*(2), 191–210.

Carter-Morris, P., & Faulkner, G. (2003). A football project for service users: The role of football in reducing social exclusion. *Journal of Mental Health Promotion, 2,* 24–30.

Chadwick, P. (1997). Recovery from psychosis: Learning more from patients. *Journal of Mental Health, 6,* 577–588.

Craft, L.L. (2005). Exercise and clinical depression: Examining two psychological mechanisms. *Psychology of Sport and Exercise, 6,* 151–171.

Crone, D. (2007). Walking back to health: A qualitative investigation into service users' experiences of a walking project. *Issues in Mental Health Nursing, 28*(2), 167–183.

Crone, D., & Guy, H. (2008). "*I know it is only exercise, but to me it is something that keeps me going*": A qualitative approach to understanding mental health service users' experiences of sports therapy. *International Journal of Mental Health Nursing, 17,* 197–207.

Davidson, L., & Roe, D. (2007). Recovery from versus recovery in serious mental illness: One strategy for lessening confusion plaguing recovery. *Journal of Mental Health, 16*(4), 459–470.

Duclos, M., Gouarne, C., & Bonnemaison, D. (2003). Acute and chronic effects of exercise on tissue sensitivity to glucocorticoids. *Journal of Applied Physiology, 94,* 869–875.

Ellis, N., Crone D., Davey, R., & Grogan, S. (2007). Exercise interventions as an adjunct therapy for psychosis: A critical review. *British Journal of Clinical Psychology, 46,* 95–111.

Faulkner, G. (2005). Exercise as an adjunct treatment for schizophrenia. In G. Faulkner & A. Taylor (Eds.), *Exercise, health and mental health: Emerging relationships* (pp. 27–46). London: Routledge.

Faulkner, G., & Biddle, S. (2001). Exercise and mental health: It's not just psychology! *Journal of Sports Sciences*, *19*, 433–444.

Faulkner, G., & Biddle, S.J.H. (2004). Exercise and depression: Considering variability and contextuality. *Journal of Sport and Exercise Psychology*, *26*, 3–18.

Faulkner, G., & Sparkes, A. (1999). Exercise as therapy for schizophrenia: An ethnographic study. *Journal of Sport and Exercise Psychology*, *21*, 52–69.

Fox, K.R. (2000). The effects of exercise on self-perceptions and self-esteem. In S.J.H. Biddle, K.R. Fox, & S.H. Boutcher (Eds.), *Physical activity and psychological well-being* (pp. 88–117). London: Routledge.

Grant, T. (2000). *Physical activity and mental health – national consensus statements and guidelines for practitioners*. London: Health Education Authority.

Mead, G.E., Morley, W., Campbell, P., Greig, C.A., McMurdo, M., & Lawlor, D.A. (2009). Exercise for depression. *Cochrane Database of Systematic Reviews*, *4*, CD004366.

Mutrie, N. (1997). The therapeutic effects of exercise on the self. In K.R. Fox (Ed.), *The physical self: From motivation to well-being* (pp. 287–314). Champaign, IL: Human Kinetics.

Mutrie, N. (2000). The relationship between physical activity and clinically defined depression. In S.J.H. Biddle, K.R. Fox, & S.H. Boutcher (Eds.), *Physical activity and psychological well-being* (pp. 46–62). London: Routledge.

National Institute for Health and Clinical Excellence. (2007). *Depression (amended): Management of depression in primary and secondary care*. Clinical Guideline 23 (amended). London: National Collaborating Centre for Medical Health.

O'Neal, H.A., Dunn, A.L., & Martinsen, E.W. (2000) Depression and exercise. *International Journal of Sport Psychology*, *31*, 110–135.

Priest, P. (2007). The healing balm effect: Using a walking group to feel better. *Journal of Health Psychology*, *12*, 36–52.

Raine, P., Truman, C., & Southerst, A. (2002). The development of a community gym for people with mental health problems: Influences on psychological accessibility. *Journal of Mental Health*, *11*(1), 43–53.

Rees, T., & Hardy, L. (2000). An investigation of the social support experiences of high-level sports performers. *The Sport Psychologist*, *14*, 327–347.

Repper, J., & Perkins, R. (2003). *Social inclusion and recovery*. Edinburgh: Balliere Tindall.

Ryff, C.D. (1989). Happiness is everything or is it? Explorations on the psychological meaning of psychological well-being. *Journal of Personality and Social Psychology*, *57*, 1069–1081.

Sonstroem, R.J., & Morgan, W.P. (1989). Exercise and self-esteem: Rationale and model. *Medicine and Science in Sports and Exercise*, *21*, 329–337.

Stathopolou, G., Powers, M., Berry, A., Smits, J., & Otto, M. (2006). Exercise interventions for mental health: A quantitative and qualitative review. *Clinical Psychology – Science and Practice*, *13*(2), 179–193.

The Mental Health Foundation. (2009). *Moving on up: Exercise on prescription for mental health*. London: Author.

Correspondence: Oliver J. Mason, Research Department of Clinical, Educational and Health Psychology, 1-19 Torrington Place, University College London, London WC1N 6BT, UK. Tel: 020 7697 8230. Fax: 020 7916 1989. E-mail: o.mason@ucl.ac.uk

7) Matarazzo, B., Barnes, S.M., Pease, J. L., Russell, L.M., Hanson, J.E., Soberay, K.A. & Gutierrez, P.M. (2014). Suicide risk among lesbian, gay, bisexual, and transgender military personnel and veterans: What does the literature tell us? *Suicide and Life-Threatening Behavior*, 44(2), 200–217.

Research suggests that both the military and veteran and the lesbian, gay, bisexual, and transgender (LGBT) populations may be at increased risk for suicide. A literature review was conducted to identify research related to suicide risk in the LGBT military and veteran populations. Despite the paucity of research directly addressing this issue, themes are discussed evident in the literature on LGBT identity and suicide risk as well as LGBT military service members and veterans. Factors such as social support and victimization appear to be particularly relevant. Suggestions are made with respect to future research that is needed on this very important and timely topic.

While serving in the U.S. military has historically been regarded as a protective factor against mortality (Rothberg, Bartone, Holloway, & Marlowe, 1990; Kang & Bullman, 1996), recent evidence (e.g., Army Suicide Prevention Task Force, 2010) suggests this may no longer be accurate as it relates to death by suicide. Suicide has become a formidable problem among U.S. military personnel. Since the beginning of the conflicts in Iraq and Afghanistan, suicide rates have doubled among active-duty military members (Army Suicide Prevention Task Force, 2010). In 2008, the prevalence of suicide in the Army and Marines surpassed that of the age-adjusted general population for the first time (Army Suicide Prevention Task Force, 2010; Frueh & Smith, 2012). Suicide is now second only to unintended injury as cause of death in the U.S. military (Department of Defense Task Force on Prevention of Suicide by Members of the Armed Forces, 2010; Ritchie, Keppler, & Rothberg, 2003). Although there is evidence to suggest that veteran suicide rates are decreasing in recent years, suicide among veterans continues to surpass rates of the general population, with males aged 30 to 64 at the highest risk (Blow et al., 2012). One reaction to this growing prevalence has been increased research on the risk factors for suicide, identification of at-risk subpopulations, and the development of suicide prevention interventions.

One population within the military that has the potential to be particularly vulnerable to suicide, but that has not been the focus of much research, is the lesbian, gay, bisexual, and transgender (LGBT) community.[1] For close to half a century, reports have documented the elevated risk for suicide among LGBT populations (Haas et al., 2011), and epidemiological studies have provided evidence that the LGBT community is at an increased risk for suicide and self-directed violent behaviors (Garofalo, Wolf, Wissow, Woods, & Goodman, 1999; King et al., 2008; Remafedi, French, Story, Resnick, & Blum, 1998). Nevertheless, there is no

Appendix B

consistent and reliable way to determine the prevalence of suicide among this population because death records do not routinely record sexual orientation (Haas et al., 2011). Psychological autopsy has been used to capture death by suicide and sexual orientation, but increased death rates among LGBT populations were not found in these studies (McDaniel, Purcell, & D'Augelli, 2001; Renaud, Berlim, Begolli, McGirr, & Turecki, 2010; Shaffer, Fisher, Hicks, Parides, & Gould, 1995). The results should be regarded as tentative due to small sample sizes and underreporting by those interviewed. One study that used Danish registries to examine same-sex partnership and death by suicide did find that individuals with same-sex partnership were 3 to 4 times more likely to die by suicide than married heterosexual individuals (Qin, Agerbo, & Mortensen, 2003).

Although it cannot be determined unequivocally that death by suicide is higher among the LGBT community, the relationship between attempted suicide and sexual orientation has been established in population-based studies in the United States and worldwide (Cochran & Mays, 2000; Fergusson, Horwood, Ridder, & Beautrais, 2005; Mathy, 2002a). Discrepancies in prevalence vary, but among adults who reported same-sex behavior, rates of attempted suicide have been consistently found to be between three and five times higher than those who never reported same-sex behavior (Cochran & Mays, 2011; Paul et al., 2002). In addition, there have been reports that combine ideation and attempts, with important differences by gender. Gay and bisexual women have reported much higher rates of suicidal ideation, and gay and bisexual men have reported significantly higher suicide attempt rates (King et al., 2008).

Fewer data are available on death by suicide and suicidal ideation and behaviors among the transgender population (Mathy, 2002b). Some data exist that suggest death by suicide and suicide attempts are much higher in individuals who have had sex reassignment surgery (Dixen, Maddever, Van Maasdam, & Edwards, 1984; Pfäfflin & Junge, 1998). However, a review of consequences of sex reassignment in Europe found that suicide attempts and suicidal ideation may decrease from 20% before surgery to a much lower rate (0.5–1.9%) after (Michel, Ansseau, Legros, Pitchot, & Mormont, 2002). Factors associated with being at risk for suicidal thoughts and behavior in the transgender population include common risk factors, such as substance abuse, depression, and anxiety (Clements-Nolle, Marx, & Katz, 2006; Xavier, Honnold, & Bradford, 2007), as well as job-related stressors (National Center for Transgender Equality & the National Gay & Lesbian Task Force, 2009). Evidence suggests that certain risk factors are specific to transgender individuals, including a history of forced sex, gender-based discrimination and victimization (Clements-Nolle et al., 2006), and rejection by their family of origin (Grossman & D'Augelli, 2008).

Given these findings, being a member of the U.S. military, as well as identifying as LGBT, could potentially constitute a double-edged risk for suicide. At the time of this writing, the authors of this paper were only able to identify two studies regarding suicide risk among LGBT military personnel. The paucity of research on the LGBT community within the U.S. military is understandable given the military's historical policies with respect to gays and lesbians serving in the military. The repeal in 2011 by President Obama of the Don't Ask Don't Tell policy (Policy Concerning Homosexuality in the Armed Forces, 2004) presents an opportunity to examine risk among sexual minority military personnel and explore ways to optimize their wellbeing and functioning. In this article we review the existing literature on the LGBT community and suicide as well as the LGBT community within the military. A conceptualization regarding the implications of these findings for military personnel is offered, gaps in the literature are identified, and recommendations for future research are discussed.

Methods

Search Strategy for the Identification of Relevant Studies

A broad search strategy for potential articles was used. Electronic searches were completed using PubMed, ERIC, Sociological Abstracts, Social Work Abstracts, and PsychInfo. Search terms were identified across three different content areas: LGBT identity, suicide, and the military. Combinations of the following terms were searched: gay, lesbian, bisexual, transgender, homosexual, transsexual, suicid*, military, and veteran. Terms related to LGBT identity, the military, and suicide were searched as a triad, terms related to LGBT identity and suicide were searched as a dyad, and terms related to LGBT identity and the military were also searched as a dyad. Each database was independently searched by two team members utilizing the entire search strategy. Any unique results yielded were included in an EndNote database.

Abstract and Full-Text Review

After duplicate articles were removed, team members reviewed all abstracts in the EndNote database. Articles were included if they were published in a peer-reviewed journal in the English language, the main focus of the article was on adults (the review only included studies in which participants' mean age was at least 18 years old), and content was related to either: LGBT identity, the military, and suicide; or LGBT identity and the military; or LGBT identity and suicide. Articles were excluded if they focused on nonsuicidal self-directed violence or did not report original research (e.g., literature reviews, opinion papers). The articles that met these criteria were divided among the team for full-text review. Articles were then removed if upon full-text review, they did not meet criteria as outlined above.

Appendix B

Synthesis of the Literature

Relevant information (e.g., abstract, results, recommendations) from each remaining original research article was entered into an Access database. Each research team member reviewed this information for each article to identify themes in the literature. Team members met to discuss themes present in the literature and decided on the most common and relevant themes to the topic area.

Results

The initial search yielded 3,810 abstracts. Following the removal of duplicate articles and those that did not meet inclusion or exclusion criteria, 187 abstracts remained. After the full-text review of these 187 articles, 117 original research articles were available for analysis. The primary reasons for exclusion were that the article did not report original research or that the primary content of the article was not related to the required content categories. The final 117 articles were classified into three groups based on content area: LGBT identity, suicide, and the military ($n = 1$); LGBT status and suicide ($n = 95$); and the military and LGBT status ($n = 21$). While searching for supporting literature, one additional original research article was identified after the initial search was conducted. This article was specifically related to LGBT identity, suicide, and military. Results from the body of literature are presented in narrative form. Information regarding prevalence data and risk and protective factors is described.

Prevalence of Suicidal Ideation and Behavior among the LGBT Population

Numerous articles reported the prevalence of suicidal thoughts and behaviors among LGBT individuals (see Table 1 for U.S. studies). These rates differed somewhat across samples and study methodologies, but all studies reported noteworthy rates of suicidal ideation and attempts among LGBT individuals. Two studies reported findings specifically related to sexual minority veterans and suicidal ideation and attempts. Blosnich, Bossarte, and Silenzio (2012) found that 11.48% of sexual minority veterans reported that they had seriously considered attempting suicide within the past year, whereas only 3.48% of heterosexual veterans reported having seriously considered attempting suicide during the past year. Herrell et al. (1999) analyzed national data from the Vietnam Era Twin Registry and reported that among veterans who had at least one same-gendered sexual partner in their lifetime, 55.3% reported suicidal ideation compared to 25.2% of those with no reported same-gender partners. Among veterans with at least one same-gender partner, 14.7% reported that they had attempted suicide compared to 3.9% of veterans with no same-gender partner.

In addition to these two studies specifically focused on LGB veterans, the search yielded multiple studies related to LGBT samples that were not specified as military or veteran. Most U.S. studies found that approximately 40% of LGB participants reported a lifetime history of suicidal ideation. Lifetime suicidal ideation was reported by 41% to 43% of mixed LGBT participant samples (Garcia, Adams, Friedman, & East, 2002; McBee-Strayer & Rogers James, 2002); approximately 41% of gay males (Balsam, Beauchaine, Mickey, & Rothblum, 2005; Cochran & Mays, 2000); 38% to 57% of lesbian women (Balsam, Beauchaine, et al., 2005; Bradford, Ryan, & Rothblum, 1994); and 31% to 39% of bisexual individuals (Balsam, Beauchaine, et al., 2005). Fifty to 64% of transgender individuals reported a lifetime history of suicidal ideation (Imbimbo et al., 2009; Kenagy & Bostwick, 2005). In keeping with these high rates of suicidal ideation, when prevalence across studies was examined, a mean of approximately 17% of LGB participants reported having attempted suicide (e.g., Balsam, Beauchaine, et al., 2005; Balsam, Rothblum, & Beauchaine, 2005; Remafedi, 2002). Transgender individuals generally reported a higher prevalence of suicide attempts, with approximately 30% having attempted suicide (Clements-Nolle, Marx, Guzman, & Katz, 2001; Kenagy, 2005; Kenagy & Bostwick, 2005).

Many studies also compared the prevalence of suicidal thoughts and behaviors between LGBT and heterosexual populations. The research shows that LGBT populations are at elevated risk of suicide relative to heterosexual populations. Blosnich and Bossarte (2012) analyzed a representative sample of 11,046 college-attending 18- to 24-year-olds and found significantly more LGB students reported suicidal ideation (gay or lesbian = 15%, bisexual = 21%) and suicide attempts (gay or lesbian = 3.3%, bisexual = 4.6%) within the past year than heterosexual students (ideation = 5.5%, attempts = 0.9%). Needham and Austin (2010) analyzed follow-up data from 11,153 participants (18–26 years old) initially recruited in a nationally representative U.S. school-based study. They also found significantly greater rates of suicidal ideation among LGB participants. Approximately 21% of lesbians, 17% of gay males, 18% of bisexual females, and 13% of bisexual males endorsed seriously considering suicide within the past year, whereas only 6.3% of heterosexual females and 5.7% of heterosexual males reported seriously considering suicide. Finally, Bolton and Sareen (2011) analyzed data from 34,653 respondents to the National Epidemiologic Survey on Alcohol and Related Conditions, a representative probability survey of U.S. civilians. Gay and bisexual men had approximately a fourfold increase in suicide attempts after controlling for demographic variables. Similarly, lesbian women evidenced a nearly threefold increase in risk and bisexual women had approximately a sixfold greater risk. No studies comparing prevalence of suicidal ideation or behavior within the transgender population to the general population were identified.

Appendix B

TABLE 1
Prevalence of Suicidal Thoughts and Behaviors among U.S. Samples

Study	Participants	Design	Prevalence
Mixed samples			
Balsam, Beauchaine, et al. (2005)	533 heterosexual, 558 lesbian or gay, and 163 bisexual individuals approximate *M* age = 35	LGB individuals were recruited via convenience sampling and then they recruited their siblings. Questionnaires completed via the mail.	History of suicidal ideation (≥ age 18): 41.1% of gay men, 31.4% bisexual men, 38.4% lesbian women, and 39.3% bisexual women. History of suicide attempt (≥ age 18): 10.5% of gay men, 11.4% bisexual men, 7.9% lesbian women, and 10.7% bisexual women.
Blosnich and Bossarte (2012)	11,046 LGB, unsure, and heterosexual college students ages 18–24; *M* = 20.1	Self-report, national college health assessment (NCHA)	History of suicidal ideation (past year): 15% gay or lesbian, 21% bisexual, and 5.5% heterosexual. History of suicide attempt (past year): 3.3% gay or lesbian, 4.6% bisexual, and 0.9% heterosexual.
Blosnich et al. (2012)	61 LGB veterans, 1,639 heterosexual veterans ages 18–64+	Statewide survey conducted in Massachusetts that contained questions about history of active-duty status, LGBT identity, and suicidal ideation	11.48% of LGB veterans reported serious suicidal ideation within past year. 3.48% of heterosexual veterans reported serious suicidal ideation within past year.
Bolton and Sareen (2011)	34,653 LGB, unsure, and heterosexual individuals age ranges by group: 20 to 39, 40 to 55, and 56 and older	Lay interviewers: National Epidemiologic Survey on Alcohol and Related Conditions	History of suicide attempt (lifetime): 9.8% gay men, 10% bisexual men, 8.5% unsure men, 2.1% heterosexual men; 10.9% lesbian women, 24.4% bisexual women, 9.9% unsure women, and 4.2% heterosexual women.
D'Augelli and Grossman (2001)	416 LGBT individuals ages 60–91; *M* = 68.5	Snowball sampling via LGB agencies and groups for older adults	13% reported a past suicide attempt (lifetime).

(continued)

TABLE 1
(continued)

Study	Participants	Design	Prevalence
Garcia et al. (2002)	138 LGBT college students, ages 18–30	Cross-sectional survey; college students	43% of respondents reported past SI, 11% reported a past suicide attempt (lifetime).
Hershberger et al. (1997)	194 lesbian or gay youth group members ages 15–21; $M = 18.86$	Survey; convenience sample Brief Symptom Inventory #9 asked about suicidal ideation	42% reported at least one lifetime suicide attempt. 39% reported suicidal thinking in the past week.
House, Van Horn, Coppeans, and Stepleman (2011)	1,126 LGBT individuals ages 18–80; $M = 37.6$	Internet-based survey	23.7% attempted suicide at least once (lifetime). 26.7% of female participants attempted suicide (lifetime). 34.8% of transgender participants attempted suicide (lifetime). 17.7% of male participants attempted suicide (lifetime).
McBee-Strayer and Rogers James (2002)	162 LGB individuals ages 18–64	Self-report surveys The Suicide Behavior Questionnaire	91% reported a history of suicidal ideation (lifetime). 37% reported a history of suicide attempt (lifetime).
Meyer, Dietrich, and Schwartz (2008)	388 LGB individuals ages 18–59	World Health Organization World Mental Health Survey Initiative of the Composite International Diagnostic Interview	7.9% of gay or lesbian participants made a lifetime suicide attempt. 10.0% of bisexual participants had made a lifetime suicide attempt.
Needham and Austin (2010)	11,153 LGB and heterosexual individuals ages 18–26	In-home interviews conducted in 2 waves with students as part of the Add Health Study	Suicidal ideation reported in the past year: 21% of lesbian women 17% of gay men 18% of bisexual females 13% of bisexual men

(continued)

Appendix B

TABLE 1
(continued)

Study	Participants	Design	Prevalence
Russell et al. (2011)	245 LGBT individuals ages 21–25	Participants recruited from 249 LGBT venues (e.g., organizations, bars, clubs). Young adult survey from The Family Acceptance Project composed of self-report scales.	41% reported history of lifetime suicide attempt. 22% needed medical attention after a suicide attempt.
Gay and bisexual men			
Berg, Mimiaga, and Safren (2008)	92 gay and bisexual men ages 18–58; $M = 35.6$	Chart review of intake procedures and assessments at an LGBT health clinic	18.5% reported suicidal ideation at time of intake.
Kipke et al. (2007)	526 gay, bisexual, and questioning men ages 18–24	Self-report surveys	10% reported they had seriously considered suicide (past 12 months). 4% reported that they had developed a plan (past 12 months). 4% reported that they had attempted suicide (past 12 months).
Paul et al. (2002)	2,881 urban gay and bisexual men ages 18–86; $M = 37$	A probability sample was interviewed over the phone Multicenter AIDS Cooperative Study; questionnaire received by mail and returned to study site	21% had made a suicide plan (lifetime). 12% had attempted suicide (lifetime). 27% reported suicidal ideation in the past 6 months.
Schneider, Taylor, Hammen, Kemeny, and Dudley (1991)	778 bisexual and gay males M age = 36		
Gay men			
Herrell et al. (1999)	4,774 male–male twin pairs of Vietnam Era veterans; those who had a same-gender partner and those who had not (No age reported)	Interview as part of the Harvard Twin Study of Substance Abuse, which included 4 questions from the Diagnostic Interview Schedule-III Revised	14.7% with any same-gender partners (whose twin did not have any same-gender partners) attempted suicide (lifetime). 55.3% reported suicidal ideation (lifetime).

(continued)

TABLE 1
(continued)

Study	Participants	Design	Prevalence
Remafedi (2002)	255 gay men ages 16–25; $M = 20$	Structured clinical interview in popular venues	34% reported a history of lifetime suicide attempt. 4.7% reported an attempt in the past year. 19% reported suicidal ideation in the past month.
Lesbian or bisexual women			
Bradford et al. (1994)	1,925 lesbian women ages 17–80; 80% were between 25 and 44 years of age	Surveys were sent to lesbian and gay health and mental health organizations and practitioners across the country. Snow-ball sampling was also used.	43% indicated they never had thought about suicide, 35% reported rarely, 19% sometimes, 2% reported often having suicidal thoughts; 18% had attempted suicide (lifetime).
Corliss et al. (2009)	1,253 lesbian or bisexual women M age = 40	Surveys completed by women who identified as lesbian, bisexual, or reported being sexually active or attracted to other women. Multiple-participant recruitment methods were used (e.g., outreach at gay community events).	10.2% reported a history of suicide attempt prior to age 18.
Matthews, Hughes, Johnson, Razzano, and Cassidy (2002)	550 lesbian women M age = 43	Surveys were sent to participants as part of the Chicago Lesbian Community Cancer Project. Questionnaire contained questions related to mental and physical health.	51% had seriously considered suicide (lifetime). 22% reported a lifetime suicide attempt.
Morris et al. (2001)	2,401 lesbian women ages 15–83; M age = 36	National Lesbian Wellness Survey data	21.5% reported a lifetime suicide attempt. 46% reported lifetime suicidal ideation.
Transgender individuals			

(continued)

Appendix B

TABLE 1
(continued)

Study	Participants	Design	Prevalence
Clements-Nolle et al. (2001)	523 transgender individuals, male to female and female to male median age: 34 for male to female (range 18–67), 36 for female to male (range 19–61)	Recruitment conducted in neighborhoods identified to have a high concentration of transgender persons. Trained transgender interviewers, included physical and mental health measures.	32% of both male to female and female to male individuals reported a lifetime history of suicide attempt.
Imbimbo et al. (2009)	139 transgender (male to female) individuals who had undergone sex reassignment surgery M age = 31.36	Questionnaire 12–18 months after surgery	50% contemplated suicide (lifetime), 2% attempted suicide (pre-surgery), 0.7% attempted suicide (postsurgery).
Kenagy (2005)	182 transgender individuals male to female and female to male age 17–68	Face-to-face interview and self-report	30.1% had attempted suicide (lifetime). 2 or 3 said they attempted due to being transgender.
Kenagy and Bostwick (2005)	111 transgender individuals male to female and female to male ages 19–70	Self-report, structured interview	64% had thought about suicide (lifetime). 60% reported having these thoughts due to being transgender. 27% had attempted suicide (lifetime). 52% reported attempting suicide due to being transgender.
Nuttbrock et al. (2010)	571 transgender individuals male to female ages 19–59	Recruited from streets, clubs, organizations, and advertising. Self-report, structured interview.	For ages 19–39 (lifetime): 53.0% had thought about suicide 34.9% had planned for suicide 31.2% had attempted suicide For ages 39–59 (lifetime): 53.5% had thought about suicide 34.9% had planned for suicide 28.0% had attempted suicide

L = lesbian, G = gay, B = bisexual, T = transgender, M = mean.

Some evidence suggests that bisexual individuals may be particularly at risk for suicide. After controlling for mental disorders, Bolton and Sareen (2011) found that bisexual men and women still demonstrated a threefold increase in risk and were the only groups that significantly differed from heterosexuals. Steele, Ross, Dobinson, Veldhuizen, and Tinmouth (2009) analyzed data from a Canadian national population based survey including 354 lesbian, 424 bisexual, and 60,937 heterosexual women. Bisexual women were significantly more likely than lesbian and heterosexual women to report lifetime suicidal ideation.

Suicide Risk and Protective Factors Identified in the Literature

The present literature review identified one study related to suicide risk factors specific to LGB individuals who have served in the military. Blosnich et al. (2012) found that sexual minority veterans had significantly less social and emotional support and higher rates of suicidal ideation than heterosexual veterans. Although this literature search only identified one study specific to the LGB military or veteran populations, there are numerous studies that identify risk factors associated with LGBT identity and self-directed violence in the general population. A summary of these studies is provided as well as an elaboration on two specific factors that are well documented in the literature identified for this article: victimization and social support.

Results of some international studies suggest that sexual minority identity is a greater risk factor for men than women (Fergusson et al., 2005; de Graaf, Sandfort, & Have, 2006). For example, de Graaf et al. (2006) found a stronger association between suicidality (i.e., ideation and behavior) and sexual orientation among men than women, particularly after controlling for psychiatric conditions. However, results regarding the potential moderating effect of gender have not been entirely consistent (Van Heerin gen & Vincke, 2000).

In addition to gender, trauma, mental health disorders, and substance use have all been associated with suicide. Although these risk factors are shared both by LGBT individuals and those who identify as heterosexual, the prevalence of these risk factors is elevated among the LGBT community. With regard to mental health disorders, multiple large scale surveys found elevated rates of mental disorders, including substance use disorders, among the LGBT community (Conron, Mimiaga, & Landers, 2010; Fergusson et al., 2005; Gilman et al., 2001). For example, King et al. (2008) reported that depression, anxiety, and substance use disorders are 1.5 times more common in the LGBT community. There is also a large body of evidence suggesting that members of the LGBT population who have experienced physical, sexual, and emotional trauma are at increased risk for suicide (Balsam, Rothblum, et al., 2005; Botnick et al., 2002; Paul et al., 2002). Literature providing evidence of the relationship between victimization and suicide risk is elaborated on below.

Appendix B

The current literature search yielded no studies exploring protective factors among the LGBT military or veteran populations. In fact, little research has been conducted in the general LGBT population on factors that protect this community from suicide. One study found that social norms, high levels of support, identification with role models, and high self-esteem help protect gay men from suicide (Fenaughty & Harre, 2003). Another study reports that support within the lesbian community is considered a protective factor (Bradford et al., 1994). Literature related to the construct of social support and its impact on suicide risk is also more fully discussed.

Victimization and Suicide Risk. Twenty-six articles retrieved discussed the relationship between victimization and suicide risk within the LGBT community. For example, Rivers and Cowie (2006) reported that 53% of their LGB sample reported suicidal or self-harm ideation as a direct result of victimization related to sexual orientation and 40% had attempted suicide or self-harm for the same reason. Some researchers suggest that sexual minority identity is not an independent risk factor for suicide; rather, the outcomes of socially based stressors such as bullying strengthen the risk (Blosnich & Bossarte, 2012). Russell, Ryan, Toomey, Diaz, and Sanchez (2011) found that LGBT young adults who reported a high level of victimization during adolescence were 5.6 times more likely to have attempted suicide than those who reported a low level of victimization. Additional research found that higher rates of gender abuse among male-to-female transgender individuals were significantly associated with suicidality. This relationship varied across the life span such that it declined postadolescence and strengthened again in middle age. Importantly, gender abuse significantly decreased over the life span, but continued to be associated with significant levels of suicidality (Nuttbrock et al., 2010). Other research showed that lesbian and bisexual women reporting antigay harassment and maltreatment were more likely than those without these experiences to report that they had attempted suicide before 18 years of age (Corliss, Cochran, Mays, Greenland, & Seeman, 2009). However, victimization does not always lead to psychological distress. Reduction in self-esteem may impact this relationship such that if self-esteem is not reduced as a result of bullying, psychological distress and suicidal thoughts and/or behaviors may not occur (Waldo, Hesson-McInnis, & D'Augelli, 1998). Research suggests, however, that low self-esteem often occurs in the context of social discrimination (e.g., Huebner, Rebchook, & Kegeles, 2004), perhaps making this relationship likely. The majority of these studies focused on verbal abuse. However, it is important to note that other research also found that a history of suicide attempt was reported more frequently among adults who were physically attacked than those who were verbally victimized because of their sexual orientation (D'Augelli & Grossman, 2001).

Victimization in the LGBT Military Community. Our literature review also yielded studies that specifically relate to victimization of LGBT individuals who served in the military. The experience of LGBT individuals in the military is likely not well documented in the literature because of past regulations (e.g., the Don't Ask Don't Tell policy; Policy Concerning Homosexuality in the Armed Forces, 2004), but a study exploring the experiences of lesbians being removed from the Canadian military showed psychological distress upon being sought out, which was likened to a "witch hunt" (Poulin, Gouliquer, & Moore, 2009; p. 498). High rates of LGBT harassment are also reported in the U.S. armed forces (Bowling, Firestone, & Harris, 2005). Not surprisingly, LGBT military members reported the negative impact of sexual orientation-based harassment. Moradi (2009) found that sexual orientation-based harassment is significantly associated with decreased social cohesion and task cohesion among U.S. military veterans (Moradi, 2009). Another study conducted by Moradi and Miller (2010) reported that a main reason why veterans of the wars in Iraq and Afghanistan supported policy banning openly gay or lesbian military personnel was because the veterans feared that this group would face harassment and bullying from other military personnel.

Social Support and Suicide Risk. The present review of the literature yielded one study that discussed social support and suicide risk in the LGB veteran population and 15 in the general LGBT population. Results presented provide evidence that factors related to social support are associated with risk for suicidal ideation and attempts. Blosnich et al. (2012) found that increased rates of suicidal ideation among sexual minority veterans were explained by poor mental health and decreased social and emotional support. With respect to the non-military or veteran population, Botnick et al. (2002) found that among a sample of gay and bisexual men, those who had attempted suicide reported significantly lower levels of social support than those who had not attempted suicide. Van Heeringen and Vincke (2000) reported that rating of homosexual friendships as unsatisfactory was associated with a history of suicide attempt.

The literature also provided evidence that factors related to the experience of coming out to family and friends appear to impact suicide risk. Research provides evidence that disclosing sexual orientation can be protective. In a study of lesbian and bisexual women, being "out" was negatively related to psychological distress, which was positively related to suicidal ideation and attempts (Morris, Waldo, & Rothblum, 2001). Moradi (2009) found that veterans who had disclosed their sexual orientation while in the military perceived higher social cohesion within their units. While this study did not assess suicide risk per se, increased social cohesion may be protective against self-directed violence as social support has been found to be protective (Botnick et al., 2002). While coming out in general may be protective, the reactions of friends impact suicide risk as well. In a study of gay youth, those who had lost friends due to disclosing their sexual orientation were three times more likely to report a suicide attempt than those who had not lost a friend in the coming out process (Hershberger, Pilkington, & D'Augelli, 1997).

Appendix B

Discussion

In this review we aimed to identify literature related to suicide within the LGBT military and veteran populations. Research suggests that active-duty service members (Army Suicide Prevention Task Force, 2010) and veterans receiving care through the Veterans Health Administration (VHA; e.g., Blow et al., 2012; McCarthy et al., 2009) are at increased risk for suicide. The literature search conducted for the present review confirmed that the LGBT community is at increased risk for suicide as well, with rates of suicidal thoughts and behaviors generally exceeding those of the heterosexual community. Additionally, two articles were identified that provided data suggesting increased prevalence of suicidal ideation and attempts in LGB veterans. No studies related to transgender veterans and suicide risk were found.

This literature begs the question, *Why are LGBT military personnel and veterans potentially at increased risk for suicide?* The results of the literature search provide evidence with respect to risk and protective factors within the general LGBT community that help shed light on this question. Evidence suggests that risk factors, such as mental health disorders and substance abuse, are important for both the general population and LGBT communities. The body of literature identified focused on two risk factors that appear to be particularly relevant to suicide risk in the LGBT population: victimization and decreased social support. Decreased social support and worse mental health were specifically identified as risk factors for LGB veterans (Blosnich & Bossarte, 2012). Importantly, these factors explained the relationship between LGB identity and suicide risk such that LGB identity alone was not shown to be a risk factor.

Joiner's (2005) Interpersonal-Psychological Theory of Suicidal Behavior (IPTS) offers a framework from which to understand how the two important risk factors identified in the LGBT literature (i.e., victimization and social support) may help further explain suicide risk in the LGBT military and veteran populations. This theory purports that a person is at increased risk for suicide if they have acquired the capability to kill themselves and have the desire to die. Acquired capability is described as habituation that can occur in the context of past self-injury, pain, and/or other injury (Joiner, 2005). The theory holds that the presence of two constructs, perceived burdensomeness and failed belongingness, results in the desire for death. Perceived burdensomeness exists when one sees themselves as a permanent burden to others. One has a sense of failed belongingness when they do not feel that they belong to any community or have connections with others (Joiner, 2005).

The research identified in this review relates to two of the three constructs that comprise Joiner's (2005) theory. Data demonstrating that a history of victimization places LGBT individuals at increased risk for suicide can be understood with respect to acquired capability for lethal self-harm. People who identify as members of sexual minority communities report experiencing more abuse than their heterosexual counterparts because of the societal stigma they experience. This can result in increased exposure, and potentially habituation to, physical and psychological pain. Furthermore, research findings suggest that veterans with experiences in combat are at increased risk for suicide as compared to those who have not served in combat, which may relate to acquired capability gained from combat (Kleespies et al., 2011). Thus, LGBT military service members and veterans may already be at increased risk of acquired capability related to military combat and/or training and further habituation to pain via experiences of victimization.

Additionally, research supports that another important suicide risk factor for LGBT individuals, and LGB veterans specifically, is decreased social support. In the context of Joiner's (2005) theory, decreased social support can be understood as a manifestation of a crucial ingredient for the desire for death (i.e., failed belongingness). Thus, the literature provides some indirect support for the applicability of this component of the IPTS. Belongingness is a particularly important consideration for the LGBT military and veteran populations as unit cohesion is such an important component of military service. Lesbian, gay, bisexual, and transgender military service members' sense of belongingness may be impacted by their experience of coming out in the military. It is unknown how this experience may or may not be impacted by the recent repeal of the Don't Ask Don't Tell policy. It is recommended that future research explores the impact that coming out in the military has on suicide risk.

The literature identified in this review does not, however, provide information regarding perceived burdensomeness, the other factor that contributes to the desire for death, in the LGBT military and veteran populations specifically or the broader LGBT population. Perceived burdensomeness was found to be positively correlated with suicidal ideation among a sample of military personnel who had been deployed (Bryan, Ray-Sannerud, Morrow, & Etienne, 2012) and thus may be a construct of interest to those trying to understand suicide risk among the LGBT military and veteran populations. An important step for researchers is to explore whether LGBT military service members or veterans who are at risk for suicide also have higher rates of perceived burdensomeness. This can be assessed via the Interpersonal Needs Questionnaire (Van Orden, Witte, Gordon, Bender, & Joiner, 2008). Thus, the IPTS offers a conceptualization of the research reported in this article, but no empirical evidence supports this understanding.

In addition to conducting future research to explore the applicability of IPTS to this population, the field would benefit greatly from more research regarding the prevalence of suicidal ideation and attempts in the LGBT military and veteran populations. Specifically, research focused on suicide risk among transgender service members and veterans is needed. Additionally, no research was identified that reports data related to suicide death among the LGBT military or veteran communities. Along with prevalence research, it would be beneficial to assess when suicide attempts occur with respect to military service (i.e., before, during, or after) as most studies have only collected data on lifetime history of suicide attempts. Research regarding the lethality of attempts and nature of suicidal ideation is also of interest. These data might provide the field with information regarding the impact of military service on suicide risk in this population. Additionally, researchers should work to identify risk and protective factors that may be unique to the LGBT military and veteran populations. Research in this area may be facilitated by the repeal of Don't Ask Don't Tell as service members and veterans may feel more comfortable to disclose their LGB identity. Research with transgender individuals who serve in the military, however, may continue to be challenged as the repeal of Don't Ask Don't Tell does not address this group. These are important first steps with respect to learning more about increased or unique risk associated with this population.

The research presented here should be considered with respect to some important limitations. For example, inconsistencies exist within the reviewed articles in regard to the methods of investigating suicidal behavior. The research assesses suicidal ideation and behavior with methods ranging from one to a few questions on each, with little consistency in the assessment methods or questions used. The time periods assessed vary between studies, with both recent and lifetime suicidal behavior explored, while rarely addressing persistent thoughts of suicide. Other methodological issues should be considered as well. Many studies employed biased sampling techniques that may limit the generalizability of the findings. For example, some studies only recruited from LGBT organizations and therefore may not be assessing individuals who choose to not affiliate with such groups. Inconsistent terminology regarding suicidal ideation and behavior and LGBT status is used throughout the research as well, which impacts the ability to accurately synthesize this body of literature. The literature reviewed utilized samples that included a wide range of ages. While an advantage of this is that many different age groups are represented, our methods employed do not allow for differentiation to be made as to how suicide risk may vary across age groups. Additionally, the definition of *sexual orientation* (e.g., behavior versus attraction) varies across studies, confounding our ability to compare between groups. Perhaps most importantly, it is entirely unclear how well research on the general LGBT population applies to experiences of the LGBT military or veteran populations. The expansion of research in this area is recommended and encouraged.

BRIDGET B. MATARAZZO and SEAN M. BARNES, Veterans Integrated Service Network (VISN) 19 Mental Illness, Research, Education and Clinical Center (MIRECC), Denver, CO, USA, and Department of Psychiatry, School of Medicine, University of Colorado, Denver, CO, USA; JAMES L. PEASE and LEAH M. RUSSELL, VISN 19 MIRECC, Denver, CO, USA; JETTA E. HANSON and KELLY A. SOBERAY, VISN 19 MIRECC, Denver, CO, USA, and Military Suicide Research Consortium (MSRC), Denver, CO, USA; PETER

M. GUTIERREZ, VISN 19 MIRECC, Denver, CO, USA, Department of Psychiatry, School of Medicine, University of Colorado, Denver, CO, USA, and MSRC, Denver, CO, USA.

This article is based on work supported, in part, by the Department of Veterans Affairs, but does not necessarily represent the views of the Department of Veterans Affairs, the Department of Defense, or the U.S. Government. This work was supported, in part, by grants awarded to the Denver VA Medical Center by the Department of Defense. The Department of Defense had no further role in the study design; in the collection, analysis, and interpretation of data; in the writing of the report; and in the decision to submit the paper for publication. Denver VA Medical Center Grant Number: W81XWH-10-2-0178.

Address correspondence to: Bridget B. Matarazzo, VISN 19 MIRECC, 1055 Clermont Street, Denver, CO 80220; E-mail: Bridget. Matarazzo@va.gov

Notes

1 The terms *lesbian*, *gay*, and *bisexual* refer to one's sexual identity, whereas *transgender* refers to gender identity or expression. Of note, the authors use the term *LGBT community* to broadly refer to the heterogeneous group of individuals who identify as LGBT, knowing that there are many distinct communities within this larger group. Specifically, LGBT individuals are included in the same acronym when appropriate and at other times are differentiated (e.g., LGB) to accurately reflect the terminology used in the literature.

References

Army Suicide Prevention Task Force. (2010). *Army health promotion, risk reduction, suicide prevention: Report 2010.* Washington, DC: Department of Defense.

BALSAM, K. F., BEAUCHAINE, T. P., MICKEY, R. M., & ROTHBLUM, E. D. (2005). Mental health of lesbian, gay, bisexual, and heterosexual siblings: Effects of gender, sexual orientation, and family. *Journal of Abnormal Psychology, 114,* 471–476. doi:10.1037/0021-843X.114.3.471.

BALSAM, K. F., ROTHBLUM, E. D., & BEAUCHAINE, T. P. (2005). Victimization over the life span: A comparison of lesbian, gay, bisexual, and heterosexual siblings. *Journal of Consulting and Clinical Psychology, 73,* 477. doi:10.1037/0022006X.73.3.477.

BERG, M. B., MIMIAGA, M. J., & SAFREN, S. A. (2008). Mental health concerns of gay and bisexual men seeking mental health services. *Journal of Homosexuality, 54,* 293–306. doi:10. 1080/00918360801982215.

BLOSNICH, J., & BOSSARTE, R. (2012). Drivers of disparity: Differences in socially based risk factors of self-injurious and suicidal behaviors among sexual minority college students. *The Journal of American College Health, 60,* 141–149. doi:10.1080/0744 8481.2011.623332.

BLOSNICH, J. R., BOSSARTE, R. M., & SILENZIO, V. M. B. (2012). Suicidal ideation among sexual minority veterans: Results from the 20052012 Massachusetts Behavioral Risk Factor Surveillance Survey. *American Journal of Public Health, 102,* S44–S47. doi:10.2105/AJPH.2011. 300565

BLOW, F. C., BOHNERT, A., ILGEN, M. A., IGNACIO, R., MCCARTHY, J. F., VALENSTEIN, M. M., et al. (2012). Suicide mortality among patients treated by the veterans health administration from 2000 to 2007. *American Journal of Public Health, 102*, S98–S104. doi:10.2105/AJPH. 2011.300441.

BOLTON, S. L., & SAREEN, J. (2011). Sexual orientation and its relation to mental disorders and suicide attempts: Findings from a nationally representative sample. *Canadian Journal of Psychiatry, 56*, 35–43.

BOTNICK, M. R., HEATH, K. V., CORNELISSE, P. G., STRATHDEE, S. A., MARTINDALE, S. L., & HOGG, R. S. (2002). Correlates of suicide attempts in an open cohort of young men who have sex with men. *Canadian Journal of Public Health, 93*, 59–62.

BOWLING, K. L., FIRESTONE, J. M., & HARRIS, R. J. (2005). Analyzing questions that cannot be asked of respondents who cannot respond. *Armed Forces & Society, 31*, 411–437. doi:10.1177/0095327X0503100305.

BRADFORD, J., RYAN, C., & ROTHBLUM, E. D. (1994). National lesbian health care survey: Implications for mental health care. *Journal of Consulting and Clinical Psychology, 62*, 228–242. doi:10.1037/0022-006X.62.2.228.

BRYAN, C. J., RAY-SANNERUD, B., MORROW, C. E., & ETIENNE, N. (2012). Guilt is more strongly associated with suicidal ideation among military personnel with direct combat experience. *Journal of Affective Disorders, 1–5.* doi:10. 1016/j.jad.2012.11.044.

CLEMENTS-NOLLE, K., MARX, R., GUZMAN, R., & KATZ, M. (2001). HIV prevalence, risk behaviors, health care use, and mental health status of transgender persons: Implications for public health intervention. *American Journal of Public Health, 91*, 915–921.

CLEMENTS-NOLLE, K., MARX, R., & KATZ, M. (2006). Attempted suicide among transgender persons: The influence of gender-based discrimination and victimization. *Journal of Homosexuality, 51*, 53–69. doi:10.1300/J082v51n03_04.

COCHRAN, S. D., & MAYS, V. M. (2000). Lifetime prevalence of suicide symptoms and affective disorders among men reporting same sex sexual partners: Results from NHANES III. *American Journal of Public Health, 90*, 573–578.

COCHRAN, S. D., & MAYS, V. M. (2011). Sexual orientation and mortality among US men aged 17 to 59 years: Results from the National Health and Nutrition Examination Survey III. *American Journal of Public Health, 101*, 1133–1138. doi:10.2105/AJPH. 2010.300013.

CONRON, K. J., MIMIAGA, M. J., & LANDERS, S. J. (2010). A population-based study of sexual orientation identity and gender differences in adult health. *American Journal of Public Health, 100*, 1953.

CORLISS, H. L., COCHRAN, S. D., MAYS, V. M., GREENLAND, S., & SEEMAN, T. E. (2009). Age of minority sexual orientation development and risk of childhood maltreatment and suicide attempts in women. *American Journal of Orthopsychiatry, 79*, 511–521. doi:10.1037/a0017163.

D'AUGELLI, A. R., & GROSSMAN, A. H. (2001). Disclosure of sexual orientation, victimization, and mental health among lesbian, gay, and bisexual older adults. *Journal of Interpersonal Violence, 16*, 1008–1027. doi:10.1177/088626001016010003.

Department of Defense Task Force on Prevention of Suicide by Members of the Armed Forces. (2010). *Executive summary.* Retrieved December 19, 2012, from http://www.health.mil/dhb/downloads/TaskForce2010/Suicide%20Prevention%20Task%20Force_EXEC%20SUM_08-20-10%20v6.doc. Published August 2010.

DIXEN, J. M., MADDEVER, H., VAN MAASDAM, J., & EDWARDS, P. W. (1984). Psychosocial characteristics of applicants evaluated for surgical gender reassignment. *Archives of Sexual Behavior, 13*, 269–276. doi:10.1007/BF01541653.

FENAUGHTY, J., & HARRE, N. (2003). Life on the seesaw: A qualitative study of suicide resiliency factors for young gay men. *Journal of Homosexuality, 45*, 1–22. doi:10.1300/J082v45n01_01.

FERGUSSON, D. M., HORWOOD, L. J., RIDDER, E. M., & BEAUTRAIS, A. L. (2005). Sexual orientation and mental health in a birth cohort of young adults. *Psychological Medicine, 35*, 971– 981. doi:10.1017/S0033291704004222.

FRUEH, B. C., & SMITH, J. A. (2012). Suicide, alcoholism, and psychiatric illness among union forces during the U.S. Civil War. *Journal of Anxiety Disorders, 26*, 769–775. doi.org/10. 1016/j.janxdis.2012.06.006.

GARCIA, J., ADAMS, J., FRIEDMAN, L., & EAST, P. (2002). Links between past abuse, suicide ideation, and sexual orientation among San Diego college students. *Journal of American College Health, 51*, 9–14. doi:10.1023/A:1016204417910.

GAROFALO, R., WOLF, C., WISSOW, L. S., WOODS, E. R., & GOODMAN, E. (1999). Sexual orientation and risk of suicide attempts among a representative sample of youth. *Archives of Pediatrics and Adolescent Medicine, 153*, 487–493. doi:10-1001/pubs.Pediatr Adolesc Med.-ISSN1072-4710-153-5-poa8293.

GILMAN, S. E., COCHRAN, S. D., MAYS, V. M., HUGHES, M., OSTROW, D., & KESSLER, R. C. (2001). Risk of psychiatric disorders among individuals reporting same-sex sexual partners in the National Comorbidity Survey. *American Journal of Public Health, 91*, 933–939.

DE GRAAF, R., SANDFORT, T. G. M., & HAVE, M. T. (2006). Suicidality and sexual orientation: Differences between men and women in a general population-based sample from the Netherlands. *Archives of Sexual Behavior, 35*, 253–262. doi:10.1007/s10508-006-9020-z.

GROSSMAN, A. H., & D'AUGELLI, A. R. (2008). Transgender youth and life-threatening behaviors. *Suicide and Life-Threatening Behavior, 37*, 527–537.

HAAS, A. P., ELIASON, M., MAYS, V. M., MATHY, R. M., COCHRAN, S. D., D'AUGELLI, A. R., et al. (2011). Suicide and suicide risk in lesbian, gay, bisexual, and transgender populations: Review and recommendations. *Journal of Homosexuality, 58*, 10–51. doi:10.1080/00918369.2011.534038.

HERRELL, R., GOLDBERG, J., TRUE, W. R., RAMAKRISHNAN, V., LYONS, M., EISEN, S., et al. (1999). Sexual orientation and suicidality: A co-twin control study in adult men. *Archives for General Psychiatry, 56*, 867–874. doi:10.1001/ archpsyc.56.10.867.

HERSHBERGER, S. L., PILKINGTON, N. W., & D'AUGELLI, A. R. (1997). Predictors of suicide attempts among gay, lesbian, and bisexual youth. *Journal of Adolescent Research, 12*, 477–497. doi:10.1177/0743554897124004.

HOUSE, A. S., VAN HORN, E., COPPEANS, C., & STEPLEMAN, L. M. (2011). Interpersonal trauma and discriminatory events as predictors of suicidal and nonsuicidal self-injury in gay, lesbian, bisexual, and transgender persons. *Traumatology, 17*, 75–85. doi:10.1177/1534765610395621.

HUEBNER, D. M., REBCHOOK, G. M., & KEGELES, S. M. (2004). Experiences of harassment, discrimination and physical violence among young gay and bisexual men. *American Journal of Public Health, 94*, 1200–1203.

IMBIMBO, C., VERZE, P., PALMIERI, A., LONGO, N., FUSCO, F., ARCANIOLO, D., et al. (2009). A report from a single institute's 14-year experience in treatment of male-to-female transsexuals. *Journal of Sexual Medicine, 6*, 2736–2745. doi:10.1111/j.1743-6109.2009.01379.x.

Appendix B

JOINER, T. (2005). *Why people die by suicide*. Cambridge: Harvard University Press.

KANG, H., & BULLMAN, T. (1996). Mortality among U.S. veterans of the Persian Gulf War. *New England Journal of Medicine, 335*, 1498–1504.

KENAGY, G. (2005). Transgender health: Findings from two needs assessment studies in Philadelphia. *Health & Social Work, 30*, 19–26. doi:10.1093/hsw/30.1.19.

KENAGY, G. P., & BOSTWICK, W. B. (2005). Health and social service needs of transgender people in Chicago. *International Journal of Transgenderism, 8*, 57–66. doi:10.1300/J485v08n 02_06.

KING, M., SEMLYEN, J., TAI, S. S., KILLASPY, H., OSBORN, D., POPELYUK, D., et al. (2008). A systematic review of mental disorder, suicide, and deliberate self harm in lesbian, gay and bisexual people. *BMC Psychiatry, 8*, 70. doi:10.1186/1471-244X-8-70.

KIPKE, M. D., KUBICEK, K., WEISS, G., WONG, C., LOPEZ, D., IVERSON, E., et al. (2007). The health and health behaviors of young men who have sex with men. *Journal of Adolescent Health, 40*, 342–350. doi:10.1016/j.jadohealth.2006.10.019.

KLEESPIES, P. M., AHNALLEN, C. G., KNIGHT, J. A., PRESSKREISCHER, B., BARRS, K. L., BOYD, B. L., et al. (2011). A study of self-injurious and suicidal behavior in a veteran population. *Psychological Services, 8*, 236. doi:10.1037/a0024881.

MATHY, R. M. (2002a). Suicidality and sexual orientation in five continents: Asia, Australia, Europe, North America, and South America. *International Journal of Sexuality and Gender Studies, 7*, 215–225. doi:10.1023/ A:1015853302054.

MATHY, R. M. (2002b). Transgender identity and suicidality in a nonclinical sample: Sexual orientation, psychiatric history, and compulsive behaviors. *Journal of Psychology and Human Sexuality, 14*, 47–65. doi.org/10.1300/ J056v14n04_03.

MATTHEWS, A. K., HUGHES, T. L., JOHNSON, T., RAZZANO, L. A., & CASSIDY, R. (2002). Prediction of depressive distress in a community sample of women: The role of sexual orientation. *American Journal of Public Health, 92*, 1131–1139. doi:10.2105/AJPH.92.7.1131.

MCBEE-STRAYER, S. M., & ROGERS, J. R. (2002). Lesbian, gay, and bisexual suicidal behavior: Testing a constructivist model. *Suicide and Life-Threatening Behavior, 32*, 272–283. doi:10. 1521/suli.32.3.272.22171.

MCCARTHY, J. F., VALENSTEIN, M., KIM, H. M., ILGEN, M., ZIVIN, K., & BLOW, F. C. (2009). Suicide mortality among patients receiving care in the Veterans Health Administration health system. *American Journal of Epidemiology, 169*, 1033–1038. doi:10.1093/aje/kwp010.

MCDANIEL, J., PURCELL, D., & D'AUGELLI, A. R. (2001). The relationship between sexual orientation and risk for suicide: Research findings and future directions for research and prevention. *Suicide and Life-Threatening Behavior, 31* (Suppl), 84–105. doi: 10.1521/suli.31.1.5.84.24224.

MEYER, I. H., DIETRICH, J., & SCHWARTZ, S. (2008). Lifetime prevalence of mental disorders and suicide attempts in diverse lesbian, gay, and bisexual populations. *American Journal of Public Health, 98*, 1004–1006. doi:10.2105/AJPH. 2006.096826.

MICHEL, A., ANSSEAU, M., LEGROS, J. J., PITCHOT, W., & MORMONT, C. (2002). The transsexual: What about the future? *European Psychiatry, 17*, 353–362. doi:10.1016/S0924-9338(02)00703-4.

MORADI, B. (2009). Sexual orientation disclosure, concealment, harassment, and military cohesion: Perceptions of LGBT military veterans. *Military Psychology, 21*, 513–533. doi:10. 1080/08995600903206453.

Moradi, B., & Miller, L. (2010). Attitudes of Iraq and Afghanistan war veterans toward gay and lesbian service members. *Armed Forces and Society, 36,* 397–419. doi:10.1177/0095327X09352960.

Morris, J. F., Waldo, C. R., & Rothblum, E. D. (2001). A model of predictors and outcomes of outness among lesbian and bisexual women. *American Journal of Orthopsychiatry, 71,* 61–71. doi:10.1037/0002-9432.71.1.61.

National Center for Transgender Equality and the National Gay and Lesbian Task Force. (2009). *National Transgender Discrimination Survey.* Retrieved January 1, 2013, from http://transequality. org/ Resources/Trans_Discrim_Survey.pdf.

Needham, B. L., & Austin, E. L. (2010). Sexual orientation, parental support, and health during the transition to young adulthood. *Journal of Youth and Adolescence, 39,* 1189–1198. doi:10.1007/s10964-010-9533-6.

Nuttbrock, L., Hwahng, S., Bockting, W., Rosenblum, A., Mason, M., Macri, M., et al. (2010). Psychiatric impact of genderrelated abuse across the life course of male-to-female transgender persons. *Journal of Sex Research, 47,* 12–23. doi:10.1080/00224490903062258.

Paul, J. P., Catania, J., Pollack, L., Moskowitz, J., Canchola, J., Mills, T., et al. (2002). Suicide attempts among gay and bisexual men: Lifetime prevalence and antecedents. *American Journal of Public Health, 92,* 338–1345. doi:10.2105/AJPH.92.8.1338.

Pfäfflin, F., & Junge, A. (1998). Sex reassignment. Thirty years of international follow-up studies. *International Journal of Transgenderism.* Retrieved from http://www.symposion.com/ijt/books/index.htm#Sex%20Reassignment. Policy Concerning Homosexuality in the Armed Forces, 10 U.S.C. Section 654 (2004).

Poulin, C., Gouliquer, L., & Moore, J. (2009). Discharged for homosexuality from the Canadian military: Health implications for lesbians. *Feminism & Psychology, 19,* 496–516. doi:10. 1177/0959353509342772.

Qin, P., Agerbo, E., & Mortensen, P. B. (2003). Suicide risk in relation to socioeconomic, demographic, psychiatric, and familial factors: A national register-based study of all suicides in Denmark, 1981-1997. *American Journal of Psychiatry, 160,* 765–772. doi:10.1176/appi.ajp.160.4.765.

Remafedi, G. (2002). Suicidality in a venue-based sample of young men who have sex with men. *Journal of Adolescent Health, 31,* 305–310. doi:10.1016/S1054-139X(02)00405-6.

Remafedi, G., French, S., Story, M., Resnick, M. D., & Blum, R. (1998). The relationship between suicide risk and sexual orientation: Results of a population-based study. *American Journal of Public Health January, 88,* 57–60. doi:10.2105/AJPH.88.1.57.

Renaud, J., Berlim, M. T., Begolli, M., McGirr, A., & Turecki, G. (2010). Sexual orientation and gender identity in youth suicide victims: An exploratory study. *Canadian Journal of Psychiatry, 55,* 29–34.

Ritchie, E. C., Keppler, W. C., & Rothberg, J. M. (2003). Suicidal admission in the United States military. *Military Medicine, 168,* 177–181.

Rivers, I., & Cowie, H. (2006). Bullying and homophobia in UK schools: A perspective on factors affecting resilience and recovery. *Journal of Gay and Lesbian Issues in Education, 3,* 11–43. doi:10.1300/J367v03n04_03.

Rothberg, J. M., Bartone, P. F., Holloway, H. C., & Marlowe, D. H. (1990). Life and death in the US Army. *Journal of the American Medical Association, 264,* 2241–2244.

Russell, S. T., Ryan, C., Toomey, R. B., Diaz, R. M., & Sanchez, J. (2011). Lesbian, gay, bisexual, and transgender adolescent school victimization: Implications for young adult health and adjustment. *Journal of School Health, 81,* 223–230. doi: 10.1111/j.1746-1561.2011.00583.x.

Schneider, S. G., Taylor, S. E., Hammen, C., Kemeny, M. E., & Dudley, J. (1991). Factors influencing suicide intent in gay and bisexual suicide ideators: Differing models for men with and without human immunodeficiency virus. *Journal of Personality and Social Psychology, 61,* 776–788. doi:10.1037/0022-3514.61.5.776.

Shaffer, D., Fisher, P., Hicks, R. H., Parides, M., & Gould, M. (1995). Sexual orientation in adolescents who commit suicide. *Suicide and Life-Threatening Behavior, 25,* 64–71. doi:10. 1111/j.1943-278X.1995.tb00491.x.

Steele, L. S., Ross, L. E., Dobinson, C., Veldhuizen, S., & Tinmouth, J. M. (2009). Women's sexual orientation and health: Results from a Canadian population-based survey. *Women and Health, 49,* 353–367. doi:10.1080/03630240903238685.

Van Heeringen, C., & Vincke, J. (2000). Suicidal acts and ideation in homosexual and bisexual young people: A study of prevalence and risk factors. *Social Psychiatry and Psychiatric Epidemiology, 35,* 494–499. doi:10.1007/s001270050270.

Van Orden, K. A., Witte, T. K., Gordon, K. H., Bender, T. W., & Joiner, T. E., Jr. (2008). Suicidal desire and the capability for suicide: Tests of the interpersonal-psychological theory of suicidal behavior among adults. *Journal of Consulting and Clinical Psychology, 76,* 72. doi:10.1037/0022-006X.76.1.72.

Waldo, C. R., Hesson-McInnis, M. S., & D'Augelli, A. R. (1998). Antecedents and consequences of victimization of lesbian, gay, and bisexual young people: A structural model comparing rural university and urban samples. *American Journal of Community Psychology, 26,* 307–334. doi:10.1023/A:1022184704174.

Xavier, J., Honnold, J., & Bradford, J. (2007). *The health, health-related needs, and lifecourse experiences of transgender Virginians.* Richmond: Division of Disease Prevention through the Centers for Disease Control and Prevention, Virginia Department of Health.

8) **Pereira, F., Lopes, A. & Marta, M. (2015). Being a teacher educator: Professional identities and conceptions of professional education. *Educational Research,* 57(4), 451–469. Copyright © 2015 by NFER. All rights reserved. Reprinted with permission.**

Being a Teacher Educator

Introduction

Contemporary social and educational conditions are characterised by deep and rapid changes. Over recent decades, these have destabilised the institutions and reference points which are the foundations for the construction of social and professional identities in Western countries (Dubet, 2002). The complexity of work in education makes a holistic and profound understanding of these changes difficult; their nature, causes and consequences are not immediately apparent (see Pereira, 2010). Material, organizational and behavioural changes on the surface emerge from invisible changes in values, society and attitudes—not to mention the economy. To put it more abstractly, they arise from the axiological, relational and subjective aspects which are implied in the concept of "teaching as a helping profession."

The consideration of teaching as a helping profession is based on phenomenological perspectives of the profession that emphasises the experiential dimension (relative to life experience), as well as the ethics of the process of professionalisation (Sommers-Flanagan & Sommers-Flanagan, 2007). In the particular instance of first CEB teachers (Teachers in the Primeiro Ciclo de Ensino Básico, i.e. Primary Education [the first four years of school]), the object of their work—the education of children—places a very particular emphasis on the affective dimension of the profession and its ethical, relational and support components (Pereira, 2009). Therefore, initial teacher education (regarded as a secondary socialisation process) is responsible for the creation of the conditions of access to the profession, as well as of learning the knowledge related to the specialised field of teaching. In addition, it leads to the formation of a basic professional identity or "first" identity (see Dubar, 1996; Lopes & Pereira, 2012).

This article intends to present and discuss one area of findings from a wider project entitled "Initial teacher education of helping professionals and the identity of the educators—the cases of teaching and of nursing."[1] In this context, the project seeks to acquire knowledge about teacher educators' identities as situated identity (the way in which the social and personal identity is translated into concrete identities). It builds knowledge about teaching as a helping profession and makes proposals for training modalities and organisation. In this text, we focus on the conceptions that teacher educators have about their work. Also, we seek to identify the specific features of the teaching profession in primary education that may show the trainees how their professional skills, knowledge and attitudes are shaped by their relationship with the identities of their trainers.

In this article, we present the main focus of the theoretical framework used, the research methodology and the findings. We end with a discussion of those findings.

Teaching as a Helping Profession and the New Challenges for Teachers in Primary Education

Teaching as a Helping Profession

Viewing teaching as a "helping profession" is justified by the understanding that it is an activity generated in complex multidimensional interaction processes, where professional knowledge takes shape and is used for the promotion of individuals and societies (Hugman, 2005). "Help" (or "care") is interpreted from a psychosocial perspective that considers the activity to be within the scope of certain professions

Appendix B

as a type of work that is produced in human relations, conditioning them and determining their impact on each of the subjects that takes part in them. To this end, Fish (1998) considers that the designation "caring professions" covers all the professions where the well-being of the "client"—in terms of health, education or social aspects of life—is the primary concern of the practitioner. This approach gives pride of place to a holistic conception of the profession that takes into account not only its visible aspects but also the invisible (e.g. the practitioner's capacities, theories, beliefs and values, along with the moral dimension of her or his practice). With reference to the training of these professionals, Fish (1998, 3) highlights the dimension of critical analysis of the practice as one of the essential competencies that must be taken into account in order to "produce a critical appreciation of the practice [that] involves the practitioner in the investigation of his or her own work."[2] In this approach, we find a convergence of the concepts of "the reflective practitioner" and of "the practitioner researcher." These concepts were developed in relation to teaching professionalism, particularly in the 1980s and 1990s (Schön, 1992; Stenhouse, 1993; Zeichner 1993), and were important to the conceptual field of teacher education.

Teaching has long been categorised as a helping profession, but that concept has not been translated into the specific theory and practice of initial teacher education. The educational relationship is the essence of teaching professionalism, and according to Ribeiro (1992), it brings together aspects of authority, conflict, approval and help. This focus on the "help" aspect is related to new conceptions of the person, the citizen and society. It conveys new definitions of knowledge and appropriate behaviour, where self-expression, emotions, communication and human capacities occupy prominent positions (see Lopes, 2001; Pereira, 2013). On that subject, Tardif and Lessard (2005, 23) observe that "schooling rests basically on the daily interactions between teachers and pupils. Without those interactions the school is no more than a vast empty shell." These interactions form the basis of social relations in the school, and are the main object of the teachers' work and, consequently, we argue that they must be the focal point of the work of their trainers as well.

Narratives in Initial Teacher Education That Characterise the Professional Work of a Teacher

Describing three types of discourse (formal curriculum, teaching practice reports and interviews with teachers) that relate to the initial education of primary teachers, Pereira (2009) identified five different narratives[3] that characterise the professional work of the teacher.

(1) The pedagogue (centered on the nature of the work that he or she does with the children; with the justifications and value judgments that he or she pronounces on it, with reference to a humanist ethic);

(2) The specialist (highlighting the cognitive dimension of the teaching task; justifying a cognitive-instrumental rationale and an ethic of expertise);
(3) The mediator (focusing on the mediation between children and the social mandates governing school education, between science and pedagogy, and between the experience of infancy in the world of life and socio-educative action; appealing to an ethic of subjectivity and of service);
(4) The professional "under construction" (referring to the professional researcher; reflective, critical, questioning and self-training; capable of calling his own work into question; guided by a critical and self-transforming ethic);
(5) The professional at a critical point (highlighting the professional challenges involved in working with children and the difficulties of implementing the ideas demanded of him or her; revealing a critical and reflective attitude towards teaching; and a sense of ethical responsibility).

These narratives, which constitute heterotopic entities (see Foucault, 1986), reveal the diversity of notions about the work of teachers, on the one hand, and on the other hand, the coexistence of different referential models for initial teacher education related to the training profile of the future teachers. This also indicates the complexity that characterises the teacher's work, and the pain and distress factors caused by that complexity. This complexity is one of the main aspects that teacher educators must consider in their educational relationship with the teacher-students. Another pertinent aspect of those narratives is the fact that if the educational work of the teacher educators is more influenced by one or another of those narratives, the impact on the teacher profile is different. Therefore, it is important to identify the influence of those narratives in the teacher educators' discourses.

A State of Flux: Change in the Teaching Profession

A teacher's professional challenge must be understood in the context of the disintegration of the social and political consensus that affects the organisation of the modern school, and of the fracturing of the socio-ethical and ontological mandates for the work of teachers (Pereira, 2011). This problem translates into the daily experience of risky interactions, that is, interactions characterised by the unpredictability of the behaviour of others, and which at any moment can lead to a breakdown of order (Derouet, 1993). The professional concern of individual teachers is significant if one accepts that the teaching profession is at a critical point, and is related to a cognitive problem (see Correia, Matos, & Canário 2002). This is a problem in terms of the performances and ways of expressing meanings that teachers resort to in order to make sense of and to direct their work with children—in other words, acting and signifying in ways which are fundamental in the educational relationship.

Appendix B

The educational relationship, which is the core of the primary teacher's professional life (Pereira & Lopes, 2009), has a strong component of mutual assistance and of working with others. This component tends to have a low profile in the professional education of teachers, staying on the periphery of training programmes.

Dubet (2002) considers that school education, like health and social work, is "working on the other" (42), meaning that it is work explicitly aimed at transforming the lives of others, which was originally set up with reference to a modern institutional programme, a programme that has supported the construction of contemporary institutions. This programme is a social process from which values and principles are transformed into action and into subjectivity through a specific and organised profession. The programme consists of three levels that make up the professional action of these career teachers and are to be articulated and given direction. The three levels are social control, service and relationships. These levels are currently becoming more autonomous, and this is a process which intrinsically produces contradictory logic. This puts the task of legitimising teachers' work into their own hands (Derouet, 1993), and, therefore, makes new demands on the teachers as individuals and on their professional training and development.

In this context, the teaching profession confronts challenges that oblige the rethinking of the training conditions of teachers, with emphasis on initial education and the relationship of theory to practice that it engenders. Teaching practice is considered "an original and relatively autonomous space for learning and training" (Tardif, Lessard, & Gauthier, 2000, 23). Accordingly, the whole apprenticeship is converted into the trainee's own experience. For this reason, teacher education demands "a constant shuttling between practice and training, between professional experience and research, between teachers and university educators" (Tardif, Lessard, & Gauthier 2000, 24). In other words, it demands a shuttling between teacher-mentors in schools and teacher educators in universities.

The current neoliberal tendency concerning educational policies is an important part of the changes in the teaching profession and it puts in question its "helping" dimension. As stated by Grimaldi (2012, 1132) "notwithstanding the specificities of local re-contextualisations, the widespread influence of a heterogeneous set of neoliberal discourses has the power to weaken and divert education policies intended to pursue social justice and inclusion." In Portugal, this tendency, as in other countries where it has impact in educational policies, creates practices of governability that transfer the social and economic problems to the responsibility of the individuals. This passage is made by a self-regulatory process that makes the individuals responsible for their own care (Webb, Gulson, & Pitton, 2014). It is argued, therefore, that the impact of neoliberal policies in the teacher profession tends to produce forms of accountability pertaining to school education in general and of teachers' work in particular, that affect the educational relationship that teachers develop with the students and the professional relationships they have with colleagues.

Being a Teacher Educator and Primary Teacher Professionalisation

Changes in Primary Teacher Professionalisation in Portugal

The professionalisation of teachers in Portugal took place in a profoundly complex socio-historic process, full of tensions and contradictions of various kinds (see Nóvoa, 1995). In the case of primary teachers, their professionalisation has undergone deep changes in recent decades, in terms of the academic degree conferred, the curriculum, the training context and their relationship with the context of work (see Lopes et al., 2007). This has provoked changes in the "first" professional identity of the teachers and in their professional career. In a process clearly intended to increase the social value of the profession, initial teacher education in Portugal from 1974 onwards (the beginning of the process of democratisation) was integrated into higher education (in colleges of education in the polytechnic institutes or in the universities). Prospective teachers studied for the degree Licenciatura (the first degree earned after four or five years of study). Recently, the plan of study was restructured as a result of the Bologna Process[4] and all teachers will have to have a master's degree (the second cycle of higher education). In previous studies, it has been shown that in some cases, the progressive upgrading of initial teacher education, notably during the 1990s, had a positive impact on the "scientific" education of the teachers. But it has been argued that this brought a weakening of the "professional" training dimensions (Buchberger et al., 2000), at least in comparison to previous periods. In particular, after the democratic revolution of 25 April 1974, there was an effective investment in the professional education of teachers, or, in other words, in the education of teachers as professionals (Lopes et al., 2007).

An analysis of the course programmes of the 1990s shows that they consist mostly of theoretical content and bibliography (as opposed to accounts of what happened in previous periods). This fact allows us to advance the hypothesis that the course programmes have undergone "academicisation." In this way, they became theoretical enough to be intellectually "worthy" of a university degree. This phenomenon could have been strongly related to the emphasis that the teacher educator placed on their status as higher education teachers, or with the curricular organisation where the university ethos could have also made itself felt—or to both. In any case, independently of their professional background and identities at the start, the teacher educator, in fact, adopted behaviour more informed by the academic world than by the professional world of school teaching (Lopes and Pereira, 2012).

In fact, the Bologna Declaration (19/06/99) had profound consequences on the restructuring of higher education in Portugal and, consequently, in initial teacher education. In 2007, a new policy on teacher education was set to converge with the Bologna Process, then, a new legal system[5] of professional qualification for pre-school, primary and secondary school teachers was defined. A certification requirement of two study cycles for teaching was proposed, including, in the case of primary teachers, a bachelor's degree in elementary education (three years) and a master's degree (two years) with a certificate for teaching.

Training courses include the following components: training in general education; specific didactic education; introduction to professional practice; cultural, social and ethical education; educational research methodologies and teaching practice.

The component of "introduction to professional practice" should provide student teachers with "experience in planning, teaching and assessment in accordance with rights and duties assigned to teachers within and outside the classroom;" this component might allow for continuous professional development and the instauration of a critical and reflective attitude regarding everyday school professional challenges, processes and performance.

A teacher may teach in primary school with a master's degree in Preschool Education and Primary Education, or in Primary Education and Elementary Education (5th and 6th grades of schooling), or in Primary Education only.

Initial Teacher Education and Identities

The process of constructing professional identities is characterised by biographic and relational transactions (Dubar, 1996), and initial teacher education has a founding role in their construction (Blin, 1997). The relational transaction is established between the trainers and the training context. As a process of secondary socialisation, initial teacher education is responsible for the conditions of access to the profession, and learning what is involved in the specialised field of education. The effect of formative life experiences involved in the construction of the professional identity depends on the "situated" interactions; in other words, the way in which the social and personal identities are translated into concrete identities—"situated identities" (Hewitt, 1991). This is possible in the context of training, given the way it is structured, but also given the roles played by the participants. The perceptions and conceptions of the teacher educator about the professionalisation of teachers, the specific nature of teaching work and of the mission that is conferred upon them by society are essential aspects of a knowledge that can inform pertinent transformations in the formative dynamics of initial teacher education.

Murray and Male (2005, 126) distinguish between the work of the teachers, considering it to be "first-order practice" and the work of the trainers of future teachers, which is a "second-order practice." These professionals—practitioners of the second order—introduce their students to practices and discourses that are simultaneously relevant to school teaching itself and to training school teachers. The situation mentioned by the authors covers, in particular, the TE who began as teachers and later opted for a role in initial teacher education. Referring to this concept from Murray and Male (2005), Swennen, Volman, and Essen (2008), emphasise that, in these cases, the second-order practices, apart from being necessary for acquiring new knowledge and skills, also involve a process of reconfiguring their professional identities that may be of long duration. Along those lines, Boyd and Harris (2010) speak of a second career and dual identity. To those authors, primary education teachers who become teacher educators experience a very challenging and problematic transition. This is because of the tensions and standards that exist in higher education, including the specifics of the academic subject, relationships between equals and relationships with schools that welcome (or at least accept) trainees. This transition is reflected in the reshaping of their identities, which, in the study on which it is based, it seems, gets closer to their original identity as teachers than to a newly constituted identity. Korthagen (2005), based on the research of various authors (Schön, 1983; Munby, Russel, & Martin, 2001; Bass, Anderson-Patton, & Allender, 2002; Loughran et al., 2004), states that speaking of teacher educators covers a great diversity and multidimensionality of roles and social actors. In convergence with this idea, Zeichner (2010a) highlights the complexity of the role of teacher educators, and talks about "hybrid educators."

Initial Teacher Education and its Influence on Professional Practice

One of the main questions asked about the work of teacher educators and initial teacher education in general is about the difficulty of significantly influencing the professional practice of the future teachers. These teachers may, in fact, be more influenced by school culture and the constraints of the classroom that are commonly referred to as "practice shock." As Korthagen (2010a) observes, many studies in diverse countries have revealed that newly trained teachers confront great difficulties in dealing with the problems they experience with their classes, and implement little of what they had learned in their training. One of the main reasons for those difficulties is related to what is traditionally called the "theory-practice gap" in teacher education. Although this gap was highlighted long ago by Dewey in 1904, it remains a "central problem of teacher education world-wide" (as quoted in Korthagen 2010b, 408). Teacher education, as a university institution, has difficulty breaking the theory-to-practice model, and, although it is professional training, the hegemony of theoretical knowledge remains a problem with a difficult resolution. Zeichner (2010b, 124) observes, "One of the central problems that has plagued college and university based pre-service teacher education for many years (is) the (disconnect) between the components of the programmes in the campus and the school." The author argues that the work of creating curricular dimensions that articulate scientific and experiential knowledge in teacher education represents a paradigm shift in the epistemology of teacher education programmes. It is possible that the articulation of the academic knowledge, the practical knowledge and the knowledge that exists in the community could produce forms of teacher learning

Appendix B

that are less hierarchical in epistemological terms than they are in the current context of teacher education (Zeichner, 2010b).

Research Questions

The main research questions that informed the data analysis were: what are the perceptions that teacher educators have about their work and the work of school teachers; and how are those perceptions related to their identities?

More specifically: What type of knowledge do the teacher educators refer to and value in their discourses? What kind of beliefs and values do they have about their work and the work of school teachers? What are their perceptions about the professional activity of the teacher educators and of the school teachers? What kind of problems do teacher educators refer to when thinking about their work and the work of school teachers?

Notes

1. In this study, the concept of "narrative" refers to public or private stories that we identify and integrate into our perception and cognition of the world, conditioning the interpretation that we put upon the incidents and the social relationships, and guiding our actions and attitudes. These narratives are not restricted to a single statement or part of a text, but are formed from different texts and discourses, without the logic of the relationship that unites them in a single narrative being made explicit in any one of them (Somers & Gibson, 1994).
2. Our translation and back translation.
3. In this study, the concept of "narrative" refers to public or private stories that we identify and integrate into our perception and cognition of the world, conditioning the interpretation that we put upon the incidents and the social relationships, and guiding our actions and attitudes. These narratives are not restricted to a single statement or part of a text, but are formed from different texts and discourses, without the logic of the relationship that unites them in a single narrative being made explicit in any one of them (Somers & Gibson, 1994).
4. See European Ministers of Education 1999.
5. Law 43/2007, 22nd September.

References

Bass, L., V. Anderson-Patton, and J. Allender. 2002. "Self-study as a Way of Teaching and Learning: A Research Collaborative Re-analysis of Self-study Teaching Portfolios." In *Improving Teacher Education Practices through Self-Study*, edited by J. Lougran and T. Russel, 56–70. Londres: Routledge Falmer.

Blin, J.-F. 1997. *Représentations, Pratiques Et Identités Professionnelles* [Representations, Practices and Professional Identities]. Paris: L'Harmathan.

Boyd, P., and K. Harris. 2010. "Becoming a University Lecturer in Teacher Education: Expert School Teachers Reconstructing Their Pedagogy and Identity." *Professional Development in Education* 36 (1–2): 9–24.

Buchberger, F., B. P. Campos, D. Kallós, and J. Stephenson. 2000. *Green Paper on Teacher Education in Europe: High Quality Teacher Education for High Quality Education and Training*. Umea: TNTEE.

Correia, J. A., M. Matos, and R. Canário. 2002. "La souffrance professionnelle des enseignants et les dispositifs de compensation identitaire [The professional suffering of teachers and the devices of identity compensation]." In *L'année de la recherche en sciences de l'éducation: Des représentations*, 281–302. Afirse matrice.

Derouet, J.-L. 1993. "École et Justice: De l'égalité des chances aux compromis locaux? [School and Justice: From opportunity equality to local compromise?]" *Revue Française de Pédagogie* 104: 109–113.

Dubar, C. 1996. *La Socialisation: Construction Des Identités Sociales & Professionnelles* [The Socialisation: Building Social & Professional Identities]. Paris: Armand Colin.

Dubet, F. 2002. *Le Déclin De L'institution* [Decline of Institution]. Paris: SEUIL. European Ministers of Education. 1999. "The Bologna Declaration of 19 June 1999". The European Higher Education Area. Accessed June 23, 2015. http://www.ehea.info/Uploads/Declarations/BOLOGNA_DECLARATION1.pdf

Fish, D. 1998. *Appreciating Practice in the Caring Professions: Refocusing Professional Development & Practitioner Research*. Oxford: Reed Educational and Professional Publishing.

Foucault, M. 1986. *Vigiar e Punir* [Discipline and Punish]. Petrópolis: Vozes.

Grimaldi, E. 2012. "Neoliberalism and the Marginalisation of Social Justice: The Making of an Education Policy to Combat Social Exclusion." *International Journal of Inclusive Education* 16 (11): 1131–1154.

Hewitt, J. 1991. *Self and Society: A Symbolic Interactionist Social Psychology*. Boston, MA: Allyn and Bacon.

Hugman, R. 2005. *New Approaches in Ethics for the Caring Professions*. Basingstoke: Palgrave Macmillan.

Korthagen, F. 2005. "Teaching Teachers: Studies into Expertise of Teacher Educators: An Introduction to This Theme Issue." *Teaching and Teacher Education* 21: 107–115.

Korthagen, F. 2010a. "Situated Learning Theory and the Pedagogy of Teacher Education: Towards an Integrative View of Teacher Behavior and Teacher Learning." *Teaching and Teacher Education* 26: 98–106.

Korthagen, F. 2010b. "How Teacher Education Can Make a Difference." *Journal of Education for Teaching: International Research and Pedagogy* 36: 407–423.

Lopes, A. 2001. *Libertar O Desejo, Resgatar A Inovação: A Construção De Identidades Profissionais Docentes* [Releasing Desire, Redeeming Innovation: The Construction of Professional Teachers Identities]. Lisboa: Instituto de Inovação Educacional.

Lopes, A., and F. Pereira. 2012. "Everyday Life and Everyday Learning: The Ways in Which Pre-service Teacher Education Curriculum Can Encourage Personal Dimensions of Teacher Identity." *European Journal of Teacher Education* 35 (1): 17–38.

Lopes, A., F. Pereira, E. Ferreira, M. Silva, and M. J. Sá. 2007. Fazer Da *Formação Um Projecto: Formação Inicial E Identidades Profissionais Docentes* [Building a Project out of Training: Initial Training and Teachers Professional Identities]. Porto: Livpsic.

Loughran, J. J., M. L. Hamilton, V. K. Laboskey, and T. Russel. 2004. *International Handbook of Self-Study of Teaching and Teacher Education Practice*. Dordrecht: Kluver.

Munby, H., T. Russel, and A. K. Martin. 2001. "Teachers' Knowledge and How It Develops." In *Handbook of Research on Teaching*, edited by V. Richardson, 877–904. Washington: AERA.

Murray, J., and T. Male. 2005. "Becoming a Teacher Educator: Evidence from the Field." *Teacher and Teacher Education* 21: 125–142.

Nóvoa, A. 1995. "O Passado E O Presente Dos Professores [The Past and the Present of Teachers]." In *Profissão Professor*, edited by A. Nóvoa, 13–34. Porto: Porto Editora.

Pereira, F. 2009. "Conceptions and Knowledge about Childhood in Initial Teacher Training: Changes in Recent Decades and Their Impact on Teacher Professionality and on Schooling in Childhood." *Teaching and Teacher Education* 25 (8): 1009–1017.

Pereira, F. 2010. "Childhood Narratives in Initial Teacher Training: Childhood Government and Its Re-institutionalization." *Research in Education* 83 (1): 1–16.

Pereira, F. 2011. "In-service Teacher Education and Scholar Innovation: The Semantics of Action and Reflection on Action as a Mediation Device." *Australian Journal of Teacher Education* 36 (11): 33–50.

Pereira, F. 2013. "Concepts, Policies and Practices of Teacher Education: An Analysis of Studies on Teacher Education in Portugal." *Journal of Education for Teaching: International Research and Pedagogy* 39 (5): 474–491.

Pereira, F., and A. Lopes. 2009. "Ser criança e ser aluno: Concepções das professoras do 1º Ciclo do Ensino Básico [Being a child and being a student: Conceptions of primary school teachers]." *Educação em Revista* 25 (1): 37–62.

Ribeiro, A. 1992. "Relação educativa [Educational relationship]." In *Psicologia Do Desenvolvimento E Da Educação Dos Jovens*, edited by B. P. Campos, 133–159. Lisbon: Universidade Aberta.

Schön, D. 1983. *The Reflective Practitioner: How Professionals Think in Action*. Nova York: Basic Books.

Schön, D. 1992. *La Formación De Profesionales Reflexivos: Hacia Un Nuevo Diseño De La Enseñanza Y El Aprendizage En Las Profesiones* [Educating the Reflective Practitioner: Toward a New Design for Teaching and Learning in the Professions]. Barcelona: Paidós.

Somers, M., and G. Gibson. 1994. "Reclaiming the Epistemological 'Other': Narrative and the Social Constitution of Identity." In *Social Theory and the Politics of Identity*, edited by C. Calhoun, 37–99. Oxford: Blackwell.

Sommers-Flanagan, R., and J. Sommers-Flanagan. 2007. *Becoming an Ethical Helping Professional*. New Jersey: John Wiley & Sons.

Stenhouse, L. 1993. *La Investigación Como Base De La Enseñanza* [Research as a Basis for Teaching]. 2nd ed. Tranlated by Guillermo Solana. Madrid: Ediciones Morata.

Swennen, A., M. Volman, and M. Essen. 2008. "The Development of the Professional Identity of Two Teacher Educators in the Context of Dutch Teacher Education." *European Journal of Teacher Education* 31 (2): 169–184.

Tardif, M., and C. Lessard. 2005. *O Trabalho Docente: Elemento Para Uma Teoria Da Docência Como Profissão De Interações Humanas* [The Teaching Work: Basis for a Theory of Teaching as a Profession of Human Interactions]. Petrópolis: Vozes.

Tardif, M., C. Lessard, and C. Gauthier. 2000. *Formação Dos Professores E Contextos Sociais: Perspectivas Internacionais* [Teachers Education and Social Contexts: International Perspectives]. Porto: Rés-Editora.

Webb, T., K. Gulson, and V. Pitton. 2014. "The Neo-liberal Education Policies of Epimeleia Heautou: Caring for the Self in School Markets." *Discourse: Studies in the Cultural Politics of Education* 35 (1): 31–44.

Zeichner, K. 1993. *A Formação Reflexiva De Professores: Ideias E Práticas* [Reflective Education of Teachers: Ideas and Practices]. Lisbon: Educa.

Zeichner, K. 2010a. "Re-thinking the Connections between Campus Courses and Filed Experiences in College-and University-Based Teacher Education." *Journal of Teacher Education* 61: 89–99.

Zeichner, K. 2010b. "Nuevas epistemologias en formación del profesorado. Repensando las conexiones entre las asignaturas del campus y las experiencias de prácticas en la formación del profesorado en la universidad [New epistemologies in teacher education. Rethinking the connections between campus courses and practical experiences in teacher education at the university]." *Revista Interuniversitaria de Formación de Profesorado* 24 (2): 123–149.

9) Schenk, A.M. & Fremouw, W.J. (2012). Prevalence, psychological impact, and coping of cyberbully victims among college students. *Journal of School Violence*, 11(1), 21–37.

On January 14, 2010, 15-year-old Phoebe Prince took her life after being cyberbullied. After her death, classmates revealed that she had been relentlessly cyberbullied by text messages and posts on social networking sites (Johnson, 2010). On September 22, 2010, 18-year-old Tyler Clementi jumped to his death from the George Washington Bridge after his roommate streamed video of him and another male over the Internet (Friedman, 2010).

Traditional bullying is moving into the technological realm and cyberbullying is becoming a growing problem. As a result, 34 states have adopted or are in the process of adopting laws against cyberbullying (National Conference of State Legislatures, 2011).

Defining Traditional Bullying and Cyberbullying

Olweus (1993) defined traditional bullying as repeated exposure to negative actions by one or more other people. Bullying can be direct, such as physically beating someone up, or indirect, which includes non-face-to-face methods like spreading rumors. This definition contains components that overlap with the current definition of cyberbullying (Figure 1). Cyberbullying is a repeated, intentional act done with the purpose of harming another person through technologies such as e-mail, cell phone messaging, social networking Web sites, chat rooms, and instant messaging (Beran & Li, 2005; Bhat, 2008; Campbell, 2005; Patchin & Hinduja, 2006), which can be perpetrated by a single individual or a group of people (Smith et al., 2008). Unlike traditional bullying, cyberbullying does not require a face-to-

Appendix B

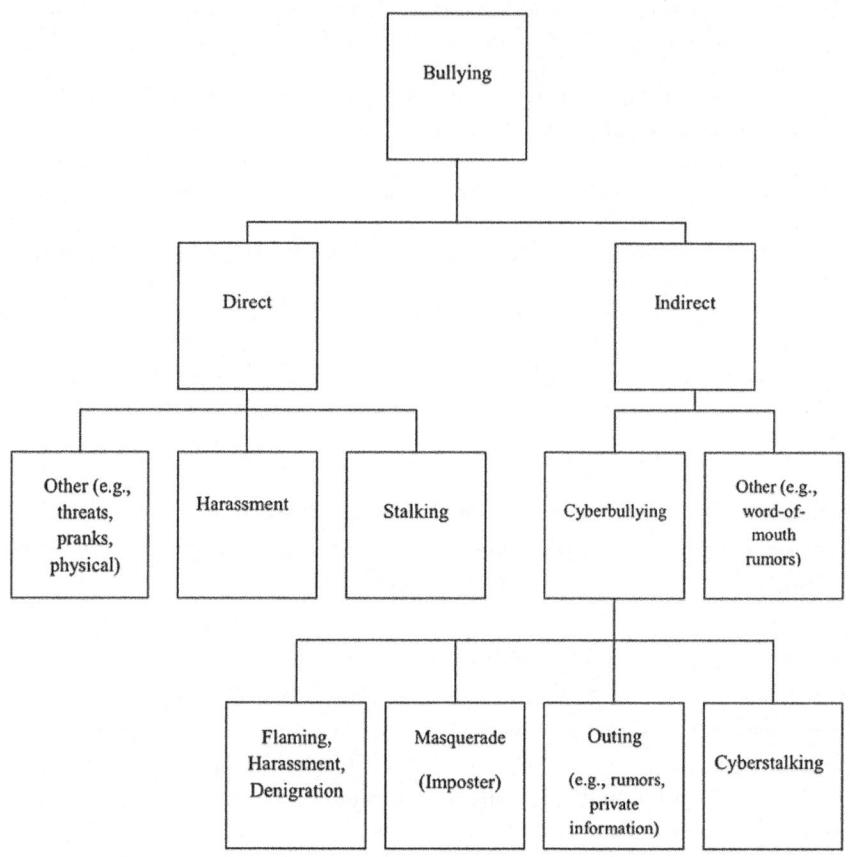

Figure 1 The relation between traditional bullying, cyberbullying, and stalking behaviors.

face confrontation or a physical location to convene and can be completely anonymous (Dehue, Bolman, & Völlink, 2008; Mason, 2008).

Most studies have defined cyberbullying in similar ways with only slight variations. For example, Mason (2008) categorized cyberbullying as a "form of psychological cruelty" that included a new form of bullying that is simply a more "covert form of verbal and written [traditional] bullying" (p. 323). Also, some researchers do not include the repetition component when defining cyberbullying (e.g., Privitera & Campbell, 2009; Raskauskas & Stoltz, 2007; Slonje & Smith, 2008). However, to leave this aspect out overgeneralizes cyberbullying by including incidents that happened only once or by chance. Other researchers also include the component of a power differential between the victim and the perpetrator of cyberbullying (Hinduja & Patchin, 2007; Mason, 2008; Privitera & Campbell, 2009). A power imbalance could be based on actual power criteria, such as physical strength, body build, age, or on technological ability (Vandebosch & Van Cleemput, 2008). However, we do not believe the power differential is a necessary element to the definition of cyberbullying due to the anonymity and security offered by cyberbullying. The anonymity provided by technology can actually help create a power advantage, where cyberbullying can be a way for smaller victims of traditional bullying to get revenge on their more powerful aggressor(s) (Campbell, 2005; Dehue et al., 2008; Li, 2007a; Ybarra & Mitchell, 2004).

Li (2007a) outlined seven different forms of cyberbullying that constitute this new phenomenon. The seven categories of cyberbullying are: flaming, online harassment, cyberstalking, denigration, masquerading, outing, and exclusion. Flaming involves the electronic transmission of angry, rude, and vulgar messages, whereas online harassment is the repeated sending of messages. Cyberstalking entails threats of harm or intimidation. Denigration (put-downs) involves sending cruel, and possibly untrue, information about a person to others. Pretending to be someone else and sharing information to damage a person's reputation or relationships is classified as masquerading. Outing is the sharing of sensitive or private information about a person to others. Finally, exclusion involves maliciously leaving someone out of a group online.

Prevalence Rates of Cyberbullying

Since studies define cyberbullying in slightly different ways and with different age groups, diverse prevalence rates have been reported. Overall, prevalence rates of cyberbully victimization ranged from 4.8% (Sourander et al., 2010) to 55.3% (Dilmac, 2009) across all age groups. The Second Youth Internet Safety Survey, a national survey collected in 2004 ($N = 1,500$), reported the overall prevalence rate for cyberbullying between the ages of 10 and 17 to be 9% (Ybarra, Mitchell, Wolak, & Finkelhor, 2006). This was a 50% increase in prevalence from a similar survey taken in 2000 (Ybarra & Mitchell, 2004). Within smaller and more specific studies the rates vary. The following summarizes the prevalence rates of cyberbullying from middle school, high school, college, and workplace samples.

At the middle school level, Canadian students completed a self-report questionnaire regarding their experiences with cyberbullying (Li, 2007a). Results showed that 24.9% of the sample ($n = 177$) were victims of cyberbullying. A sample of seventh-grade students ($n = 461$) in both Canada and China completed the same questionnaire and found one in three students had been a victim of cyberbullying (Li, 2007b). Of those victims, over 40% had been cyberbullied more than three times. In addition, Beran and Li (2005) sampled 432 Canadian middle school students and reported that 21% of students had been frequently cyberharassed (e.g., cyberbullied).

Studies have included both middle school and high school children to examine prevalence rates of cyberbullying across adolescence. Using a sample of 92 children

Appendix B

from the United States, ages 11 to 16, Smith and colleagues (2008) found that 6.6% of students had been bullied "often" (two or three times a month) and 15.6% had experienced cyberbullying at least once or twice. Among 2,215 Finland youth, ages 13 to 16, 4.8% had been cyberbullied within the last 6 months (Sourander et al., 2010). Hinduja and Patchin (2008) reported the prevalence of cyberbullying among 384 Americans, up to age 17, as 30%. Additionally, Slonje and Smith (2008) assessed experiences with cyberbullying of 360 Swedish students, ages 12 to 20. The overall cyberbullying victimization rate for that sample was 11.7%.

To date, there is little research examining cyberbullying with a college population. However, Kraft and Wang (2010) conducted one such study that investigated both cyberbullying and cyberstalking among college students in the United States (New Jersey). They reported prevalence rates of 10% for cyberbully victims and 9% for cyberstalking victims among a sample of 471 participants. Only one other study has been found that examines cyberbullying among college students. This study was conducted at a university in Turkey and found much higher prevalence rates of cyberbully victimization at 55.3% of the 666 students in the sample (Dilmac, 2009). This prevalence rate can be explained by the fact the researchers counted being a victim of cyberbullying at least once in their lifetime. More research utilizing a college-age sample is necessary to better understand the prevalence rate among this population.

In the workplace, Privitera and Campbell (2009) reported that 10.7% of male Australian Manufacturing Workers' Union employees ($n = 103$) had been cyberbullied. These results support the idea that traditional bullying is changing with technological advancements, not only in schools, but beyond.

Impact of Cyberbully Victimization

Victims of cyberbullying experience a variety of emotional impacts, with most showing an increase in emotional distress (Ybarra & Mitchell, 2004). Typical responses to cyberbully victimization included frustration, anger, and sadness. Additionally, the more cyberbullying that was experienced, the more offline problems victims exhibited (Hinduja & Patchin, 2007). Beran and Li (2005) identified feeling angry and crying as the most frequent reactions with feeling sad, hurt, anxious, embarrassed, afraid, and blaming one's self as other common emotional responses. An American-based study found victims of cyberbullying had significantly lower self-esteem than other middle school students who had no experience with cyberbullying (Patchin & Hinduja, 2010). Finkelhor, Mitchell, and Wolak (2000) found that approximately one third (32%) of cyberbully victims experienced at least one symptom of stress, 31% were upset, 19% were afraid, and 18% felt embarrassed as a result of being cyberbullied.

Specific behavioral impacts reported from Canadian cyberbully victims in Grades 7–9 were poor concentration, low school achievement, and absenteeism (Beran &

Li, 2005). Consciously avoiding the Internet, dwelling on the harassment, feeling jumpy or irritable, and losing interest in things were also found to be common experiences among cyberbullying victims. Adolescent victims were more likely to have behavior problems, consume alcohol, smoke, and have low school commitment than adolescent nonvictims (Mason, 2008). A population-based study of cyberbullying in adolescents from Finland found victims experienced emotional and peer problems, headaches, recurrent abdominal pain, problems sleeping, and not feeling safe at school compared to nonvictims (Sourander et al., 2010). Cyberbullying experienced in the workplace was typically associated with negative physical health, negative emotional well-being, impacted social and family relationships, as well as a reduction in staff morale, commitment, job satisfaction, and a breakdown of work relationships (Privitera & Campbell, 2009).

Cyberbully victimization was also associated with clinical symptomology. Ybarra (2004) found that victims of cyberbullying, ages 10 through 17, endorsed more depressive symptoms than nonvictims. Furthermore, Fauman (2008) identified common psychological consequences related to cyberbully victimization as depression, anxiety, suicidal ideation, and poor concentration, as well as a sense of helplessness and low self-esteem. Thomas (2006) also found anxiety, school phobia, depression, lowered self-esteem, emotional distress, and suicide were acknowledged as potential results of being a victim of cyberbullying among adolescents, ages 13 through 18. Raskauskas and Stoltz (2007) recognized that extreme cases of cyberbully victimization have been linked to adolescent suicide.

Empirically, Hinduja and Patchin (2010) investigated the relation between suicidal behaviors (ideation, attempts/experiences) among traditional and cyberbully victims and perpetrators. Their research revealed a link between youth who experienced traditional or cyberbullying, as either perpetrator or victim, and more suicidal thoughts and an increased likelihood of attempting suicide compared to a control group. This relation was stronger for victims, rather than perpetrators, of both forms of bullying.

Research has shown that the impact on cyberbully victims is substantial and negative. Some factors that can escalate the severity of the impact are the increased difficulty to escape the cyberbullying, as well as the countless bystanders that can view this private information due to the ease of electronic transmission (Bhat, 2008; Campbell, 2005; Slonje & Smith, 2008).

Methods for Coping With Cyberbully Victimization

Coping strategies to deal with cyberbullying varied across empirical studies. For example, some victims in the United States removed themselves from the particular Web site, stayed offline for a period of time, talked about their experience with a friend, and a few informed a teacher or an adult about what they experienced

Appendix B

(Hinduja & Patchin, 2007). Telling someone and blocking or avoiding the technological device were viewed as the best methods, although doing nothing/ignoring, blocking one's identity, keeping a record of offensive e-mails and texts, reporting the occurrence to police/authorities, contacting the service provider, asking the perpetrator to stop, and fighting back were also identified as methods for dealing with cyberbully victimization in 11 through 16 year olds in England (Smith et al., 2008). In addition, pretending to ignore it, really ignoring it, deleting all the bully's messages, and bullying the bully were other strategies identified by a sample ($n = 1,211$) of primary school children and first-year pupils of secondary schools in the Netherlands (Dehue et al., 2008).

It is evident that victims of cyberbullying negatively react to the experience and cope in a variety of ways. To date, the majority of research has been done using school-age children and adolescents. Research is necessary to identify the prevalence of cyberbullying in a college sample, how this age group is impacted by their victimization, and what coping strategies are utilized. Cyberbullying is especially relevant for this age group since they are typically just out of high school where cyberbullying is still prevalent, and they are more independent from parental influences. There also needs to be more research focusing on cyberbullying in the United States, as much of the current research has been conducted internationally.

To date, the two studies that examined cyberbullying among college students have laid important groundwork on this new phenomenon. This study builds upon those by obtaining another prevalence rate for cyberbullying among college students in the United States, as well as utilized standardized measures (e.g., SCL-90-R, Suicidal Behaviors Questionnaire-Revised [SBQ-R]) to better understand the psychological impact cyberbullying can have on victims. Additionally, this study expands others by assessing coping strategies victims employ.

Purpose

The purpose of this study was to examine the prevalence rate of cyberbullying, the psychological impact, and the coping strategies utilized by college-student victims. Differences in suicidal behaviors between victims of cyberbullying and control participants were explored. Gender differences in the results were also examined.

References

Beran, T., & Li, Q. (2005). Cyber-harassment: A study of a new method for an old behavior. *Journal of Educational Computing Research, 32,* 265–277.

Bhat, C. S. (2008). Cyber bullying: Overview and strategies for school counsellors, guidance officers, and all school personnel. *Australian Journal of Guidance and Counselling, 18,* 53–66. doi:10.1375/ajgc.18.1.53

Brown, G. K. (2001). *A review of suicide assessment measures for intervention research with adults and older adults*. Retrieved from http://sbisrvntweb.uqac.ca/archivage/15290520.pdf

Brunstein-Klomek, A., Sourander, A., & Gould, M. (2010). The association of suicide and bullying in childhood to young adulthood: A review of cross-sectional and longitudinal research findings. *Canadian Journal of Psychiatry, 55*, 282–288.

Campbell, M. A. (2005). Cyber bullying: An old problem in a new guise? *Australian Journal of Guidance and Counselling, 15*, 68–76. doi:10.1375/ajgc.15.1.68

Cole, D. A. (1988). Hopelessness, social desirability, depression, and parasuicide in two college student samples. *Journal of Consulting and Clinical Psychology, 56*, 131–136. doi:10.1037/0022-006X.56.1.131

Dehue, F., Bolman, C., & Völlink, T. (2008). Cyberbullying: Youngsters' experiences and parental perceptions. *CyberPsychology & Behavior, 11*, 217–223. doi:10.1089/cpb.2007.0008

Derogatis, L. R. (1994). *Symptom Checklist-90-R: Administration, scoring, and procedures manual* (3rd ed.). Minneapolis, MN: National Computer Systems.

Derogatis, L. R., Rickels, K., & Roch, A. F. (1976). The SCL-90 and the MMPI: A step in the validation of a new self-report scale. *The British Journal of Psychiatry, 129*, 280–289. doi:10.1192/bjp.128.3.280

Dilmac, B. (2009). Psychological needs as a predictor of cyber bullying: A preliminary report on college students. *Educational Sciences: Theory and Practice, 9*, 1307–1325.

Fauman, M. A. (2008). Review of "Cyber bullying: Bulling in the digital age." *The American Journal of Psychiatry, 165*, 780–781. doi:10.1176/appi.ajp.2008.08020226

Finkelhor, D., Mitchell, K. J., & Wolak, J. (2000). *Online victimization: A report on the nation's youth*. Alexandria, VA: National Center for Missing and Exploited Children.

Friedman, E. (2010, September 29). Victim of secret dorm sex tape posts Facebook goodbye, jumps to his death. *ABC News*. Retrieved from http://abcnews.go.com/US/victim-secret-dorm-sex-tape-commits-suicide/story?id 11758716

Hinduja, S., & Patchin, J. W. (2007). Offline consequences of online victimization: School violence and delinquency. *Journal of School Violence, 6*, 89–112. doi:10.1300/J202 v06n03_06

Hinduja, S., & Patchin, J. W. (2008). Cyberbullying: An exploratory analysis of factors related to offending and victimization. *Deviant Behavior, 29*, 129–156. doi:10.1080/01639620701457816

Hinduja, S., & Patchin, J. W. (2010). Bullying, cyberbullying, and suicide. *Archives of Suicide Research, 14*, 206–221. doi: 10.1080/13811118.2010.494133

Johnson, O. (2010, January 23). Bullying eyed in girl's death. *Boston Herald*. Retrieved from http://news.bostonherald.com/news/regional/view/ 20100123bullying_eyed_in_girls_death/srvc home&position also

Kraft, E., & Wang, J. (2010). An exploratory study of the cyberbullying and cyberstalking experiences and factors related to victimization of students at a public liberal arts college. *International Journal of Technologies, 1*, 74–91. doi:10.4018/jte.2010100106

Li, Q. (2007a). Bullying in the new playground: Research into cyberbullying and cyber victimization. *Australian Journal of Educational Technology, 23*, 435–454.

Li, Q. (2007b). New bottle but old wine: A research of cyberbullying in schools. *Computers in Human Behavior, 23*, 1777–1791. doi:10.1016/j.chb.2005.10.005

Linehan, M. M., & Nielsen, S. L. (1981). Assessment of suicide ideation and parasuicide: Hopelessness and social desirability. *Journal of Consulting and Clinical Psychology, 49*, 773–775. doi:10.1037/0022-006X.49.5.773

Appendix B

Mason, K. L. (2008). Cyberbullying: A preliminary assessment for school personnel. *Psychology in the Schools, 45*, 323–348. doi:10.1002/pits.20301

National Conference of State Legislatures. (2011, January 26). *State cyberstalking, cyberharassment, and cyberbullying laws.* Retrieved from http://www.ncsl.org/default.aspx?tabid 13495

Olweus, D. (1993). *Bullying at school: What we know and what we can do.* Oxford, England: Blackwell.

Patchin, J. W., & Hinduja, S. (2006). Bullies move beyond the schoolyard: A preliminary look at cyberbullying. *Youth Violence and Juvenile Justice, 4*, 148–169. doi:10.1177/1541 204006286288

Patchin, J. W., & Hinduja, S. (2010). Cyberbullying and self-esteem. *Journal of School Health, 80*, 614–621. doi:10.1111/j.1746-1561.2010.00548.x

Privitera, C., & Campbell, M. (2009). Cyberbullying: The new face of workplace bullying? *CyberPsychology & Behavior, 12*, 395–400. doi:10.1089/cpb.2009.0025

Raskauskas, J., & Stoltz, A. D. (2007). Involvement in traditional and electronic bullying among adolescents. *Developmental Psychology, 43*, 564–575. doi:10.1037/0012-1649. 43.3.564

Slonje, R., & Smith, P. K. (2008). Cyberbullying: Another main type of bullying? *Scandinavian Journal of Psychology, 49*, 147–154. doi:10.1111/j.14679450.2007.00611.x

Smith, P. K., Mahdavi, J., Carvalho, M., Fisher, S., Russell, S., & Tippett, N. (2008). Cyberbullying: Its nature and impact in secondary school pupils. *Journal of Child Psychology and Psychiatry, 49*, 376–385. doi:10.1111/j.14697610.2007.01846.x

Sourander, A., Brunstein-Klomek, A., Ikonen, M., Lindroos, J., Luntamo, T., Koskelainen, M., . . . Helenius, H. (2010). Psychological risk factors associated with cyberbullying among adolescents: A population-based study. *Archive of General Psychiatry, 67*, 720–728. doi:10.1001/archgenpsychiatry.2010.79

Thomas, S. P. (2006). From the editor: The phenomenon of cyberbullying. *Issues in Mental Health Nursing, 27*, 1015–1016.

Vandebosch, H., & Van Cleemput, K. (2008). Defining cyberbullying: A qualitative research into the perceptions of youngsters. *CyberPsychology & Behavior, 11*, 499–503. doi:10.1089/cpb.2007.0042

Willard, N. E. (2007). *Cyberbullying and cyberthreats: Responding to the challenge of online social aggression, threats, and distress.* Champaign, IL: Research Press.

Ybarra, M. L., & Mitchell, K. J. (2004). Youth engaging in online harassment: Associations with caregiver-child relationships, Internet use, and personal characteristics. *Journal of Adolescence, 27*, 319–336. doi:10.1016/j.adolescence. 2004.03.007

Ybarra, M. L., Mitchell, K. J., Wolak, J., & Finkelhor, D. (2006). Examining characteristics and associated distress related to Internet harassment: Findings from the second youth Internet safety survey. *Pediatrics, 118*, 1169–1177. doi:10.1542/peds.2006-0815

Ybarra, M. L. (2004). Linkages between depressive symptomatology and Internet harassment among young regular Internet users. *CyberPsychology & Behavior, 7*, 247–257. doi:10.1089/109493104323024500

Zuckerman, M. (2002). Zuckerman-Kuhlman personality questionnaire (ZKPQ): An alternative five-factorial model. In B. de Raad & M. Perugini (Eds.), *Big Five assessment* (pp. 376–392). Ashland, OH: Hogrefe & Huber.

Address correspondence to Allison M. Schenk, Department of Psychology, West Virginia University, Morgantown, WV 26505, USA. E-mail: allison.schenk@mail.wvu.edu

10) Singer, J.B. & Slovak, K. (2011). School social workers' experiences with youth suicidal behavior: An exploratory study. *Children & Schools*, 33, 215–228.

Child and adolescent suicidal behavior, including ideation, attempt, and dying, is a national and preventable public health problem (Center for Substance Abuse Treatment, 2008) and a significant concern for school staff and administrators. In 2006 (the most recent year for which statistics are available), the third leading cause of death among U.S. youths ages 5 to 19 years was suicide, with 1,774 deaths. Rates (per hundred thousand) of youth suicide increase significantly with age: 0.18 for youths ages 5 to 12 years, 2.78 for youths 13 to 15, and 8.06 for youths 16 to 19 (Centers for Disease Control and Prevention [CDC], 2010a). The death by suicide of an individual student, or multiple students in cluster suicides, can be devastating to the members of the school community; challenges the emotional, legal, and administrative resources of the school; and requires an informed and coordinated response by school staff (including school social workers [SSWs], counselors, and teachers) and administrators (Callahan, 2002; Newgass & Schonfeld, 2005). However, the relative infrequency of suicide means that many school staff will never work with a youth who dies by suicide, so a more frequent concern for school staff is the much larger number of youths who present with suicidal ideation and attempt.

Unlike death by suicide, which is reported across all age groups by the CDC, there is no single source for information on youth suicide ideation and attempt. For example, the Youth Risk Behavior Survey (YRBS), which provides the baseline for rates of suicidal behavior among middle school (MS) and high school (HS) students, is not administered to elementary school (ES) students. The prevalence of suicidal ideation among children ages 6 to 12 years has been reported to be as low as 8.9 percent in a U.S. sample (Pfeffer, Zuckerman, Plutchik, & Mizruchi, 1984) and as high as 32.2 percent in a Brazilian sample (Bandim, Fonseca, & De Lima, 1997). Reisch, Jacobson, Sawdey, Anderson, and Henriques (2008) found that among a sample of youths ages 9 to 12, 8.9 percent reported attempting suicide. According to the YRBS, MS students reported that over their lifetime approximately 20 percent seriously thought about killing themselves, 13 percent made a plan, and 8 percent tried to kill themselves (Shanklin, Brener, McManus, Kinchen, & Kann, 2007). HS students reported that within the 12 months prior to the study, 14.5 percent seriously thought about killing themselves, 11.3 percent made a plan, 6.9 percent tried to kill themselves, and 2.0 percent received medical attention for their suicide attempt (Eaton et al., 2008). Recent research has suggested that although older adolescents might report more frequency and duration of suicidal ideation, even transient suicidal ideation among ES- and MS age children is predictive of poorer outcomes in adulthood (Vander Stoep, McCauley, Flynn, & Stone, 2009). Despite the difficulties in comparing suicide risk across age groups,

Appendix B

these data indicate that youths in ES, MS, and HS think about and attempt suicide. Consequently, the prevention of and intervention in youth suicidal ideation and attempt should be a primary focus of child and adolescent professionals, with school being perhaps the most important venue for these activities (Joe & Bryant, 2007).

Youths receive more mental health services in schools than in any other service sector, including specialty mental health service settings such as psychiatric hospitals, outpatient clinics, and residential treatment facilities (Rones & Hoagwood, 2000). Schools are a particularly important venue for mental health services delivery because school staff members have unparallel access to at-risk youths. For example, a recent study reported that youths who receive special education services had significantly higher rates of suicidal ideation (previous 12 months = 31.5 percent) and suicide attempts (lifetime = 30 percent) than youths in juvenile justice, substance abuse treatment, county mental health, and child welfare (Chavira, Accurso, Garland, & Hough, 2010). According to a U.S. Department of Health and Human Services study, almost all schools have at least one staff member whose responsibilities include providing mental health services to students (Foster et al., 2005). Although these staff members are more likely to be school counselors (77 percent), nurses (69 percent), and school psychologists (68 percent) than social workers (44 percent), social workers have reported spending the largest percentage of time providing mental health services (57 percent), followed by school counselors (52 percent), school psychologists (48 percent), and nurses (32 percent). SSWs also reported spending more time providing crisis intervention services (7.4 percent) than school counselors (4.7 percent) or school psychologist (3.1 percent) (Agresta, 2004). Examples of crisis intervention services that SSWs are expected to provide include suicide prevention programming, risk assessment, counseling, referral, and facilitation of hospitalization (Constable, 2008). In addition, SSWs are expected to provide suicide education and prevention programming to faculty and staff and families and the community (Gibbons & Struder, 2008).

Although the data suggest that SSWs play an integral role in providing mental health and crisis intervention services in schools, their experiences with suicidal youths, preparation to work with suicidal students, and role in the school regarding this issue is currently undocumented. The limited scholarship on youth suicide and SSWs is most likely a natural extension of the fact that suicide has long been neglected as a focus of social work research (Joe & Neidermeyer, 2008); there is limited scholarship on school social work (Franklin, Kim, & Tripodi, 2009); researchers have traditionally focused on consumers of services and program development rather than provider characteristics in treatment outcomes (Wampold, 2001); and across all of the helping professions, there is a limited scholarship on the experiences of providers of services to suicidal youths. Therefore, to provide a context for the current study, we have summarized extant research on youth suicide and social workers and relevant knowledge from research in allied and school professions.

Literature Review

Social Workers and Youth Suicide

A review of the literature suggests that social workers have contributed empirical literature that primarily describes risk factors and characteristics of suicidal youths and conceptual literature that addresses practice, education, and policy related to social work with suicidal youths. For example, empirical studies by social workers on youth suicide since 1980 have reported on the rise in suicide rates among African American male adolescents due to firearms; increased risk for suicide due to sexual and physical abuse, depression, substance abuse, race and sexual orientation, and school exclusion; use of firearms in male adolescent suicide and medication overdose in female adolescents; and the use of, and need for, youth suicide prevention and intervention internationally (see Joe & Neidermeyer, 2008, for a review; Walls, Freedenthal, & Wisneski, 2008). A recent study in Great Britain reported that social work services were a significant factor in reducing suicide risk among socially disadvantaged youths (Pritchard & Williams, 2009). Other scholarship has addressed pedagogical and practice implications of suicide (Sanders, Jacobson, & Ting, 2008), development of evidence-based approaches to working with suicidal youths (Singer, 2006), and the role of school-based social workers in the prevention of suicide (Peebles-Wilkins, 2006; Ward, 1995). Missing from the social work literature is information on the experiences and perceptions of SSWs who work with suicidal youths.

School Staff and Youth Suicide

Although most research on suicide and schools has looked at staff training, curriculum-based programs, or screening programs (Eckert, Miller, DuPaul, & Riley-Tillman, 2003), a few studies have reported on the experiences, perceptions, attitudes, or beliefs of school counselors, school psychologists, nurses, and teachers. Whereas the majority of school counselors reported experience working with youth suicidal ideation and attempt (King, Price, Telljohann, & Wahl, 1999; King & Smith, 2000), the majority of school counselors and school psychologists reported no experience with youth suicide; those with experience reported between zero and six deaths by suicide during their employment (Debski, Spadafore, Jacob, Poole, & Hixson, 2007; King et al., 1999). Experience with suicidal youths appears to be important. King et al. (1999) found that the more experience school counselors had with suicidal youths, the more confident they were in engaging in suicide prevention and intervention services.

A number of studies reported on school staff members' knowledge, attitudes, and graduate and professional training. Knowledge of risk factors varied by study and discipline, with rates as low as 9 percent for school health teachers, 34 percent for school counselors (King & Smith, 2000), and 43 percent for school psychologists

(Debski et al., 2007) and as high as 63 percent for school counselors in an earlier study (Peach & Reddick, 1991). School staff members reported increased knowledge and skills following gatekeeper trainings like QPR (question, persuade, and refer) and ASIST (applied suicide intervention training skills) (Joe & Bryant, 2007). When school staff were part of crisis intervention teams or received specific training on suicide assessment and intervention, they reported higher levels of self-confidence in identifying and intervening in a suicidal crisis (King & Smith, 2000). However, staff members from all disciplines reported insufficient professional training in suicide prevention, intervention, and postvention (Christianson & Everall, 2008; Feldman & Freedenthal, 2006; King et al., 1999, 2000; King & Smith, 2000; Ries & Cornell, 2008). Adequate and appropriate training not only affects a school staff's ability to address youth suicide in the schools, but also may increase the likelihood of providing suicide awareness training for non-mental-health school staff. One limitation of extant literature is that there are no studies that looked at school staff at the ES level, possibly because there is no training program that covers the developmental issues that staff at the ES level face. It is unclear whether a training program developed for secondary education would improve services rendered by staff at an ES level.

Although education and training on youth suicide is crucial to preparedness in this area, research suggests it is not a standard component of the educational programming for school mental health professionals. Debski et al. (2007) found that although 99 percent of school psychologists had received some form of suicide training, only 40 percent had received any of this training while completing their graduate programs. Feldman and Freedenthal (2006) found that 79 percent of MSW-level social work graduates did not receive any formal training in their graduate curriculums, and of the 21 percent who received training in their graduate program, over three-fourths (76 percent) received four hours or fewer of suicide-related training. School staff who graduated more recently reported increased knowledge and training regarding adolescent suicide (Debski et al., 2007; Feldman & Freedenthal, 2006; King & Smith, 2000).Although this suggests a positive trend, it appears that most school staff members are likely to obtain training on suicide from sources such as professional journals, workshops, on-the-job training, and college courses (King et al., 2000). This may apply to SSWs as well.

In summary, a small body of research suggests that the level of training, experiences, and perceptions of working with suicidal youths varies by school staff discipline and that these factors influence the likelihood of school staff intervening in a suicidal crisis. Because SSWs work at all grade levels, and because they assume a variety of roles in the school system (Whitted & Dupper, 2005), extant research on non-social workers cannot be generalized to social workers. Undertaking a preliminary examination of SSWs' experiences with and perceptions of working with suicidal youths will address calls from researchers and policymakers for more research on youth suicide, particularly from social workers (Joe & Bryant, 2007; Satcher, 1999; U.S. Department of Health and Human Services, 2001); respond to a recent call for more documentation of SSWs' activities (Franklin et al., 2009); and serve as a baseline and foundation for future research on SSWs' knowledge, skills, and perceived effectiveness in suicide prevention and intervention activities.

Purpose of the Current Study

The purpose of the current study was to gather basic information on social workers' experience with and perceptions of suicidal youths across three school levels (ES, MS, and HS) that could inform practice, policy, and future research. As an exploratory study, it neither tests hypotheses nor evaluates SSWs' knowledge, skills, or effectiveness in suicide intervention.

References

Agresta, J. (2004). Professional role perceptions of school social workers, psychologists, and counselors. *Children & Schools, 26,* 151–163.

Aseltine, R. H., Jr., & DeMartino, R. (2004). An outcome evaluation of the SOS suicide prevention program. *American Journal of Public Health, 94,* 446–451.

Astor, R. A., Behre, W. J., Wallace, J. M., & Fravil, K. A. (1998). School social workers and school violence: Personal safety, training, and violence programs. *Social Work, 43,* 223–232.

Bandim, J. M., Fonseca, L., & De Lima, J. M. (1997). Prevalencia da idea ao suicida numa popula ao de escolares do nordeste Brasileiro. *Journal Brasileiro de Psiquiatria, 46,* 477–481.

Berman.A. L.,Jobes, D.A., & Silverman, M. M. (2005). *Adolescent suicide: Assessment and intervention* (2nd ed.). Washington, DC: American Psychological Association.

Bongar, B. (2002). *The suicidal patient: Clinical and legal standards of care.* Washington, DC: American Psychological Association.

Bridge, J. A., Greenhouse, J. B., Weldon, A. H., Campo, J. V., & Kelleher, K. J. (2008). Suicide trends among youths aged 10 to 19 years in the United States, 1996–2005. *JAMA, 300,* 1025–1026.

Callahan, J. (2002). School–based crisis intervention for traumatic events. In R. Constable, S. McDonald, & J. Flynn (Eds.), *School social work: Practice, policy, and research perspective* (5th ed., pp. 481–500). Chicago: Lyceum Books.

Center for Substance Abuse Treatment. (2008). *Substance abuse and suicide prevention: Evidence and implications. A white paper* (DHHS Pub. No. SMA-08-4352). Rockville, MD: Substance Abuse and Mental Health Services Administration.

Centers for Disease Control and Prevention. (2010a). *Web-based injury statistics query and reporting system.* Retrieved from http://webappa.cdc.gov/sasweb/ncipc/mortrate10_sy.html

Centers for Disease Control and Prevention. (2010b, June 4). Youth risk behavior surveillance—United States, 2009. Surveillance summaries. *Morbidity and Mortality Weekly Report, 59*(SS-5), 1-142.

Centers for Disease Control and Prevention. (n.d.). *Youth risk behavior surveillance survey: Comparisons between state or district and national results fact sheet.* Retrieved from http://www.cdc.gov/HealthyYouth/yrbs/ state_district_comparisons.htm

Chavira, D. A., Accurso, E. C., Garland, A. F., & Hough, (2010). Suicidal behavior among youth in five public sectors of care. *Child and Adolescent Mental Health, 15*(1), 44–51.

Christianson, C. L., & Everall, R. D. (2008). Constructing bridges of support: School counsellors' experiences of student suicide. *Canadian Journal of Counselling, 42*, 209–221.

Coleman, D., Quest, D., & Bae, J. (2010, January 14). *Three suicide prevention trainings: Six-month effects on suicide prevention knowledge, confidence and behavior.* Paper presented at the Society for Social Work and Research Conference, San Francisco.

Constable, R. (2008). The role of the school social worker. In C. R. Massat, R. T. Constable, S. McDonald, & J. P. Flynn (Eds.), *School social work: Practice, policy and research perspectives* (7th ed., pp. 3–29). Chicago: Lyceum Books.

Daniel, S. S., & Goldston, D. B. (2009). Interventions for suicidal youth: A review of the literature and developmental considerations. *Suicide and Life-Threatening Behavior, 39*, 252–268.

Debski, J., Spadafore, C. D., Jacob: S., Poole, D. A., & Hixson, M. D. (2007). Suicide intervention: Training, roles, and knowledge of school psychologists. *Psychology in the Schools, 44*, 157–170.

Eaton, D. K., Kann, L., Kinchen, S., Shanklin, S., Ross, J., Hawkins, J., et al. (2008, June 6). Youth risk behavior surveillance—United States, 2007. *Morbidity and Mortality Weekly Report, 57*(SS04), 1–131. Retrieved from http://www.cdc.gov/mmwr/PDF/ss/ss5704.pdf

Eckert, T. L. Miller, D. N., DuPaul, G. J., & Riley Tillman, T. C. (2003). Adolescent suicide prevention: School psychologists' acceptability of school-based programs. *School Psychology Review, 32*(1), 57–76.

Feldman, B. N., & Freedenthal, S. (2006). Social work education in suicide intervention and prevention: An unmet need? *Suicide and Life-Threatening Behavior, 36*, 467–480.

Foster, S., Rollefson, M., Doksum, T., Noonan, D., Robinson, G., & Teich, J. (2005). *School mental health services in the United States, 2002–2003* (DHHS Publication No. [SMA] 05-4068). Rockville, MD: Center for Mental Health Services, Substance Abuse and Mental Health Services Administration.

Franklin, C., Kim, J. S., & Tripodi, S. J. (2009). A metaanalysis of published school social work outcome studies: 1980–2007. *Research on Social Work Practice, 19*, 667–677.

Gibbons, M., & Struder, J. (2008). Suicide awareness training for faculty and staff: A training model for school counselors. *Professional School Counseling, 11*, 272–276.

Gould, M. S., Greenberg, T., Velting, D. M., & Shaffer, D. (2003). Youth suicide risk and preventive interventions: A review of the past 10 years. *Journal of the American Academy of Child and Adolescent Psychiatry, 42*, 386–405.

Joe, S., & Bryant, H. (2007). Evidence-based suicide prevention screening in schools. *Children & Schools, 29*, 219–227.

Joe, S., & Niedermeier, D. (2008). Preventing suicide: A neglected social work research agenda. *British Journal of Social Work, 38*, 507–530.

Joseph, A., & Broussard, A. (2001). School social workers and structured inequality: A survey of attitudes and knowledge of tracking. *School Social Work Journal, 25*(2), 59–75.

Kerr, D.C.R., Owen, L. D., Pears, K. S., & Capaldi, D. M. (2008). Prevalence of suicidal ideation among boys and men assessed annually from ages 9 to 29 years. *Suicide and Life-Threatening Behavior, 38*, 390–402.

King, K. A., Price, J. H., Telljohann, S. K., & Wahl, J. (1999). How confident do high school counselors feel in recognizing students at risk for suicide? *American Journal of Health Behavior, 23*, 457–467.

King, K. A., Price, J. H., Telljohann, S. K., & Wahl, J. (2000). Preventing adolescent suicide: Do high school counselors know the risk factors? *Professional School Counseling, 3*, 255–263.

King, K. A., & Smith, J. (2000). Project SOAR: A training program to increase school counselors' knowledge and confidence regarding suicide prevention and intervention. *Journal of School Health, 70*, 402–407.

Newgass, S., & Schonfeld, D. (2005). School crisis intervention, crisis prevention, and crisis response. In A. R. Roberts (Ed.), *Crisis intervention handbook: Assessment, treatment and research* (3rd ed., pp. 499–518). New York: Oxford University Press.

Peach, L., & Reddick, T. L. (1991). Counselors can make a difference in preventing adolescent suicide. *School Counselor, 39*(2), 107–116.

Peebles-Wilkins, W. (2006). Evidence-based suicide prevention. *Children & Schools, 28*, 195–196.

Pfeffer, C.R., Zuckerman, S., Plutchik, R., & Mizruchi, M. S. (1984). Suicidal behavior in normal school children: A comparison with child psychiatric inpatients. *Journal of the American Academy of Child Psychiatry, 23*, 416–423.

Pritchard, C., & Williams, R. (2009). Does social work make a difference? A controlled study of former 'looked-after-children' and 'excluded-from-school' adolescents now men aged 16–24 subsequent offences, being victims of crime and suicide. *Journal of Social Work, 9*, 285–307.

Reisch, S. K., Jacobson, G., Sawdey, L., Anderson, J., & Henriques, J. (2008). Suicide ideation among later elementary school-aged youth. *Journal of Psychiatric and Mental Health Nursing, 15*, 263–277.

Ries, C., & Cornell, D. (2008). An evaluation of suicide gatekeeper training for school counselors and teachers. *Professional School Counseling, 11*, 386–394.

Rones, M., & Hoagwood, K. (2000). School-based mental health services: A research review. *Clinical Child and Family Psychology Review, 3*, 223–241.

Sanders, S., Jacobson, J. M., & Ting, L. (2008). Preparing for the inevitable: Training social workers to cope with client suicide. *Journal of Teaching in Social Work, 28*, 1–18.

Satcher, D. (1999). *The surgeon general's call to action to prevent suicide*. Washington, DC: U.S. Government Printing Office.

Shanklin, S. L., Brener, N., McManus, T., Kinchen, S., & Kann, L. (2007). *Youth risk behavior survey: 2005 middle school*. Retrieved from http://www.cdc.gov/ HealthyYouth/ yrbs/middleschool2005/index.htm

Shea, S. (2002). *The practical art of suicide assessment: A guide for mental health professionals and substance abuse counselors*. Hoboken, NJ: Wiley & Sons.

Singer, J. B. (2006). Making stone soup: Evidence based practice for a suicidal youth with comorbid attention-deficit/hyperactivity disorder and major depressive disorder. *Brief Treatment and Crisis Intervention, 6*, 234–247. doi:10.1093/brieftreatment/ mhl004

Slovak, K. (2006). School social workers' perceptions of student violence and prevention programming. *School Social Work Journal, 31*(2), 30–42.

Slovak, K., & Singer, J. B. (2011). School social workers' perceptions of cyberbullying. *Children & Schools, 33,* 5–16.

Suicide Education Enhancement Project. (n.d.). Retrieved from http://www.bu.edu/ssw/research/ seep/overview.shtml

Tompkins, T. L., Witt, J., & Abraibesh, N. (2009). Does a gatekeeper suicide prevention program work in a school setting? Evaluating training outcome and moderators of effectiveness. *Suicide and Life-Threatening Behaviors, 39,* 671–681.

Tukey, J. W. (1953). The problem of multiple comparisons. In H. I. Braun (Ed.), *The collected works of John W. Tukey, Volume VIII Multiple comparisons: 1948–1983* (pp. 1–300). New York: Chapman & Hall.

U.S. Department of Health and Human Services. (2001). *National strategy for suicide prevention: Goals and objectives for action.* Washington, DC: U.S. Government Printing Office.

Vander Stoep, A., McCauley, E., Flynn, C., & Stone, (2009). Thoughts of death and suicide in early adolescence. *Suicide and Life-Threatening Behaviors, 39,* 599–613.

Walls, N. E., Freedenthal, S., & Wisneski, H. (2008). Suicidal ideation and attempts among sexual minority youths receiving social services. *Social Work, 53,* 21–29.

Wampold, B. E. (2001). *The great psychotherapy debate: Models, methods, and findings.* Mahwah, NJ: Laurence Erlbaum Associates.

Ward, B. R. (1995). The school's role in the prevention of youth suicide. *Social Work in Education, 17,* 92–100.

Whitted, K. S., & Dupper, D. R. (2005). Best practices for preventing or reducing bullying in schools. *Children & Schools, 27,* 167–175.

Jonathan B. Singer, PhD, LCSW, *is assistant professor, School of Social Work, Temple University, 1301 Cecil B. More Avenue, Philadelphia, PA 19122; e-mail: jbsinger@temple. edu.* **Karen Slovak, PhD**, *is associate professor, Social Work, Ohio University Zanesville.*

11) Volpato, F., Verin, L. & Cardinaletti, A. (2016). The comprehension and production of verbal passives by Italian preschool-age children. *Applied Psycholinguistics*, 37(4), 901–931. Copyright © 2016 by Cambridge University Press. All rights reserved. Reprinted with permission.

Comprehension and Production of Verbal Passives

The present study compares the comprehension and production of passive sentences in Italian-speaking children ranging in age from 3 years, 4 months to 6 years, 2 months (3;4 to 6;2), controlling for several variables: verb class (actional vs. nonactional), presence versus absence of the external argument expressed in the *by*-phrase, and auxiliary type (*essere* "to be" vs. *venire* "to come"). This is the first study that investigates both production and comprehension, focusing on similarities and differences in the route of acquisition of two different passive constructions in Italian, which use the auxiliaries *essere* and *venire*, respectively.

This study is at the heart of a lively debate on the acquisition of passive sentences, dating back to the end of the seventies. Since then, much linguistic and psycholinguistic research has been conducted on the acquisition of this structure across different languages in both comprehension (for English, Bencini & Valian, 2008; Borer&Wexler, 1987; Fox&Grodzinsky, 1998; Gordon&Chafetz, 1990; Hirsch &Wexler, 2006; Horgan, 1978; Maratsos, Fox, Becher, & Chalkley, 1985; O'Brien, Grolla, & Lillo-Martin, 2006; Orfitelli, 2012; Pinker, Lebeaux, & Frost, 1987; for Greek, Driva & Terzi, 2008; Terzi & Wexler, 2002; for Italian, Volpato, Verin, Tagliaferro, & Cardinaletti, 2013; for Portuguese, Rubin, 2009; for Japanese, Sano, 2000; for Russian, Babyonyshev & Brun, 2003; for Sesotho, Demuth, 1989, 1990; Demuth, Moloi, & Machobane, 2010) and production (for English, Bencini & Valian, 2008; Crain, Thornton, & Murasugi, 1987; Horgan, 1978; Messenger, Branigan, McLean, & Sorace, 2009, 2012; for German, Mills, 1985; for Hebrew, Berman & Sagi, 1981; for Sesotho, Demuth et al., 2010; for Italian, Manetti, 2013; Volpato, Verin, & Cardinaletti, 2014).

The results of these previous studies do not converge. Early studies proposed that the acquisition of passives is either semantically (Maratsos et al., 1985) or syntactically constrained (Borer & Wexler, 1987). Maratsos et al. (1985) suggested that the children's ability to comprehend the passive structure is restricted to actional verbs (1a). At 4 years of age, children show a good competence of passives with actional verbs, while nonactional passives (1b) are still problematic at the age of 5–7 years, and are fully mastered only at a later stage, by the age of 9 to 11 years:

(1) a. The boy is *kissed* (by the girl).
    b. The boy is *seen* (by the girl).

Children also show a better comprehension of passives lacking the *by*-phrase (2a) than passives containing it (2b) (Horgan, 1978):

(2) a. The window is broken.
    b. The window is broken by the wind.

In English, a short passive, as in (2a), is ambiguous between an adjectival (allowing a stative reading) and a verbal passive (allowing an eventive reading). When the *by*-phrase is added to the sentence, as in (2b), the passive is no longer ambiguous, and only an eventive reading is possible. Borer and Wexler (1987) suggest that earlier than 5 or 6, children are only able to master adjectival passives. Hence, they interpret *broken* in (2a) as an adjective rather than a verb. This strategy is possible and felicitous only with actional verbs because nonactional passive participles cannot be interpreted as adjectives.

Appendix B

The asymmetry between long and short passives was later replicated by other studies investigating children's comprehension in Greek (Terzi & Wexler, 2002), Russian (Babyonyshev & Brun, 2003), English (Hirsch & Wexler, 2006), and Portuguese (Rubin, 2009), although in some studies, the difference between the two structures is not statistically significant (Hirsch & Wexler 2006, for English; Driva & Terzi, 2008, for Greek).[1] Lack of statistical significance between long and short passives was recently replicated by Orfitelli (2012). She tested the comprehension of verbal passives in English-speaking children ranging in age from 4 to 6; 11 using a binary picture-matching task. Analyzing actional and nonactional passives with or without the *by*-phrase, she found that at the age of 4 and 5, most children showed above-chance performance on both short and long passives, and at the age of 6, children performed at ceiling. At the age of 4 and 5, actional passives were comprehended significantly better than nonactional ones, on which children's performance is not significantly different from chance. The performance on nonactional passives increases in 6-year-old children (higher than chance), although percentages remain lower than with actional ones.

However, some other studies (Crain et al., 1987; O'Brien et al., 2006; Pinker et al., 1987) found that when felicity conditions in the test administration are met, English-speaking 4-year-old children comprehend and produce long and short eventive passive sentences with both actional and nonactional verbs. By using a priming task, Bencini and Valian (2008) and Messenger et al. (2009, 2012) confirmed that the structure of passive sentences is fully represented in 3- and 4-year-old English children. Messenger et al. (2012) extensively showed that by the age of 4, children's syntactic representation of passives is adultlike in both production and comprehension tasks, and it is not semantically constrained; that is, it is independent of the verb class tested (actional vs. nonactional). Both children and adults produced more passive sentences after hearing passive primes than after hearing active primes.

Further evidence in favor of the early acquisition of passive sentences comes from studies conducted on non-Indo-European languages (for Quiche Mayan, Pye & Quixtan Poz, 1988; for Sesotho, Demuth, 1989, 1990; Demuth et al., 2010; for Inuktikut, Allen & Crago, 1993). Demuth (1989, 1990) found that in Sesotho, a language in which verbal and adjectival passives are morphologically and syntactically distinct, passive sentences are attested in child language starting from 3 years of age or even in younger children. By the same age, comprehension of long and short passives containing either actional or nonactional verbs is also adequately developed (Demuth et al., 2010).

As for Italian, few data are available on the first language acquisition of passive sentences. Ciccarelli (1998), quoted in Guasti (2007), investigated the comprehension of long passives with actional verbs, by using a sentence–picture matching task. At the age of 4, passive sentences are at chance level (57%). An improvement in performance is observed at the age of 5 and 6 (72% and 80% accuracy, respectively). Higher accuracy was found in a standardized comprehension test developed by Chilosi and Cipriani (2006), who showed that children acquire reversible passives (like *La bambina è spinta dal bambino* "the child.FEM is pushed by the child.MS") at the age of 5;6. Manetti (2013) reports an elicited production study and two syntactic priming studies with Italian children aged 3;6 to 4;6. In the former, no passive sentence was produced; in the latter, the overall rate of production of passive sentences is 33% and 16%, respectively. The rate of passives in response to passive primes was significantly higher than in response to active primes (26% vs. 15%). She concluded that at the age of 3;6, children are able to produce passive sentences, thus proving that they master this syntactic construction very early.

The goal of our study is to contribute to the debate by providing a comprehensive analysis of the acquisition of passive sentences in Italian-speaking children ranging in age from 3;4 to 6;2. We investigate both the comprehension and the production of passive sentences in the different sentence combinations analyzed in previous studies, that is, the use of actional versus nonactional verbs and the presence versus absence of the *by*-phrase. We also investigate an Italian-specific variable, that is, the use of auxiliary *essere* versus *venire*.

Like English, Italian builds passive sentences by using the auxiliary *essere*, as shown in (3). As in English, verbal and adjectival passive constructions are not morphologically distinct. Therefore, sentences with *essere* are ambiguous. Because the word *chiusa* "closed" is either an adjective or a verb, (3a) can have a stative, a resultative, or an eventive reading. When the *by*-phrase or a manner adverb is uttered, as in (3b), the sentence is unambiguously an eventive passive. The three-way ambiguity of (3a) can also be solved by replacing the auxiliary *essere* with *venire*, as in (4a), which is only compatible with the eventive (nonstative) interpretation of the sentence and *chiusa* can only be analyzed as a verb. In (4b), the insertion of the *by*-phrase or a manner adverb is also possible:

(3) a. La porta è chiusa.
    b. La porta è chiusa da Maria / violentemente.
       "The door is closed (by Mary / with violence)."

(4) a. La porta viene chiusa.
    b. La porta viene chiusa da Maria / violentemente.
       the door comes closed (by Mary / with violence)
       "The door is being closed (by Mary)."

The possibility of adding the *by*-phrase in *venire* passives confirms their eventive status: as in English, the *by*-phrase can only be used with verbal passives and not with adjectival ones (Frigeni, 2004). Another observation points to the verbal status

Appendix B

of what follows *venire*. While a superlative form of the adjective is possible with *essere* (5a), it cannot occur in verbal passives with either *essere* (5b) or *venire* (5c):[2]

(5) a. La gara è aperta / apertissima a tutti (*da Maria).
       the race is open / very open to everybody (*by Mary)
    b. La gara è stata aperta / *apertissima (da Maria).
       the race has been opened / *very open (by Mary)
    c. La gara viene aperta / *apertissima (da Maria).
       the race comes opened / *very open (by Mary)

Further evidence that an eventive interpretation is present with both *essere* and *venire* is provided by the syntactic activity of the external thematic role even when it is not pronounced (Baker, Johnson, & Roberts, 1989; Jaeggli, 1986):

(6) La nave fu / venne affondata [PRO per riscuotere l'assicurazione].
    The ship was / came sunk [PRO to collect the insurance]
       "The ship was sunk to collect the insurance."

With both *essere* and *venire*, the external argument acts as a controller for the PRO subject of the embedded clause. Hence, both sentences are compatible with an eventive reading. In this respect, *venire* passives are different from English *get* passives, whose external argument is not syntactically active.

As in passives with *essere*, in sentences containing *venire*, the internal argument of the active verb (7a) becomes the subject of the passive sentence, in either the postverbal (7b) or preverbal (7c) position, and triggers agreement on the inflected verb[3]:

(7) a. Maria chiude la porta / le porte alle cinque.
       Mary closes the door / the doors at five
    b. Viene chiusa la porta / Vengono chiuse le porte alle cinque.
    c. La porta viene chiusa / Le porte vengono chiuse alle cinque.
       The door is / doors are closed at five

Idiomatic expressions are possible in *venire* passives, as in *essere* passives:

(8) A Gianni era / veniva sempre data carta bianca.
       to John was / came always given paper white
       "Gianni was always given carte blanche."

Venire passives differ from *essere* passives in aspectual properties. The former are preferred in progressive contexts in the present tense (no aspectual difference is, however, detected in past and future tenses).

In sum, *venire* and *essere* passives behave alike as true passives according to numerous tests, as shown above. We conclude, as per much of the literature on the topic, that Italian has two variants of the passive (introduced by the two auxiliaries), which are the focus of the current paper. Italian *venire* passives are crucial to assess the competence of passives in children. If Italian children comprehend and produce passive sentences with *venire*, it can safely be concluded that they have the representation of true verbal passives from very early on.

In our study, we also investigate how the interaction of all these variables (verb class, *by*-phrase, and auxiliary) modulates the comprehension of the passive voice in Italian children in the course of language development, in light of recent research on passives. In particular, we discuss how recent research on the syntactic representation of passives (Collins, 2005) predicts and explains children's performance in the use of long and short passives. To this effect, tasks assessing memory resources are also used. Some studies (Montgomery, Magimairaj, & O'Malley, 2008) found an association between memory skills and complex sentence comprehension (also including passive sentences).

In addition to comprehension, we also investigate production. Only one modality is sometimes not sufficient to determine whether language is mastered by a child. Production provides a picture of the content and form of children's emerging language system. In contrast, comprehension makes it possible to give a picture of the grammatical knowledge of structures that are not produced yet. The use of both comprehension and production tasks provides more detailed evidence of children's linguistic knowledge. Some studies reported an asymmetry between the two modalities. In some cases, comprehension is shown to precede production in both typical (Clark, 1993) and atypical language development (Contemori & Garraffa, 2010). Some other studies reported a reversed pattern, in which production precedes comprehension, as, for instance, in the acquisition of relative clauses (Hakansson & Hansson, 2000) and of object pronouns and subject–verb–object (SVO) word order (Hendriks & Koster, 2010). Because the behaviors that children show in comprehension and production tasks investigating the same linguistic properties is particularly telling, both modalities in the acquisition of passive sentences are analyzed here.

Theoretical Background on the Acquisition of Passive Sentences

In order to explain the difficulties experienced by children with the passive structure, Borer and Wexler (1987) put forward the A-chain maturation hypothesis, according to which children manage to master verbal passives at the age of 5 or 6. Before this age, children are only able to comprehend and produce adjectival passives. Despite the same surface structure, adjectival and verbal passives have different syntactic representations. In verbal passives, the complement of *be* is a verb. Following

Appendix B

early approaches to the representation of passives (Jaeggli, 1986), in verbal passives, the internal argument raises to the subject position, and the external theta role, absorbed by the passive morphology, is optionally transmitted to the *by*-phrase. In adjectival passives, the complement of *be* is an adjective, and no movement takes place. According to Borer and Wexler, this structural difference is crucial to understand why children are delayed in the acquisition of passives. They suggested that the ability to form argument A-chains becomes available starting from the age of 5 to 6 years. Earlier, children's grammar is only able to generate adjectival (stative) passives, which do not involve A-chains. The A-chain maturation hypothesis also predicts the correct comprehension of actional passives as opposed to nonactional passives, the adjectival interpretation being only possible with actional verbs. Hirsch and Wexler (2006) slightly reformulated the hypothesis by suggesting that children's passives are resultative and contain verbs expressing a state as the result of an event. The A-chain maturation hypothesis is kept: no A-chain is built with resultatives.

However, the A-chain maturation approach is at odds with evidence coming from the acquisition of other A-movement constructions where children behave adultlike, such as reflexive–clitic constructions (Snyder & Hyams, 2014) and subject-to-subject raising (Becker, 2006; Choe, 2012; Orfitelli, 2012).

The acquisition of the passive voice has recently been reconsidered given Collins's (2005) new analysis of passives. Collins (2005) suggests that the external argument is merged with v', and *by* (for long passives) and *0* (for short passives) are merged as the heads of the passive VoiceP projection, as shown in (9):

(9) a. [VoiceP by [vP John [VP written the book]]]
    b. [VoiceP0 [vP PRO [VP written the book]]]

Unlike previous approaches, in which long and short passives are derived in different ways, under Collins' (2005) approach, long and short passives have the same derivation, and a difference between the two is not expected. We will see that this is the correct prediction for the acquisition of passives.

Given (9), locality principles block the movement of the object DP from the merge position within VP to specTP: the external argument in SpecvP represents an intervening element for the movement of the object DP to a higher position:

(10) a. [$_{TP}$ The book was [$_{VoiceP}$ by [$_{vP}$ John [$_{VP}$ written <the book>]]]]
     b. [$_{TP}$ The book was [$_{VoiceP}$ 0 [vP PRO [$_{VP}$ written <the book>]]]]
                    DP   DP   DP
         |_____ b_lo_c_k_e_d _____|

Collins's proposal is that passive sentences must be derived in more local steps: the VP chunk containing the verb and the object moves leftward to *smuggle* the subject in the vP-internal position, and a second step is necessary for the object to reach the specTP position at the left edge of the sentence:

(11) [$_{TP}$ The book was [$_{VoiceP}$ written <the book> by [$_{vP}$ John <written the book>]]]
[$_{TP}$ The book was [$_{VoiceP}$ written <the book> *0* [$_{vP}$ PRO <written the book>]]]

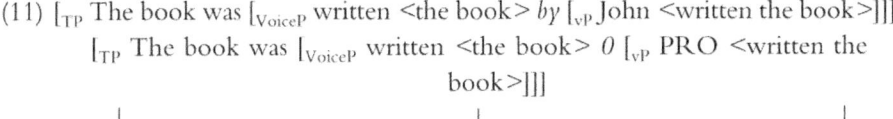

Stemming from Collins's (2005) proposal, Orfitelli (2012) put forward the argument intervention hypothesis (AIH), according to which young children are only delayed in acquiring those syntactic structures, including verbal passives, which involve A-movement of one argument over another one. The experiment conducted on passive structures shows that children are especially delayed in the comprehension of nonactional passives regardless of the presence or absence of the *by*-phrase. This phenomenon led the author to conclude, like Collins, that unpronounced *by*-phrases are syntactically active and give rise to intervention effects. However, Orfitelli's AIH needs two further hypotheses. First, it needs to assume that only the experiencer arguments of nonactional verbs give rise to intervention effects, while agentive arguments do not. Second, the AIH is subject to maturation and no longer active in adults. Similar to other maturational approaches, it predicts that children should be delayed in all languages. We will see that this is not the case for Italian children, who comprehend nonactional passives well above chance.

Adopting Collins' approach to passives, Snyder and Hyams (2014) suggest that children do not have access to *smuggling*, which matures at around age 6.5. However, in the spirit of Rizzi (2004), later adopted by Friedmann, Belletti, and Rizzi (2009), Garraffa and Grillo (2008), and Rizzi (2013) to state the link between memory resources and syntax, Snyder and Hyams suggest that intervention effects are only found when the two nominal arguments share the same features. Children are adultlike when the internal argument moved to specTP has a topic feature (as in Demuth, 1990; O'Brien et al., 2006). This proposal predicts that there should be no difference between long and short passives and between actional and non-actional passives as long as the derived subject is a topic. As we will see, while the long versus short asymmetry is not found in Italian children, the actional versus nonactional asymmetry is also found with topic-derived subjects, as in our experiment. Notice that their analysis is also at odds with the results coming from priming experiments (Bencini & Valian, 2008; Messenger et al., 2009, 2012), in which 3-year-olds produced passive sentences whose derived subjects were not topics in the discourse.

Appendix B

Notes

1. Unlike these studies, Fox and Grodzinsky (1998) found that in a group of eight children (age range = 3;6–5;5), the comprehension of long passives with actional verbs and short passives with nonactional verbs is at ceiling, while long passives with nonactional verbs are at chance level. Fox and Grodzinsky's results were not replicated by any other study.
2. Being an auxiliary and not a verb, *venire* does not have selectional properties and cannot be combined with any directional argument. Compare verbal *venire* in (ia) with auxiliary *venire* in (ib):
   (i) a. Gianni viene a Venezia ogni settimana.
           Gianni comes to Venice every week
       b. Gianni viene (*a Venezia) derubato ogni settimana.
           Gianni comes (*to Venice) robbed every week.
3. With both *essere* and *venire*, *ne*-extraction is possible out of the postverbal subject of the passive clause:
   (i) Ne furono / vennero licenziati [tre <ne>].
       of-them were / came fired three
       "Three of them were fired."

References

Babyonyshev, M., & Brun, D. (2003). *The role of aspect in the acquisition of passive constructions in Russian*. Paper presented at GALA, Utrecht.

Baker, M., Johnson, K., & Roberts, I. (1989). Passive arguments raised. *Linguistic Inquiry, 23*, 219–251.

Becker, M. (2006). There began to be a learnability puzzle. *Linguistic Inquiry, 37*, 441–456.

Bencini, G. M. L., & Valian, V. V. (2008). Abstract sentence representation in 3-year-olds: Evidence from language production and comprehension. *Journal of Memory and Language, 59*, 97–113.

Berman, R. A., & Sagi, Y. (1981). Children's word formation and lexical innovations. *Hebrew Computational Linguistics Bulletin, 18*, 31–62.

Borer, H., & Wexler, K. (1987). The maturation of syntax. In T. Roeper & E. Willliams (Eds.), *Parameter setting and language acquisition* (pp. 123–172). Dordrecht: Reidel.

Chilosi, A. M., & Cipriani, P. (2006). *TCGB: Test di comprensione grammaticale per bambini* (in collaboration with A. Giorgi, B. Fazzi, & L. Pfanner). Pisa: Edizioni del Cerro.

Ciccarelli, L. (1998). *Comprensione del linguaggio, dei processi di elaborazione e memoria di lavoro: Uno studio in et`a prescolare*. Unpublished doctoral dissertation, University of Padua.

Clark, E. (1993). *The lexicon in acquisition*. Cambridge: Cambridge University Press.

Collins, C. (2005). A smuggling approach to the passive in English. *Syntax, 8*, 81–120.

Contemori, C., & Garraffa, M. (2010). Comparison of modalities in SLI syntax: A study on the comprehension and production of non-canonical sentences. *Lingua, 120*, 1940–1955.

Crain, S., Thornton, R., & Murasugi, K. (1987). *Capturing the evasive passive*. Paper presented at the 12th Annual Boston University Conference on Language Development, Boston.

Demuth, K. (1989). Maturation and the acquisition of Sesotho passive. *Language, 65*, 56–80.

Demuth, K. (1990). Subject, topic, and Sesotho passive. *Journal of Child Language, 17*, 67–84.

Demuth, K., Moloi, F., & Machobane, M. (2010). 3-year-olds' comprehension, production, and generalization of Sesotho passives. *Cognition, 115*, 238–251.

Driva, E., & Terzi, A. (2008). Children's passives and the theory of grammar. In A. Gavarro & M. J. Freitas (Eds.), *Language acquisition and development: Proceedings of GALA 2007*. Newcastle: Cambridge Scholar Publishers.

Fox, D., & Grodzinsky, Y. (1998). Children's passive: A view from the by-phrase. *Linguistic Inquiry, 29*, 311–332.

Friedmann, N., Belletti, A., & Rizzi, L. (2009). Relativized relatives: Types of intervention in the acquisition of A-bar dependencies. *Lingua, 119*, 67–88.

Frigeni, C. (2004). "How do you miss your external argument?" Non-active voice alternations in Italian. *Toronto Working Papers in Linguistics, 23*, 47–94.

Garraffa, M., & Grillo, N. (2008). Canonicity effects as grammatical phenomena. *Journal of Neurolinguistics, 21*, 177–197.

Gordon, P., & Chafetz, J. (1990). Verb-based versus class-based accounts of actionality effects in children's comprehension of passives. *Cognition, 36*, 227–254.

Guasti, M. T. (2007). *L'acquisizione del linguaggio: Un'introduzione*. Milano: Raffaello Cortina Editore.

Håkansson, G., & Hansson, K. (2000). Comprehension and production of relative clauses: A comparison between Swedish impaired and unimpaired children. *Journal of Child Language, 27*, 313–333.

Hendriks, P., & Koster, C. (2010). Production/comprehension asymmetries in language acquisition. *Lingua, 120*, 1887–2094.

Hirsch, C., & Wexler, K. (2006). Children's passives and their resulting interpretation. In K. U. Deen, J. Nomura, B. Schulz, & B. D. Schwartz (Eds.), *The Proceedings of the Inaugural Conference on GALANA: University of Connecticut Occasional Papers in Linguistics* (Vol. 4). Cambridge, MA: University of Connecticut/MIT.

Horgan, D. (1978). The development of the full passive. *Journal of Child Language, 5*, 65–80.

Jaeggli, O. (1986). Passive. *Linguistic Inquiry, 17*, 582–622.

Manetti, C. (2013). On the production of passives in Italian: Evidence from an elicited production task and a syntactic priming study with preschool children. In S. Baiz, N. Goldman, & R. Hawkes (Eds.), *Proceedings of the 37th Boston University Conference on Language Development online supplement* (pp. 1–16). Boston: Boston University.

Maratsos, M. P., Fox, E. C., Becher, J., & Chalkley, M. A. (1985). Semantic restrictions on children's passives. *Cognition, 19*, 167–191.

Messenger, K., Branigan, H., McLean, J., & Sorace, A. (2009). Semantic factors in young children's comprehension and production of passives. In J. Chandlee, M. Franchini, S. Lord, & G.-M. Rheiner (Eds.), *Proceedings of the 33rd Boston University Conference on Language Development*. Somerville, MA: Cascadilla Press.

Messenger, K., Branigan, H., McLean, J., & Sorace, A. (2012). Is young children's passive syntax semantically constrained? Evidence from syntactic priming. *Journal of Memory and Language, 66*, 568–587.

Mills, A. E. (1985). The acquisition of German. In D. Slobin (Ed.), *The crosslinguistic study of language acquisition* (Vol. 1, pp. 141–254). Hillsdale, NJ: Erlbaum.

Montgomery, J.W., Magimairaj, B., & O'Malley, M. (2008). The role of working memory in typically developing children's complex sentence comprehension. *Journal of Psycholinguistic Research, 37*, 331–354.

Appendix B

O'Brien, K., Grolla, E., & Lillo-Martin, D. (2006). Long passives are understood by young children. In D. Bamman, T. Magnitskaia, & C. Zaller (Eds.), *Proceedings of the 30th Annual Boston University Conference on Language Development*. Somerville, MA: Cascadilla Press.

Orfitelli, R. M. (2012). *Argument intervention in the acquisition of A-movement*. Unpublished doctoral dissertation, University of California, Los Angeles.

Pinker, S., Lebeaux, D., & Frost, L. A. (1987). Productivity and constraints in the acquisition of the passive. *Cognition, 26*, 195–267.

Pye, C., & Quixtan Poz, P. (1988). Precocious passives and antipassives in Quiche Mayan. *Papers and Reports on Child Language Development, 27*, 71–80.

Rizzi, L. (2004). Locality and left periphery. In A. Belletti (Ed.), *Structures and beyond: The cartography of syntactic structure* (Vol. 3, pp. 223–251). Oxford: Oxford University Press.

Rizzi, L. (2013). Locality. *Lingua, 130*, 169–186.

Rubin, Maraci Coelho de Barros Pereira. (2009). The passive in 3- and 4-year-olds. *Journal of Psycholinguistic Research, 38*, 435–446.

Sano, T. (2000). Issues on unaccusatives and passives in the acquisition of Japanese. In Y. Otsu (Ed.), *Proceedings of the Tokyo Conference on Psycholinguistics* (Vol. 1, pp. 1–21). Tokyo: Hituzi Shobo.

Snyder, W., & Hyams, N. (2014). *Minimality effects in children's passives*. Unpublished manuscript, University of Connecticut and UCLA.

Terzi, A., & Wexler, K. (2002). A-chains and S-homophones in children's grammar: Evidence from Greek passives. In M. Hirotani (Ed.), *Proceedings of NELS 32*. University of Massachusetts, Amherst: GLSA.

Volpato, F., Verin, L., & Cardinaletti, A. (2014). The acquisition of passives in Italian: Auxiliaries and answering strategies in an experiment of elicited production. In J. Costa, A. Fíeis, M. J. Freitas, M. Lobo, & A. L. Santos (Eds.), *New directions in the acquisition of Romance languages: Selected Proceedings of the Romance Turn* (Vol. 5, pp. 371–394). Newcastle: Cambridge Scholars Publishing.

Volpato, F.,Verin, L., Tagliaferro, L.,& Cardinaletti, A. (2013). The comprehension of (eventive) verbal passives by Italian preschool age children. In S. Stavrakaki, M. Lalioti, & P. Konstantinopoulou (Eds.), *Advances in language acquisition: Proceedings of Generative Approaches to Language*.

Index

Page locators in *italic* indicate examples and figures in text; **bolded** locators indicate tables.

abstracts *34*, 180, 211–12
acronyms 140
Advanced Search feature (WorldCat) 23–4, *24*
Allen, E.S. 167–72
alphabetizing reference lists 154, *155*
analyzing literature: assessing methodology 58–9, *58*, *59*; checklist for 162–3; citing statistics 55–6, *55*; currency of references 62; evaluating author's evidence 59, *59–60*; finding research trends 60, *60*; focusing on review articles 56, *56*; identifying research gaps 46–7, *47*, 61, *61*; overview 14; quotations 57–8, *57*; relationships among studies 61; relevance to your topic 61–2, *62*, 162–3; terms used in research 53–5, *53–5*
anecdotal reports 8
annotations 126–7, *127*
APA *see* Publication Manual of the American Psychological Association
argument: checking flow of 130, 163; organizing notes for 100; summarizing 126; thesis of 99
articles *see* literature review articles
assertions vs. evidence 59, *59–60*
auditors 80
avoiding plagiarism 148–51, *150*
Ayna, D. 180–9

backups of paper files 146
Balderrama-Durbin, C.M. 167–72

Being a teacher educator (Pereira, Lopes, and Marta) 246–57
bibliographic software 153–4
Burrell, L.V. 172–9

capitalization 156–7
Cardinaletti, A. 272–82
categories of core ideas 85
cause-and-effect issues 68
Chicago Manual of Style, The 137
Children as earwitnesses (Burrell, Johnson, and Melinder) 172–9
citations: APA style for books 159, *159*; avoiding plagiarism with 148–51, *150*; checklist for 164; creating 121; landmark studies 114–15, *115*; online tools for checking 159; relevance of 61–2, *62*, 162–3; *see also* sample literature reviews
citing: landmark studies 114–15, *115*; online journals 157, *157*, *158*; statistics 55–6, *55*
coherency *see* developing coherent essays
colloquialisms 141
compiling research notes 47–9, *48–9*
Comprehension and production of verbal passives by Italian preschool-age children, The (Volpato, Verin, and Cardinaletti) 272–82
computer technology: backing up paper files 146; bibliographic software 153–4; checking citations with online tools 159;

Index

compiling research notes on 47–9, *48–9*; creating hanging indents 154, 155, *155*; *see also* online resources

conclusions: considering implications and 104–5, *104*, *105*; overview used as 208; samples of 180, 187, 221–2; writing 129–30, *129*, 164

concurrent criterion-related validity 71, *71*

consensual qualitative research (CQR) methodology 84–5

construct validity 71, *72*

consulting experts 80, *81*

content validity 72, *72*

contractions 140, *141*, 165

contrasting terms 55

core ideas 85

CQR (consensual qualitative research) methodology 84–5

criterion-related validity 70–1, *71*

Cronbach's alpha 70

databases: EBSCOhost database platform 37–9, *37*, *38*, *39*; finding 25–6, *27*; learning to use 21–5; library workshops on 19; unpublished studies listed on, 33, 42n2; *see also* online resources

degrees of evidence 76

delimitations of reviews 125, *125*

Demand and withdraw behaviors (Balderrama-Durbin, Allen, and Rhoades) 167–72

demographics: defined, 78n14; qualitative use of 83, *84*; quantitative use of 74–5

developing coherent essays: about 124; avoiding annotations 126–7, *127*; checking argument flow 130, 163; checklist for 163; clarifying point of view 125–6, *126*; managing multiple disciplines 128–9; overviews helping 124, *124–5*; stating review delimitations 125, *125*; subheadings 127; transitions for 127, *127*; writing conclusions 129–30, *129*, 164

dissertations: citations for 121; voice for 9, 11–12; *see also* writing reviews

double-checking references 160

EBSCOhost database platform 37–9, *37*, *38*, *39*

editing drafts: acronyms 140; checklist for 161–6; coined terms 141; common conventions for manuscripts 142–3; comparing draft to outline 138; contractions 140, *141*, 165; grammar checks 165; help for 151; incorporating feedback 135–7; Latin abbreviations 142; overview 15, 135–6; parallelism in writing 138, 163; plagiarism 148–51, *150*; preparing for review 144–6; proofreading 144, 165, 166; quotations 138–9, 146–8, *146*, *147*; reconciling contradictions 137; reference lists 159; slang, colloquialisms, and idioms 141; special tips for 166; style issues 137, 164–5; synonyms for recurring words 139, *139*, *140*; titles 143–4, *145*; tools for checking citations 159; *see also* first drafts; manuscripts; outline

Effect of student discussion frequency, The (Kosko and Miyazaki) 202–11

effect size 78n15

empirical observation 4, 17n3

empirical research reports 3–6

evidence 59, *59–60*, 76

experiments: experimental vs. nonexperimental studies 67; random assignment to treatment 67–8

feedback: incorporating 135–7; from instructors 41, 136; reconciling contradictory 137

first drafts: checklist for 161; citing landmark studies 114–15, *115*; comparing to outline 138; defining research gaps 102, 117, *117–18*, 163; establishing time frames 113–14, *113–14*; highlighting importance of studies 112–13, *112–13*; identifying research findings in 111–12, *111*, *112*; inconsistencies in 119, *120*; indicating importance of topics 110–11, *110*, *111*; justifying study 121, *121–2*; mentioning related issues 116, *116–17*; overview 14–15, 109; references in 118–19, *118*, 121; showing scope of problems 109–10, *110*; *see also* developing coherent essays; editing drafts

flawed research 4–6, 76
formatting *see* manuscripts
Fremouw, W.J. 257–64

Google Scholar 20
grammatical accuracy 165
Grekin, E.R. 180–9
Gulbrandsen, C. 190–201

hanging indents 154, 155, *155*
historical studies 35–7, *36*
Holt, R. 211–24
How and When to Cite (University of Washington Psychology Writing Center) 148

idioms 141
inconsistent research results 119, *120*
instructor feedback 41, 136
internal consistency reliability 69–70, *70*
introductions 162
italics 155–6, *156*

Johnson, M.S. 172–9

keywords: locating articles with 32, *32*, 33–4, *34*; samples of 180, 212; searching with 24–5, 29–30, *30*
Kosko, K.W. 202–11

landmark studies: citing 114–15, *115*; identifying 35–7, *36*
Latin abbreviations 142
libraries *see* university libraries
literal enumeration 85
literature review articles: annotation methods for reading 47; assessing methodology of 58–9, *58*, *59*; categorizing 44–6, *45*, *46*; creating citations for 121; currency of 62; database searches for 25–6, *26*; definitions of key terms in 53–5, *53–5*; evaluating evidence of 59, *59–60*; focusing on 56, *56*; locating, 34-5, *35*, 42n5; prereading 43–4, *44*; as primary source, 7-8, 17n2; spotting gaps in collection of 46–7, *47*, 61, *61*; trends or patterns in 60, *60*; *see also* reviews

literature searches: finding unpublished studies, 32-33, 42n2; increasing results for 31–2; overview 13–14; selecting search engines 20; tips for 33; *see also* keywords; online resources
Lopes, A. 246–57

manuscripts: abstracts for *34*, 180, 211–12; checklist for 164; grammatical accuracy of 165; notes in printed 170, 187, 241, 254, 280; numbering and titling tables 93; page numbers 156, 164; preparing for review 144–6; punctuation in 157, 165; reference lists 154–6, *155*, *156*; style issues for 137, 164–5; titles and title pages 143–4, *145*; *see also* conclusions; references; tables
Marta, M. 246–57
Mason, O.J. 211–24
Matarazzo, B. 225–46
measurement: defined 69; errors in 4; quantitative process for 73, *73*, *74*
Measuring older women's resilience (Gulbrandsen) 190–201
mechanics of writing *see* manuscripts
Melinder, A. 172–9
member checking 81–2, *81*
Mental health and physical activity interventions (Mason and Holt) 211–24
meta-comments 128, *128*, 163
methodological assessments 57–8, *58*
methodology: description in qualitative research 84, *84–5*; tables delineating 89–93, **89**, **90**, *91*, *92*
Microsoft Word hanging indents 155
Miyazaki, Y. 202–11
MLA Handbook 137

narrowing topics 31, *31*, 40, *40*, *41*
nonexperimental studies 68
non-native English writers 166
notes: in manuscripts 170, 187, 241, 254, 280; *see also* research notes
numbering and titling tables 93

omitting issues 116, *116–17*
online bibliographic tools 158

Index

Online Computer Library Center (OCLC) 20
online resources: advanced searches of 23–4, *24*; citing online journals 157, *157, 158*; date and URL of 158, *158, 159*; keyword searches in 24–5; navigation of 21; online databases 21–5; selecting search engines 20; verifying credentials for 18–19
organizing research: categorizing articles 44–6, *45, 46*; compiling research notes 47–9, *48–9*; grouping notes 88–93, 98, *99–100, 100*; prereading articles 43–4, *44*; setting up annotation methods before reading 47; spotting possible gaps in articles 46–7, *47*, 61, *61*; using quotations 49; *see also* tables
outline: comparing draft to 138; creating topic 99, *99–100*; fitting notes to 100; fleshing out 106–7, *107*

page numbers 156, 164
papers *see specific type of review*
parallelism 138, 163
parentheses around Latin abbreviations 142
participants: demographics of 74–5, 83, *84*; member checking of 81–2, *81*; random assignment to treatment 67–8; sampling of 74
peer review process 80
Pereira, F. 246–57
plagiarism 148–51, *150*
point of view 125–6, *126*
predictive criterion-related validity 71, *71*
preparing to write: conclusions and implications 104–5, *104, 105*; considering voice and purpose 97–8, *98*; creating topic outline 99, *99–100*; fitting notes to argument 100; fleshing out outline 106–7, *107*; including periodic summaries 103–4; outlining differences among studies 101, *101*; overview 15; planning descriptions of theories 102, *102–3*; relating studies to theories 103; reviewing notes 98; suggesting future research 105, *106*; *see also* organizing research; research gaps; writing reviews
prereading articles 43–4, *44*
Prevalence, psychological impact, and coping of cyberbully victims among college students (Schenk and Fremouw) 257–64
primary sources: accessing online articles 25–6; adding to reference list 154; anecdotal reports 8; empirical research reports 3–6; identifying landmark studies and theorists 35–7, *36*; literature review articles 7–8; online availability of 18; reports on professional practices and standards 8; theoretical articles 6–7; writing reviews from 8–16
problems: errors identifying research 4–5; showing scope of research 109–10, *110*
professional practices and standards reports 8
proofreading drafts 144, 165, 166
Psychological Bulletin 42n6
Publication Manual of the American Psychological Association (APA): following style of, 15, 17n5 137; quotation guidelines 146–8; *see also* references
punctuation 157, 165
purposive samples 82–3, *82–3*

qualitative research: consulting experts 80, *81*; defining quantities in 85, *85*; demographics in 83, *84*; member checking in 81–2, *81*; method of obtaining results 79; methodologies in 84, *84–5*; quantitative vs. 66; sampling in 82, *82, 83*
quantitative research: assessing relative validity of 72; cause-and-effect issues in 68; characteristics of 65–7; demographics in 74–5; evaluating size in statistical variations 75, *75*; experimental or nonexperimental studies in 67; flaws in 76; internal consistency reliability in 69–70, *70*; measurement process in 73, *73, 74*; measuring validity 70–3, *71, 72*; sampling in 74; test-retest reliability 69, *69*
quotation marks 141

quotations: editing 146–8, *146*, *147*; using 49, 57–8, *57*, 138–9

random assignment to treatment 67–8
reader's comments 136
references: alphabetizing 154, *155*; APA style for books 159, *159*; avoiding nonspecific 118–19, *119*; bibliographic software creating 153–4; checklist for 164; citing online journals 157, *157*, *158*; creating citations for 121; currency of 62; date and URL of online materials 158, *158*, *159*; double-checking 160; formatting 154–6, *155*, *156*; increasing size of list 31–2, *32*; placement in drafts 154; sources needed for 154; tools for checking 159; *see also* citations; sample literature reviews
related issues 116, *116–17*
relational theory of loneliness 6-7, 16n1
relationships among studies 61
reliability 69–70, *69*, *70*
replicated landmark studies 115, *115*
research: flaws in empirical 4–6, 76; highlighting importance of study 112–13, *112–13*; identifying findings in first drafts 111–12, *111*, *112*; inconsistent results in 119, *120*; justifying 121, *121–2*; qualitative methods for collecting 79; searching 33; suggestions for future 105, *106*; *see also* landmark studies
researchers: clarifying point of view 125–6, *126*; compiling research notes 47–9, *48–9*; defining general topic 28; formalizing library affiliation 18; identifying landmark theorists 35–7, *36*; learning to use databases 19, 21–7; narrowing topics 31, *31*, 40, *40*, *41*; quantitative, 77n1, 77n2, 77n3; reconciling contradictions 137; selecting search engines 20; *see also* organizing research; writing reviews
research gaps: defining your 102, 117, *117–18*, 163; finding in reviews 46–7, 61, *61*
research notes: compiling research 47–9, *48–9*; organizing 88–93, 98, *99–100*, *100*; reviewing 98

research teams 79–81, *80*, *81*
Review of Educational Research 42n6
reviews *see* literature review articles; writing reviews
Rhoades, G.K. 167–72

sample literature reviews: *Being a teacher educator* 246–57; *Children as earwitnesses* 172–9; *Comprehension and production of verbal passive* 272–82; *Demand and withdraw behaviors* 167–72; *Effect of student discussion frequency, The* 202–11; *Measuring older women's resilience* 190–201; *Mental health and physical activity interventions* 211–24; *Prevalence, psychological impact, and coping of cyberbully victims* 257–64; *School social worker's experiences with youth suicidal behavior* 265–72; *Suicide risk among LGBT military personnel and veterans* 225–46; *Waterpipe smoking among college students* 180–9
sampling: errors in empirical research 4; evaluating method of participant 74; purposive 82–3, *82–3*; quantitative vs. qualitative 65–7; sample of convenience 82, *83*
Schenk, A.M. 257–64
School social worker's experiences with youth suicidal behavior (Singer and Slovak) 265–72
search engines 20
searches *see* literature searches
secondary sources 3–4
self-editing checklist 161–6
Singer, J.B. 265–72
slang 141
Slovak, K. 265–72
spelling: acronyms in full 140; checking drafts for 144, 164
spreadsheets 47–9, 55
statistics: citing 55–6, *55*; evaluating variations 75, *75*
style: checklist for 137, 164–5; following APA, 15, 17n5 137; reference citation 159, *159*; *see also Publication Manual of the American Psychological Association*; quotations; references
subheadings 127

suggestions for future research 105, *106*
Suicide risk among LGBT military personnel and veterans (Matarazzo and others) 225–46
summarizing research results 90–1, **90**
synonyms 139, *139*, *140*
synthesis 14
systematic observation 4

tables: delineating methodology in 89–90, **89, 90,** *91, 92*; numbering and titling 93; samples of **182, 215–16, 230–4**; split across pages 93; summarizing results in 90–1, **90**; table of definitions 88, **88**, *89*; when to use 92–3, *92*
terminology 53–5, *53–5*
term papers: avoiding plagiarism in 148–51, *150*; finding voice for 9–11; formats for 144–6; placement of references in 154; quotations used in 146–8, *146*, *147*; *see also* writing reviews
test-retest reliability 69, *69*
theoretical articles: locating 33–4, *34*; as primary source 6–7
theories: brief descriptions of 102, *102–3*; defined 6; how studies relate to 103
theses: citations for 121; finding voice for 9, 11–12; *see also* writing reviews
thesis of argument 99
timeline for writing reviews *10*
titles and title page 143–4, *145*
topics: checklist for 162; defining 28, *84–5*; drafting first statement of 39–40, *39*; feedback on 41; focusing articles on 61; general to specific reviews 109–10, *110*; importance of 110–11, *110, 111*; increasing search results for 31–2; keyword searches for 29–30, *30*; landmark studies and theorists on 35–7, *36*; learning about data online 29; narrowing 31, *31*, 40, *40, 41*; online sources for 37–9, *37, 38, 39*; outline of 99, *99–100*; review articles on, *35*, 34–35, 42n5; separating into disciplines 128–9; summarizing 103–4; theoretical articles on 33–4, *34*; timeliness of 113–14, *113–14*; *see also* outline; research gaps
Turnitin 150, 151

university libraries: formalizing use of 18; keyword searches at 24–5; online resources of 18, 19, 21; workshops exploring 19; *see also* WorldCat
unpublished studies 32–33, 42n2
URLs of online resources 158, *158, 159*

validity 70–3, *71, 72*
validity coefficient 70–1; 69–70, 78n12
Verin, L. 272–82
voice: considering purpose and 97–8, *98*; finding 9, 11–12
Volpato, F. 272–82

Waterpipe smoking among college students (Grekin and Ayna) 180–9
workshops on library databases 19
WorldCat: about 20; Advanced Search feature 23–4, *24*; learning to use 21–3, *21, 22, 23*
writing reviews: acronyms when 140; conclusions 129–30, *129*, 164; contractions 140, *141*, 165; dealing with flawed research 4–6; editing drafts 15, 135–6, 137; finding voice 9, 11–12, 97–8, *98*; first drafts 14–15, 109; identifying gaps in 46–7, *47*, 61, *61*; managing literature searches 13–14; manuscript preparation 144–6; parallelism when 138, 163; periodic summaries when 103–4; process for 8–16, 161; reference lists for 154–6, *155, 156*; self-editing checklist for 161–6; slang, colloquialisms, and idioms 141; style issues in 137, 164–5; subheadings when 127; timeline for *10*, 137; topic statements 39–40, *39*; transitions 127, *127*; *see also* manuscripts; sample literature reviews